SOFTWARE ENGINEERING WITH OBJ
Algebraic Specification in Action

Advances in Formal Methods

Michael Hinchey
Series Editor

SOFTWARE ENGINEERING WITH OBJ
Algebraic Specification in Action

edited by

Joseph Goguen
University of California at San Diego

Grant Malcolm
University of Liverpool

KLUWER ACADEMIC PUBLISHERS
Boston / Dordrecht / London

Distributors for North, Central and South America:
Kluwer Academic Publishers
101 Philip Drive
Assinippi Park
Norwell, Massachusetts 02061 USA
Telephone (781) 871-6600
Fax (781) 871-6528
E-Mail <kluwer@wkap.com>

Distributors for all other countries:
Kluwer Academic Publishers Group
Distribution Centre
Post Office Box 322
3300 AH Dordrecht, THE NETHERLANDS
Telephone 31 78 6392 392
Fax 31 78 6546 474
E-Mail <orderdept@wkap.nl>

 Electronic Services <http://www.wkap.nl>

Library of Congress Cataloging-in-Publication Data

Software engineering with OBJ : algebraic specification in action / edited by Joseph Goguen, Grant Malcolm.
    p. cm. -- (Advances in formal methods)
  Includes bibliographical references and index.
  ISBN 0-7923-7757-5 (alk. paper)
    1. Software engineering. 2. Functional programming languages. 3. Object oriented programming (Computer science) I. Goguen, Joseph. II. Malcolm, Grant. III. Series.

QA76.758. S65615 2000
005.1--dc21

                                                                00-022759

Series Foreword
Advances in Formal Methods

Michael Hinchey
Series Editor

University of Nebraska-Omaha
College of Information Science and Technology
Department of Computer Science
Omaha, NE 68182-0500 USA

Email: mhinchey@unomaha.edu

As early as 1949, computer pioneers realized that writing a program that executed as planned was no simple task. Turing even saw the need to address the issues of program correctness and termination, foretelling groundbreaking work of Edsger Dijkstra, John McCarthy, Bob Floyd, Tony Hoare, Sue Owicki and David Gries, among others, two and three decades later.

The term *formal methods* refers to the application of mathematical techniques for the specification, analysis, design, implementation and subsequent maintenance of complex computer software and hardware. These techniques have proven themselves, when correctly and appropriately applied, to result in systems of the highest quality, which are well documented, easier to maintain, and promote software reuse.

With emerging legislation, and increasing emphasis in standards and university curricula, formal methods are set to become even more important in system development. This Kluwer book series, Advances in Formal Methods, aims to present results from the cutting edge of formal methods research and practice.

Books in the series will address the use of formal methods in both hardware and software development, and the role of formal methods in the development of safety-critical and real-time systems, hardware-software co-design, testing, simulation and prototyping, software quality assurance, software reuse, security, and many other areas. The series aims to include both basic and advanced textbooks, monographs, reference books and collections of high quality papers which will address managerial issues, the development process, requirements engineering, tool support, methods integration, metrics, reverse engineering, and issues relating to formal methods education.

It is our aim that, in due course, Advances in Formal Methods will provide a rich source of information for students, teachers, academic researchers and industrial practitioners alike. And I hope that, for many, it will be a first port-of-call for relevant texts and literature.

Professor Mike Hinchey

Contents

Preface

There has recently been greatly increased interest in the possibility that formal methods can significantly enhance the development process for both software and hardware, in such ways as the following:

- making specifications more precise and easier to read;

- making designs more precise and easier to read;

- facilitating the production of accurate natural language documentation;

- provide capabilities for rapid prototyping through executable specifications;

- reducing errors in the later stages of software development;

- making maintenance easier and more accurate;

- facilitating proving properties of designs; and

- facilitating proving correctness of code.

Such advances would help reduce the cost of designing, producing and maintaining systems, and seem particularly promising for so-called *safety critical* systems.

Algebraic specification is one of the more recently developed formal methods, known for its entirely rigorous and mathematically simple foundations in equational logic, and for its relatively highly developed mechanical support environments. These properties contrast with those of older and better known methods, which tend to lack formal semantics and support for execution.

This book presents case studies in the use of OBJ by leading practitioners in the fields of formal methods and software engineering. The book is novel in concentrating on the use of the executable specification language OBJ which, in contrast to most other popular approaches to formal methods, is an *executable* algebraic specifiction language with a simple yet rigorous mathematical foundation. The book gives a detailed introduction to the language, including such features as its support for error handling, overloading, and its powerful generic modules which support large grain 'hyperprogramming', reusablity and software composition. The case studies cover such diverse application areas as computer graphics, hardware development and verification, concurrent systems, and an interpreter for OBJ designed using OBJ itself.

These case studies demonstrate that OBJ can be used in a wide variety of ways to achieve a wide variety of practical aims in the system development process. The papers on various OBJ systems demonstrate that the language is relatively easy to understand and to use, and supports formal reasoning in a straightforward way.

INTRODUCTION

Joseph Goguen and Grant Malcolm

Information is the life-blood of modern society. It is largely controlled, distributed and manipulated through software systems that drive communications networks, mediate financial transactions and operate databases of almost anything from recipes, through vehicle registrations and corporate finances, to criminal records. These systems range in scope from personal organizers to networks that girdle the earth. They control access to buildings, allow researchers to communicate results and share ideas, format documents such as financial reports and this book; they monitor and control particle accelerators, production lines, nuclear reactors, satellite trajectories and ballistic missiles, as well as cash dispensers and the family car brakes. Participating in society without encountering such systems is as difficult as cutting a pound of flesh from a man's breast without shedding a jot of blood.

Information can be effectively recorded, controlled and used only insofar as it is *about* something, whether money, braking distances, mouse buttons or production quotas. How information is interpreted depends on many things, including dynamic technical, social, psychological, legal, and commercial factors. This is the *situated*, social aspect of information [19, 21] that feeds the muscles, organs, nerves and brains of society. Another important aspect of information, particularly as embodied in software systems, is that it is as precisely delineated and *structured* as a hemoglobin molecule, or the DNA that controls the body's manufacture of hemoglobin. For example, the debit and credit values in a spreadsheet are represented as sequences of zeroes and ones, and adding columns is achieved by manipulating these sequences. To design and build effective software systems, the software engineer must master both the technical and the social aspects of the relevant information [19, 37].

Large complex software systems fail much more often than seems to be generally recognized. Perhaps the most common case is that a project is simply cancelled before completion; this may be due to time and/or cost overruns or other management difficulties that seem insurmountable. For example, the US

Federal Aviation Agency (FAA) recently cancelled an $8 billion contract with IBM to build the next generation air traffic control system for the entire United States. This is perhaps the biggest software cancellation in history, but there are many more examples, including cancellation of a $2 billion contract with IBM to provide modern information systems to replace myriads of obsolete, incompatible systems being used by the US Department of Defense. The highly publicized failure of IBM software to deliver real time sports data to the media at the 1996 Olympic Games in Atlanta, the self-destruction of the European satellite launch Ariane 5, costing $2 billion, the 1994 failure of the United Airlines baggage delivery system at Denver International Airport, which delayed its opening by one and a half years costing about $15 million [16], and 1989 cancellation of the $2 million Taurus system, which was supposed to bring the London Stock Exchange into the 20th century and instead led to a diminution of its power. Much more information of this kind can be found in the Risks Forum run by Peter Neumann (see his column in *Communications of the ACM*, as well as `www.csl.sri.com/risks.html` and [43]).

Anyone who has worked for some time in the software industry has seen numerous examples of projects that were over time, over cost, or failed to meet crucial requirements, and hence were cancelled, curtailed, diverted, replaced, or released anyway, sometimes with dire consequences. For obvious reasons, the organizations involved usually try to hide such failures, but experience suggests that half or more of large complex systems fail in one way or another, and that the frightening list in the previous paragraph is just the tip of an enormous iceberg.

Experience also shows that many of these failures are due to a mismatch between the social and technical aspects of a supposed solution, i.e., due to the tension between information as situated and as structured representation. Traditionally, software engineering has been biased towards this latter, formalistic, view of information. Understandably so, because computer programs consist of precise instructions that manipulate formally defined structured representations of data, and this is what software engineers are trained to deal with, as opposed to relatively more messy social situations.

This book presents case studies in software design using the high-level specification and prototyping language OBJ. The emphasis in these studies is on the formal aspects of design, particularly the formal specification and verification of systems; however, the preceding discussion of the situatedness of information and software highlights some reasons we feel OBJ is appropriate for these endeavors. The following three sections address various aspects of this.

0.1   OBJ IS A SPECIFICATION LANGUAGE

In the early days of computing, coding arithmetic routines involved a considerable investment of time and effort; nowadays the task is considered trivial, and building a (small) compiler is considered a suitable task for undergraduate students. The main reason behind this increased efficiency of software production, without which the pervasiveness of information systems would be impossible, is the development of high-level programming languages. These allow programmers to ignore many details and concentrate on more abstract properties of their software. For example, these languages allow a more abstract conceptualization of the data the program manipulates, e.g., numbers rather than their binary representations. Indeed, much of the history of computing can be seen as a series of advances in *abstraction* mechanisms of various kinds for various purposes, for example, from subroutines, through procedures, to modules, and now objects and repositories.

The need for abstraction is illustrated by Jonathan Swift's parody on the Academy of Lagado, where the professors communicate not with words but with the objects that they represent[1]:

> many of the most learned and wise adhere to the new scheme of expressing themselves by *things*, which hath only this inconvenience attending it, that if a man's business be very great, and of various kinds, he must be obliged in proportion to carry a greater bundle of *things* upon his back, unless he can afford one or two servants to attend him. I have often beheld two of these sages almost sinking under the weight of their packs... who when they meet in the streets would lay down their loads, open their sacks and hold conversation for an hour together; then put up their implements, help each other to resume their burthens, and take their leave.

Specification languages allow a more abstract view than programming languages. They concentrate on functionality and design structure, leaving algorithmic aspects for a later coding phase. Declarative specification languages like OBJ allow an incremental approach to developing specifications. The first stage might consist of merely naming the kinds of entity that compose the system, while later stages refine the functionalities of these entities. Algebraic specification is perhaps the best developed strain of formal specification, both in its supporting theory and in its very efficient implementation technology. As such it seems especially suitable for expressing standards, such as GKS (Chapter 5).

Of course, this is still a long way from capturing the situatedness of the end product, but we believe it is an important step in the right direction, not just

---

[1] From *Gulliver's Travels*. Although Swift's satire is largely directed against seventeenth century ideals of conciseness in language, it is also in part directed against ideal universal languages like that proposed by Leibniz (see Section 0.5 below); we do not think he was satirizing object oriented programming.

because of the abstractness offered by OBJ, but also because the executability of its specifications supports prototype-driven incremental development methods.

0.2   OBJ IS A FUNCTIONAL PROGRAMMING LANGUAGE

OBJ specifications consist of names for kinds of entities (sorts), and operations on those entities whose functionality is specified by equations. These equations look similar to the definitions in functional programming languages (though they are more general), and they can be used to experiment with a specification. Therefore a specification can be seen as a *prototype* of its eventual implementation, so that designers, and more importantly end users, can experiment with specifications, to discover flaws and gaps in the specification or requirements statements. These can then be rectified before the expensive coding process begins. Thus OBJ can be used in an iterative prototype-driven development process, where key aspects are incrementally improved on the basis of user feedback throughout the lifecycle. Moreover, today's hardware allows many small to medium applications to be written and run directly in OBJ, without any coding at all.

0.3   OBJ IS A THEOREM PROVER

Although its support for prototyping allows designers to take some account of the situatedness of the systems they design, OBJ is primarily intended to support the structured representation aspect of software systems. OBJ was designed for algebraic semantics: its declarations introduce symbols for sorts and functions, its statements are equations, and its computations are equational proofs. Thus, an OBJ specification actually *is* an equational theory, and every OBJ computation actually *proves* some theorem about such a theory. In the same way that equational reasoning can be used to prove properties of numbers or sets, this allows designers to prove (using OBJ itself!) properties of their specifications. Many examples appear in our book, *Algebraic Semantics of Imperative Programs* [24], along with the relevant mathematical theory, we hope in a relatively digestible form. The following chapters provide many more examples; a further example worth mentioning is the use of OBJ to specify and prove the correctness of an optimizing compiler [35]; this involves proving that one specification refines another, i.e., provides (at least) the same behavior.

0.4   OBJ HAS A PAST AND A FUTURE

Most of the relevant historical information can be found in Section 1.1 of Chapter 1 of this book. Here we fill in some earlier and later developments, including some information about the origins of this book.

Perhaps the most important enabling event for OBJ was Goguen's gradual realization, during the period from 1968 to 1972, that Lawvere's characterization of the natural numbers as a certain initial algebra [39] could be extended to other data structures of interest to computer science; reading Knuth's compendium [38] in a seminar at the IBM T.J. Watson Research Center organized by Jim Thatcher was a great help, and the influence of Sanders Mac Lane was also important during this period.

This insight led to the development of the mathematical theory of abstract data types as initial algebras [32], as well as the somewhat earlier general theory of abstract syntax and compositional semantics [17, 31]. The attempt to develop the computational side of abstract data types led to considering term rewriting theory, and indeed an early draft of [32] made extensive use of these ideas. However, term rewriting theory was still in a primitive state at that time, and a more abstract viewpoint was found expedient. Nevertheless, this early foray into term rewriting was an essential precondition for OBJ. (For much more historical information on the so-called ADJ group, see [18].)

This book grew out of a project to implement a new version of OBJ in the UK, and use it in a number of industrial experiments. This effort was led by Derek Coleman and Robin Gallimore at UMIST (University of Manchester Institute of Science and Technology), with Victoria Stavridou as Research Assistant, supported by the UK SERC (Science and Engineering Research Council, recently renamed EPSRC); UMIST OBJ was used in several of the studies reported in this book. It was later commercialized, renamed OBJ-Ex, and supported by Gerrard Software, a small UK firm; OBJ-Ex appears to be still in use within the UK government. Meanwhile, Coleman and Gallimore moved from UMIST to Hewlett-Packard at Bristol, and developed another variant of OBJ, called Axis [14], while the UMIST project came under the direction of Colin Walter. An OBJ users group was formed in the UK, and held a number of meetings with participation by many of the authors in this book.

Several post-OBJ3 developments seem especially noteworthy. One is Maude [7, 6], an extension of OBJ to rewriting logic [41], which is particularly suited to specifying concurrent systems. This project is led by Dr. José Meseguer at SRI International in Menlo Park, California, where most of the original OBJ3 development was done, and indeed, Dr. Meseguer co-led the later phases of the OBJ3 implementation effort, while Goguen was chief designer, and supervised further enhancements at Oxford University. As this is written, there is a preliminary release of Maude, with a very efficient implementation and several interesting features, including support for meta-programming [5] based on reflection, and for order sorted membership equational logic [42], a recent extension of order sorted equational logic.

The second system, called CafeOBJ [11, 12], has been implemented at JAIST (Japan Advanced Institute of Science and Technology) in Hokuriku, Japan, under the direction of Professor Kokichi Futatsugi, supported on a large scale by MITI, the Japanese Ministry of Industry and Technology. This system includes features to handle both rewriting logic (as in Maude) and hidden algebra [25, 26, 10], which provides powerful proof techniques for behavioral specification and verification.

A third group called "CoFI," consisting (largely) of European theoretical computer scientists, is designing and building a "common" algebraic specification language called CASL. Participants include Bernd Krieg-Bruckner, who designed the Ada module system (influenced by OBJ), Don Sannella, Peter Mosses, Till Mossakowsky, Maura Cerioli, Michel Bidoit, and Andre Tarlecki. Although it is not clear that they would like CASL to be called a descendent of OBJ, the language certainly does have significant similarities to OBJ3; perhaps its most distinctive feature is its advocacy of partial first order logic. The latest design documents can be found at www.brics.dk/Projects/CoFI/.

We are also pleased to report a significant event for the OBJ community, a "OBJ/CafeOBJ/Maude" workshop held at FM'99 (World Congress on Formal Methods in Toulouse, France) in September 1999, where presentations were made on many exciting new developments [15]; in addition, there was a OBJ/CafeOBJ/Maude mini-track as part of the main FM'99 event, the papers from which were published in its proceedings [47].

Finally, we should mention that part of the spirit of OBJ also lives on in the module system of several modern programming languags, including ML [36], C++, and Ada [8], since the designers of the languages were all influenced by OBJ3, and/or its predecessor Clear [4].

0.5   OBJ IS NOT THE LAST WORD

The case studies in this book show that OBJ can be used to specify, prototype and reason about both software and hardware systems; that it can be used to define formal semantics of languages and standards; and that it can provide support for mechanical theorem proving. Because of the clarity of its semantics, OBJ is also a useful educational tool, and it has been used at UCSD, Oxford and other universities in courses on theorem proving and on the semantics of imperative programs [40]. All this is not to suggest that we view OBJ as the *characteristica universalis* envisioned by Gottfried Leibniz in the seventeenth century:

> All our reasoning is nothing but the joining and substituting of characters, whether these characters be words or symbols or pictures... if we could find characters

or signs appropriate for expressing all our thoughts as definitely and as exactly as arithmetic expresses numbers... we could in all subjects in so far as they are amenable to reasoning accomplish what is done in arithmetic and geometry. For all inquiries that depend on reasoning would be performed by the transposition of characters and by a kind of calculus.... And if someone would doubt my results, I should say to him: 'let us calculate, Sir,' and thus by taking to pen and ink, we should soon settle the question.

Leibniz was not concerned merely with a language for formal reasoning in mathematics. Anticipating by more than three hundred years the kind of predictions that earned Artificial Intelligence a reputation for hyperbole [13], Leibniz wrote:

I believe that a number of chosen men can complete the task within five years; within two years they will exhibit the common doctrines of life, that is, meta-physics and morals, in an irrefutable calculus[2].

Nonetheless, we believe that OBJ is particularly well-suited to specifying and reasoning about the formal structures of software systems. Chapter 1 of this book gives an introduction to OBJ, describing precisely how its declarations relate to equational theories, how its specifications can be executed, how it allows error specification and recovery, how its powerful module facilities support hierarchical design, and much more. The ensuing chapters show how this translates into practice.

OBJ's elegant declarative, algebraic approach makes it appropriate to many paradigms in software engineering, and it has been applied to the logic paradigm in Eqlog [28, 9], and to the object paradigm in FOOPS [29]. Chapter 1 explains how OBJ's module features support what is called *parameterized pro-gramming*, which is particularly appropriate for large-grain specification, and provides facilities for prototyping at the system design level. It also provides support for reuse of code and designs [33].

Some recent research is directed to unifying the functional, logic, constraint and object paradigms in a way that takes better account of the situatedness of software [27]. Although some elements of this paradigm are already prefig-ured in the use of FOOPS in TOOR [44], an object oriented environment for requirements tracing, much exciting work remains to be done. Other current research is using OBJ in the Kumo project, to verify distributed concurrent systems [22, 23], using techniques from hidden algebra [45, 30, 46, 25, 26].

The dismaying pattern of ongoing, and indeed escalating, software failure described earlier suggests that the real software crisis lies not so much in producing software as in producing software appropriate to the situation where it will actually be used. Alasdair Gray's short story 'The Crank that Turned the

---

[2]These quotations from Leibniz are taken from a fascinating discussion of mathematical formalism in Barrow [3].

Revolution' [34] tells the cautionary tale of Vague McMenamy, a thoughtful and precocious child who

> would stand for long hours on the edge of the duck-pond wondering how to improve his Granny's ducks.... He thought that since ducks spend most of their days in water they should be made to do it efficiently. With the aid of a friendly carpenter he made a boat-shaped container into which a duck was inserted. There was a hole at one end through which the head stuck out, allowing the animal to breathe, see and even eat; nonetheless it protested against the confinement by struggling to get out and in doing so its wings and legs drove the cranks which conveyed motion to a paddle-wheel on each side. On its maiden voyage the duck zig-zagged around the pond at a speed of thirty knots, which was three times faster than the maximum speed which the boats and ducks of the day had yet attained. McMenamy had converted a havering all-rounder into an efficient specialist.

Encouraged by his success, McMenamy constructs a larger craft, "to be driven by every one of his Granny's seventeen ducks", powered by a screw propeller.

> Quacking hysterically, it crossed the pond with such velocity that it struck the opposite bank at the moment of departure from the near one. Had it struck soil it would have embedded itself. Unluckily, it hit the root of a tree, rebounded to the centre of the pond, overturned and sank. Every single duck was drowned.

This light-hearted illustration of the dangers of an overly formalistic view of ducks as swimming-systems should not distract us from the more serious illustrations mentioned earlier. The situatedness of information and software, and the role that this plays in system design, is an active research area. At present, most research is directed at the initial stages of requirements analysis and capture, but some recent work is directed at the relationships between the situated and formalistic aspects of software, such as the theory of situated abstract data types [19, 20, 21].

The latest information on OBJ and its progeny can be obtained over the World Wide Web, at

> `http://www.cs.ucsd.edu/users/goguen/sys/obj.html`

and subscription to an OBJ mailing list is available by emailing to

> `objforum@csc.liv.ac.uk`.

0.6   CONTENTS OF THIS BOOK

We now briefly describe the papers in this volume, in some cases indicating how they relate to themes sketched earlier in this introduction.

Part I of the book consists of *Introducing OBJ*, by Joseph Goguen, Timothy Winkler, José Meseguer, Kokichi Futatsugi and Jean-Pierre Jouannaud. This is the official OBJ3 manual, with many examples and applications, including proofs as well as specifications.

Part II contains a number of OBJ specifications. Victoria Stavridou uses OBJ and REVE in the development of hardware and proofs of properties of digital systems that evolve through time. Ataru Nakagawa, Kokichi Futatsugi, S. Tomura and T. Shimizu present a specification of a sophisticated interactive graphics package, and an example of a systematic way to check specifications during the design process. David Duce applies OBJ to the GKS graphics standard, showing that executable specifications can help to find errors, and that algebraic specifications can be relatively easy to read and modify.

Part III demonstrates the specification of formal semantics in OBJ. Joseph Goguen uses OBJ to specify a new kind of parallel computer architecture based on term rewriting, called the *Rewrite Rule Machine*; this is perhaps the first formal specification of a computer architecture. The rewrite rule machine is intended to provide a platform for an efficient implementation of OBJ's executable sublanguage [1, 2]. Claude Kirchner, Hélène Kirchner and Aristide Mégrelis describe their experience building the OBJ3 interpreter using OBJ2 as a specification language; the OBJ2 code supported coding, as well as communication among a diverse team of programmers and designers. Eugenio Battison, Fiorella de Cindio and Gian-Carlo Mauri also consider parallelism in their paper, which uses OBJ to add data types and data abstraction to the Petri net approach to concurrent system specification; in particular, OBJ is used to specify the data types to which individual tokens belong.

Part IV closes the book with two papers on Parameterized Programming. Kazuhito Ohmaki, Koichi Takahashi and Kokichi Futatsugi present a LOTOS simulator in OBJ. This is used to check behavioral properties of LOTOS specifications, and includes a discussion of extending LOTOS with some of OBJ's support for modularity such as parameterized modules. Finally, Joseph Goguen and Grant Malcolm document some higher order features of OBJ's module system that were somehow omitted from Part I, and illustrate the use of these advanced features for programming and theorem proving.

Looking over this set of papers, it seems to us both surprising and impressive that OBJ can be effectively used in so many different ways for so many different purposes. Surely there is an important lesson here for the emerging field of Formal Methods: there is no single best way to use any given notation or tool; instead, great flexibility is needed to adapt to the incredible variety of projects and their social contexts. The experiences reported in these papers also reinforce our strongly held view that a formal notation or tool used for specification should be executable, and not merely printable.

References

[1] Hitoshi Aida, Joseph Goguen, Sany Leinwand, Patrick Lincoln, José Meseguer, Babak Taheri, and Timothy Winkler. Simulation and performance estimation for the Rewrite Rule Machine. In *Proceedings, Fourth Symposium on the Frontiers of Massively Parallel Computation*, pages 336–344.

IEEE, October 1992.

[2]   Hitoshi Aida, Joseph Goguen, and José Meseguer. Compiling concurrent rewriting onto the rewrite rule machine. In Stéphane Kaplan and Misuhiro Okada, editors, *Conditional and Typed Rewriting Systems*, pages 320–332. Springer, 1991. Lecture Notes in Computer Science, Volume 516; also, Technical Report SRI-CSL-90-03, Computer Science Lab, SRI International, February, 1990.

[3]   John D. Barrow. *Pi in the Sky: counting, thinking and being*. Penguin, 1992.

[4]   Rod Burstall and Joseph Goguen. Putting theories together to make specifications. In Raj Reddy, editor, *Proceedings, Fifth International Joint Conference on Artificial Intelligence*, pages 1045–1058. Department of Computer Science, Carnegie-Mellon University, 1977.

[5]   Manuel Clavel, Francisco Duran, Steven Eker, José Meseguer, and M.-O. Stehr. Maude as a formal meta-tool. In *Proceedings, FM'99 - Formal Methods, Volume II*, pages 1684–1701. Springer, 1999. Lecture Notes in Computer Science, Volume 1709.

[6]   Manuel Clavel, Steven Eker, Patrick Lincoln, and José Meseguer. Principles of Maude. In José Meseguer, editor, *Proceedings, First International Workshop on Rewriting Logic and its Applications*. Elsevier Science, 1996. Volume 4, *Electronic Notes in Theoretical Computer Science*.

[7]   Manuel Clavel, Steven Eker, and José Meseguer. Current design and implementation of the Cafe prover and Knuth-Bendix tools, 1997. Presented at CafeOBJ Workshop, Kanazawa, October 1997.

[8]   Department of Defense. Reference manual for the Ada programming language. United States Government, Report ANSI/MIL-STD-1815A, 1983.

[9]   Răzvan Diaconescu. *Category-based Semantics for Equational and Constraint Logic Programming*. PhD thesis, Programming Research Group, Oxford University, 1994.

[10] Răzvan Diaconescu. Behavioural coherence in object-oriented algebraic specification. Technical Report IS–RR–98–0017F, Japan Advanced Institute for Science and Technology, June 1998. Submitted for publication.

[11] Răzvan Diaconescu and Kokichi Futatsugi. *CafeOBJ Report: The Language, Proof Techniques, and Methodologies for Object-Oriented Algebraic Specification*. World Scientific, 1998. AMAST Series in Computing, Volume 6.

[12] Răzvan Diaconescu and Kokichi Futatsugi. Logical foundations of CafeOBJ, 1999. Submitted for publication.

[13] Hurbert L. Dreyfus. *What Computers Still Can't Do*. MIT, 1992.

[14] Derek Coleman *et al.* The Axis papers. Technical report, Hewlett-Packard Labs, Bristol, September 1988.

[15] Kokichi Futatsugi, Joseph Goguen, and José Meseguer, editors. *OBJ/-CafeOBJ/Maude at Formal Methods '99.* Theta (Bucharest), 1999. Proceedings of a workshop held in Toulouse, France, 20 and 22 September 1999.

[16] W. Wyat Gibbs. Software's chronic crisis. *Scientific American*, pages 72–81, September 1994.

[17] Joseph Goguen. Semantics of computation. In Ernest Manes, editor, *Proceedings, First International Symposium on Category Theory Applied to Computation and Control*, pages 151–163. Springer, 1975. (San Fransisco, February 1974.) Lecture Notes in Computer Science, Volume 25.

[18] Joseph Goguen. Memories of ADJ. *Bulletin of the European Association for Theoretical Computer Science*, 36:96–102, October 1989. Guest column in the 'Algebraic Specification Column.' Also in *Current Trends in Theoretical Computer Science: Essays and Tutorials*, World Scientific, 1993, pages 76–81.

[19] Joseph Goguen. Requirements engineering as the reconciliation of social and technical issues. In Marina Jirotka and Joseph Goguen, editors, *Requirements Engineering: Social and Technical Issues*, pages 165–200. Academic, 1994.

[20] Joseph Goguen. Formality and informality in requirements engineering. In *Proceedings, International Conference on Requirements Engineering*, pages 102–108. IEEE Computer Society, April 1996.

[21] Joseph Goguen. Towards a social, ethical theory of information. In Geoffrey Bowker, Leigh Star, William Turner, and Les Gasser, editors, *Social Science, Technical Systems and Cooperative Work: Beyond the Great Divide*, pages 27–56. Erlbaum, 1997.

[22] Joseph Goguen, Kai Lin, Akira Mori, Grigore Roşu, and Akiyoshi Sato. Distributed cooperative formal methods tools. In Michael Lowry, editor, *Proceedings, Automated Software Engineering*, pages 55–62. IEEE, 1997.

[23] Joseph Goguen, Kai Lin, Akira Mori, Grigore Roşu, and Akiyoshi Sato. Tools for distributed cooperative design and validation. In *Proceedings, CafeOBJ Symposium.* Japan Advanced Institute for Science and Technology, 1998. Namazu, Japan, April 1998.

[24] Joseph Goguen and Grant Malcolm. *Algebraic Semantics of Imperative Programs.* MIT, 1996.

[25] Joseph Goguen and Grant Malcolm. A hidden agenda. Technical Report CS97–538, UCSD, Dept. Computer Science & Eng., May 1997. To

appear in special issue of *Theoretical Computer Science* on Algebraic Engineering, edited by Chrystopher Nehaniv and Masamo Ito. Extended abstract in *Proc., Conf. Intelligent Systems: A Semiotic Perspective, Vol. I*, ed. J. Albus, A. Meystel and R. Quintero, Nat. Inst. Science & Technology (Gaithersberg MD, 20–23 October 1996), pages 159–167.

[26] Joseph Goguen and Grant Malcolm. Hidden coinduction: Behavioral correctness proofs for objects. *Mathematical Structures in Computer Science*, 9(3):287–319, June 1999.

[27] Joseph Goguen, Grant Malcolm, and Tom Kemp. A hidden Herbrand theorem: Combining the object, logic and functional paradigms. In Catuscia Palamidessi, Hugh Glaser, and Karl Meinke, editors, *Principles of Declarative Programming*, pages 445–462. Springer Lecture Notes in Computer Science, Volume 1490, 1998. Full version to appear in *Electronic Journal of Functional and Logic Programming*, MIT, 1999.

[28] Joseph Goguen and José Meseguer. Eqlog: Equality, types, and generic modules for logic programming. In Douglas DeGroot and Gary Lindstrom, editors, *Logic Programming: Functions, Relations and Equations*, pages 295–363. Prentice-Hall, 1986. An earlier version appears in *Journal of Logic Programming*, Volume 1, Number 2, pages 179–210, September 1984.

[29] Joseph Goguen and José Meseguer. Unifying functional, object-oriented and relational programming, with logical semantics. In Bruce Shriver and Peter Wegner, editors, *Research Directions in Object-Oriented Programming*, pages 417–477. MIT, 1987. Preliminary version in *SIGPLAN Notices*, Volume 21, Number 10, pages 153–162, October 1986.

[30] Joseph Goguen and Grigore Roşu. Hiding more of hidden algebra. In Jeannette Wing, Jim Woodcock, and Jim Davies, editors, *FM'99 – Formal Methods*, pages 1704–1719. Springer, 1999. Lecture Notes in Computer Sciences, Volume 1709, Proceedings of World Congress on Formal Methods, Toulouse, France.

[31] Joseph Goguen and James Thatcher. Initial algebra semantics. In *Proceedings, Fifteenth Symposium on Switching and Automata Theory*, pages 63–77. IEEE, 1974.

[32] Joseph Goguen, James Thatcher, and Eric Wagner. An initial algebra approach to the specification, correctness and implementation of abstract data types. In Raymond Yeh, editor, *Current Trends in Programming Methodology, IV*, pages 80–149. Prentice-Hall, 1978.

[33] Joseph Goguen and William Tracz. An implementation-oriented semantics for module composition. In Gary Leavens and Murali Sitaraman, editors, *Foundations of Component-based Systems*. Cambridge, To appear 1999.

[34] Alasdair Gray. *Unlikely Stories, Mostly*. Penguin, 1984.

[35] Lutz Hamel. *Behavioural Verification and Implementation of an Opti-mizing Compiler for OBJ3*. PhD thesis, Oxford University Computing Lab, 1996.

[36] Robert Harper, David MacQueen, and Robin Milner. Standard ML. Tech-nical Report ECS-LFCS-86-2, Department of Computer Science, Univer-sity of Edinburgh, 1986.

[37] Marina Jirotka and Joseph Goguen. *Requirements Engineering: Social and Technical Issues*. Academic, 1994.

[38] Donald Knuth. *The Art of Computer Programming, Volume 1: Funda-mental Algorithms*. Addison-Wesley, 1971.

[39] F. William Lawvere. An elementary theory of the category of sets. *Pro-ceedings, National Academy of Sciences, U.S.A.*, 52:1506–1511, 1964.

[40] Grant Malcolm and Joseph Goguen. An executable course on the al-gebraic semantics of imperative programs. In Michael Hinchey and C. Neville Dean, editors, *Teaching and Learning Formal Methods*, pages 161–179. Academic, 1996.

[41] José Meseguer. Conditional rewriting logic: Deduction, models and con-currency. In Stéphane Kaplan and Misuhiro Okada, editors, *Conditional and Typed Rewriting Systems*, pages 64–91. Springer, 1991. Lecture Notes in Computer Science, Volume 516.

[42] José Meseguer. Membership algebra as a logical framework for equational specification. In Francisco Parisi-Presicce, editor, *Proceedings, WADT'97 – Workshop on Abstract Data Types*, pages 18–61. Springer, 1998. Lecture Notes in Computer Science, Volume 1376.

[43] Peter G. Neumann. *Computer-Related Risks*. ACM (Addison-Wesley), 1995.

[44] Francisco Pinheiro and Joseph Goguen. An object-oriented tool for trac-ing requirements. *IEEE Software*, pages 52–64, March 1996. Special issue of papers from ICRE'96.

[45] Grigore Roşu. Behavioral coinductive rewriting. In Kokichi Futatsugi, Joseph Goguen, and José Meseguer, editors, *OBJ/CafeOBJ/Maude at For-mal Methods '99*, pages 179–196. Theta (Bucharest), 1999. Proceedings of a workshop held in Toulouse, France, 20 and 22 September 1999.

[46] Grigore Roşu and Joseph Goguen. Hidden congruent deduction. In Ricardo Caferra and Gernot Salzer, editors, *Proceedings, 1998 Workshop on First Order Theorem Proving*, pages 213–223. Technische Universität Wien, 1998. (Schloss Wilhelminenberg, Vienna, November 23-25, 1998). Full version to appear in *Lecture Notes in Artificial Intelligence*, Springer, 1999.

[47] Jeannette Wing, Jim Woodcock, and Jim Davies, editors. *FM'99 – Formal Methods*. Springer, 1999. Lecture Notes in Computer Sciences, Volumes 1078 and 1709, Proceedings of World Congress on Formal Methods, Toulouse, France.

I
AN INTRODUCTION TO OBJ

Chapter 1

INTRODUCING OBJ

Joseph A. Goguen

Department of Computer Science & Engineering, University of California at San Diego, La Jolla CA 92093-0114, USA.

Timothy Winkler

SRI International, Menlo Park CA 94025, USA.

José Meseguer

SRI International, Menlo Park CA 94025, USA.

Kokichi Futatsugi

Japan Advanced Institute of Science and Technology, 1-1 Asahidai, Tatsunokuchi, Ishakawa, Japan.

Jean-Pierre Jouannaud

Université de Paris-Sud, 91405 Orsay, France.

Abstract   This is an introduction to the philosophy and use of OBJ, emphasizing its operational semantics, with aspects of its history and its logical semantics. Release 2 of OBJ3 is described in detail, with many examples. OBJ is a wide spectrum first-order functional language that is rigorously based on (order sorted) equational logic and parameterized programming, supporting a declarative style that facilitates verification and allows OBJ to be used as a theorem prover.

   Order sorted algebra provides a notion of *subsort* that rigorously supports multiple inheritance, exception handling and overloading. *Parameterized programming* gives powerful support for design, verification, reuse, and maintenance, using two kinds of module: *objects* to encapsulate executable code, and in particular to define abstract data types by initial algebra semantics; and (loose) *theories* to specify both syntactic and semantic properties of modules. Each kind of module can be parameterized, where actual parameters may be modules. For parameter instantiation, a *view* binds the formal entities in an interface theory to actual entities in a module, and also asserts that the target module satisfies the semantic conditions of the interface theory. *Module expressions* allow complex combinations of already defined modules, including sums, instantiations, and transformations; moreover, evaluating a module expression actually constructs the described software (sub)system from the given components. *Default views* can greatly reduce the effort of instantiating modules, by allowing obvious correspondences to be left out. We argue that first-order parameterized programming includes much of the power of higher-order programming, in a form that is often more convenient.

Although OBJ executable code normally consists of equations that are interpreted as rewrite rules, OBJ3 objects can also encapsulate Lisp code, e.g., to provide efficient built-in data types, or to augment the system with new capabilities; we describe the syntax of this facility, and provide some examples. In addition, OBJ provides rewriting modulo associative, commutative and/or identity equations, as well as user-definable evaluation strategies that allow lazy, eager, and mixed evaluation strategies on an operator-by-operator basis; memoization is also available on an operator-by-operator basis. In addition, OBJ3 supports the application of equations one at a time, either forwards or backwards; this is needed for equational theorem proving. Finally, OBJ provides user-definable mixfix syntax, which supports the notational conventions of particular application domains.

1   INTRODUCTION

This paper motivates and describes the use of OBJ, based on Release 2.04 of the OBJ3 system. OBJ3 is the latest in a series of OBJ systems, each of which has been rigorously based upon equational logic; however, the semantic basis of OBJ is not developed here in full detail. The OBJ3 system is implemented in Common Lisp, and is based on ideas from order sorted algebra and parameterized programming. OBJ3 provides mixfix syntax, flexible subsorts, parameterized modules, views, and rewriting modulo associativity, commutativity, and/or identity. With its module database and its ability to incorporate Lisp code, this provides a very flexible and extensible environment that is convenient for specification and rapid prototyping, as well as for building new systems, such as experimental languages and theorem proving environments. For example, OBJ3 has been used for building FOOPS, an object oriented specification and programming system [74, 87], the Eqlog system [71, 72, 25] for equational logic (or relational) programming, OOZE [3], an object oriented specification language influenced by Z [142], the 2OBJ metalogical framework theorem prover [81], and TOOR [130], a system for tracing requirements.

OBJ has been used for many applications, including debugging algebraic specifications [77], rapid prototyping [69], defining programming languages in a way that directly yields an interpreter (see Appendix Section C.2, as well as [79] and some elegant work of Peter Mosses [120, 121]), specifying software systems (e.g., the GKS graphics kernel system [28], an Ada configuration manager [40], the MacIntosh QuickDraw program [126], and OBJ itself [20]), hardware specification, simulation, and verification (see [144] and Section 4.8), specification and verification of imperative programs [66], specification of user interface designs [60, 58], and theorem proving [53, 66, 59]; several of these were done under a UK government grant. OBJ has also been combined with Petri nets, thus allowing structured data in tokens [5], and was used to verify compilers for parallel programming languages in the ESPRIT sponsored PRO-COS project [137, 138]. In addition, OBJ serves as a programming language for the massively parallel Rewrite Rule Machine, which executes rewrite rules directly [63, 152, 106, 75, 107, 2, 54, 1]; in fact, given equal silicon floorspace and development effort, OBJ on such a machine could out-perform a conventional language on a conventional machine, because of the direct concurrent execution of rewrite rules. Some examples using OBJ3 for theorem proving and hardware verification from [51] and [59] are given in Appendix Section C.4. In [66], OBJ3 is used for teaching the semantics of imperative programming languages, and all the proofs in [66] are actually executable OBJ3 programs; see [109] for a more detailed discussion of the educational uses of OBJ.

1.1   A BRIEF HISTORY OF OBJ

OBJ was designed in 1976 by Goguen [43], using "error algebras" to extend algebraic abstract data type theory with error handling and partial functions; this first design also used ideas from Clear [8, 10] for parameterized modules, thus giving birth to parameterized programming. The first implementations of OBJ were done from 1977 to 1979 at UCLA by Joseph Tardo and Joseph Goguen. OBJ0 [45] was based on unsorted equational logic, while OBJT used error algebras plus an "image" construct for parameterization [148, 82]. David Plaisted implemented OBJ1, building on OBJT during 1982–83 at SRI, based on theoretical and design work carried out with Joseph Goguen and José Meseguer; improvements of OBJ1 over OBJT included rewriting modulo associativity and/or commutativity, hash coded memo functions, the use of theories with loose semantics as well as objects with initial semantics, and new interactive features [77] which made the system more convenient for users.

OBJ2 [35, 36] was implemented using parts of OBJ1 during 1984-85 at SRI by Kokichi Futatsugi and Jean-Pierre Jouannaud, following a design in which José Meseguer and Joseph Goguen also participated, based on order sorted algebra [44, 76, 62, 73, 141] rather than error algebra; also, OBJ2 provided Clear-like parameterized modules, theories, and views, although not in full generality. Another influence on OBJ3's design and implementation was the HISP system [38, 39, 30] of Kokichi Futatsugi.

OBJ3 was first developed at SRI by Timothy Winkler, José Meseguer, Joseph Goguen, Claude and Hélène Kirchner, and Aristide Megrelis; Release 2 was developed at SRI by Timothy Winkler, Patrick Lincoln, José Meseguer, and Joseph Goguen, and later extended by Winkler and Goguen at the Programming Research Group of the Oxford University Computing Lab; version 2.04 includes further small bug fixes made at Oxford. Although the syntax of OBJ3 is close to that of OBJ2, it has a different implementation based on a simpler approach to order sorted rewriting [101], and it also provides much more sophisticated parameterized programming. OBJ2 and OBJ3 can be seen as implementations of Clear [8, 10], where the chosen logic is order sorted equational logic.

Other implementations of OBJ1 include UMIST-OBJ from the University of Manchester Institute of Science and Technology [20], Abstract Pascal from the University of Manchester [105], and MC-OBJ from the University of Milan [14]; the first two are written in Pascal and the third in C. In addition, there is a Franz Lisp OBJ2 done at Washington State University [143]. UMIST-OBJ has been made available as a proprietary software product from Gerrard Software, under the name ObjEx.

OBJ has been extended in many directions, including logic (or relational) programming (the Eqlog system [71, 72, 25]), object oriented programming (the FOOPS system [74, 87]), object oriented specification (OOZE [3]), requirements tracing (TOOR [130]), higher-order functional programming [97, 110], and LOTOS-style specification for communication protocols [127, 128].

Recent developments within the OBJ community include CafeOBJ, Maude, and CASL. CafeOBJ [26, 27] is being built at the Japan Institute of Science and Technology under the direction of Prof. Kokichi Futatsugi; it extends OBJ3 with hidden algebra [55, 80, 68, 67] for behavioral specification, and with rewriting logic [113, 114] for applications programming. Maude [112, 16] is being built at SRI International under the direction of Dr. José Meseguer; it extends OBJ with rewriting logic, and has been successfully used for metaprogramming, reflection, and algorithm implementation [17, 18]. CASL [19] is being developed by a European consortium called CoFI, whose members include Maura Cerioli, Till Mossakowsky, Peter Mosses, Don Sannella, Bernd Krieg-Bruckner, Michel Bidoit, and Andre Tarlecki; this system is loosely based on OBJ ideas, including parameterized programming, but is more oriented towards specification than verification and prototyping, and is intended to support experimentation with a variety of logics. As this document is being finished, a system called Kumo is being installed at UCSD. Kumo is a proof assistant for first order hidden logic, that also generates websites to document the proofs obtained [65, 64, 78, 60]; it greatly extends the theorem proving power of OBJ, in the logics supported, in the level of automation obtained, and in the user interface, including proof documentation.

1.2   A BRIEF SUMMARY OF PARAMETERIZED PROGRAMMING

OBJ has three kinds of entity at its top level: objects, theories, and views. An **object** encapsulates executable code, while a **theory** defines properties that may (or may not) be satisfied by another object or theory. Both objects and theories are **modules**. A **view** is a *binding* of the entities declared in some theory to entities in some other module, and also an assertion that the other module satisfies the properties declared in the theory. Theories and views are found in no other implemented language with which we are familiar; however, Standard ML has been influenced by this approach.

Modules can import other previously defined modules, and therefore an OBJ program is conceptually a *graph* of modules. Modules have **signatures** that introduce new sorts[1] and new operators[2] among both new and old sorts. In addition, **variables** with declared sorts are introduced. **Terms** are built up from variables and operators, respecting their sort declarations. Modules can be parameterized, and parameterized modules use theories to define both the syntax and the *semantics* of their interfaces. Views indicate how to instantiate a parameterized module with an actual parameter.

This kind of module composition is, in practice, more powerful than the purely functional composition of traditional functional programming, because a single module instantiation can compose together many different functions all at once, in complex ways. For example, a parameterized complex arithmetic module CPXA can easily be instantiated with any of several real arithmetic modules as actual parameter:

- single precision reals, CPXA[SP-REAL],

- double precision reals, CPXA[DP-REAL],

- multiple precision reals, CPXA[MP-REAL],

where SP-REAL, DP-REAL, and MP-REAL are modules for single-precision, double-precision, and multiple precision floating point arithmetic. Each instantiation may involve substituting dozens of functions into the definitions of dozens of other functions. While something similar is possible in higher-order

---

[1] Here and hereafter, we generally use the word "sort" instead of "type" because of the very many different meanings that have been assigned to the word "type."

[2] Although we generally use the word "operator," in this paper it usually means "function" because we are dealing with a functional language.

functional programming by coding up modules as records, it seems much less natural, particularly if this encoding also specifies the semantics of the interface of CPXA. Furthermore, parameterized programming allows the logic to remain first-order, so that understanding and verification can be simpler. Section 4.7 shows that many typical higher-order functional programming techniques can be implemented with OBJ parameterized modules, often with essentially the same flexibility and with greater clarity, while Section 4.8 shows that a typical application of higher-order functions, namely hardware verification, is readily captured in the simpler formalism.

1.3   AN OVERVIEW OF THIS DOCUMENT

OBJ3's top level accepts declarations (for objects, theories and views), and commands to reduce terms, to show various status and structural information, to set various conditions, and to do various actions. A **reduction** evaluates a given term with respect to a given object, and OBJ supports reduction modulo associativity, commutativity, and/or identity. Section 2 describes objects, Section 4.1 describes theories, Section 4.2 describes views, and Section 2.3.1 describes reduction. The show, set and do commands are discussed in various places, but are collected in Appendix A. OBJ's approach to imported modules and to built-in sorts and operators is described in Section 3, with many further details of the latter in Appendix D. Built-ins can be useful, for example, in adding new built-in data types to OBJ, or in extending or modifying OBJ in various other ways. Section 5 discusses how to apply rewrite rules one at a time, forwards or backwards, which is needed for theorem proving. Section 6 tries to discuss what OBJ is and is not. Appendix A gives some hints on how to use OBJ, Appendix B gives OBJ3's syntax, and Appendix C gives many examples. We have tried to give a fairly comprehensive bibliography of papers that use OBJ.

1.4   ACKNOWLEDGEMENTS

We wish to thank: Professor Rod Burstall for his extended collaboration on Clear and its foundations, which inspired the parameterization mechanism of OBJ; Professor David Plaisted for his many suggestions about the design of OBJ, and for his implementation of OBJ1; Dr. Joseph Tardo for his pioneering and courageous implementation of OBJT; Drs. James Thatcher, Eric Wagner and Jesse Wright for their initial collaboration on abstract data types; Dr. Peter Mosses for his valuable suggestions and his efforts to use a very early version of OBJ3; Dr. Victoria Stavridou for her use of OBJ3 in hardware specification and verification; Dr. Claude Kirchner for his work on the pattern matching routines and rule generation for OBJ3; Dr. Hélène Kirchner for her work on the rule generation for OBJ3; Dr. Adolfo Socorro for help checking the details of OBJ3 syntax; Dr. Patrick Lincoln for help with the routines for rewriting modulo equations used in Release 2 of OBJ3; Mr. Aristide Megrelis for his work on the OBJ3 parser; and several generations of students at Oxford and UCSD for their feedback on using OBJ3 in courses on theorem proving, and on the semantics of programming languages [57]. Much of this paper is based upon [47, 52, 86] and [35].

The research reported in this paper has been supported in part by: Office of Naval Research Contracts N00014-85-C-0417, N00014-86-C-0450, and N00014-90-C-0086; NSF Grant CCR-8707155; grants from the Science and Engineering Research Council; a gift from the System Development Foundation; and a grant from Fujitsu Laboratories.

2   OBJECTS

The most important OBJ unit is the **object**[3], which encapsulates executable code. Syntactically, an object begins with the keyword obj and ends with endo[4]. The name of the object occurs immediately after the obj keyword; following this comes is, and then the **body** of the object. For unparameterized objects, the name is a simple identifier, such as STACK-OF-INT, PHRASE or OBJ14. Parameterized objects have an interface specification in place of a simple name, as discussed in Section 4. Schematically, the form is

    obj ⟨ModId⟩ is
    · · · · ·
    endo

where ⟨ModId⟩ is a metasyntactic symbol for a module identifier, by convention all upper case, possibly including special characters; however, this convention is not enforced, and any character string not containing blanks (i.e., spaces) or special characters can be used. OBJ keywords are lower case.

2.1   STRONG SORTING AND SUBSORTS

We believe that languages should have strong but flexible "type systems." Among the advantages of "strong typing," which of course we call **strong sorting**, are: to catch meaningless expressions before they are executed; to separate logically and intuitively distinct concepts; to enhance readability by documenting these distinctions; and, when the notion of subsort is added, to support multiple inheritance, overloading (a form of subsort polymorphism),

---

[3] Objects in this sense are not very closely related to objects in the sense of object-oriented programming; rather, they provide executable algebraic specifications for abstract data types.
[4] OBJ3 has the uniform convention that ending keywords can be of the form "end<x>" where "<x>" is the first letter, or first two letters, of the corresponding initial keyword. The initial keyword spelled backwards, as in jbo, is an archaic form for some keywords preserved from earlier versions of OBJ.

coercions, multiple representations, and error handling, without the confusion, and lack of semantics, found in many programming languages (see [73] for a more detailed discussion of these issues). In particular, overloading can allow users to write simpler expressions, because context can often determine which possibility is intended. Of course, strong sorting may require additional declarations, but with a modern editor, it is little trouble to insert declarations, and many could even be generated automatically.

Ordinary unsorted logic offers the dubious advantage that anything can be applied to anything; for example,

$$\text{first-name(not(age(3 * false)))}$$
$$\text{iff }_2\text{ birth-place(temperature(329))}$$

is a well formed expression. Although beloved by Lisp and Prolog hackers, unsorted logic is too permissive. Unfortunately, the obvious alternative, many sorted logic, is too restrictive, because it does not support overloaded function symbols, such as _+_ for integer, rational, and complex numbers. Moreover, strictly speaking, an expression like (-4 / -2)! does not even parse (assuming that factorial only applies to natural numbers), because (-4 / -2) looks to the parser like a rational rather than a natural. In Section 2.3.3 below, we show that order sorted algebra with *retracts* provides sufficient expressiveness, while still banishing truly meaningless expressions.

Let us now be specific. Sorts are declared in OBJ3 with the syntax

    sorts ⟨SortIdList⟩ .

where ⟨SortIdList⟩ is a list of ⟨SortId⟩s, as in

    sorts Nat Int Rat .

When there is just one sort, it may be more fluent to write

    sort ⟨SortId⟩ .

However, sort and sorts are actually synonymous.

Warning: Sort declarations must be terminated with a blank followed by a period.

Order sorted algebra, sometimes abbreviated **OSA** in the following, is designed to handle cases where things of one sort are also of another sort (e.g., all natural numbers are also rational numbers), and where operators or expressions may have several different sorts. The essence of order sorted algebra is to provide a *subsort* partial ordering among sorts, and to interpret it semantically as subset inclusion among the carriers of models; for example, Nat < Rat means that $M_{\text{Nat}} \subseteq M_{\text{Rat}}$, where M is a model, and M_s is its set of elements of sort s. (Note that OBJ uses < instead of ≤ simply for typographical convenience.) OSA also supports **multiple inheritance**, in the sense that a given sort may have *more than one* distinct supersort.

Although many sorted algebra has been quite successful for the theory of abstract data types, it can produce some very awkward code in practice, primarily due to difficulties in handling erroneous expressions, such as dividing by zero in the rationals, or taking the top of an empty stack. In fact, there *is no* really satisfying way to define either rationals or stacks with (unconditional) many sorted algebra: [83] and [29] contain some examples which show just how awkward things can get, and [73] actually proves that certain kinds of specifications cannot be expressed at all in many sorted equational logic.

OSA overcomes these obstacles with its subsorts and overloaded operators, and it allows functions to be total that would otherwise have to be partial, by restricting them to a subsort. Two pleasant facts are that OSA is only slightly more difficult than many sorted algebra, and that essentially all results generalize without difficulty from the many sorted to the order sorted case. Although this paper omits the technical details, OSA is a rigorous mathematical theory. OSA was originally suggested by Goguen in 1978 [44], and is further developed in [76] and [73]; some alternative approaches have been given by Gogolla [41, 42], Mosses [122], Poigne [133, 134], Reynolds [135], Smolka *et al.* [140, 141], Wadge [150], and others. A survey as of 1993 appears in [61], along with some new generalizations. Meseguer has recently proposed a new generalization, called membership equational logic [115].

OBJ3 directly supports *subsort polymorphism*, which is operator overloading that is consistent under subsort restriction (this is further discussed in Section 2.2). By contrast, languages like ML [91], Hope [13] and Miranda [149] support *parametric polymorphism*, following ideas of Strachey [147] as further developed by Milner [119]. OBJ3's parameterized modules also provide a parametric capability, but instantiations are determined by views, rather than by unification; see Section 4.7 for further discussion.

The basic syntax for a subsort declaration in OBJ3 is

```
subsort ⟨Sort⟩ < ⟨Sort⟩ .
```

which means that the set of things having the first ⟨Sort⟩[5] is a subset (not necessarily proper) of the things having the second ⟨Sort⟩. Similarly,

```
subsorts ⟨SortList⟩ < ⟨SortList⟩ < ... .
```

means that each sort in the first ⟨SortList⟩ is a subsort of each sort in the second ⟨SortList⟩, and so on. (Actually **subsort** and **subsorts** are synonyms.)

---

[5] Note that ⟨Sort⟩s differ from ⟨SortId⟩s in allowing qualification by module name; see Appendix B for details of the notation for syntax that is used in this paper.

Warning: The elements of each list must be separated by blanks, and the declaration must be terminated with a blank followed by a period. OBJ3 complains if any sort in a subsort declaration doesn't appear in a previous sort declaration, or if there are cycles in the graph of the subsort relation. Subsort cycles may produce strange behavior.

2.2   OPERATOR AND EXPRESSION SYNTAX

We believe it is worth some extra implementation effort and processing time to support syntax that is as flexible, as informative, and as close as possible to users' intuitions and standard usage in particular problem domains. Thus, users of OBJ can define any syntax they like for operators, including prefix, postfix, infix, and most generally, **mixfix**; this is similar to ECL [15]. Obviously, there are many opportunities for ambiguity in parsing such a syntax. OBJ's convention is that a term is **well formed** if and only if it has exactly one parse, or more precisely, a unique parse of *least sort*; it is intended that the parser give information about difficulties that it encounters, including multiple parses of least sort.

Warning: Due to the treatment of user-supplied operator precedence (see Section 2.4.3), the parser in Release 2 of OBJ3 may sometimes fail to find a parse, even though an unambiguous parse exists. This can usually be repaired by adding parentheses.

Let us now discuss operator syntax. The argument and value sorts of an operator are declared at the same time that its **syntactic form** is declared. There are two kinds of syntactic form declaration in OBJ. We call the first kind the **standard form**, because it defines the parenthesized-prefix-with-commas syntax that is standard in mathematics. For example,

```
op push : Stack Int -> Stack .
```

declares syntax for terms of the form push(X,Y) of sort Stack, where X has sort Stack and Y has sort Int. If the top operator of a term has standard syntactic form, then its arguments (i.e., its first level subterms) must be separated by commas and be enclosed within a top level matching pair of parentheses, for the entire term to be well formed. OBJ3's syntax for a standard operator declaration is

op ⟨*OpForm*⟩ : ⟨*SortList*⟩ -> ⟨*Sort*⟩ .

where ⟨*OpForm*⟩ is a nonempty string of characters, possibly consisting of multiple (blank-separated) tokens. Operators in standard form should not include the underbar character, "_" (some further syntactic requirements for ⟨*OpForm*⟩ are discussed below).

Warning: An operator declaration must be terminated with a blank followed by a period[6], and all of the sorts (and operators — see the discussion of id declarations below) used in it must have been previously declared.

The second kind of OBJ syntax for operator declarations is called **mixfix form**, and it allows declaring arbitrary mixfix syntax. This kind of declaration uses place-holders, indicated by an underbar character, to indicate where arguments should appear; the rest of the operator form consists of the keywords associated with the operator. For example, the following is a prefix declaration for top as used in terms like top push(S,5):

```
op top_ : Stack -> Int .
```

Similarly, the "outfix" form of the singleton set formation operator, as in { 4 }, is declared by

```
op {_} : Int -> Set .
```

and the infix form for addition, as in 2 + 3, is given by

```
op _+_ : Int Int -> Int .
```

while a mixfix declaration for conditional is

```
op if_then_else_fi : Bool Int Int -> Int .
```

Between the : and the -> in an operator declaration comes the **arity** of the operator, and after the -> comes its **value sort** (sometimes called "co-arity"); the ⟨arity, value sort⟩ pair is called the **rank** of the operator. The general syntax for mixfix form operator declarations is

```
op ⟨OpForm⟩ : ⟨SortList⟩ -> ⟨Sort⟩ .
```

where ⟨OpForm⟩ is a non-empty string of characters, possibly consisting of multiple (blank-separated) tokens, possibly including blanks and matching pairs of parentheses. Blanks in the form have no effect when they are contiguous to an underbar. The following shows a form with a blank:

```
op _is in_ : Int IntSet -> Bool .
```

Warning: A mixfix operator form should be neither entirely blank, nor consist of just one underbar. Also, it must contain *exactly* as many underbars as there are sorts in its arity.

---

[6] An exception is if the last character is a left bracket, "]", which will occur if there are attributes (see Section 2.4).

The entire ⟨*OpForm*⟩ of an operator can be enclosed in parentheses. This can be used to avoid syntactic ambiguity. For example, in the following declaration for division of rational numbers by non-zero rationals,

```
op (_:_) : Rat NzNat -> Rat .
```

failure to enclose the operator name in parentheses could cause the first ":" to be erroneously treated as the delimiter for the ⟨*SortList*⟩ of the declaration. Such enclosing parentheses are not considered part of the ⟨*OpForm*⟩, but rather provide a way to avoid this kind of syntactic ambiguity. The rule is that if the first token encountered after the "op" in an operator declaration is a left parenthesis that is matched by a right parenthesis before the delimiting ":", then these parentheses are interpreted as delimiters, rather than as part of the ⟨*OpForm*⟩. This does not preclude using parentheses as tokens in the syntax of an operator. However, the first token in the syntax of an operator should never be a left parenthesis. For example, one can declare an "apply" operator in a data type of lambda expressions with the syntax

```
op _(_) : Lambda Lambda -> Lambda .
```

Constant declarations have no underbars and have empty arity. For example,

```
op true : -> Bool .
```

Operators with the same rank but different forms can be declared together using the keyword ops; for example,

```
ops zero one : -> S .
ops (_+_) (_*_) : S S -> S .
```

The parentheses are required in the second case, to indicate the boundary between the two forms.

Warning: op and ops are *not* synonymous.

Here is a simple example illustrating some of the syntax given so far; it defines strings of bits.

```
obj BITS is
  sorts Bit Bits .
  ops 0 1 : -> Bit .
  op nil : -> Bits .
  op _._ : Bit Bits -> Bits .
endo
```

A typical term over the syntax declared in this object is 0 . 1 . 0 . nil.

Warning: The period character, ".", is special in OBJ3, because it is used to terminate operator and equation declarations, among other constructions (although it is not required in simple situations where the input is self-delimiting). Sometimes you may need to enclose terms in parentheses to prevent an internal period from being interpreted as a final period. Tokens, such as ".", that are used to delimit syntactic units only function as delimiters when not enclosed in parentheses.

The parse command, with syntax

    parse ⟨*Term*⟩ .

can be used at the top level of OBJ3, and also inside modules, to check the parsing of terms. It causes a fully parenthesized form of ⟨*Term*⟩ to be printed with its sort, provided it can be parsed.

When parsing fails, the system gives some diagnostic information that may help to discover the problem. For example,

    red in INT : 1 + 10 div 2 .

produces the following

```
No successful parse for the input:
1 + 10 div 2
partial descriptions:
 _ _ _ div _
1 + 10 _[div]_ 2
```

Two different "partial descriptions" are given of problematic tokens. In the first, the problematic tokens are replaced by "_". In the second, all tokens are displayed, but the problematic ones are enclosed within a matching "_[" and "]_" pair. This information can be very useful in detecting misspelled variable names and operator tokens. For example, the token "div" above should have been "quo". Tokens are considered problematic if they do not appear in any partial parse, where partial parses are generated by considering the prefixes of each suffix of the input string. In general, this only gives approximate information. For example, "1 + 10" is parsed as a prefix in the above expression, which may not be what the user intended.

When strong sorting is not sufficient to prevent ambiguity in a term that uses overloaded operators and subsorts, then **qualification** notation can be useful. For example, to distinguish the bit 0 in the object BIT above from the natural number zero, one can write 0.Bit and 0.Nat. Sort qualifiers can also be applied to mixfix operators; for example, (X is in Set1 or Set2).Nat could be used to distinguish a natural number valued operator is in (as used for bags) from a truth valued operator is in (as used for sets); the parentheses are not optional in this case.

Sometimes sort qualification doesn't work, but module qualification does, because different instances of the operator syntax have been introduced in different modules. For example, one might write (when X is in Set2 do Act25).LANG, where LANG is the name of a module. Sort names can also be qualified by module names, as in Nat.NAT, Elt.X, Elt.Y, etc. Quali-fication by module can be distinguished from qualification by sort as long as distinct names are involved, which happens naturally by using the convention suggested in this paper, that module names are all upper case, while sort names only have an upper case letter at the beginning (but note that this convention is not enforced by OBJ3).

Warning: Complete module names must be used, and the complete names of modules that have been created by evaluating module expressions can be surprisingly long; see Section 4.5.

Because OBJ3 is based on order sorted algebra, it supports **overloading**, so that the same operator symbol can have several different ranks. For example, addition might have the following declarations:

```
op _+_ : Nat Nat -> Nat .
op _+_ : Rat Rat -> Rat .
```

When the arity sorts of one operator declaration are less than those of another for the same function symbol, then in the models, the function interpreting the operator with smaller arity is the *restriction* to the smaller arity of the function interpreting the operator with larger arity. For example, the natural number addition of natural numbers should yield the same result as the rational number addition of the same natural numbers, provided we have declared Nat < Rat.

The **signature** of a module consists of the sorts, subsort relation, and op-erators available in it, where each operator has a form, arity, and value sort. Under the natural assumption of regularity, each order sorted term has a well defined least sort, where a signature is **regular** iff for any operator $f : w \to s$ and any $w' \leq w$ there is a least rank $\langle w'', s'' \rangle$ among all $f : w'' \to s''$ sat-isfying $w' \leq w''$, where the ordering of ranks $\langle w, s \rangle$ is pointwise [62, 76]. A signatureinxxsignature,coherent is **coherent** if each connected component of the set of sorts ordered by the subsort ordering has a top element, where the connected components are the equivalence classes under the equivalence relation obtained from the relation

$$ sRs' \text{ iff } s \leq s' \text{ or } s' \leq s $$

by closure under transitivity. To guarantee that OBJ3 works correctly, all signatures should be regular and coherent, and each connected component should have a top element; however, OBJ3 does not check these assumptions.

Using subsorts, and representing list concatenation by juxtaposition, we can now give a somewhat better representation for bit strings than that above:

```
obj BITS1 is
  sorts Bit Bits .
  subsorts Bit < Bits .
  ops 0 1 : -> Bit .
  op __ : Bit Bits -> Bits .
endo
```

A typical term using this syntax is 0 1 0 .

2.3   EQUATIONS AND SEMANTICS

We now turn to semantics. OBJ has both an abstract denotational semantics based on order sorted algebra, and a more concrete operational semantics based on order sorted term rewriting. The semantics of an object is determined by its equations. Equations are written declaratively, and are interpreted operationally as rewrite rules, which replace substitution instances of left sides by the corresponding substitution instances of right sides. Operational and denotational semantics are discussed in the next two subsections.

The following is a rather typical equation,

```
eq M + s N = s(M + N) .
```

where M and N are *variable symbols*, while + and s are operator symbols. The keyword "eq" introduces the equation, and the equality symbol "=" separates its left and right sides.

The syntax for declaring variables is

```
vars ⟨VarIdList⟩ : ⟨Sort⟩ .
```

where the variable names are separated by blanks. For example,

```
vars L M N : Nat .
```

The keyword var can also be used, and is more idiomatic when there is just one variable, but it is actually synonymous with vars.

Warning: The final blank and period are required for variable declarations.

The syntax for an ordinary equation in OBJ3 is

```
eq ⟨Term⟩ = ⟨Term⟩ .
```

where the two ⟨*Term*⟩s must be well formed OBJ3 terms in the operators and variables available in the current context, and must have a common (super-) sort.

Warning: Equations must be terminated by a blank followed by a period[7]. OBJ will think a "loose" period within an equation marks the end of the equation, and then will probably generate a parse error and other chaos. However, it is easy to avoid this by placing parentheses around an expression that contains the offending period. For similar reasons, any use of = in the left side must be enclosed in parentheses.

Warning: All variables in an equation must have been previously declared. For equations appearing in objects[8], each variable that occurs in the right side must also occur in the left side, and the left side must not be a single variable. All these conditions are checked, and warnings are issued if they fail.

Warning: Correctness of OBJ3's operational semantics normally requires that the least sort of the left side of each equation is greater than or equal to that of its right side. If this condition is not satisfied by an equation, then OBJ3 will add retracts in parsing the right side, but not the left side. Sections 2.3.3 and 2.3.4 below discuss this in more detail and also introduce a refinement.

There is a shorthand notation for giving a name to a ground term. The syntax is

```
let ⟨Sym⟩ = ⟨Term⟩ .
let ⟨Sym⟩ : ⟨Sort⟩ = ⟨Term⟩ .
```

The name used must be single simple symbol (such as x, @2, or ThePoint). The second form above is equivalent to

```
op ⟨Sym⟩ : -> ⟨Sort⟩ .
eq ⟨Sym⟩ = ⟨Term⟩ .
```

In the first form, the sort of the top operator is taken to be the sort of the term (as discovered by the parser). For example,

```
let t = 1 0 1 .
```

defines t to be the list 1 0 1. A variation of let that is suitable for use when applying equations by hand is discussed in Section 5.1.

Warning: The symbol given to a let declaration must be a single token.

---

[7] The blank can be omitted if the last character is "special", i.e., a parenthesis or bracket.
[8] This requirement is not made for theories (see Section 4.1).

Warning: When a symbol defined by a `let` is used in a term being reduced, it is replaced by its original definition. Hence, if the symbol is used more than once, the definition will also be reduced more than once.

OBJ also has **conditional equations**, which have the syntax

cq ⟨*Term*⟩ = ⟨*Term*⟩ if ⟨*Term*⟩ .

where the first two ⟨*Term*⟩s must have a common sort, and the third ⟨*Term*⟩, which is called the **condition**, must have sort `Bool`, a predefined sort that is automatically provided in every module. A conditional rewrite rule can be thought of as a "conditional pattern-driven demon" that awakens when the pattern in its left side is matched and when its condition evaluates to `true`, using values for variables determined by the match. The keyword `ceq` is synonymous with `cq`.

Warning: For conditional equations appearing in objects, all variables that occur in the condition must also occur in the left side, otherwise a warning is issued. Also, any occurrence of `if` in the right side must be enclosed in parentheses, or else OBJ will assume that what follows it is the condition.

The command

show rules [⟨*ModExp*⟩] .

will show the rules for the named module (see Section 4.5 for details about module expressions) or for the current module if none is named. Each rule is associated with a positive integer by the system[9]. The rules of certain predefined modules, in particular `BOOL`, will not be displayed unless the command

set all rules on .

has been executed, in which case all rules from all imported modules are shown. Of course,

set all rules off .

restores the default. The command

show all rules .

shows rules as if both the `verbose` (see Section 3) mode and the `all rules` were set on.

A label can be given to a rule by using the syntax

---

[9] This is useful for specifying rules in `apply` commands (see Section 5).

[⟨*LabelList*⟩] ⟨*Rule*⟩

where ⟨*LabelList*⟩ is a comma or blank separated list of identifiers, which must not contain a "." or begin with a digit. For example,

    [sum0,id+] eq M + 0 = M .

(Actually, the label need not immediately precede the rule, and the form [label] can be thought of as setting the label for the next rule to be created.) For example,

    [def1] let x = 1 0 0 .

works as expected, i.e., the label "def1" is associated with the rule "x = 100" that is generated internally by the use of let.

Labels are shown when rules are shown. Certain automatically generated rules have automatically generated labels.

The command

    show rule ⟨*RuleSpec*⟩ .

shows the specified rule, where ⟨*RuleSpec*⟩ is defined as follows:

    ⟨*RuleSpec*⟩ ::= [-][⟨*ModId*⟩].⟨*RuleId*⟩
    ⟨*RuleId*⟩   ::= ⟨*Nat*⟩ | ⟨*Id*⟩

(The syntactic notation used here is explained in Appendix B below.) For example,

    show rule .def1 .

in the context of the module containing the let considered above, shows the rule

    [def1] eq x = 1 0 0

and the variant

    show all rule ⟨*RuleSpec*⟩ .

shows a specific rule in verbose mode.

Warning: The initial period in .def1 is required, but square brackets (e.g., .[def1]) must not be used.

Warning: It is possible that rules, as displayed by the show command, will be renumbered in curious ways when modules are combined.

2.3.1   Operational Semantics is Reduction.   We illustrate computation by term rewriting with a simple LIST-OF-INT object. (The line protecting INT in the example below indicates that the INT module, for integers, is imported; module importation is discussed in Section 3.1 below.)

```
obj LIST-OF-INT is
  sort List .
  protecting INT .
  subsort Int < List .
  op __ : Int List -> List .
  op length_ : List -> Int .
  var I : Int .    var L : List .
  eq length I = 1 .
  eq length(I L) = 1 + length L .
endo
```

The subsort declaration "Int < List" yields a syntax in which single integers, such as "5", are valid lists. Omitting the parentheses in the last equation above creates a relatively subtle parsing ambiguity, which as an exercise, the reader is invited to discover.

Let us now evaluate some terms over this object. A term ⟨*Term*⟩ to be evaluated is presented with the syntax

reduce [in ⟨*ModExp*⟩ :] ⟨*Term*⟩ .

which is evaluated in the context of the module currently in focus, unless the optional "in ⟨*ModExp*⟩" is given, in which case it is evaluated in the context of ⟨*ModExp*⟩. Usually the module currently in focus is the last module entered into the system, but this can be changed by using the select command, as described in the beginning of Section 3. The keyword reduce can be abbreviated to red. The term given for reduction may contain variables, in which case a warning is given, but the reduction is carried out with the variables being treated as constants of the declared sorts.

Warning: The period after a term to be reduced is required, and "loose" periods inside the term will confuse the parser and may cause chaos. For example, in

reduce 0 . 1 . 0 . nil .

OBJ first reduces just "0", and then tries to interpret "1 . 0 . nil ." as further top level commands; this fails, and produces some further error messages. This can be avoided by enclosing the entire term to be reduced in parentheses. A command like "red in(1) ." also fails, because OBJ assumes that the "in" introduces a module name. Parentheses can also be used to resolve this ambiguity, as in "red (in(1)) ."

A reduce command is executed by matching the given term with the left sides of equations, and then replacing the matched subterm with the corresponding substitution instance of the right side; i.e., evaluation proceeds by applying rewrite rules. For example, the command

```
reduce length(17 -4 329).
```

causes the given term to be evaluated in the module LIST-OF-INT if it follows that module, and in this case, the following is printed,

```
==============================================
reduce in LIST-OF-INT : length (17 (-4 329))
rewrites: 5
result NzNat: 3
==============================================
```

as a result of the following sequence of rewrite rule applications,

```
length(17 -4 329) =>
1 + length(-4 329) =>
1 + (1 + length 329) =>
1 + (1 + 1) =>
1 + 2 =>
3
```

which we call a **trace** of the computation. Here, the first step uses the second rule, with the left side length(I L) matching I to 17 and L to -4 329. The second step also uses this rule, but now matching I to -4 and L to 329; this match works by regarding the integer 329 as a List, because Int is a subsort of List. The third step simply uses the first rule, and the last steps use the built-in arithmetic of INT. Execution proceeds until reaching a term to which no further rules can be applied, called a **normal** (or **reduced**) **form**[10]. The command

```
set trace on .
```

causes a local trace to be printed as a reduction is executed. This displays information describing the application of each rule. Global tracing is produced by the command

---

[10] Most functional programming languages require users to declare **constructors** such that a term is reduced iff it consists entirely of constructors. OBJ3 does not make any use of constructors, and thus achieves greater generality; however, constructor declarations could be used, e.g., for compiler optimization; and they are also used in Kumo to support induction [65].

```
set trace whole on .
```

which displays the whole term being reduced at each rule application. Similarly, the commands

```
set trace off .
set trace whole off .
```

return OBJ3 to its default state of not printing traces.

The operational semantics for a conditional rewrite rule is as follows: first find a match for the left side; then evaluate the condition, after substituting the bindings determined by the match; if it evaluates to true, then do the replacement by the right side, again using the values for the variables determined by the match. Note that evaluating the condition could require non-trivial further rewriting in some cases. This requires OBJ to keep track of bindings, because a term may match a rule in more than one way, and we do not want to keep trying the same match over and over; this bookkeeping can be highly non-trivial for associative/commutative matching (see Section 2.4).

OBJ3 has a built-in (i.e., predefined) polymorphic binary infix Bool-valued **equality** operator which specializes as neeeded to any sort S; its syntax is

```
op _==_ : S S -> Bool .
```

This operator tests whether or not two ground terms are equal, by reducing the two terms to normal form, and then comparing the normal forms for syntactic identity[11]. For example, _==_ on Bool itself is just _iff_. The operator == really is equality on a sort provided that the rules for terms of that sort are Church-Rosser, that the rules are terminating with respect to the given evaluation strategy, and that the evaluation strategy is non-lazy (these notions are discussed in Sections 2.3.4 and 2.4.4 below), because these conditions guarantee that normal forms will be reached. The negation _=/=_ of _==_ is also available, and so is polymorphic if_then_else_fi; these polymorphic operators are all provided by the predefined module BOOL, which is automatically imported into each module (unless this default is specifically disabled).

Release 2 of OBJ3 allows variables that are declared in the current context to occur in terms that are presented to the reduce and parse commands; a warning is issued in the case of reduction. Of course, a parse error will occur if there are variables that have not been declared. For example,

```
reduce length I .        ***> should be: 1
reduce length (I I).     ***> should be: 2
```

---

[11] If == is used for two terms with incompatible sorts, then a parse error occurs.

```
reduce length (I I I).  ***> should be: 3
```

(A parsing error will result from omitting the parentheses, for reasons to be discussed in Section 2.4; "***>" indicates that what follows is a comment that should be printed.)

It is possible to perform a number of reductions over the same module in a "reduction loop", with the syntax

$$\langle RedLoop \rangle \ ::= \ \mathtt{rl} \ \{. \ | \ \langle ModId \rangle\} \ \{ \ \langle Term \rangle \ .\}... \ .$$

The terms are read, and the reduction results printed, one at a time. If "." is given instead of a ⟨*ModId*⟩, then the current module is used. A synonym for rl is red-loop.

For example,

```
rl NAT
   5 + 5 .
   3 * 6 + 18 .
   (21 - 8) * 3 . .
```

(the last term will fail to parse, because - is not defined in NAT).

Sometimes when we want to execute test cases for some code, it may be convenient to use the "test reduction" command, which has the syntax

$$\mathtt{test \ reduction} \ [\mathtt{in} \ \langle ModExp \rangle \ :] \ \langle Term \rangle \ \mathtt{expect:} \ \langle Term \rangle \ .$$

and checks whether the result is as expected, and then issues an error message if it isn't. For example,

```
test reduction in NAT : 5 + 5 expect: 10 .
```

But it is often easier to use a comment, such as

```
***> should be: 10
```

or to execute

```
red 5 + 5 == 10 .
```

where == is the predefined polymorphic equality function (as described in Section 2.3.1).

2.3.2   Denotational Semantics.

Whereas an *operational* semantics for a language should show how its computations are done, a *denotational* semantics should give precise mathematical meanings to programs in a way that is as conceptually clear and simple as possible, and that supports proving properties of programs. If a language is rigorously based upon logic, then the already established proof and model theories of the underlying logical system apply *directly* to its programs, and complex formalisms like Scott-Strachey semantics or Hoare logics are not needed. The denotational semantics of OBJ is algebraic, as in the algebraic theory of abstract data types [84, 83, 153, 90], and in particular, the denotation of an OBJ object is an **algebra**, a collection of sets with functions among them[12]. The initial algebra approach [83, 116] takes the unique (up to isomorphism) **initial** algebra as the "standard," or "most representative" model of a set of equations (there may of course be many other models), i.e., as the representation-independent standard of comparison for correctness. It is shown in [11] (see also [116]) that an algebra is initial if and only if it satisfies the following properties:

1. **no junk:** every element can be named using the given constant and operator symbols; and

2. **no confusion:** all ground equations true of the algebra can be proved from the given equations.

For canonical systems (as defined in Section 2.4.4 below), the rewrite rule operational semantics agrees with initial algebra semantics, in the sense that the reduced forms constitute an initial algebra (this result was shown in [46]; see also [116, 151]). Because OBJ3 is based on order sorted algebra, it is important to note that this result easily extends to this context. OSA, and thus OBJ3, provides a completely general programming formalism, in the sense that any partial computable function can be defined[13]. The formalism is especially convenient and natural for non-numerical processing, but in fact, it also handles numerical applications quite felicitously.

2.3.3 Exceptions and Retracts.

Exceptions have both inadequate semantic foundations and insufficient flexibility in most programming and specification languages, including functional programming languages. Algebraic specification languages sometimes use partial functions, which are simply undefined under exceptional conditions. Although this can be developed rigorously, as in [98], it is unsatisfactory in practice because it does not allow error messages or error recovery. For some time, we have been exploring rigorous approaches that allow users to define their own exception conditions, error messages, and exception handling. OBJT and OBJ1 used error algebras [43], which sometimes fail to have initial models [131]; however, the current approach based on OSA seems entirely satisfactory to us.

---

[12] We will see later that the denotation of an OBJ theory is a class of algebras, that are not in general isomorphic to one another.

[13] See [6, 116] for similar results about total computable functions.

As a simple example, let's consider the natural and rational numbers, with sorts Nat < Rat. If _+_ is only defined for rationals, then (2 + 2) is fine because 2 is a natural number and Nat < Rat. On the other hand, given the term (-4 / -2)!, where ! is only defined for natural numbers, the parser must consider the subterm (-4 / -2) to be a rational, because at parse time it cannot know whether this term will evaluate to a natural number; thus, the term (-4 / -2)! does not parse in the conventional sense. However, we can "give it the benefit of the doubt" by having the parser insert a **retract**, which is a special operator symbol (in this case denoted r:Rat>Nat and having arity Rat and coarity Nat) that is removed at run time if the subterm evaluates to a natural, but otherwise remains behind as an informative error message. Thus, the parser turns the term (-4 / -2)! into the term (r:Rat>Nat(-4 / -2))!, which at runtime becomes first (r:Rat>Nat(2))! and then (2)!, using the (built-in) **retract equation**

    r:Rat>Nat(X) = X

where X is a variable of sort Nat. The retract operator symbols are automatically generated by the OBJ3 system, along with the corresponding retract equations. Retracts are inserted, if needed, by the parser, and will not be seen by the user in ordinary examples. However, the user who wants to see retracts can give the command

    set show retracts on .

which causes the OBJ3 system to print them, both when showing equations in modules, and also when showing the results of rewriting. Of course,

    set show retracts off .

restores the default mode in which retracts are not shown.

We will see later that retracts can be used to handle rewrite rules that are not sort decreasing (see Section 2.3.4); also, equations with retracts on their left sides are useful for defining "coercions" among various data types, and data with multiple representations, as explained in [73] and illustrated in [50] and [61].

Turning to theory for a moment, retracts are new operators $r_{s,s'} : s \to s'$, one for each pair s, s' of sorts in the same connected component; these give an extension of the original signature provided by the user. For each $r_{s,s'}$, a retract equation $r_{s,s'}(x) = x$ is also added, where x is a variable of sort s. Then (a slight extension of) the "conservative extension" theorem proved in [76] shows that under some mild assumptions, adding these operators and equations does not create any confusion among terms that do not involve retracts. The OBJ3 implementation uses the notation r:s>s' for the operator $r_{s,s'} : s \to s'$. Details of the mathematical and operational semantics of retracts, using order sorted algebra and order sorted term rewriting, are given in [62] and [76]; see [56] for recent applications of retracts to theorem proving for partial functions.

Warning: Release 2 of OBJ3 does not allow qualified sort names in retracts within terms provided by the user.

Now some code that illustrates retracts. Stacks are a well known benchmark in this area, because the example is simple, but raises the interesting problem of what a term like top(empty) actually means, and indeed, whether it has any meaning. The OBJ3 code given below not only handles the exceptions in a natural way, but also seems about as simple as one could hope. The approach is to define a subsort NeStack of non-empty stacks, and then say that top *is only defined* on this subsort.

```
obj STACK-OF-NAT is sorts Stack NeStack .
  subsort NeStack < Stack .
  protecting NAT .
  op empty : -> Stack .
  op push : Nat Stack -> NeStack .
  op top_ : NeStack -> Nat .
  op pop_ : NeStack -> Stack .
  var X : Nat .    var S : Stack .
  eq top push(X,S) = X .
  eq pop push(X,S) = S .
endo
```

Then evaluating

```
reduce top push(1,empty) .
```

yields the natural number 1, while

```
reduce pop push(1,empty) .
```

yields empty, and

```
reduce top empty .
```

yields

```
result Nat: top r:Stack>NeStack(empty)
```

with empty retracted to the sort NeStack. Similarly,

```
reduce top pop empty .
```

yields

```
result Nat:
top r:Stack>NeStack(pop r:Stack>NeStack(empty))
```

If the show retracts mode is on, when OBJ3 shows the term to be reduced in the above example, then it will contain retracts; in fact, it will show the same term given above as output, because no reduction is possible.

An alternative approach to exceptions involves introducing supersorts that contain specific error messages for exceptional conditions, as in the following:

```
obj STACK-OF-NAT is
  sorts Stack Stack? Nat? .
  subsort Stack < Stack? .
  protecting NAT .
  subsort Nat < Nat? .
  op empty : -> Stack .
  op push : Nat Stack -> Stack .
  op push : Nat Stack? -> Stack? .
  op top_ : Stack -> Nat? .
  op pop_ : Stack -> Stack? .
  op topless : -> Nat? .
  op underflow : -> Stack? .
  var X : Nat .   var S : Stack .
  eq top push(X,S) = X .
  eq pop push(X,S) = S .
  eq top empty = topless .
  eq pop empty = underflow .
endo
```

Here are some sample reductions for this code:

```
reduce top push(1,empty) .   ***> should be: 1
reduce pop push(1,empty) .   ***> should be: empty
reduce top empty .           ***> should be: topless
reduce pop empty .           ***> should be: underflow
reduce top pop empty .
        ***> should be: top r:Stack?>Stack(underflow)
```

Sometimes we may want a certain operator, or a certain term, to have a lower sort than it otherwise would. **Sort constraints** [62, 73] are declarations of this kind. Release 2 of OBJ3 has syntax for a kind of sort constraint that restricts the domain of a multi-argument operator to arguments that satisfy some equational conditions. For example, the code in Section C.8 contains the operator declaration

```
op-as _;_ : Mor Mor -> Mor for M1 ; M2
    if d1 M1 == d0 M2 [assoc] .
```

which means that M1 ; M2 has sort Mor if d1 M1 == d0 M2, and otherwise has sort Mor?, which is an automatically provided error supersort of Mor; the attribute [assoc] says that _;_ is associative (the [assoc] attribute is discussed in the following subsection).

Warning: Release 2 of OBJ3 only supports the *syntax*, but not the semantics, of sort constraints. In particular, error supersorts (such as Mor?) are *not* automatically generated for each user declared sort. However, we hope that some future version of OBJ will fully implement this feature, as it seems to have many interesting applications. In fact, in Release 2 of OBJ3, the semantics of the above op-as declaration is equivalent to that of the following ordinary operator declaration:

```
op _;_ : Mor Mor -> Mor [assoc] .
```

A related feature allows defining a subsort by a Boolean expression. For example,

```
sort PosRat .
subsort PosRat < Rat .
var N : Rat .
as PosRat : N if N > 0 .
```

defines PosRat < Rat to have as its elements the rationals N such that N > 0. The syntax is

```
as ⟨Sort⟩ : ⟨Term⟩ if ⟨Term⟩ .
```

Warning: This feature is not yet implemented, and attempting to use it produces the message

```
Error:
general sort constraint not currently handled (ignored)
```

2.3.4 More on the Operational Semantics.
This section gives an informal introduction to some delicate aspects of OBJ3's operational semantics; fuller treatments of order sorted rewriting, order sorted equational deduction, and retract equations can be found in [101, 76, 141]. The aim here is to familiarize OBJ3 users with the basic properties that equations should have for term reduction to behave properly. As already mentioned in Section 2.2, OBJ3 assumes that signatures are regular and coherent, and we maintain this assumption throughout this subsection. We first discuss the Church-Rosser property

and termination, and then we explain some additional conditions required to handle subsorts.

Often, the order of applying rules does not affect the result, in the sense that whenever a term t_0 is rewritten in two different ways, obtaining terms t_1 and t_2, then there is another term t_3 such that both t_1 and t_2 rewrite to t_3. A rule set with this desirable property is called **Church-Rosser**; OBJ3 assumes that the rules in objects are Church-Rosser. Another desirable property for a rule set is **termination**, in the technical sense that there are *no* infinite sequences of rewrite rule applications. A rule set that is terminating (in this sense) can be checked for the Church-Rosser property by the Knuth-Bendix algorithm [104]; a rule set that is both terminating and Church-Rosser is called **canonical**. Although we cannot assume that all rule sets are terminating, rules that define total computable operators over total computable sets can always be chosen to be both Church-Rosser and terminating [6]; this includes the typical case of abstract data types. However, further functions defined over these structures can fail to have terminating rule sets, for example, if they implement procedures for problems that are only semi-decidable, such as full first-order theorem proving, higher-order unification, or combinator reduction[14]. The Knuth-Bendix algorithm extends to a completion procedure that may produce a canonical rule set from one that is terminating. Note that an order sorted version of Knuth-Bendix is needed for OBJ3 [141]. Huet and Oppen give a nice survey of rewrite rule theory which develops some connections with general algebra [93]; Klop [102, 103] and Dershowitz and Jouannaud [24] have also written useful surveys of this area, that are more up to date. OSA foundations for the issues discussed above may be found in [117, 62, 101, 141]. Chapter 5 of [59] gives a recent algebra-oriented survey of term rewriting, and [4] is a recent elementary textbook on this subject.

We have run many thousands of reductions on many hundreds of examples, often in dozens of variations, and we have hardly ever encountered problems with canonicity. We believe that OBJ users almost always write equations for abstract data types that are canonical, because they tend to think of equations as programs, and therefore they write primitive recursive definitions for operators. A practical implication of this is that tests for canonicity are not of critical importance. This is fortunate, because the problem is undecidable.

In summary, the intuition of the Church-Rosser property is that when it holds, reduction can be seen as evaluating a functional expression to a unique result that does not depend on the order of evaluation. The termination property ensures that this result always exists.

---

[14] In order not to add new values to the underlying abstract data type, the value sorts of such potentially non-terminating operators should be error supersorts; then retracts will be added when they are used as ordinary values in terms.

We now discuss some issues concerning subsorts in rewriting. Intuitively, the more we advance in evaluating a functional expression, the more information we should have about its result. This should also apply to information about the *sort* of the result, and the smaller the sort that we can associate to a data element, the more information we have about that data element. For example, by syntactic analysis we can only associate to the expression (7 + (- 3))/ 2 the sort Rat, but after evaluation we know that its result has sort NzNat.

This suggests that rewrite rules should be **sort decreasing**, i.e., that if a term t can be rewritten to a term t', then the least sort of t' should always be less than or equal to the least sort of t. This is very often the case in the many examples that we have studied; however, there are some quite reasonable rewrite rules that can violate this requirement *temporarily*. For example, in the number hierarchy described in Appendix C.7, the rule

```
eq | C |^2 = C * (C #) .
```

which defines the square modulus of a complex number with rational coordinates as the product of the number by its conjugate, has a left side with sort Rat and a right side with sort Cpx. In the end, this will (in the appropriate sense clarified below) not matter because the requirement of rewriting down is only violated temporarily, and the reduced expression is always a rational number.

But in general, the careless treatment of rules that are not sort decreasing could result in unsound deductions. For example, consider the object

```
obj PROBLEMS is
    sorts A B .
    subsorts A < B .
    op a : -> A .
    op b : -> B .
    ops f g : A -> A .
    var X : A .
    eq f(X) = g(X) .
    eq a = b .
endo
```

and suppose that we want to reduce the term f(a). By applying the first equation, we can reduce it to g(a), and by applying the second equation, we can reduce it to g(b). The problem here is that g(b) is not a well-formed term! In fact, the second step of deduction is not allowed under the rules of order sorted equational deduction [76], and is unsound in this precise sense. The problem is that while the deduction a = b is sound in itself, it becomes unsound in the context of the enclosing function symbol g.

Retracts allow a correct and sound treatment of rules like that for the square modulus of a complex number discussed above. In this treatment, rewriting works even if the rules are not sort decreasing, provided they are "reasonable" in a sense that is made precise below. Moreover, if the rules are not reasonable, then the retracts will help to detect flaws in the specification. The idea is as follows: suppose that a term t of least sort s can be rewritten at the top by applying a rule $u = v$ to yield a term t', i.e., suppose there is a substitution θ (respecting the sorts of the variables) such that $t = \theta(u)$ and $t' = \theta(v)$. Next, suppose that the least sort s' of t' is not less than or equal to s. This could be a problem if our term t were enclosed in a subterm that made its replacement by t' ill-formed. A way to guarantee that this never happens, regardless of the embedding context, is to check the least sorts of t and t', and whenever the sort of t is not greater than or equal to the sort of t', to replace t not by t' but by the term $r:s'{>}s(t')$. We then call the rewrite from t to $r:s'{>}s(t')$ a **safe rewrite** using the rule $u = v$. Rewrites in which retract symbols are eliminated by applying the built-in retract rules (see Section 2.3.3), and also rewrites with $s \geq s'$, where no retract is needed, are also considered safe.

The key point about safe rewrites is that they are *sound*, i.e., they are correct logical deductions. First, as discussed in Section 2.3.3, adding retracts and retract rules to the original specification is conservative, in the sense that no new equalities between terms without retracts can be derived after the addition of retracts and retract rules. The soundness of safe rewriting then follows from the observation that the rewrite from t to $r:s'{>}s(t')$ using the rule $u = v$ is a combination of two sound steps of deduction, namely, we can first derive $r:s'{>}s(t) = r:s'{>}s(t')$ using $u = v$, and then derive $t = r:s'{>}s(t')$ by applying to the term on the left the retract rule $r:s'{>}s(x) = x$ with x a variable of sort s.

Notice that if the original rules are sort decreasing, then safe rewrites and ordinary rewrites coincide, in the sense that there is never any need to introduce retracts on the right side after applying a rule. Safe rewriting allows us to broaden the class of rules that OBJ3 can handle properly, to include all intuitively "reasonable" rules. Without safe rewriting, we would have to require that all rules are sort decreasing. But with safe rewriting it is enough to require that if a ground term t without retracts can be safely rewritten to a term t' to which no rules can be applied, then

(1) t' has no retracts; and

(2) any sequence of safe rewrites from t to t'' can be continued by a sequence of safe rewrites from t'' to t'.

We call rules satisfying conditions (1) and (2) **reasonable** rules. Notice that, by the definition of safe rewriting, an irreducible term t', as well as any intermediate term, will have a least sort less than or equal to the least sort of the original term *t*. Notice also that any rules that are Church-Rosser and sort decreasing are obviously reasonable. The rules for the complex number example are reasonable (and also terminating). The rules in the PROBLEMS example are unreasonable, and the user will get evidence of this by performing reductions. For example, the reduction of a will yield the result r:B>A(b), and the reduction of f(a) will yield the result g(r:B>A(b)), both of which violate condition (1).

One last word of caution. Failure to be reasonable may not be apparent from a cursory inspection of the rules. For example, consider the object

```
obj MORE-PROBLEMS is
  sorts A B C .
  subsorts A < B < C .
  op f : C -> C .
  ops f h : A -> A .
  op g : B -> B .
  op a : -> A .
  var X : B .
  eq f(X) = g(X) .
endo
```

Here, f(X) has a sort C that is greater than B, the sort of g(X). However, this specification is unreasonable. For example, the term h(f(a)) reduces to the term h(r:B>A(g(a))), violating condition (1). The problem is that the rule

```
eq f(Y) = g(Y) .
```

obtained from the original rule by "specializing" the variable X of sort B to a variable Y of sort A violates the sort decreasing property. Therefore, not just the original rules, but also all of their "specializations" to rules with variables having smaller sorts may have to be considered; see [101].

2.4   ATTRIBUTES

It is natural and convenient to consider certain properties of an operator as **attributes** that are declared at the same time as its syntax. These properties include axioms like associativity, commutativity, and identity that have both syntactic and semantic consequences, as well as others that affect order of evaluation, parsing, etc. In OBJ3, such attributes are given in square brackets after the syntax declaration. You can see what attributes an operator actually has with the show command, which has the following syntax:

```
show op ⟨OpRef⟩ .
```

where ⟨*OpRef*⟩ describes the operator (see Appendix B for its details). The operator will be described in the context of the module currently in focus.

2.4.1   Associativity and Commutativity.   Let us first consider associativity. For example,

```
op _or_ : Bool Bool -> Bool [assoc] .
```

indicates that or is an associative binary infix operator on Boolean values. This implies that the parser does not require full parenthesisation. For example, we can write (true or false or true) instead of (true or (false or true)); moreover, the term printer will omit unnecessary parentheses. Of course, the assoc attribute also gives the semantic effect of an associativity axiom, which is implemented by associative rewriting and associative extensions, as described below.

Warning: The assoc attribute is only meaningful for a binary operator with arity A B and value sort C when C < A and C < B; however, retracts might be inserted if either A < C or B < C.

Binary infix operators can be declared commutative with the attribute comm, which is semantically a commutativity axiom, implemented by commutative rewriting (as described below). Note that a binary operator can be given both commutative and associative attributes.

Warning: The commutative attribute is only meaningful when the two sorts in the arity have a common supersort; also, some retracts may be added if these two sorts are unequal.

Warning: Because associative/commutative matching is an NP-complete problem, a *uniformly fast* implementation is impossible.

The present implementation, based on work of Lincoln [108] extended to OSA along the lines of [62, 101], is reasonably efficient, but cannot be expected to run quickly for really large problems; see also [96].

2.4.2   Identity and Idempotence.   An identity attribute can be declared for a binary operator. For example, in

```
op _or_ : Bool Bool -> Bool [assoc id: false] .
```

the attribute id: false gives the effects of the identity equations (B or false = B) and (false or B = B). Identity attributes can be *ground terms* and not just constants.

Warning: All the operators occurring in the value term of an identity attribute must have been previously declared.

If it only makes sense to have a left or a right identity, then that is all that is generated. For example, in

```
op nil : -> List .
op __ : Int List -> NeList [id: nil] .
```

only a right identity equation is added. A left identity equation is added if the sort of the identity is a subsort of the left arity sort, and a right identity equation is added if the sort of the identity is a subsort of the right arity sort.

Warning: OBJ3 implements rewriting modulo identity by a combination of direct matching modulo identity, and a partial completion process that may generate further equations. Matching modulo identity very often leads to problems with termination and efficiency, as discussed in Section 3.1.1 below.

The attribute `idr:` introduces only the identity equations themselves, without invoking any completion process. This can be convenient for avoiding the termination problems associated with the `id:` attribute.

Warning: Associative, commutative and identity attributes are inherited downward, from an overloaded operator to all operators having the same form and lower rank.

Operators can also be declared idempotent, by using the attribute `idem`; this is implemented simply by adding the idempotent equation.

Warning: The effect of rewriting modulo idempotence is neither attempted nor achieved.

It is possible to give *any* operator symbol any of the attributes `assoc`, `comm`, `id:`, `idr:` and/or `idem`; warnings are issued when the attributes do not make sense.

Let us now consider a more sophisticated integer list object with associative and identity attributes,

```
obj LIST-OF-INT1 is
  sorts List NeList .
  protecting INT .
  subsorts Int < NeList < List .
  op nil : -> List .
  op __ : List List -> List [assoc id: nil] .
  op __ : NeList List -> NeList [assoc id: nil] .
  op head_ : NeList -> Int .
  op tail_ : NeList -> List .
```

```
    var I : Int .    var L : List .
    eq head(I L) = I .
    eq tail(I L) = L .
endo
```

and some test cases using this object. For example,

```
reduce 0 nil 1 nil 3 .
```

is carried out in LIST-OF-INT1 by applications of the identity equation modulo associativity, as follows,

```
0 nil 1 nil 3 =>
0 1 nil 3 =>
0 1 3
```

and it prints

```
result NeList: 0 1 3
```

Similarly, we may consider

```
reduce head(0 1 3) .        ***> should be: 0
reduce tail(0 1 3) .        ***> should be: 1 3
reduce tail(nil 0 1 nil 3) . ***> should be: 1 3
```

2.4.3   Precedence and Gathering.   Ambiguity in the parsing of terms can be reduced by using precedence and gathering. The **precedence** of an operator is a number (in the range 0 to 127), where a lower value indicates "tighter binding" in the sense that is discussed below. For example, the predefined object INT contains the declarations

```
op _+_ : Int Int -> Int [assoc comm id: 0 prec 33] .
op _*_ : Int Int -> Int [assoc comm id: 1 prec 31] .
```

The precedence of a *term* is the precedence of its top operator, unless it is enclosed in parentheses or qualified, in which case it has precedence 0. Ordinarily, the arguments of an operator must have precedence less than or equal to its precedence. Therefore, (1 + 2 * 3) is not parsed as ((1 + 2) * 3), but instead is parsed as (1 + (2 * 3)) under the above declarations, because the precedence of the arguments to * must be less than or equal to 31. Intuitively, we can think of the "tighter binding" indicated by lower precedence as the strength with which an operator "pulls" on its arguments; in this example, the constant 2 has been pulled on more strongly by * than by +.

The default precedence for an operator with standard (i.e., prefix-with-parentheses) form is 0. If an operator pattern begins and ends with something other than an underbar, then its precedence also defaults to 0. Unary prefix operators have default precedence 15. In all other cases, the default precedence is 41.

This default behavior can be modified. The **gathering pattern** of an operator is a sequence of elements e, E, or & (one element for each argument position) that restricts the precedences of terms that are allowed as arguments: e indicates that the corresponding argument must have strictly lower precedence, E allows equal or lower precedence, and & allows any precedence. For example, parentheses could be described as having precedence 0 and gathering pattern (&); also, the gathering pattern (E e) forces left association for a binary operator.

An interesting example that needs this gathering pattern is combinatory algebra, the code for which (see Appendix C.6) includes the following declaration:

```
op __ : T T -> T [gather (E e)] .
```

For example, under this declaration, a b c will be parsed as (a b) c, rather than as a (b c).

The default gathering pattern for an operator with standard form is all &s. If an underbar for an argument position is not adjacent to another underbar, then the default gathering value for that position is &. In all other cases, the default gathering value is E.

Warning: The current OBJ3 parser sometimes "jumps to conclusions" based on precedence and gathering information, and then simply fails if its initial assumption is wrong. This means that sometimes a term that really does have a unique parse of least sort may fail to parse. Although the defaults are surprisingly effective, sometimes it is necessary to explicitly give carefully chosen precedence and gathering attributes, and/or to insert some parentheses into terms, in order to get the parsing behavior that you want.

2.4.4   Order of Evaluation.

In general, a large tree will have many different sites where rewrite rules might apply, and the choice of which rules to try at which sites can strongly affect efficiency, and can also affect termination. Most modern functional programming languages have a uniform lazy (i.e., top-down, or outermost, or call-by-name) semantics. But because raw lazy evaluation is slow, lazy evaluation enthusiasts have built clever compilers that figure out when an "eager" (i.e., bottom-up or call-by-value) evaluation can be used with exactly the same result; this is called "strictness analysis" [123, 95]. OBJ3 is more flexible, because each operator can have its own evaluation strategy. Moreover, the OBJ3 programmer gets this flexibility with minimum effort, because OBJ3 determines a default strategy if none is explicitly given.

This default strategy is computed very quickly, because only a very simple form of strictness analysis is done, and it is surprisingly effective, though of course it does not fit all possible needs.

Syntactically, an **E-strategy** (E for "evaluation") is a sequence of integers in parentheses, given as an operator attribute following the keyword `strat`. For example, OBJ's built-in conditional operator has the following E-strategy,

```
op if_then_else_fi : Bool Int Int -> Int [strat (1 0)] .
```

which says to evaluate the first argument until it is reduced, and then apply rules at the top (indicated by "0"). Similarly,

```
op _+_ : Int Int -> Int [strat (1 2 0)] .
```

indicates that `_+_` on `Int` has strategy (1 2 0), which says to evaluate both arguments before attempting to add them.

The default E-strategy for a given operator is determined from its equations by requiring that all argument places that contain a non-variable term in some rule are evaluated before equations are applied at the top. If an operator with a user-supplied strategy has a tail recursive rule (in the weak sense that the top operator occurs in its right side), then OBJ3 may apply an optimization that repeatedly applies that rule, and thus violates the strategy. In those rare cases where it is desirable to prevent this optimization from being applied, you can just give an explicit E-strategy that does not have an initial 0.

There are actually two ways to get lazy evaluation. The simplest approach is to omit a given argument number from the strategy; then that argument is not evaluated unless some rewrite exposes it from underneath the given operator. For example, this approach to "lazy cons" gives

```
op cons : Sexp Sexp -> Sexp [strat (0)] .
```

The second approach involves giving a negative number $-j$ in a strategy, which indicates that the jth argument is to be evaluated "on demand," where a "demand" is an attempt to match a pattern to the term that occurs in the jth argument position. This approach to lazy cons is expressed as

```
op cons : Sexp Sexp -> Sexp [strat (-1 -2)] .
```

Then a `reduce` command at the top level of OBJ3 is interpreted as a top-level demand that may force the evaluation of certain arguments. This second approach cannot be applied to operators with an associative or commutative attribute. Appendix C.5 gives a further example of lazy evaluation, using the Sieve of Erasthothenes to find all prime numbers.

A strategy is called **non-lazy** if it requires that all arguments of the operator are reduced in some order, and either the operator has no rules, or the strategy ends with a final "0". In general, in order for all subterms of a reduction result to be fully reduced, it is necessary that all evaluation strategies be non-lazy. The default strategies computed by the system are non-lazy.

2.4.5   Memoization. Giving an operator the memo attribute causes the results of evaluating a term headed by this operator to be saved; thus the work of reduction is not repeated if that term appears again [118]. In OBJ3, the user can give any operators that he wishes the memo attribute, and this is implemented efficiently by using hash tables. More precisely, given a memoized operator symbol f and given a term f(t1,...,tn) to be reduced (possibly as part of some larger term), a table entry for f(t1,...,tn) giving its fully reduced value is added to the memo table. Moreover, entries giving this fully reduced value are also added for each term f(r1,...,rn) that, according to the evaluation strategy for f, could arise while reducing f(t1,...,tn) just before a rule for f is applied at the top; this is necessary because at that moment the function symbol f could disappear. In some cases, memoizing these intermediate reductions is more valuable than memoizing just the original expression.

For example, suppose that f has the strategy (2 3 0 1 0), let r be the reduced form of the term f(t1,t2,t3,t4), and let ri be the reduced form of ti for $i = 1, 2, 3$. Then the memo table will contain the following pairs:

```
(f(t1,t2,t3,t4),r)
(f(t1,r2,r3,t4),r)
(f(r1,r2,r3,t4),r)
```

Memoization gives the effect of structure sharing for common subterms, and this can greatly reduce term storage requirements in some problems. Whether or not the memo tables are re-initialized before each reduction can be controlled with the top level commands

```
set clear memo on .
set clear memo off .
```

The default is that the tables are *not* reinitialized. However, they can be reinitialized at any time with the command

```
do clear memo .
```

Each of these commands must be terminated with a blank followed by a period. Of course, none of this has any effect on the *result* of a reduction, but only on its speed. A possible exception to this is the case where the definitions of operators appearing in the memo table have been altered. (When rules are added to an open module, previous computations may become obsolete. Therefore, you may need to explicitly give the command "do clear memo .";" see Section 3.2.) Memoization is an area where term rewriting based systems seem to have an advantage over unification based systems like Prolog.

2.4.6   Propositional Calculus Example.   This subsection gives a decision procedure for a theory of real interest, the propositional calculus. The procedure is due to Hsiang [92], and makes crucial use of associative/commutative rewriting. The OBJ3 code for PROPC below evolved from OBJ1 code written by David Plaisted [77]. It reduces tautologuous propositional formulae, in the usual connectives (and, or, implies, not, xor (exclusive or) and iff) to the constant true, and reduces all other formulae to a canonical form (modulo the commutative and associative axioms) in the connectives xor, and, true and false. The TRUTH object used here contains just true and false (plus the basic true, false-valued operators _==_, _=/=_ and if_then_else_fi), while QID provides identifiers that begin with an apostrophe, e.g., 'a. The module import modes extending and protecting are discussed in Section 3.1 below. The rules in this object have been shown by Hsiang [92] to be Church-Rosser and terminating modulo the commutative and associative axioms.

```
obj PROPC is
  sort Prop .
  extending TRUTH .
  protecting QID .
  subsorts Id Bool < Prop .
    *** constructors ***
  op _and_ : Prop Prop -> Prop
      [assoc comm idem idr: true prec 2] .
  op _xor_ : Prop Prop -> Prop
      [assoc comm idr: false prec 3] .
  vars p q r : Prop .
  eq p and false = false .
  eq p xor p = false .
  eq p and (q xor r) = (p and q) xor (p and r) .
    *** derived operators ***
  op _or_ : Prop Prop -> Prop [assoc prec 7] .
  op not_ : Prop -> Prop [prec 1] .
  op _implies_ : Prop Prop -> Prop [prec 9] .
  op _iff_ : Prop Prop -> Prop [assoc prec 11] .
  eq p or q = (p and q) xor p xor q .
  eq not p = p xor true .
  eq p implies q = (p and q) xor p xor true .
  eq p iff q = p xor q xor true .
endo
```

Now some sample reductions in the context of this object:

```
reduce 'a implies 'b iff not 'b implies not 'a .
***> should be: true
reduce not('a or 'b) iff not 'a and not 'b .
***> should be: true
reduce 'c or 'c and 'd iff 'c .
***> should be: true
reduce 'a iff not 'b .
***> should be: 'a xor 'b
reduce 'a and 'b xor 'c xor 'b and 'a .
***> should be: 'c
reduce 'a iff 'a iff 'a iff 'a .
***> should be: true
reduce 'a implies 'b and 'c iff
       ('a implies 'b) and ('a implies 'c) .
***> should be: true
```

Thus, the first three and last two expressions are tautologies, while the fourth is true if and only if exactly one of 'a and 'b is true, and the fifth is true iff 'c is true. Note that 'a, 'b, 'c are **propositional variables** in the sense that anything of sort Prop can be substituted for them while still preserving truth; in particular, true and false can always be substituted. Of course, deciding tautologies in the propositional calculus is an NP-complete problem, so we cannot expect this code to run very fast for large problems.

This example illustrates a striking advantage of using a logical language: every computation is a proof, and interesting theorems can be proved by applying the right programs to the right data. Even if the given equations do not define a decision procedure for a given theory, so long as they are all correct with respect to this theory, then the results of reduction will be correct. For this purpose, we don't even need the Church-Rosser property. For example, even if we didn't know that PROPC was canonical, we could still be certain that any term that reduces to true is a tautology. Thus, OBJ code can be used for theorem proving, as illustrated by the examples in [51] and [59], a sample from which is given in Section 4.8 below. Some more elaborate theorem proving examples are given in Appendix C.4, and much more detail is available in [66, 59].

3   MODULE HIERARCHIES

Conceptual clarity and ease of understanding are greatly facilitated by breaking a program into modules, each of which is mind-sized and has a natural purpose. This in turn greatly facilitates both debugging and reusability. When there are many modules, it is helpful to make the hierarchical structure of module dependency explicit, so that whenever one module uses sorts or operators declared in another, the other is explicitly imported to the first, and is also defined earlier in the program text. A program developed in this way has the abstract structure of an *acyclic graph* of abstract modules[15]. We will use the word **context** to describe such a graph of modules, later extending it to include views, as discussed in Section 4.3.

More exactly now, a directed edge in an acyclic graph of modules indicates that the higher (target) module **imports** the lower (source) module, and the **context** of a given module is the subgraph of other modules upon which it depends, i.e., the subgraph of which it is the top. Parameterized modules can also occur in such a hierarchy, and are treated in essentially the same way as unparameterized modules; they may also have instantiations, and these are considered to be distinct from the parameterized module itself.

In addition to representing program structure in a clear and convenient way, the module hierarchy can have some more specific applications, such as maintaining multiple mutually inconsistent structures as subhierarchies, which could be useful for keeping available more than one way to do the same or related things, for example, in a family of partially overlapping system designs; that is, the module hierarchy can be used for configuration management. It can also be used to keep information from different sources in different places, and to maintain multiple inconsistent worlds, which would be useful in Artificial Intelligence applications exploring the consequences of various mutually inconsistent assumptions, where there may also be some shared assumptions. Hierarchical structure could also be used to reflect access properties of a physically distributed database, as suggested in [48].

The command

```
show modules .
```

shows a list of all modules in the current OBJ working context. If a module with an atomic name has been redefined, then it may appear more than once in the output from this command.

One can save the current context with the command

```
do save ⟨ChString⟩ .
```

where ⟨*ChString*⟩ is any character string, possibly containing blanks; you can then return to a previously named context with the command

---

[15] Such a hierarchy differs from what is sometimes called a "Dijkstra-Parnas" hierarchy, because lower level modules do not *implement* higher level (less abstract) modules, but rather, lower level modules are *included in* higher level modules; both kinds of hierarchy are supported in the LILEANNA system [85].

```
do restore ⟨ChString⟩ .
```

Warning: The commands `save` and `restore` do not work correctly in an OBJ3 system that has been constructed using Kyoto Common Lisp; however, they do work correctly in a system built using (for example) Lucid Common Lisp.

Warning: The command `openr` (as described in Section 3.2) can retroactively change a saved context.

The initial OBJ context, which has exactly what the standard prelude provides, can be restored at any time with the command

```
do restore init .
```

Simply reading in the standard prelude again will restore the modules in the standard prelude to their original state, but will not delete any modules that have been subsequently added.

OBJ3 has a notion of "the module currently in focus", and the module name `THE-LAST-MODULE` evaluates to that module; ordinarily, this is the last module mentioned to the system, but it can be changed to any desired module by using the command

```
select [⟨ModExp⟩] .
```

(The old form `show select` ⟨*ModExp*⟩ still works.)

The following synonymous commands

```
show [⟨ModExp⟩] .
show mod [⟨ModExp⟩] .
```

display the structure of the given module, or of the current module if no ⟨*ModExp*⟩ is given.

Warning: When a module is displayed, some details may omitted, and other details may be shown that the user did not input, for example, some declarations that properly belong to submodules.

The command

```
show all [⟨ModExp⟩] .
```

shows a module in more detail than the default form. The commands

```
set verbose on .
set verbose off .
```

control whether modules are displayed in detailed form by default. (It also controls whether a trace of the id processing is displayed; this is discussed later.)

OBJ3 automatically generates abbreviated names for modules and module expressions; they can be very useful, because sometimes the "official" name of a module can be very long indeed. These abbreviations have the form "MOD⟨*Nat*⟩" where ⟨*Nat*⟩ is a natural number, and can serve as names for modules in many top-level commands. One can see the abbreviation for a module's name with the command

        show abbrev [⟨*ModExp*⟩] .

For example,

        show abbrev PROPC .

gives the abbreviation for PROPC, which at the current point in processing the OBJ3 code in this paper is MOD40. Names of the form MOD⟨*Nat*⟩ can also be used in show commands and many other contexts. These names are considered abbreviations, rather than a formal part of the syntax of OBJ3.

3.1   IMPORTING MODULES

OBJ3 has four **modes** for importing modules, with the syntax

        ⟨*ImportKw*⟩ ⟨*ModExp*⟩ .

where ⟨*ImportKw*⟩ is one of protecting, extending, including, or using, and ⟨*ModExp*⟩ is a module expression, such as INT; the abbreviations pr, ex, inc, and us can be used for the corresponding mode keywords.

By convention, if a module M imports a module M' that imports a module M'', then M'' is also imported into M; that is, "imports" is a *transitive* relation. A given module M' can only be imported into M with a single mode; modules that are multiply imported due to transitivity are ordinarily considered to be "shared."

The meaning of the import modes is related to the initial algebra semantics of objects, in that an importation of module M' into M is:

1. **protecting** iff M adds no new data items of sorts from M', and also identifies no old data items of sorts from M' (no junk and no confusion);

2. **extending** iff the equations in M identify no old data items of sorts from M' (no confusion);

3. **including** or **using** if there are no guarantees at all (see below for the difference between these).

A protecting importation has the advantage that it guarantees that no newly generated rules need to be added to the imported module, and also, the E-strategies of imported operators do not need to be recomputed; thus, the code from protecting imported modules can just be shared.

Warning: OBJ3 does not check whether the user's import declarations are correct, because this could require arbitrarily difficult theorem proving that would render the language impractical.   However, the consequences of an incorrect import mode declaration can be serious: incomplete reductions in some cases, and inefficient reductions in others.

Warning: If an object A has a sort S, and an object B imports A and introduces a new subsort S' of S, then things may not work as you expect, even if mathematically A is protected in B. In particular, if B introduces a new overloading of an operator of sort S from A that restricts to S', then the protecting declaration may cause failure to generate rules that are needed for matching for some cases, such as rules associated with an identity attribute. Also, retracts may appear on right sides because of equations that appear to be sort increasing (this issue was discussed in Section 2.3.4).

For example, the module

```
obj A is
   sort S .
   op f : S -> S .
   ops a b : -> S .
   vars X : S .
   eq f(X) = b .
endo
```

is certainly protected from the mathematical point of view in the module

```
obj B is
   protecting A .
   sort S' .
   subsorts S' < S .
   op f : S' -> S' .
   op a : -> S' .
endo
```

However, in the context of B, the equation f(X) = b, which was trivially sort decreasing in A, is no longer sort decreasing, and evaluating the term f(a) in the context of the module B now gives the result r:S>S'(f(b)). Thus, introducing new sorts under previous sorts should be avoided in *protecting* importations.

For an `extending` importation, the E-strategies associated to imported operators are recomputed, according to the following rules:

1. if an imported operator has an explicit, user-supplied strategy, then use it;

2. if not, and if there are no new equations, then use the inherited computed strategy; and

3. if there are new equations, then recompute the strategy and use the new one.

Including is implemented as incorporation without copying, and in this respect is similar to `protecting`; if a module is included twice in a given module, only one version is created (if it doesn't already exist) and all references are to the same shared instance.

Warning: The `using` mode is implemented by copying the imported module's top-level structure, sharing all of the submodules that it imports. It is required that all copied sorts within a given module have distinct names, and that all copied operators are uniquely identified by their name and rank. This means operators that require qualification will be a problem. Such operators may be mistakenly collapsed into a single operator.

Warning: "`using BOOL`" is not meaningful, because a `using` importation that is not an `extending` importation will identify `true` with `false`, which is not only not useful, but also will interfere with the predefined operators `_==_` and `if_then_else_fi`.

Sometimes it is desirable to copy not only the top-level structure of a module, but also that of some of its submodules, for example, to ensure that the associative or identity completion process is carried out, or that evaluation strategies are recomputed. This can be done using the following syntax,

$$\text{using } \langle ModExp \rangle \text{ with } \langle ModExp \rangle \ \{\text{and } \langle ModExp \rangle\}\ldots$$

which causes the listed submodules to be copied instead of shared. This feature is illustrated in the unification example in Appendix C.3. Note that all automatically created submodules[16] are automatically copied by `using`, so the multi-level using declaration is not needed for such cases.

The module that introduces a given sort often establishes a convention for naming variables of that sort, and introduces a number of variables for it. The following command makes it easy to reuse variable names, and thus to maintain such conventions. Thus,

---

[16] This notion is discussed in Section 4.5 below.

```
vars-of ⟨ModExp⟩ .
```

introduces all the variables from ⟨*ModExp*⟩; these have the same names and sorts as in ⟨*ModExp*⟩.

Warning: Only the variables declared in ⟨*ModExp*⟩ are introduced, and not variables from modules imported by ⟨*ModExp*⟩, even if their variables had been introduced into ⟨*ModExp*⟩ using `vars-of`.

OBJ3 permits redefining any module, simply by introducing a new module with the old name. A warning is issued, indicating that redefinition has occurred, and then all future mentions of this name refer to the new definition. This can be very useful in theorem proving; for example, you may want to replace a predefined module for numbers that is efficient, by another that is less efficient but more logically complete; Appendix C.4 contains several examples of this.

Warning: Redefining a module does not cause the redefinition of modules that have been previously built from it. For example, if we define A to be an enrichment of INT, then redefine INT, and then look at A, it will still involve the old definition of INT. The same happens with parameterized modules.

BOOL is implicitly `protecting` imported into every module, to ensure that conditional equations can be used, unless an explicit `extending` BOOL declaration is given instead; TRUTH can be imported instead of BOOL by giving an explicit declaration, as in the PROPC example in Section 2.4.6. Usually it is convenient that BOOL has been imported, because conditional equations often make use of the operators that are provided in BOOL, such as ==, and, or not. But sometimes, especially in applications to theorem proving, this can be inconvenient, because it does not provide enough rules to correctly decide all equalities about truth values, even though it does correctly specify the initial algebra of Boolean truth values. The command

```
set include BOOL off .
```

causes not importing BOOL to become the default. The original default can be restored with the command

```
set include BOOL on .
```

When `include` BOOL is on, then BOOL is included in a module before anything except a `using`, `protecting`, `extending` or `sort` declaration, unless TRUTH-VALUE, TRUTH, or BOOL itself has been included already. (This will affect the determination of the principal sort of a module, as described in Section 4.3.)

3.1.1   Identity Completion and Associative Extensions.   Pattern match-ing for operators with identities is implemented in OBJ3 using a process called **id processing** that consists of a "partial identity completion" process that may generate some new rules, and an "id processing" process that may add some so-called "id conditions" to rules. Identity completion generates instances of a rule by considering "critical pairs" between the rule and the identity equations, in order to give the effect of rewriting modulo identity. For example, consider the first equation from the module `LIST-OF-INT1` in Section 2.4, `head(I L) = I`. This equation has `head I = I` as the special case where `L = nil`, and identity completion considers adding it to the rulebase; however, it is not actually added in this case, because the rule is matched in such a way that terms are rewritten as if this rule had been added. Id processing restricts the standard identity completion process to avoid simple cases of non-termination by adding id conditions to rules, so that obviously problematic instances are disallowed, and also by discarding rule instances whose left sides are variables (because their implementation as rules is problematic); in addition, generated rules that are subsumed by other rules are deleted for the sake of efficiency.

Warning: Experience shows that matching modulo identity often results in problems with non-termination. It is safer to use the attribute `idr:` and then add any desired identity completion equations by hand.

Warning: Strategies of operators are not taken into account when testing for non-termination. It is possible that a rule will be considered non-terminating, when this condition is actually avoided because of the evaluation strategies.

For example, in the object `PROPC` of Section 2.4.6, if you replace the at-tributes `idr:` by `id:`, then identity completion will substitute q = false into the distributive law,

```
eq p and (q xor r) = (p and q) xor (p and r) .
```

and (in effect) add the new equation

```
eq p and r = (p and false) xor (p and r) .
```

which would make it likely that terms containing and would fail to terminate. However, OBJ3's id processing will discard the problematic equations and add an id condition to the rule, so that it looks as follows:

```
eq p and (q xor r) = (p and q) xor p and r
        if not (r === false or p === true or q === false) .
```

Id conditions are normally not displayed. But when rules are displayed either in `verbose` mode, or with a `show all` command, then the id conditions

are shown. For example, you can see what id completion does to PROPC with
id:, including those generated by identity completion, by using the command

    show PROPC .

or more specifically, the command

    show eqs PROPC .

Also, when a module is processed in verbose mode, some details of the completion process are shown, including the new rule instances that are generated, and indications of modifications or additions to rules. This extra information can help to understand non-termination problems. The rules that are automatically added by id processing have automatically generated labels of the form "compl⟨*Nat*⟩".

The object BSET of Appendix Section C.1 illustrates a different approach, which is to explicitly make the distributive law a *conditional* equation. This approach can also be useful in many other cases. The object IDENTICAL in the standard prelude is used in this example; it consists of BOOL plus the operators _===_ and _=/==_, which test for syntactic identity and non-identity, respectively.

For another example, if the following module is processed in verbose mode,

```
obj TST is
  sort A .
  ops c d e 0 1 : -> A .
  vars X Y : A .
  op _+_ : A A -> A [assoc comm id: 0] .
  eq X + Y = c .
endo
```

then OBJ3 will produce this output:

```
==============================================
obj TST
Performing id processing for rules
For rule: eq X + Y = c
  Generated valid rule instances:
  eq X + Y = c
  Generated invalid rule instances:
  eq Y = c
  eq X = c
  Modified rule:
  eq X + Y = c if not (Y === 0 or X === 0)
```

```
Done with id processing for rules
==============================================
```

No new rules are generated here, but an id condition is added to the given rule. A rule instance is considered invalid if its left side is a variable, or if it would "obviously" cause non-termination, e.g., if its left and right sides are the same term; such rules are discarded. The following commands

```
show rule .1 .
show all rule .1 .
```

produce the following output:

```
==============================================
show rule .1 .
rule 1 of the last module
   eq X + Y = c
==============================================
show all rule .1 .
rule 1 of the last module
   eq X + Y = c if not (Y === 0 or X === 0)
==============================================
```

The following is a somewhat more complicated example:

```
obj TST is
   protecting TRUTH-VALUE .
   sort A .
   op 0 : -> A .
   op _+_ : A A -> A [assoc id: 0] .
   op 1 : -> A .
   op _*_ : A A -> A [assoc id: 1] .
   op f : A -> A .
   ops a b c d e f : -> A .
   var X Y : A .
   eq (X * Y) + f(X * Y) = f(X) .
endo
```

Its verbose output is:

```
==============================================
obj TST
Performing id processing for rules
For rule: eq (X * Y) + f(X * Y) = f(X)
   Generated valid rule instances:
```

```
eq (X * Y) + f(X * Y) = f(X)
eq X + f(X) = f(X)
eq Y + f(Y) = f(1)
eq f(0) = f(1)
Generated invalid rule instances:
eq f(0) = f(0)
Added rule: [compl16] eq f(0) = f(1)
Added rule: [compl17]
    eq X + f(X) = f(X) if not X === 0
Modified rule:
    eq (X * Y) + f(X * Y) = f(X)
        if not (X === 0 and Y === 1)
Done with id processing for rules
================================================
```

The rule compl16 must be added because the top operator of its left side is
f rather than _+_, and OBJ3 stores rules according to the top symbol of their
left side. Notice that the left side of rule compl17 is a generalization of the
original left side, and in fact, is a strict generalization because with OBJ3's
built-in matching, the original rule's left side cannot match X + f(X), the left
side of the new rule. Therefore, it might make sense to delete the original rule;
however, OBJ3 does not do this, to avoid the potential confusion of having rules
given by the user disappear. The id completion process may not be correct
unless the original rule set is confluent, in the sense that the set of rules available
after id completion is confluent modulo OBJ3's built-in matching (which is
basically associative, or associative-commutative, matching, plus some quite
limited identity matching). In this example, the confluence assumption implies
that it is valid not to add the rule eq Y + f(Y) = f(1). Note that in this
rather contrived example, the original system was not confluent. The following
is a simpler example of a single rule that is not confluent:

```
eq f(X) + f(Y) = X .
```

where + is commutative.

Warning: Although Release 2.04 of OBJ3 handles associative rewriting in
part through special internal data structures, its way of dealing with subsorts
may generate new "extension" equations from given equations that involve
associative operators; see [99] for further details. In many cases, these new
equations are not only unnecessary, but can also greatly slow down reduction.
For example, if you read in the objects NAT and INT from Appendix Section
C.7 and then ask OBJ to show you the equations, among them you will find

```
[×] eq 0 + I + ac_E = ac_E + I .
```

Although this equation can be very expensive to match, it adds nothing to the power of the equation that it extends, namely

        eq 0 + I = I .

Unfortunately, the current implementation of associative rewriting does sometimes require equations like [×] to be generated, and it can be hard to tell when they are useless. The issues involved in implementing rewriting modulo associativity and identity are surprising subtle, and it is likely that improvements on the techniques that we have used in OBJ3 could be found; see [99, 96] for further discussion.

3.2   OPENING AND CLOSING MODULES

A module can be temporarily enriched after it has been defined, by using the command

        open ⟨*ModExp*⟩ .

or, for the last module, just the command

        open .

This is useful for many applications, and in particular for theorem proving.

Warning: The blank and period are required here.

Exactly the same syntax can be used for adding declarations to an open module as for originally introducing them into modules; thus, operators can be added with the op command, sorts with the sort command, and so on. All other top level commands (e.g., in, set, show, select, and do) also work as usual.

Normally a module that has been opened should eventually be closed, using the command

        close

Warning: There is no period after this command; it is considered self-delimiting.

The command open creates a hidden object (called "%") that includes the given object, and the command close causes the hidden object "%" to be deleted. All enrichments to an opened module "disappear" when it is closed. This allows an object to temporarily have more structure than when it was originally defined, which can be very useful in theorem proving examples, as illustrated many times in Section C.4.

OBJ3 separately keeps track of the "last" module and the "open" module (if any). Therefore, it is possible (for example) to show the module INT while the module LIST is open; this will make INT the "last" module, but all newly declared elements will still go into the open LIST module. The "last" module can be identified by the command "show name" and the open module can be identified by "show name open".

The variables declared in a module are no longer available when it is opened, but they can be made available with the command

        vars-of .

The variables that are available can be seen by using the command

        show vars [⟨*ModExp* ⟩] .

An alternate version of open called openr (to suggest "open retentive") retains additions after closure; it is closed with just close. This can be useful for including lemmas when OBJ3 is used for theorem proving.

Warning: If an enriched module has been incorporated into some other module, either directly (e.g., by protecting) or indirectly (by appearing in a module expression), then the incorporating module may no longer be valid with respect to the enriched version of the incorporated module.

The command

        select open .

makes the open module the last module (i.e., the default for show commands, etc.). In fact, "open" can be used as a short name for the open module in any of the show commands.

Warning: If you show the open module, OBJ will display the name of the underlying module, but marked with "*** open" as a reminder.

3.3   BUILT-INS AND THE STANDARD PRELUDE

Usually, languages have some built-in data types, such as numbers and identifiers. OBJ is sufficiently powerful that it does not need built-ins, because it can define any desired data type; but building in the most frequently used data types can make a great difference in efficiency and convenience. OBJ3 has predefined objects TRUTH-VALUE, TRUTH, BOOL, IDENTICAL, NAT, NZNAT, INT, RAT, FLOAT, QID, QIDL, and ID, plus the parameterized tuple objects described in Section 4.2, the theory TRIV described in Section 4.1, and some other objects that serve a technical purpose.

TRUTH-VALUE provides just the truth values true and false, while TRUTH enriches TRUTH-VALUE with _==_ , _=/=_ and if_then_else_fi, and BOOL adds the expected syntax and semantics for Booleans, e.g., infix associative and, or, and `iff`, infix `implies`, prefix `not`. Indeed, the object `PROPC` of Section 2.4.6 above can be considered a *specification* for these features of the Booleans, except of course, that quoted identifiers are not provided, but `_==_`, `_=/=_` and `if_then_else_fi` are provided; also, note that these last three operators are polymorphic, in the sense that they apply to any appropriate sorts. This can help, for example, with parsing problems when a condition is of the form `E == C`, where `C` is an ambiguous constant (i.e., there is more than one constant with that name) and `E` is has a well-defined unique sort.

The object `IDENTICAL` can be used in place of `BOOL`; it provides the operators `_===_` and `_=/==_` which check for literal identity of terms without evaluating them.

`NAT`, `NZNAT`, `INT` and `RAT` provide natural numbers, non-zero naturals, integers and rationals, respectively, while `FLOAT` provides floating point numbers, each with the usual operators, having the expected attributes. You can discover exactly what any predefined object provides by using the `show` command, or else by looking at the file that defines OBJ3's predefined objects, which is `obj/lisp/prelude/obj3sp.obj` in the standard distribution of OBJ3; this file is executed as a standard prelude whenever a new instance of OBJ3 is constructed.

`QID`, `QIDL` and `ID` provide identifiers. `QID` and `QIDL` identifiers begin with the apostrophe symbol, e.g., `'a`, `'b`, `'1040`, and

   `'aratherlongidentifier` .

`QID` has no operators, while `QIDL` and `ID` have equality, disequality, and lexicographic order, which is denoted `_<_`, and also include everything that `BOOL` does.

Warning: Data elements from `ID` lack the initial apostrophe, and therefore must be used very carefully to avoid massive parsing ambiguities.

Some of OBJ3's predefined modules were implemented by encapsulating Lisp code in objects, as can be seen by looking at the OBJ3 standard prelude. The possibility of implementing other efficient built-in data structures and algorithms remains available to sophisticated users, and has many potential applications, such as building graphics interfaces. Details of the syntax for built-in sorts and equations appear in Appendix Section D.

3.4   FILES AND LIBRARIES

To reuse code, it and anything that it relies upon (its context) must be available. Files provide a convenient way to store and retrieve modules along with their contexts. The context of a given file of modules and views can be preserved by prefacing the file with a command that fetches whatever it depends upon. Thus, an OBJ file may contain modules, views, and other top level OBJ commands, including reduction commands and the in (or input) command, which reads in and executes a file. For example,

    in mysys

reads the file mysys.obj, adding its modules and views to the current context, executing whatever commands it may contain, including nested in commands, and checking that a consistent context is formed as they are added to the database. This "batch mode" use of OBJ3 is in fact more convenient in practice than using it interactively.

If eof appears as a top level command in a file, then everything after it is ignored. This can be convenient during debugging.

Allowing files to include top level commands is very convenient and flexible. For example, after constructing a particular multi-module context, one can execute some illustrative examples. UNIX directories provide a convenient way to organize files into libraries, because a given directory can have subdirectories named by keywords, with further named subdirectories, etc. For example, the propositional calculus decision procedure may be found in file obj/exs/propc.obj, its test cases in obj/exs/propc-exs.obj, and the results of running them might be in obj/exs/propc-exs.lg. Note that a given file can be included in many other files, located in many different subdirectories.

The command cd

    cd ⟨*Directory*⟩

can be executed at the top level of OBJ3, and will change the current directory for OBJ3 to be the given directory. The command cd ⁓ can be used to change to one's home directory. A file name beginning with "⁓/" will be expanded to the user's home directory in most contexts.

The command pwd reports the current working directory. The command ls lists the files in the current working directory.

Warning: These commands do not have final periods.

3.5 COMMENTS

OBJ has two kinds of comment, those that print when executed, and those that don't. The former are lines that begin with "***>", and the latter are lines that begin with "***". In many cases, these comment indicators can also appear part way through a line, in which case the remainder of the line is treated as a comment. "---" is a synonym for "***" for comments. The printing comments can be useful when OBJ is used in "batch mode." These comments must either be at the outer-most level or the top level of a module and cannot appear inside of other basic syntactic units; specifically, they cannot appear in terms (and hence equations) or views.

If the first non-blank character after "***" is a "(", then the comment extends from that character up to the next balancing ")". This makes it easy to comment out several lines at once. For example,

```
*** (
  eq X * 0 = 0 .
  eq X + X = X .
  )
```

Warning: Be careful of comments that have parentheses in them; for example, in

```
*** (This is the idempotent law:)  eq X + X = X .
```

the comment only extends to the balancing ")", and does not include the equation. This treatment is inconsistent with release 1, and may cause errors in some older specifications.

4   PARAMETERIZED PROGRAMMING

Both the costs and the demands for software are enormous, and are growing rapidly. One way to diminish these effects is to maximize the **reuse** of software, through the systematic use of what we call **parameterized programming** (see [85, 47, 52, 49, 36, 37, 55, 77]). Successful software reuse depends upon the following tasks being sufficiently easy:

1. finding old parts that are close enough to what you need;

2. understanding those parts;

3. getting them to do what you need now; and

4. putting them all together correctly.

Under these conditions, the total effort, and especially debugging and maintenance effort, can be greatly reduced. Objects, theories, views and module expressions provide formal support for these tasks. The basic idea of parameterized programming is a strong form of *abstraction*: to break code into highly parameterized mind-sized pieces. Then one can construct new programs from old modules by instantiating parameters and transforming modules. Actual parameters are modules in this approach, and interface specifications include semantic as well as syntactic information.

Ada [22] generic packages provide only part of what would be most useful. In particular, Ada generic packages provide no way to document the *semantics* of interfaces, although this feature can greatly improve the reliability of software reuse and can also help to retrieve the right module from a library, as discussed in [49]. Also, Ada provides only very weak facilities for combining modules. For example, only one level of module instantiation is possible at a time; that is, one cannot build F(G(A)), but rather one must first define B to be G(A), and then build F(B).

Parameterized modules are the basic building blocks of parameterized programming, and its theories, views and module expressions go well beyond the capabilities of Ada generics. A **theory** defines the interface of a parameterized module, that is, the structure and properties required of an actual parameter for meaningful instantiation. A **view** expresses that a certain module satisfies a certain theory in a certain way (note that some modules can satisfy some theories in more than one way); that is, a view describes a *binding* of an actual parameter to an interface theory. **Instantiation** of a parameterized module with an actual parameter, using a particular view, yields a new module. **Module expressions** describe complex interconnections of modules, potentially involving instantiation, addition, and renaming of modules.

A useful insight (see [7]) is that programming in the large can be seen as a kind of *functional programming*, in which evaluating (what we call) a module expression is indeed a kind of expression evaluation; in particular, there are no variables, no assignments, and no effects, side or otherwise, just functions applied to arguments; this can provide a formal basis for software reuse [12]. However, there are also some significant differences between ordinary functional programming and module expression evaluation in parameterized programming, including semantic interfaces, the use of views, and evaluation *in context*, producing not just a single module, but also embedding it in its context, i.e., placing it within a graph of modules.

As an example of parameterized programming, consider a parameterized module LEXL[X] that provides lists of Xs with a lexicographic ordering, where the parameter X can be instantiated with any partially ordered set. Thus, given QIDL that provides identifiers (and in particular, words) with their usual (lexicographic) ordering, then LEXL[QIDL] provides a lexicographic ordering on lists of words (i.e., on "phrases," such as book titles). And LEXL[LEXL[QIDL]] provides a lexicographic ordering on list of phrases (such as lists of book titles) by instantiating the ordering that LEXL[X] requires with the one that LEXL[QIDL] provides, namely lexicographic ordering[17]. Similarly, given a module SORTING[Y] for sorting lists of Ys (again for Y any partially or-

---

[17] In practice, the two kinds of list should use different notation, to avoid parse ambiguities, as in Section 4.5 below.

dered set, and assuming that SORTING[Y] imports LEXL[Y]), we can let Y be LEXL[QIDL] to get a program SORTING[LEXL[QIDL]] that sorts lists of book titles.

Let us examine this example a little more closely. In general, a module can define one or more data structures, with various operators among them, possibly importing some data structures and operators from other modules[18]. For example, LEXL[X] should define or import lists of Xs and provide a binary relation, say L1 << L2, meaning that list L1 is the same as or comes earlier in the ordering than L2. The interface theory for LEXL is POSET, the theory of partially ordered sets, and hereafter we will use the notation LEXL[X :: POSET] to indicate this. To instantiate a formal parameter with an actual parameter, it is necessary to provide a **view**, which *binds* the formal entities in the interface theory to actual ones. If there is a default view of a module M as a partial order, we can just write LEXL[M]; for example, if M = QIDL, there is an obvious view that selects the predefined lexicographic ordering relation on identifiers. LEXL[QIDL] in turn provides another lexicographic ordering, and a default view from POSET using this ordering makes it legal to write SORTING[LEXL[QIDL]]. (Code for this example is given in Sections 4.4 and 4.5.) The next two subsections discuss theories and views, respectively.

4.1   THEORIES

Theories are used to express properties of modules and module interfaces. In general, OBJ3 theories have the same structure as objects; in particular, theories have sorts, subsorts, operators, variables and equations, can import other theories and objects, and can even be parameterized. Semantically, a theory denotes a "variety" of models, containing all the (order sorted) algebras that satisfy it, whereas an object defines just one model (up to isomorphism), its initial algebra. As a result of this, theories are allowed to contain equations that are prohibited in objects, because they cannot be interpreted as rewrite rules. In particular, equations in theories may have variables in their right side and conditions that do not occur in their left side; also the left side may be a single variable. Nonetheless, Release 2 of OBJ3 allows reductions to be executed in the context of theories, and simply ignores any equations that cannot be interpreted as rewrite rules. However, the apply feature (described in Section 5) does fully support equational deduction with such non-rewrite-rule equations. Another difference is that built-in rules (see Appendix D.1.3) are not allowed in theories.

---

[18] In general, modules may have internal states; although this feature is not discussed in this paper, the reader can consult [85, 70, 55] and [74] for further information about approaches to this important topic, which is implemented in the FOOPS [74, 87], OOZE [3], and LILEANNA [85] systems.

Now some examples, declaring some interfaces with properties that might have to be satisfied for certain modules to perform correctly. The first is the trivial theory TRIV, which requires nothing except a sort, designated Elt.

```
th TRIV is
   sort Elt .
endth
```

This theory is predefined in OBJ3, as part of the standard prelude.

The next theory is an extension of TRIV, requiring that models also have a given element of the given sort, here designated "*".

```
th TRIV* is
   using TRIV .
   op * : -> Elt .
endth
```

Of course, this enrichment is equivalent to

```
th TRIV* is
   sort Elt .
   op * : -> Elt .
endth
```

which may seem clearer. These first two theories impose only syntactic requirements.

Next, the theory of pre-ordered sets; its models have a binary infix Bool-valued operator <= that is reflexive and transitive.

```
th PREORD is
   sort Elt .
   op _<=_ : Elt Elt -> Bool .
   vars E1 E2 E3 : Elt .
   eq E1 <= E1 = true .
   cq E1 <= E3 = true if E1 <= E2 and E2 <= E3 .
endth
```

Note the use of and in the condition of the last equation, used to express transitivity; it has been imported from BOOL. Recalling that previously declared variables can occur in terms submitted for reduction, the term

```
   reduce E1 <= E1 .
```

reduces to true (after producing a warning about the presence of variables).

Similarly, the theory of partially ordered sets, with models having a binary infix Bool-valued operator < that is anti-reflexive and transitive, can be expressed as follows:

```
th POSET is
  sort Elt .
  op _<_ : Elt Elt -> Bool .
  vars E1 E2 E3 : Elt .
  eq E1 < E1 = false .
  cq E1 < E3 = true if E1 < E2 and E2 < E3 .
endth
```

The theory of an equivalence relation has a binary infix Bool-valued operator, here denoted _eq_, that is reflexive, symmetric and transitive.

```
th EQV is
  sort Elt .
  op _eq_ : Elt Elt -> Bool [comm].
  vars E1 E2 E3 : Elt .
  eq (E1 eq E1) = true .
  cq (E1 eq E3) = true if (E1 eq E2) and (E2 eq E3) .
endth
```

Note the use of the [comm] attribute here; of course, we could instead have given the equation for symmetry,

```
  eq E1 eq E2 = E2 eq E1 .
```

Finally, the theory of monoids, which in Section 4.7 will serve as an interface theory for a general iterator that in particular gives sums and products over lists.

```
th MONOID is
  sort M .
  op e : -> M .
  op _*_ : M M -> M [assoc id: e] .
endth
```

The possibility of expressing *semantic* properties, such as the associativity of an operator, as part of the interface of a module is a significant advantage for parameterized programming over traditional functional programming. For example, traditional functional programming can easily provide a (second-order) function to iterate any given binary function (such as integer addition) over lists, but it cannot express the condition that the binary function must be associative, although this property is necessary for certain optimizations to be correct (see Section 4.7 for the details of this example). There is no reason why the language used to express assertions in theories couldn't be full first-order logic (including quantifiers); in fact, this might be a very desirable extension of OBJ3. However, the expressive power of the `protecting` importation of objects into theories (which requires that the given object must be interpreted with initial algebra semantics) and in particular the use of such importations for the `BOOL` object, allows quite sophisticated theories to be defined in OBJ3 even with its current restriction to equational logic. For example, the theory `FIELD` of fields, which is well known not to be equationally definable, can easily be defined as follows[19]

```
th FIELD is
   sorts Field NzField .
   subsorts NzField < Field .
   protecting BOOL .
   op 0 : -> Field .
   op 1 : -> NzField .
   op _+_ : Field Field -> Field [assoc comm id: 0].
   op _*_ : Field Field -> Field [assoc comm id: 1].
   op _*_ : NzField NzField -> NzField
                                    [assoc comm id: 1].
   op -_ : Field -> Field .
   op _^-1 : NzField -> NzField .
   op nz : Field -> Bool .
   vars X Y Z : Field .
   vars X' Y' : NzField .
   as NzField : X if nz(X) .
   eq X + (- X) = 0 .
   eq X' * (X' ^-1) = 1 .
   eq X * (Y + Z) = (X * Y) + (X + Z) .
   cq X = 0 if not nz(X) .
endth
```

4.2   PARAMETERIZED MODULES

Let us now consider some parameterized modules. First, a parameterized `LIST` object, with `TRIV` as its interface theory:

```
obj LIST[X :: TRIV] is
   sorts List NeList .
```

---

[19] However, as pointed out in Section 2.3.3, general sort constraints like the one given in this theory are not yet implemented.

```
      subsorts Elt < NeList < List .
      op nil : -> List .
      op __ : List List -> List [assoc id: nil prec 9] .
      op __ : NeList List -> NeList [assoc prec 9] .
      op head_ : NeList -> Elt .
      op tail_ : NeList -> List .
      op empty?_ : List -> Bool .
      var X : Elt .
      var L : List .
      eq head(X L) = X .
      eq tail(X L) = L .
      eq empty? L = L == nil .
    endo
```

Warning: The interface theories of parameterized modules must have been defined earlier in the program text. For example, TRIV must have been defined before the above LIST module; this is not a problem in this case, because TRIV is predefined.

Modules can have more than one parameter. A two parameter module has an interface with the syntax [X :: TH1, Y :: TH2], and if the two theories are the same, we can just write [X Y :: TH]. Now a parameterized theory, vector spaces over a field:

```
    th VECTOR-SP[F :: FIELD] is
      sort Vector .
      op 0 : -> Vector .
      op _+_ : Vector Vector -> Vector [assoc comm id: 0] .
      op _*_ : Field Vector -> Vector .
      vars F F1 F2 : Field .
      vars V V1 V2 : Vector .
      eq (F1 + F2) * V = (F1 * V) + (F2 * V) .
      eq (F1 * F2) * V = F1 * (F2 * V) .
      eq F * (V1 + V2) = (F * V1) + (F * V2) .
    endth
```

For $2 \leq n \leq 4$, the predefined parameterized nTUPLE modules provide n-tuples, with all n interface theories being TRIV. Here is the code for $n = 2$:

```
    obj 2TUPLE[C1 :: TRIV, C2 :: TRIV] is
      sort 2Tuple .
      op <<_;_>> : Elt.C1 Elt.C2 -> 2Tuple .
      op 1*_ : 2Tuple -> Elt.C1 .
      op 2*_ : 2Tuple -> Elt.C2 .
```

```
      var E1 : Elt.C1 .
      var E2 : Elt.C2 .
      eq 1* << E1 ; E2 >> = E1 .
      eq 2* << E1 ; E2 >> = E2 .
    endo
```

Note the use of the qualifications in the sorts Elt.C1 and Elt.C2.

4.3 VIEWS

A module can satisfy a theory in more than one way, and even if there is a unique way, it can be arbitrarily difficult to find. We therefore need a notation for describing the particular ways that modules satisfy theories. For example, NAT can satisfy POSET with the usual "less-than" ordering, but "divides-and-unequal" and "greater-than" are also possible; each of these corresponds to a different view. Thus, an expression like LEXL [NAT] (where LEXL has interface theory POSET, as in Section 4.1) would be ambiguous if there were not certain definite conventions for default views.

More precisely now, a **view** ϕ from a theory T to a module M, indicated $\phi : T \Rightarrow M$, consists of a mapping from the sorts of T to the sorts of M preserving the subsort relation, and a mapping from the operators of T to the operators of M preserving arity, value sort, and the meanings of the attributes assoc, comm, idem, id: and[20] idr: (to the extent that these attributes are present), such that every equation in T is true of every model of M (thus, a view from one theory to another is called a "theory interpretation" in logic [9]). The mapping of sorts is expressed with the syntax

```
    sort S1 to S1' .
    sort S2 to S2' .
    ...
```

and the mapping of operators is expressed with the syntax

```
    op o1 to o1' .
    op o2 to o2' .
    ...
```

Warning: The final blank and period are required. Comments may not appear anywhere inside of views.

Thus, the mapping of sorts and the mapping of operators can each be seen as sets of pairs. The operators o1, o1', o2, ..., may be designated by operator

---

[20] For this purpose, id: and idr: are treated as equivalent.

forms, or operator forms plus value sort and arity, possibly qualified by sort and/or module, as needed for disambiguation. As explained below, the target operators o1', o2', ..., can also be derived operators, i.e., terms with variables.

These two sets of pairs together are called a **view body**. The syntax for defining a view at the top level of OBJ3 requires giving names for the source and target modules, and (usually) a name for the view. For example,

```
view NATG from POSET to NAT is
  sort Elt to Nat .
  op _<_ to _>_ .
endv
```

defines a view called NATG from POSET to NAT, interpreting _<_ in POSET as _>_ in NAT.

Now some views that involve derived operators. First, consider

```
view NATLEQ from PREORD to NAT is
  vars L1 L2 : Elt .
  op L1 <= L2 to L1 < L2 or L1 == L2 .
endv
```

This maps <= in PREORD to "less-than-or-equal" in NAT, which for illustrative purposes is defined here from < and ==, even though <= is already defined in NAT. Similarly, the following view maps < in POSET to the relation "divides-and-unequal" in NAT (note that divides-and-unequal is a partial ordering that is not a total ordering):

```
view NATD from POSET to NAT is
  vars L1 L2 : Elt .
  op L1 < L2 to L1 divides L2 and L1 =/= L2 .
endv
```

Warning: The variables must be declared, using sorts from the source theory, while the target terms in operator pairs must be of the corresponding sorts from the target module. For parsing the target terms, the variables are re-declared with the appropriate sorts.

When the user feels that there is an obvious view to use, it can be annoying to have to write out that view in full detail. **Default views** often allow omitting views within module expressions, by capturing the intuitive notion of "the obvious view." A default view is a **null view**[21], which is the extreme case of an

---

[21] Some further conventions for default views are described in [52], but these are not implemented in Release 2 of OBJ3; also, the discussion in [52] does not reflect some improvements to OBJ3 made after that paper was written.

abbreviated view in which the view is abbreviated to nothing. Given a view $\phi : \mathrm{M} \Rightarrow \mathrm{M}'$, there are two rules for abbreviating sorts:

1. Any pair of the form S to S can be omitted, except in the case that the target sort S is a sort in a parameter theory.

2. A pair S to S' can be omitted if S and S' are each the principal sort of their module. The **principal sort** of a module is intuitively the first sort introduced into its body. More precisely, it is defined as follows:

   (a) the first sort explicitly declared in the module, if there is one;

   (b) or else the principal sort of the first imported module, if there is one;

   (c) or else the principal sort of the first parameter theory, if there is one;

   (d) or else Bool, provided that implicit importation of Bool has not been disenabled.

   If none of these conditions hold, then the module has no sorts!

Warning: The handling of default views described above is slightly different from that in Release 1, and some default views may be computed differently.

As a special case, every module has a default view from TRIV with its principal sort as the target for Elt. For another example, the default view from POSET to NAT is

```
view NATV from POSET to NAT is
  sort Elt to Nat .
  op _<_ to _<_ .
endv
```

In the following abbreviated view

```
view NATG from POSET to NAT is
  op _<_ to _>_ .
endv
```

the pair Elt to Nat has been omitted.

The sort to be used as the principal sort of a module can be explicitly set with a declaration in the module of the form

```
principal-sort ⟨Sort⟩ .
```

where `principal-sort` may be abbreviated to `psort`. Note that this does not create a sort, but just declares that a certain existing sort should be taken as the principal sort of the module. This feature is not usually needed, because the default choice of principal sort, as the first sort "mentioned", is quite good, but it is needed (for example) if the sort desired to be principal comes from an interface theory.

The commands

> show psort [⟨*ModExp*⟩] .

and

> show psort .

show the principal sort of a given module, or of the current module if none is given.

There are also conventions for omitting operator pairs from a view:

1. Any pair of the form o to o can be omitted.

2. If o to o' is a pair in a view, and if o and o' have attributes id: e (or idr: e) and id: e' (or idr: e') respectively, then e to e' can be omitted.

For example, the default view from POSET to NAT has Elt to Nat and `_<_` to `_<_`, and the default view from MONOID to NAT is

```
view NAT* from MONOID to NAT is
  sort M to Nat .
  op _*_ to _*_ .
  op e to 1 .
  endv
```

where e maps to 1 because the identity attribute of ∗ is preserved. The following is a non-default view of NAT as a MONOID,

```
view NAT+ from MONOID to NAT is
  op _*_ to _+_ .
  op e to 0 .
  endv
```

where e to 0 could also be omitted by preservation of the identity attribute.

It can be shown [52] that if ψ is an abbreviation of each of two views ϕ and ϕ', then $\phi = \phi'$. From this, it follows that there is at most one null view from any module to any other.

Warning: Although our default view conventions work well for simple examples, it cannot be expected that they will always produce exactly the view that a user wants in more complex examples. Also, there is more going on behind the scenes than meets the eye.

Next, a view where the target module involves a parameter:

```
view LISTM from MONOID to LIST is
  op _*_ to __ .
  op e to nil .
endv
```

This view can actually be abbreviated to the following null view:

```
view LISTM from MONOID to LIST is endv
```

Warning: Although the source components of the operator mapping of a view $\phi: M \longrightarrow M'$ involve only operators from M itself, the target components can be terms that involve anything that M' imports; indeed, they do not have to involve operators from M' itself at all. Also notice that ϕ could be meaningless if some modules imported by M are not also imported by M', because then the translations of some of the equations in M might not make sense in M'.

We wish to emphasize the documentation aspect of views, because it is unique to OBJ and also seems very practical. In principle, theorem proving technology could be used to verify that a given mapping really is a view, that is, that the semantic properties specified in the source theory are in fact satisfied by the target module; presumably, this could be done using OBJ itself as a theorem prover, using techniques from [51, 53], or the Kumo system [65, 64, 78, 60]. However, this often may not be worth the effort in practice, and non-verified views should be seen as documenting the programmer's intentions and beliefs about the semantic properties of modules. Going a little further, a level of assurance could be associated with a view, reflecting the degree to which it has been validated, ranging from "pious hope" to "mechanically verified theorem." An intermediate level of assurance that may often be practical is that a paper and pencil proof has been given with the usual informal rigor of mathematics. Some form of automatic testing could also be provided.

4.4   INSTANTIATION

This subsection discusses instantiatinginstantiation the formal parameters of a parameterized module with actual modules. This construction requires a view from each formal interface theory to the corresponding actual module. The result of such an instantiation replaces each interface theory by its corresponding actual module, using the views to bind actual names to formal names, and avoiding multiple copies of shared submodules.

Let us consider the `make` command, which evaluates a module expression, and then adds the result to the OBJ3 database. This can be used to instantiate a parameterized module with an actual module *via* a view, and if a module name is used instead of a view, then the default view of that module from the interface theory of the parameterized module is used, if there is one. For example, given the parameterized object LEXL[X :: POSET], we can write

        make LEXL-NATG is LEXL[NATG] endm

using the explicit view NATG, while

        make NAT-LIST is LIST[NAT] endm

uses the default view from TRIV to NAT to instantiate the parameterized module LIST with the actual parameter NAT. Similarly, we might have

        make RAT-LIST is LIST[RAT] endm

where RAT is the field of rational numbers, using a default view from TRIV to RAT, or

        make RAT-VSP is VECTOR-SP[RAT] endm

using the default view from FIELD to RAT. More interestingly,

        make STACK-OF-LIST-OF-RAT is STACK[LIST[RAT]] endm

uses two default views. Expressions like LEXL[NATG], LIST[NAT], and STACK[LIST[RAT]] are **module expressions**, as discussed further in Section 4.5 below.

In general,

        make M is P[A] endm

is equivalent to

        obj M is protecting P[A] . endo

where A may be either a module or a view. Thus, `make` is redundant, and in fact it was not implemented in OBJ2.

If a non-null view is only used once, say to instantiate a parameterized module, it can be defined "on the fly" where it is used, with the syntax

        view to ⟨*ModExp*⟩ is {⟨*SortMap*⟩ | ⟨*OpMap*⟩}... endv

For example, if the view NATG were not already defined, then we could get the same effect from

```
make LEXL-NATG is
  LEXL[view to NAT is op _<_ to _>_ . endv]
endm
```

as we did from making `LEXL[NATG]`.

A sort name (possibly preceded by the keyword sort) given as an actual parameter to a parameterized module, is treated as an abbreviation for a default view mapping the principal sort of the source theory to the given sort. For example, the object

```
obj LEXL-NAT is  protecting NAT .
                 protecting LEXL[Nat] .
endo
```

uses the sort Nat as an abbreviation for the view

```
view from POSET to NAT is
  sort Elt to Nat .
  op _<_ to _<_ .
endv
```

When the interface theory is TRIV, it is enough just to give a sort name to define a view. For example, 2TUPLE[Int,Bool] is a module expression whose principal sort consists of pairs of an integer and a truth value. A more complex example is 3TUPLE[Int,Bool,LIST[Int]].

An operator name, possibly preceded by the keyword op, given as an actual parameter to a parameterized module, is treated as an abbreviation for a default view mapping the operator of similar rank in the source theory to the given operator. For example, the module expression MAP[(sq_).FNS] is used in Section 4.7.

Sometimes it is convenient to import a module expression with its formal parameters instantiated by (some of) those of a parameterized module into which it is imported, as in

```
obj LEXL[X :: POSET] is
protecting LIST[X] .
op _<<_ : List List -> Bool .
vars L L' : List .
vars E E' : Elt .
eq L << nil = false .
eq nil << E L = true .
eq E L << E L' = L << L' .
cq E L << E' L' = E < E' if E =/= E' .
endo
```

where LIST[X] uses the default view of X as TRIV. Thus,

```
make LEXL-NAT is LEXL[NAT] endm
```

uses the default view of NAT as POSET to give a lexicographic ordering on lists
of natural numbers, and also instantiates LIST with NAT. Similarly,

```
make LEXL-NATD is LEXL[NATD] endm
```

orders lists of NATs by the divisibility ordering on NATs, while

```
make PHRASE is LEXL[QIDL] endm
```

uses the lexicographic ordering on QIDL to give a lexicographic ordering on
lists of identifiers, and thus (for example) on titles of books. (This example,
which builds upon one from [77], is continued in the following subsection.)

Now consider the case where a view that is abbreviated to just a sort name
occurs in a module, and the sort name used has been declared above it, in the
same module. OBJ3 treats this harmless form of self-reference by automatically creating a submodule that contains all of the definitions in the current
module, up to the module expression containing the self-reference. This newly
created module is then used as the target module for the view. For example,

```
obj SELF-REF is
  sort A .
  op a : -> A .
  protecting LIST[A] .
endo
```

causes the automatic generation of a submodule containing the sort A and the
constant a.

Warning: These automatically created modules are considered hidden. Although they are assigned names, these names cannot appear in user-supplied
input. However, users can display them with a command of the form "show
sub 2 ." (this feature is described in Appendix Section A).

Environments for ordinary programming languages are usually functions
from names to values (perhaps with an extra level of indirection); but OBJ
environments, which we call **contexts**, must also store views, which are relationships between modules, and must record module importation relationships.
Section 3 discussed the submodule inclusion relation that arises from module
importation, giving rise to an acyclic graph structure. Contexts with views as
edges from source to target module give a general graph structure. If submodule inclusions are also included, then the submodule hierarchy appears as a
particular subgraph of this overall graph.

4.5   MODULE EXPRESSIONS

Module expressions permit defining, constructing, and instantiating complex combinations of modules, as well as modifying modules in various ways, thus making it possible to use a given module in a wider variety of contexts. The major combination modes are instantiation (as discussed above), sum, and renaming. No other implemented language that we know has such features in the language itself.

The simplest module expressions are simple named modules, which are either the predefined data types TRUTH-VALUE, TRUTH, BOOL, IDENTICAL, NAT, NZNAT, INT, ID, QIDL, ID and FLOAT, or any unparameterized user-defined modules available in the current context.

Renaming uses a sort mapping and an operator mapping, to create a new module from an old one; the syntax is

$$(\{\langle SortMap \rangle \ | \ \langle OpMap \rangle \} \ldots)$$

where each map can be empty, or consist of pairs of the form sort S to S' or op o to o', respectively, with the pairs separated by commas. A renaming is applied to a module expression postfix after *, and creates a new module with the syntax of the preceding module expression modified by applying the given pairs to it. For example, we can use renaming to modify the PREORD theory to get the theory of an equivalence relation, as follows:

```
th EQV is
  using PREORD * (op _<=_ to _eq_) .
  vars E1 E2 : Elt .
  eq (E1 eq E2) = (E2 eq E1) .
endth
```

Within a module,

```
dfn ⟨SortId⟩ is ⟨ModExp⟩ .
```

acts as an abbreviation for

```
protecting ⟨ModExp⟩ * (sort ⟨PSort⟩ to ⟨SortId⟩) .
```

where ⟨PSort⟩ is the principal sort of ⟨ModExp⟩. We can use define as a synonym for dfn. This feature is put to good use in the programming language example in Appendix Section C.2.

Warning: Renaming parts of a parameterized module that is instantiated with a self-referential actual parameter (i.e., with a sort or operator that was defined earlier in an enclosing module), will also affect any other instantiations of the same parameterized module that occur earlier in the program text of that enclosing module. Therefore, one should rename parts of the parameterized module before its instantiation, rather than after. For example, one should write

```
obj NO-PROB is
   protecting LIST[INT] .
   sort A .
   op a : -> A .
   protecting (LIST * (op __ to _*_))[A] .
endo
```

instead of

```
obj TROUBLE is
   protecting LIST[INT] .
   sort A .
   op a : -> A .
   protecting LIST[A] * (op __ to _*_) .
endo
```

That is, one should use the form

$$((\langle Mod \rangle \ * \ (\langle Rename \rangle)))[\langle ModExp \rangle]$$

rather than the form

$$\langle Mod \rangle [\langle ModExp \rangle] * (\langle Rename \rangle)$$

In NO-PROB, the module LIST is renamed *before* it is instantiated with a sort declared earlier in the enclosing module; therefore the renaming does not affect the earlier LIST[INT]. But in TROUBLE, the renaming is also applied to LIST[INT], because this is implicitly part of the parameter and within the scope of the renaming. (Section 4.4 discusses the automatically generated module that is involved here.)

Another important module building operator is **sum**. This has the syntax

$$\langle ModExp \rangle \ + \ \ldots \ + \ \langle ModExp \rangle$$

which creates a new module that combines all the information in its summands. For example, the expression A + B creates a module that is the same as AB having the following definition

```
obj AB is
    pr A .
    pr B .
endo
```

The module that results from a sum of other modules is considered an extension
of its summands. An important issue here is the treatment of submodules that
are imported by more than one summand; for example, in A + B, both A and
B may protect or extend BOOL, NAT, INT or other modules; such multiply
imported modules should be *shared*, rather than repeated.

Earlier versions of OBJ had an **image** transformation with capabilities of
renaming and instantiation; but because it did not use theories to describe
interfaces, it now seems somewhat undisciplined, and has been abandoned,
even though it can be given a respectable semantics using colimits [77]. Clear
[8, 10] had a construction to *enrich* a given module, but this would be redundant
in OBJ, because we need only import the given module into a new module,
and then add the desired sorts, operators and equations.

Let us now continue the lexicographic ordering example from the previous
section. To be able to sort lists of book titles, we might want to form something
like

```
make PHRASE-LIST is LEXL[LEXL[QIDL]] endm
```

which extends the lexicographic ordering on phrases, from LEXL[QIDL], to a
lexicographic ordering on lists of phrases. However, this may not work quite
as expected, because the two instances of list have exactly the same syntax,
and thus, for example, we could not tell whether 'a 'b was a single phrase, or
a list of two phrases. We can overcome this difficulty by renaming the append
constructor of one of the lists, for example, as follows:

```
make PHRASE-LIST is
    LEXL[LEXL[QIDL]*(op __ to _._)]
endm
```

Then the two cases ('a)('b) and ('a . 'b) are clearly different; for a more
complex phrase list, consider ('a . 'b)('c . 'd . 'e).

We can carry this example a bit further by giving a naive sorting algorithm
for lists over a partial order < that relies on the power of associative rewriting.
Correct behavior for such a sorting algorithm requires that, given a list L
such that a and b occur in L with a < b, then a occurs earlier than b in the list
sorting(L), i.e., the list a b should be a sublist of sorting(L); but if neither
a < b nor b < a, then a may occur either before or after b. A tricky point
about the code below is its use of a conditional equation to define the predicate

unsorted by searching for a counter-example; note that unsorted does not reduce to false when it is false, but merely fails to reduce to true; this works because it is used in the condition of the equation. (Strictly speaking, this example extends BOOL, but we do not bother to say so explicitly, because we do not need to generate any new E-strategies or rules; instead, we just rely on the default extending importation of BOOL.)

```
obj SORTING[X :: POSET] is
  protecting LIST[X] .
  op sorting_ : List -> List .
  op unsorted_ : List -> Bool .
  vars L L' L'' : List .    vars E E' : Elt .
  cq sorting L = L if unsorted L =/= true .
  cq sorting L E L' E' L'' = sorting L E' L' E L''
     if E' < E .
  cq unsorted L E L' E' L'' = true if E' < E .
endo
```

Now some test cases, and some more complex module expressions:

```
reduce in SORTING[INT] : unsorted 1 2 3 4 .
  ***> should not be: true
reduce unsorted 4 1 2 3 .
  ***> should be: true
reduce sorting 1 4 2 3 .
  ***> should be: 1 2 3 4

make SORTING-PH-LIST is
  SORTING[LEXL[QIDL]*(op __ to _._)]
endm
reduce sorting (('b . 'a)('a . 'a)('a . 'b)) .
  ***> should be: ('a . 'a)('a . 'b)('b . 'a)

reduce in SORTING[NATD] : sorting(18 6 5 3 1) .
  ***> should contain: 1 3 6 18
```

The last comment means that the list 1 3 6 18, which is sorted by divisibility should appear as a sublist of the result of reducing sorting(18 6 5 3 1); the location of 5 is not determined. It is perhaps also worth noting that the conditional equation

```
cq sorting L E L' E' L'' = sorting L E' L' E L''
   if E' < E .
```

can often be matched against a given list in many different ways; some of these may succeed and others may fail. Also, note that the above code makes use of the fact that the command

```
reduce in SORTING[INT] : unsorted 1 2 3 4 .
```

changes the module in focus from the parameterized SORTING module to its instance SORTING[INT].

A bubble sorting algorithm can be obtained from the above code by replacing the key equation

```
cq sorting L E L' E' L'' = sorting L E' L' E L''
   if E' < E .
```

by its special case

```
cq sorting L E E' L'' = sorting L E' E L'' if E' < E .
```

which is obtained by letting L' = nil. However, this new program only works correctly when the actual parameter satisfies the stronger condition of being *totally ordered*; a theory for totally ordered sets may be obtained from the theory POSET of partially ordered sets by adding the equation

```
cq E1 < E2 or E2 < E1 = true if E1 =/= E2 .
```

In this setting, we can directly define a predicate sorted that evaluates to true when its argument is sorted.

This example illustrates the importance of semantic conditions for module interfaces: the bubble sorting algorithm is *only valid for total orders*, and if a user insists on instantiating it with an ordering that is only partial, then it may give incorrect results; this is illustrated below. (Recall that OBJ does not enforce the correctness of such user beliefs, but only allows them to be recorded in a systematic manner.) Now the code:

```
th TOSET is
  using POSET .
  vars E1 E2 E3 : Elt .
  cq E1 < E2 or E2 < E1 = true if E1 =/= E2 .
endth
```

```
obj BUBBLES[X :: TOSET] is
  protecting LIST[X] .
  op sorting_ : List -> List .
  op sorted_ : List -> Bool .
  vars L L' L'' : List .
  vars E E' : Elt .
  cq sorting L = L if sorted L .
  cq sorting L E E' L'' = sorting L E' E L''
    if E' < E .
  eq sorted nil = true .
  eq sorted E = true .
  cq sorted E E' L = sorted E' L if E < E' or E == E' .
endo
```

The following illustrates correct and incorrect behavior for BUBBLES, and also introduces a new module expression that allows naming module expressions, with the following syntax,

⟨*Id*⟩ is ⟨*ModExp*⟩

which can be used inside of modules, as well as inside a reduce command, as below. This expression creates an "alias" for the module corresponding to the module expression.

```
reduce in A is BUBBLES[NAT]   : sorting(18 5 6 3) .
  ***> should be: 3 5 6 18
reduce sorting(8 5 4 2) .
  ***> should be: 2 4 5 8
reduce in B is BUBBLES[NATD] : sorting(18 5 6 3) .
  ***> mightnt contain: 3 6 18
reduce sorting(8 5 4 2) .
  ***> mightnt contain: 2 4 8
reduce in C is SORTING[NATD] : sorting(18 5 6 3) .
  ***> should contain: 3 6 18
reduce sorting(8 5 4 2) .
  ***> should contain: 2 4 8
reduce in A : sorting(9 6 3 1) .
  ***> should be: 1 3 6 9
reduce in B : sorting(9 6 3 1) .
  ***> mightnt be: 1 3 6 9
reduce in C : sorting(9 6 3 1) .
  ***> should be: 1 3 6 9
```

Here the first, second and seventh reductions are done in the context of BUBBLES[NAT], while the third, fourth and eighth are done in the context of BUBBLES [NATD]. In fact, executing the reductions in B shows that violating the interface theory really can lead to incorrect results.

4.6   TOP-DOWN DEVELOPMENT

It might seem at first that parameterized programming is limited to a bottom-up development style, but in fact, there are many ways to realize a top-down style using OBJ:

1. Write a theory T that describes some desired behavior, and then write a module M with a view $T \Rightarrow M$. Here M may be either an object or another theory.

2. Write a module that realizes the desired behavior if the right modules are imported; write "stubs" (i.e., skeletal code) for the modules to be imported, and then elaborate them later (see [36, 37, 34]). One may be able to use the interface theories themselves as "stubs," because reductions can be executed over OBJ3 theories.

3. Write a parameterized module that realizes the desired behavior if its parameters are instantiated according to their interface theories. Then later, write modules that satisfy these interface theories, and do the instantiation.

Of course, a given step of top-down development could involve any two, or even all three of these strategies, and any number of steps can be taken. In addition, it could be useful to combine views, using the same operators that we have discussed for combining modules; however, this is not supported in Release 2 of OBJ3.

4.7   HIGHER-ORDER PROGRAMMING WITHOUT HIGHER-ORDER FUNCTIONS

Higher-order logic seems useful in many areas, including the foundations of mathematics (e.g., type theory [111]), extracting programs from correctness proofs of algorithms, describing proof strategies (as in LCF tactics [89]), modeling traditional programming languages (as in Scott-Strachey semantics [139]), and studying the foundations of the programming process. One important advantage of higher-order programming over traditional imperative programming is its capability for structuring programs (see [94] for some cogent arguments and examples).

However, a language with sufficiently powerful parameterized modules *does not need* higher-order functions. We do not *oppose* higher-order functions as such; however, we do claim that higher-order functions can lead to code that is very difficult to understand, and that higher-order functions should be avoided where they are not necessary. We further claim that parameterized programming provides an alternative basis for higher-order programming that has certain advantages. In particular, the following shows that typical higher-order functional programming examples are easily coded as OBJ3 programs that are quite structured and flexible, and are rigorously based upon a logic that is *only first-order* and does not require reasoning about functions. The use of first-order logic makes programs easier to understand and to verify. Moreover, OBJ can use theories to document any semantic properties that may be required of functions.

One classic functional programming example is motivated by the following two instances: `sigma` adds a list of numbers; and `pi` multiplies such a list. To encompass these and similar examples, we want a function that applies a binary function recursively over suitable lists. Let's see how this looks in vanilla higher-order functional programming notation. First, a polymorphic list type is defined by something like

```
type list(T) = nil + cons(T,list(T))
```

and then the function that we want is defined by

```
function
   iter : (T -> (T -> T)) -> (T -> (list(T) -> T))
axiom iter(f)(a)(nil) => a
axiom iter(f)(a)(cons(c,lst)) =>
         f(c)(iter(f)(a)(lst))
```

so[22] that we can define our functions by

```
sigma(lst) => iter(plus)(0)(lst)
pi(lst) => iter(times)(1)(lst)
```

For some applications of `iter` to work correctly, f must have certain *semantic* properties. For example, if we want to evaluate `pi(lst)` using as few multiplications as possible and/or as much parallelism as possible (by first converting a list into a binary tree, and then evaluating all the multiplications at each tree level in parallel), then f must be *associative*. Associativity of f implies the following "homomorphic" property, which is needed for the correctness proof of the more efficient evaluation algorithm,

---

[22] Most people find the rank of `iter` rather difficult to understand. It can be simplified by uncurrying with products, and convention also permits omitting some parentheses; but these devices do not help much. Actually, we feel that products are more fundamental than higher-order functions, and that eliminating products by currying can be misleading and confusing.

(H)   iter(f)(a)(append(lst)(lst')) =
                f(iter(f)(a)(lst))(iter(f)(a)(lst')

where lst and lst' have the same type, list(T). Furthermore, if we want the empty list nil to behave correctly in property (H), then a must be an identity for f.

Now let's do this example in OBJ3. First, using mixfix syntax _*_ for f improves readability somewhat; but much more significantly, we can use the interface theory MONOID to assert associativity and identity axioms for actual arguments of a generic iteration module,

```
obj ITER[M :: MONOID] is
  protecting LIST[M] .
  op iter : List -> M .
  var X : M .    var L : List .
  eq iter(nil) = e .
  eq iter(X L) = X * iter(L) .
endo
```

where e is the monoid identity. Note that LIST[M] uses the default view from TRIV to MONOID. (This code uses an associative List concatenation, but it is also easy to write code using a cons constructor if desired.) Notice that all of the equations involved here are first-order.

We can now instantiate ITER to get our two example functions[23]. First,

```
make SIGMA is ITER[NAT+] endm
```

sums lists of numbers; for example,

```
reduce iter(1 2 3 4) .
```

yields 10. Similarly,

```
make PI is ITER[NAT*] endm
```

multiplies lists of numbers, and so

```
reduce iter(1 2 3 4) .
```

now yields 24. Of course, we could use renaming to get functions that are literally named sigma and pi. For example, the following module provides *both* sigma and pi.

---

[23] The views used below were defined in Section 4.3 above; however, a default view could be used for making PI.

```
make SIGMA+PI is
  ITER[NAT+]*(op iter to sigma)
  + ITER[NAT*]*(op iter to pi)
endm
```

(Incidentally, this is a nice example of a complex module expression.)

Any valid instance of ITER has the property (H), which in the present notation is written simply

```
iter(L L') = iter(L) * iter(L')
```

and it is natural to state this fact with a theory and a view, as follows:

```
th HOM[M :: MONOID] is
  protecting LIST[M] .
  op h : List -> M .
  var L L' : List .
  eq h(L L') = h(L) * h(L') .
endth

view ITER-IS-HOM[M :: MONOID]
    from HOM[M] to ITER[M] is
endv
```

This view is parameterized, because property (H) holds for all instances; to obtain the appropriate assertion for a given instance ITER[A], just instantiate the view with the same actual parameter module A.

Warning: Release 2 of OBJ3 does not implement parameterized views.

Because semantic conditions on argument functions cannot be stated in a conventional functional programming language, all of this would have to be done *outside* of such a language. But OBJ3 can not only assert the monoid property, it can even be used to *prove* that this property implies property (H), using methods first described in [51, 53] and further developed in [66, 59].

Many researchers have argued that it is much easier to use type inference for higher-order functions to get such declarations and instantiations automatically. However, the notational overhead of encapsulating a function in a module is really only a few keywords, and the appropriate definitions could even be generated automatically by a structural editor from a single keystroke; moreover, this overhead is often shared among several function declarations. Also, the overhead due to variable declarations could be reduced to almost nothing by two techniques: (1) let sort inference give a variable the highest possible sort; and (2) declare sorts "on the fly" with a qualification notation. Our position has been that the crucial issue is to make the *structure* of *large programs* as clear as possible; thus, tricks that slightly simplify notation for small examples are of little importance, and are of negative value if they make it harder to read large programs. Consequently, we have not implemented such tricks in OBJ3, because explicit declarations can save *human* program readers much effort in doing type inference.

On the other hand, our notation for instantiation can often be significantly simplified, particularly in cases where non-default views are needed, or where renaming is needed to avoid ambiguity because there is more than one instance of some module in a given context. For example,

```
make ITER-NAT is
   ITER[view to NAT is op _*_ to _+_ . endv]
endm
```

is certainly more complex than `iter(plus)(0)`. However, in OBJ3 just `ITER[(_+_).NAT]` denotes the same module[24] because default view conventions map Elt to Nat in NAT, and e to 0.

For a second example, let us define the traditional function map, which applies a unary function to a list of arguments. Its interface theory requires a sort and a unary function on it (more generally, we could have distinct source and target sorts, if desired).

```
th FN is
   sort S .
   op f : S -> S .
endth

obj MAP[F :: FN] is protecting LIST[F] .
   op map : List -> List .
   var X : S .   var L : List .
   eq map(nil) = nil .
   eq map(X L) = f(X) map(L) .
endo
```

Now we can instantiate MAP in various ways. The following object defines some functions to be used in examples below:

---

[24] We could go a little further and let `iter[(_+_).NAT]` actually denote the `iter` function on naturals, with the effect of creating the module instantiation that defines it, unless it is already present. Indeed, this is essentially the same notation used in functional programming, and it avoids the need to give distinct names for distinct instances of `iter`. This "abbreviated operator notation" could also be used when there is more than one argument, as well as for sorts. In Release 2 of OBJ3 one can get much the same effect by using qualified references to operators, as illustrated in this section.

```
obj FNS is
 protecting INT .
 ops (sq_)(dbl_)(_*3) : Int -> Int .
 var N : Int .
 eq sq N = N * N .
 eq dbl N = N + N .
 eq N *3 = N * 3 .
endo
```

Now some reductions in objects using some non-default in-line views:

```
reduce in MAP[(sq_).FNS] : map(0 nil 1 -2 3) .
 ***> should be: 0 1 4 9
reduce in MAP[(dbl_).FNS] : map(0 1 -2 3) .
 ***> should be: 0 2 -4 6
reduce in MAP[(_*3).FNS] : map(0 1 -2 nil 3) .
 ***> should be: 0 3 -6 9
```

In [51] there is a complete proof that the nth element of map(list) is f(e), where e is the nth element of list, using OBJ3 itself as a theorem prover.

The following module does another classical functional programming example, applying a given function twice; some instantiations are also given.

```
obj 2[F :: FN] is
 op xx : S -> S .
 var X : S .
 eq xx(X) = f(f(X)) .
endo

reduce in 2[(sq_).FNS] : xx(3) .
 ***> should be: 81
reduce xx(4) .
 ***> should be: 256
reduce in 2[(dbl_).FNS] : xx(3) .
 ***> should be: 12
reduce in 2[2[(sq_).FNS]*(op xx to f)] : xx(2) .
 ***> should be: 65536
reduce xx(3) .
 ***> should be: 43046721
```

Let us consider these examples more carefully. Because xx applies f twice, the result function xx of the first instantiation applies sq_ twice, i.e., it raises to the 4th power; then the next to last instantiation applies that twice, i.e., it raises to the 16th power.

To summarize, the difference between parameterized programming and higher-order functional programming is essentially the difference between programming in the large and programming in the small. Parameterized programming does not just combine functions, it combines modules. This parallels one of the great insights of modern abstract algebra, that in many important examples, functions should not be considered in isolation, but rather in association with other functions and constants, with their explicit sources and targets, plus the equations that they satisfy. Thus, the invention of abstract algebras (for vector spaces, groups, etc.) parallels the invention of program modules (for numbers, vectors, windows, etc.); parameterized programming makes this parallel more explicit, and also carries it further, by introducing theories and views to document semantic conditions on function arguments and on module interfaces, as well as to assert provable properties of modules (such as the property (H) above). As we have already noted, it can be more convenient to combine modules than to compose functions, because a single module instantiation can compose many conceptually related functions at once, as in the complex arithmetic (CPXA) example mentioned near the beginning of Section 1. On the other hand, the notational overhead of theories and views is excessive for applying just one function. However, this is exactly the case where our abbreviated operator notation can be used to advantage.

We should also note that it can be much more difficult to reason with higher-order functions than with first-order functions; in fact, the undecidability of higher-order unification means that it will be very difficult to mechanize certain aspects of such reasoning[25]. Reasoning about first-order or higher-order functions can each take place in either first-order or higher-order logic. The simplest case is first-order functions with first-order logic, and this is the case that parameterized programming focuses upon. Also, it is much easier to compile and interpret first-order programs. It is worth noting that Poigné [132] has found some significant difficulties in combining subsorts and higher-order functions, and we hope to have been convincing that subsorts are very useful; however, see also [110] where significant progress has been made. Finally, note the experience of many programmers, and not just naive ones, that higher-order notation can be difficult to understand and to use.

What can we conclude from all this? We might conclude that it is better to "factorize" code with parameterized modules than with higher-order functions, and in fact, that it is better to avoid higher-order functions whenever possible. From this, one could conclude that the essence of functional programming cannot be the use of higher-order functions, and therefore it must be the lack

---

[25] Similar difficulties arise for first-order unification modulo equations, such as those for the combinators, so this difficulty is not particular to higher-order logic. It is worth noting that higher-order specifications can be implemented by higher-order rewriting [97].

of side effects. However, the true essence of functional programming may well reside in its having a solid basis in equational logic, because this not only avoids side effects, but also allows the kind of equational reasoning about programs and transformations that is needed to support powerful programming environments.

4.8   HARDWARE SPECIFICATION, SIMULATION AND VERIFICATION

This subsection develops a computer hardware verification example. The crucial advantage of using a logical programming language is that the reductions really are *proofs*, because the programs really are logical theories and computation really is deduction. This code uses the propositional calculus decision procedure object (from Section 2.4.6), thus providing an excellent example of software reuse, because PROPC was written in OBJ1 by David Plaisted in 1982, years before we thought of using it for hardware verification [77]. Next, Time is defined for use in input and output streams, which are functions from Time to Prop. An interface theory WIRE is defined, and then a NOT gate using it. The object F introduces two "symbolic variables," t and f0, which are a "generic" time and input stream, respectively. Finally, two NOT gates are composed and instantiated with F. Evaluating expressions in this context corresponds to proving certain theorems, in this case that the double NOT gate acts on input streams as a two unit delayor.

```
obj TIME is
  sort Time .
  op 0 : -> Time .
  op s_ : Time -> Time .
endo

th WIRE is
  protecting TIME + PROPC .
  op f1 : Time -> Prop .
endth

obj NOT[W :: WIRE] is
  op f2 : Time -> Prop .
  var T : Time .
  eq f2(0) = false .
  eq f2(s T) = not f1(T) .
endo
```

```
obj F is
  extending TIME + PROPC .
  op t : -> Time .
  op f0 : Time -> Prop .
endo

make 2NOT is NOT[NOT[F]*(op f2 to f1)] endm
reduce f2(s s t) iff f0(t) .  ***> should be: true
```

See [51] for a precise statement of the theorem proved here, as well as a detailed justification that the given reduction really proves that theorem. Parameterized modules make this code much more readable than it would be otherwise. The same techniques seem effective for much more complex examples of hardware specification, simulation and verification, and many more examples are given in [51] and [53], along with supporting theory. The application of 2OBJ [81] to hardware verification is described in [145] and [146].

5   APPLYING RULES

Release 2 of OBJ3 allows users to apply rules one at a time to a given term, either "forwards" or "backwards" (i.e., either replacing an instance of the left side by the corresponding instance of the right side, or else *vice versa*). This capability is needed for many common examples of equational reasoning; for example, Appendix Section C.4.5 gives a proof from group theory that requires applying equations backwards.

The syntax is necessarily somewhat complex, as an *action* (which may be a rule), an optional *substitution*, a *range*, and a *selected subterm* may be involved. Each of these elements is discussed below. The following is an overview of the syntax:

apply ⟨*Action*⟩ [⟨*Substitution*⟩] ⟨*Range*⟩ ⟨*Selection*⟩ .

5.1   START AND TERM

The `start` command introduces a term to which rules can then be applied; its syntax is

start ⟨*Term*⟩ .

The system keeps track of the current term, called `term`, which is either the result of the last term reduction, the term given in the last `start` command, or else is undefined. It is used as the focus for the controlled application of rules. The value of the current term can be seen by using the command

show term .

This command can also be used to see the structure of term in greater detail if the print with parens mode is on.

A variant of the let feature allows the user to give a more permanent name to term, using the syntax

$$\texttt{let } \langle Sym \rangle \ [:\ \langle Sort \rangle] \ = \ .$$

The current module must be open for this to be effective.

5.2   ACTIONS

An action is a request to print a selected subterm, to reduce it, or to apply a selected rule (possibly backwards) to it. The following shows some of the syntax:

$$\texttt{reduction} \mid \texttt{red} \mid \texttt{print} \mid \texttt{[-]} \ [\langle \mathit{ModId} \rangle].[\langle \mathit{Nat} \rangle \mid \langle \mathit{Id} \rangle]$$

The action reduction (or equivalently, red) calls for full reduction of the selected term. The action print displays the selected subterm. The last action requests applying (possibly backwards) the $\langle \mathit{Nat} \rangle^{th}$ rule, or else the rule having $\langle \mathit{Id} \rangle$ as one of its labels, (optionally) from the module $\langle \mathit{ModId} \rangle$. Because $\langle \mathit{ModId} \rangle$ must be a simple module name, abbreviated module names can be very useful here. If no $\langle \mathit{ModId} \rangle$ is given, then the currently selected module is used.

Warning: If more than one rule has the same label, and you try to apply that label, then a warning is issued, no rule is applied, and control is returned to the top level.

There are two special actions for dealing with the built-in retract rules,

$$\texttt{retr} \mid \texttt{-retr with sort} \ \langle Sort \rangle$$

The first action tries to apply a built-in retract rule of the form

$$\texttt{r:A>B(X) = X}$$

where X has sort B, and the second action allows introducing a retract by applying this rule backwards.

5.3   SUBSTITUTIONS

The following rule has a variable in its left side that does not appear in its right side,

$$\texttt{eq X * 0 = 0 .}$$

so that its backwards version is

```
eq 0 = X * 0 .
```

which has a variable in its right side that does not appear in its left side. In such cases, it is necessary to specify a binding for the variables not in the left side (X in this case) in order to be able to apply the rule backwards. If these variables are not instantiated, then they are just copied into the current term. It is also natural to allow substituting variables in all cases, including forward rule applications; this is especially convenient when proving equations in the context of a theory.

A substitution gives terms as bindings for some variables in the form of a list of equations separated by commas (after the rule specification and delimited by with). More precisely, the syntax is

with ⟨*Var*⟩ = ⟨*Term*⟩ {, ⟨*Var*⟩ = ⟨*Term*⟩}...

where each variable mentioned must appear somewhere in the rule.

Warning: No warning is given if no binding is given for some variable that appears in the right side but not the left side of the rule. However, this condition can be detected, because a variable will have been introduced into the resulting term.

A substitution given to print or reduce is ignored.

5.4   SELECTING A SUBTERM

There are three basic kinds of selection: for an *occurrence*, a *subsequence* (used for associative operators), and a *subset* (used for associative commutative operators).

The syntax for occurrence selection is

(⟨*Nat*⟩...)

Starting from a given term, occurrence selection progressively selects the argument positions specified by the given numbers, where both subterms and argument positions are numbered from 1. For example, if the term is (a + (c * 2)), then the occurrence (2 1) selects the subterm c. The empty list of numbers () is a selector, and it selects the whole term.

Subsequence selection has the two forms

[⟨*Nat*⟩ .. ⟨*Nat*⟩] | [⟨*Nat*⟩]

where blanks are required around the "..". This kind of selection is only appropriate for terms whose top operator is associative (or associative and commutative). For such operators, a tree of terms formed with that operator is naturally viewed as the sequence of the terms at the leaves of this tree.

Selecting [k] is the same as selecting [k .. k], and it selects the kth subterm from the sequence (it does not form a sequence of length one). The form [⟨*Nat*⟩ .. ⟨*Nat*⟩] forces restructuring the term so that the specified range of terms form a proper subterm of the whole term, and then it selects that term as the next current subterm. This implies that a selection may change the structure of the term, and hence that a print could affect the structure of the term. For example, if the current module is INT, and the current term (when fully parenthesized) is "(1 * (2 * (3 * (4 * 5))))", then the command

    apply print at [2 .. 4] .

will cause term "(1 * ((2 * (3 * 4)) * 5))" to be printed.

Subset selection has the syntax

    {⟨*Nat*⟩ [, ⟨*Nat*⟩]...}

where "{" and "}" are not syntactic meta-notation, but rather stand for the corresponding characters. No blanks are required in this notation. This kind of selection is only appropriate for terms with top operators that are associative and commutative. Repetitions of numbers in the list are ignored. This selector forces the given subset of the list (or more properly "bag") of terms under the top operator to be a proper subterm, and then selects that term as the next current subterm. The order of the subterms within "{}"s affects the order of appearance of these terms in the selected subterm. For example, if the current module is INT, and the current term (when fully parenthesized) is "(1 * (2 * (3 * (4 * 5))))", then the command

    apply print at 1,3,5 .

causes term structure "((1 * (3 * 5)) * (2 * 4))" to be printed.

You can specify the top or whole of the current term by using either of the selectors term or top. It only makes sense to use these once, and often they can be omitted. One of these is required if there is no other selector, but the selector () could be used instead.

Selectors can be composed by separating them by of, as in

    {3,1,2} of [4] of (2 3 1) of [2 .. 5] of (1 1) of term

Such a composition is interpreted like functional composition: the selection on the right is done first, then the second one on the result of that selection, and so on, until finally the selector on the left is done. Note that this order is the opposite of that used for the elements of an occurrence, such as (2 1).

5.5   THE APPLY COMMAND

The form of an apply command is `apply` followed (in order) by the action, possibly a substitution, `within` or `at`, and a composition of selectors:

apply { reduction | red | print | retr |
    -retr with sort ⟨*Sort*⟩ |
    ⟨*RuleSpec*⟩ [with ⟨*VarId*⟩ = ⟨*Term*⟩
        {, ⟨*VarId*⟩ = ⟨*Term*⟩}...] }
  { within | at }
⟨*Selector*⟩ {of ⟨*Selector*⟩}...

(Here, "{" and "}" are used for syntactic grouping.)

A user can either request a rule to be applied exactly "`at`" a selected subterm (as described the next subsection), or else to be applied "`within`" a selected subterm. In the latter case, the indicated rule is at most once. Reduction and printing always act on a whole subterm.

Sometimes, giving a substitution may make it possible to apply a rule without specifying any specific subterm, by using `within` as the range.

The resulting value of the current term is always printed after an apply command has been performed. Here are some examples of rule applications.

```
apply G.1 at term .
apply -G.1 at term .
apply -G.2 with X = a at term .
apply print at term .
apply reduction at (2 1) .
apply G.1 at () .
apply X.3 at {2} .
apply X.3 at {3,1,2} .
apply G.2 at [2 .. 4] .
apply G.1 at [2] .
apply X.1 at {2,4} of [4] of (2 2) .
apply X.1 at {2,4} of [4 .. 4] of (2 2) of top .
```

The command

```
apply ? .
```

shows a summary of the apply command syntax.

5.6   CONDITIONAL RULES

Applying conditional rules in general requires shifting the focus of reduction to the (instantiated) condition of a rule, so that rules can be applied to it. This is done by using a stack of pending actions, pushing a rule application onto the stack if its left side matches, but it has a condition the evaluation of which is still pending. When a condition has been reduced to "true," then the pending rule application is executed, and focus shifts to its result term. If the condition reduces to "false," then the rule is not applied, and focus returns to the previous term.

It is possible to request that conditions of conditional equations be directly reduced, using the command

```
set reduce conditions on .
```

The default behavior can then be restored by the command

```
set reduce conditions off .
```

(Either all nontrivial conditions must be evaluated by hand, or else none.) One reason to prefer evaluating conditions directly is that, if the top operator of the left side is associative and/or commutative, then when the rule is applied, all possible matches are tested against the condition until a successful case is found; but with controlled application, only one match is attempted. However, all potential matches can be specified by using the selection notation.

Here is a small example:

```
obj X is sort A .
  pr QID .
  subsort Id < A .
  op f : A -> A .
  var X : A .
  cq f(X) = f(f(X)) if f(X) == 'a .
  eq f('b) = 'a .
endo
```

for which the following is an output trace, illustrating how conditional rule application works:

```
==============================================
start f('b) .
==============================================
apply X.1 at term .
shifting focus to condition
condition(1) Bool: f('b) == 'a
==============================================
apply X.2 within term .
condition(1) Bool: 'a == 'a
```

```
===========================================
apply red at term .
condition(1) Bool: true
condition is satisfied, applying rule
shifting focus back to previous context
result A: f(f('b))
===========================================
```

Note that when actions are pending, `condition` is printed instead of `result`, and the number of conditions being reduced (i.e., the number of pending actions) is printed in parentheses.

If you are evaluating a condition and want to force either success or failure, then you can use the following commands:

```
start true .
start false .
```

For example, the above example could have continued from "apply X.1 at term" with

```
===========================================
start false .
condition(1) Bool: false
condition is not satisfied, rule not applied
shifting focus back to previous context
result A: f('b)
===========================================
```

This can be used to abandon reductions that you no longer wish to perform. Note that using "`start true .`" can easily produce incorrect results, i.e., results that are not sound under order sorted equational deduction. Also, you cannot perform a controlled reduction in the middle of doing another one, and then continue the first reduction, because a new `start` causes the current state of the previous term to be lost.

The command

```
show pending .
```

shows details about the terms, rules, conditions, and replacements that are currently pending. The following is sample output from this command:

```
pending actions
  1| in f('b)  at top
  | rule cq f(X) = f(f(X)) if f(X) == 'a
  | condition f('b) == 'a  replacement f(f('b))
```

```
2| in f('b) == 'a  at f('b)
 | rule cq f(X) = f(f(X)) if f(X) == 'a
 | condition f('b) == 'a  replacement f(f('b))
   3| in f('b) == 'a  at f('b)
    | rule cq f(X) = f(f(X)) if f(X) == 'a
    | condition f('b) == 'a  replacement f(f('b))
```

If you use the range specification within and the rule is conditional, then the rule will be applied at most once, and a warning will be issued like the following:

```
applying rule only at first position found: f('b)
```

6   DISCUSSION AND CONCLUSIONS

Although we are very fond of OBJ, and believe that it introduced some valuable new ideas, we certainly do not wish to claim that it is the perfect language for all applications. In particular, Release 2 of OBJ3 has a number of limitations of which we are aware:

1. OBJ3 is not a compiler, but is rather closer to an interpreter.

2. Associative/commutative rewriting can be very inefficient for large terms; but this is an inevitable result of AC matching being an NP-complete problem.

3. The parser applies precedence and gathering information *a priori*, and thus may fail on some terms that in fact are well formed.

4. Release 2 of OBJ3 gives warnings about meaningless or erroneous input, but these warning are less comprehensive than some might desire, and are not always easy to interpret.

5. OBJ3 does not have so-called "logical variables," the values for which are supplied by the system through "solving" systems of constraints, although its extension to Eqlog does [71, 72, 25].

6. OBJ3 does not keep track of whether a given equation has the status of an assumption, a conjecture, or a proven conclusion, as a good theorem proving environment should do. Similar comments apply to the ability to undo changes to modules and many other features; on the other hand, OBJ3 was not initially conceived as a theorem prover. The Kumo system [65, 64, 78, 60] was developed for this purpose, and does provide such capabilities; in addition, it generates web-based documentation for its proofs.

On the positive side, Release 2 of OBJ3 lets you experiment with a combination of parameterized programming, subsorts, rewriting modulo attributes, E-strategies, and memoization, which together allow styles that are quite different from conventional languages. We hope that you will enjoy this!

OBJ3 also provides a very workable platform for implementing other system; in particular, it has been used to implement the combined functional and object oriented system FOOPS [74], the object oriented specification language OOZE [3], a generic (i.e., metalogical) theorem prover called 2OBJ [81], and the combined logic and functional language Eqlog [71]. FOOPS and OOZE support objects with states (where we mean "objects" in the sense of object oriented programming, rather than in the sense of OBJ), and Eqlog has logical variables. OBJ3 terms can have state in some sense, but they can only be used through built-in equations. An alternative approach to object-oriented programming, supporting concurrent objects and general concurrent systems programming, is being developed at SRI in the language Maude [112, 16], which uses *rewriting logic* [113, 114] as a basis for very direct systems modeling. Someday, we may implement FOOPlog [74] or MaudeLog, which combine the functional, logic, and object oriented paradigms. We find that it is relatively easy to build such systems on top of OBJ3, and we expect that others will be able to build many other interesting systems in much the same way.

In summary, we feel that the OBJ3 system should be useful for the following applications:

1. **Teaching**, especially in the areas of algebraic specification, programming language semantics, and theorem proving [109];

2. **Rapid prototyping**, especially for relatively small but sophisticated systems;

3. **Implementing experimental languages**, especially declarative languages that have features like associative/commutative pattern matching, subtypes, views, theories, and parameterized modules;

4. **Building theorem provers**, for example, an efficient metalogical framework based on equational logic; and

5. **Designing, specifying and documenting** large systems; for example, we used OBJ2 in designing OBJ3, and much of this specification is included in the OBJ3 source code as documentation [100]; see also the recent work on specifying user interface designs via algebraic semiotics [60, 58].

Probably there are other applications that readers have found; please let us know!

Appendix A : Use of OBJ3

OBJ3's top level statements for declaring objects, modules and views can all be seen as commands whose effect is to add something to the OBJ3 database, which is constructed incrementally. A general "engine" for term rewriting actually does the reductions, consulting the database to get the rules for a given context. Reductions do not change the database in any way (although they may change memo tables).

To get started, the only commands you really need are obj, in and q (or quit), which get you into OBJ3 from the operating system level, read a file within OBJ3, and quit OBJ3, respectively. The recommended way to work is to first edit a file, then start up OBJ3, and read in the file. If you are using an editor like Emacs with buffers that are also UNIX shells, then you can get a log of the execution, containing a record of any problems that arise to help you go back and re-edit the file. If you prefer an editor that does not support shells, then it may be more convenient to use a shell script, and/or to redirect input and output.

As a summary, OBJ3 definitions are assumed to have these properties: the signature should be regular and coherent [76] (coherence means that connected components of sorts must have tops); and the rule set for objects should be Church-Rosser, and if possible, terminating with respect to the given evaluation strategies.

The command ? (note that there is no ".") produces the following top-level help information

```
    Top-level definitional forms include:
        obj, theory, view, make
    The top level commands include:
      q; quit --- to exit from OBJ3
      show .... . --- for further help: show ? .
      set .... . --- for further help: set ? .
      do .... . --- for further help: do ? .
      apply ..... --- for further help: apply ? .
      other commands:
        in <filename>
        red <term> .
        select <module-expression> .
        cd <directory>; ls; pwd
        start <term> .; show term .
        open [<module-expression>] .
        openr [<module-expression>] .; close
        ev <lisp>; evq <lisp>
```

Here ";"s are only used to separate alternatives.

OBJ3 has classes of commands to show aspects of the current context, to set various system parameters and to do certain actions; in addition, one can evaluate Lisp expressions. Given the argument "?", the commands show, set, and do displays a summary of legal arguments to that command.

The show commands are the most numerous. The first group of them have the syntax

        show ⟨*ModPart*⟩ [⟨*ModExp*⟩] .

where ⟨*ModPart*⟩ is one of sorts, psort, ops, vars, eqs, mod, params, subs, name, sign, rules, abbrev and where ⟨*ModExp*⟩ is an optional module expression argument; if there is no module expression, then the module in focus is used. show can be abbreviated to sh, and show ⟨*ModExp*⟩ is short for show mod ⟨*ModExp*⟩. The command select ⟨*ModExp*⟩ resets the current module to be ⟨*ModExp*⟩, without printing anything. An instance of a ⟨*ModExp*⟩ may also be preceded by sub ⟨*Nat*⟩ or param ⟨*Nat*⟩ to specify the corresponding sub-module or interface theory, respectively, of the following module; you can even give several of these selectors in a sequence. show psort shows the principal sort, show sign shows the signature of the selected module, i.e., its sorts and operators; show params shows its parameters, if any, show subs shows the names of its sub-modules, and show name shows its full name. To get more detailed information on a particular sort or operator, you can use the forms

        show sort ⟨*Sort*⟩ .
        show op ⟨*OpRef*⟩ .

which can also be qualified by a module name (see Appendix Section B for details). The command show all ⟨*ModExp*⟩ displays the module in a more detailed form. The command show all rules [⟨*ModExp*⟩] displays more comprehensively the rules that are used for rewriting in a module. The command show abbrev [⟨*ModExp*⟩] shows the abbreviation of the specified module as used when qualifications are being abbreviated).

Warning: If the ⟨*ModExp*⟩ contains a ".", you will almost always have to enclose the whole module expression in parentheses.

The command

        show modules .

lists all modules in the current context. The command

        show time .

prints the elapsed time since the last use of this command, or since the start of execution if there has been no prior use. The command show term .

shows the current term (the last term reduced, or the last term started), while

        show [all] rule ⟨*RuleSpec*⟩

shows a specified rule, possibly in detailed form. The command

        show pending .

shows the pending rule applications, while

        show modes .

shows the settings of the settable system parameters, and

        show all modes .

gives more detail. These parameters can all be set with commands of the form

        set ⟨*Param*⟩ ⟨*Polarity*⟩ .

where ⟨*Polarity*⟩ is either on or off, and ⟨*Param*⟩ is one of trace, blips, gc show, print with parens, show retracts, abbrev quals, include BOOL, clear memo, stats, trace whole, all eqns, show var sorts, reduce conditions, or verbose. If trace is on, then rule applications are displayed during reduction. If blips is on, then a "!" is printed whenever a rule is applied, and a "-" is printed whenever an attempt to apply a rule fails. If gc show is on, then a message is printed at each start and completion of garbage collection. If print with parens is on, then many parentheses are used in printing terms, making the structure much more explicit. If show retracts is on, then retracts are shown in the right sides of equations. If abbrev quals is on, then qualifications on printed terms or sorts are abbreviated to MOD⟨*Nat*⟩. These qualifications are only printed if there are two sorts with the same name or two operators with the same name or pattern and the same arity. If include BOOL is on, as it is by default, then BOOL is automatically included in modules. If clear memo is on, then the memo table is cleared before each reduction. If stats is on (which it is by default), then the number of rules applied in each reduction is printed. If trace whole is on, then the whole term is printed for each reduction. If all eqns is on, then all rule extensions are printed when showing equations. If show var sorts is on, then the sorts of variables are printed along with their names, in the form X:Int. If the verbose mode is on, then modules are displayed in a more detailed form, and id processing will be traced as it is performed.

    For commands with the syntax

do ⟨*Act*⟩ .

⟨*Act*⟩ may be one of gc or clear memo, or save ⟨*ChString*⟩, or restore ⟨*ChString*⟩. "gc" forces a garbage collection, "clear memo" clears the memo table, and save and restore save the current context, and restore a named context, respectively.

Common Lisp expressions can be evaluated with the syntax

ev ⟨*LispExpr*⟩

and the command

evq ⟨*LispExpr*⟩

can be used to evaluate a Lisp form with the minimum of output during processing. Longer forms for each of these are eval and eval-quiet, respectively. These are useful for loading functions used in built-in right sides.

Warning: There are no final periods for these commands, because the Lisp input is considered self-delimiting.

The UNIX interrupt character (typically ^C) can be used to interrupt OBJ3, which will leave you in the lisp break handler. In Austin Kyoto Common Lisp (AKCL), you can return to the top level of OBJ3 with the break command :q, or you can continue the computation with the command :r. You can see the current structure of the term being reduced (even if tracing is off) by interrupting OBJ3 (e.g., with ^C), and then typing (show), followed by a return; then you can resume with :r. You can use the command :h to get a AKCL break-loop command summary.

In the AKCL version of OBJ3, there are some special command line arguments. These are pairs of these forms

-in ⟨*FileName*⟩
-inq ⟨*FileName*⟩
-evq ⟨*FileName*⟩

The first two forms cause a file to be read in as OBJ3 starts up, either with a trace or quietly. The last form will quietly load a Lisp file on startup.

LATEX source files containing OBJ examples can be executed using a shell script called obj3-tex, by enclosing the OBJ code between matching \bobj and \eobj commands; everything else is treated as a comment. You will need to have defined the LATEX commands

```
\newcommand{\bobj}{\begin{alltt}}
\newcommand{\eobj}{\end{alltt}}
```

in your LATEX source file, and have called the `alltt` style file. A tricky point is that { and } must be written \{ and \}, respectively, or else they will not be printed by LATEX. In fact, initial \s are stripped off, in these cases, to prepare the text for OBJ execution (this explains why \{ and \} do not appear in\tt font in Appendix C.8); this approach extends to allowing arbitrary TEX symbols in OBJ code; for example, $\ast$ will produce *. This is very useful for writing papers about OBJ3, which we of course encourage everyone to do; it was used in preparing this paper. The code appears in the distribution tape as `obj/aux/bin/obj3-tex` and the C program is in `obj/aux/c/examples.c`; when `obj3-tex` is run on a file `foo.tex`, it produces a file `foo.obj` containing all the OBJ code that it runs.

Another tricky point is that sometimes code that you want to print relies on some other code that you don't want to print. The shell script saves the day by also executing invisible code, placed between a matching `%\bobj` and `%\eobj` pair, with `obj-tex` stripping off an initial `%` from each line in between.

The distribution tape for Release 2 of OBJ3 comes with all the examples in this paper, in the directory `/obj/exs/`. OBJ3 was implemented on Sun workstations, using Austin Kyoto Common Lisp (AKCL). AKCL has been ported to many different machines, the main requirements being a C compiler and an adequate amount of memory. Release 2.04 of OBJ3 in AKCL has some specific implementation dependent details, but it has been ported to other versions of Common Lisp, including gnu Common Lisp. You can ftp the entire distribution from `ftp://www.cs.ucsd.edu/pub/fac/goguen`. The latest information about the OBJ Family can be obtained from the OBJ homepage at UCSD, at `http://www.cs.ucsd.edu/users/goguen/sys/obj.html`.

Appendix B : OBJ3 Syntax

This appendix describes the syntax of OBJ3 using the following extended BNF notation: the symbols { and } are used as meta-parentheses; the symbol | is used to separate alternatives; [ ] pairs enclose optional syntax; . . . indicates 0 or more repetitions of preceding unit; and "x" denotes x literally. As an application of this notation, A{,A}. . . indicates a non-empty list of A's separated by commas. Finally, `---` indicates comments in the syntactic description, as opposed to comments in OBJ3 code.

```
--- top-level ---
```

⟨*OBJ-Top*⟩ ::=
    {⟨*Object*⟩ | ⟨*Theory*⟩ | ⟨*View*⟩ | ⟨*Make*⟩ | ⟨*Reduction*⟩ |
    in ⟨*FileName*⟩ | quit | eof |
    start ⟨*Term*⟩ . |
    open [⟨*ModExp*⟩] . | openr [⟨*ModExp*⟩] . | close |
    ⟨*Apply*⟩ | ⟨*OtherTop*⟩}...

⟨*Make*⟩ ::= make ⟨*Interface*⟩ is ⟨*ModExp*⟩ endm

⟨*Reduction*⟩ ::= reduce [in ⟨*ModExp*⟩ :] ⟨*Term*⟩ .

⟨*Apply*⟩ ::=
    apply {reduction | red | print | retr |
      -retr with sort ⟨*Sort*⟩ |
      ⟨*RuleSpec*⟩ [with ⟨*VarId*⟩ = ⟨*Term*⟩
                      {, ⟨*VarId*⟩ = ⟨*Term*⟩}...]}
    {within | at}
    ⟨*Selector*⟩ {of ⟨*Selector*⟩}...

⟨*RuleSpec*⟩ ::= [-][⟨*ModId*⟩].⟨*RuleId*⟩
⟨*RuleId*⟩ ::= ⟨*Nat*⟩ | ⟨*Id*⟩

⟨*Selector*⟩ ::= term | top |
    (⟨*Nat*⟩...) |
    [⟨*Nat*⟩ [.. ⟨*Nat*⟩]] |
    "{" ⟨*Nat*⟩ {, ⟨*Nat*⟩}... "}"
  --- note that "()" is a valid selector

⟨*OtherTop*⟩ ::= ⟨*RedLoop*⟩ | ⟨*Commands*⟩ | call-that ⟨*Id*⟩ . |
  test reduction [in ⟨*ModExp*⟩ :] ⟨*Term*⟩ expect: ⟨*Term*⟩ . |
  ⟨*Misc*⟩
  --- "call-that ⟨*Id*⟩ ." is an abbreviation for
  --- "let ⟨*Id*⟩ = ."

⟨*RedLoop*⟩ ::= rl {. | ⟨*ModId*⟩} { ⟨*Term*⟩ .}... .

⟨*Commands*⟩ ::= cd ⟨*Sym*⟩ | pwd | ls |
    do ⟨*DoOption*⟩ . |
    select [⟨*ModExp*⟩] . |
    set ⟨*SetOption*⟩ . |
    show [⟨*ShowOption*⟩] .
  --- in select, can use "open" to refer to the open module

⟨*DoOption*⟩ ::= clear memo | gc | save ⟨*Sym*⟩... |
    restore ⟨*Sym*⟩... | ?

⟨*SetOption*⟩ ::= {abbrev quals | all eqns | all rules | blips |
    clear memo | gc show | include BOOL | obj2 | verbose |
    print with parens | reduce conditions | show retracts |
    show var sorts | stats | trace | trace whole} ⟨*Polarity*⟩
    | ?

⟨*Polarity*⟩ ::= on | off

⟨*ShowOption*⟩ ::=
    {abbrev | all | eqs | mod | name | ops | params |
      principal-sort | [all] rules | select | sign |
      sorts | subs | vars}
      [⟨*ParamSpec*⟩ | ⟨*SubmodSpec*⟩] [⟨*ModExp*⟩] |
    [all] modes | modules | pending | op ⟨*OpRef*⟩ |
    [all] rule ⟨*RuleSpec*⟩ | sort ⟨*SortRef*⟩ | term |
    time | verbose | ⟨*ModExp*⟩ |
    ⟨*ParamSpec*⟩ | ⟨*SubmodSpec*⟩ | ?
  --- can use "open" to refer to the open module

⟨*ParamSpec*⟩ ::= param ⟨*Nat*⟩
⟨*SubmodSpec*⟩ ::= sub ⟨*Nat*⟩

⟨*Misc*⟩ ::= eval ⟨*Lisp*⟩ | eval-quiet ⟨*Lisp*⟩ | parse ⟨*Term*⟩ . |
    ⟨*Comment*⟩

⟨*Comment*⟩ ::= *** ⟨*Rest-of-line*⟩ | ***> ⟨*Rest-of-line*⟩ |
    *** ((⟨*Text-with-balanced-parentheses*⟩))
⟨*Rest-of-line*⟩ --- the remaining text of the current line

--- modules ---

⟨*Object*⟩ ::= obj ⟨*Interface*⟩ is {⟨*ModElt*⟩ | ⟨*Builtins*⟩}... endo

⟨*Theory*⟩ ::= th ⟨*Interface*⟩ is ⟨*ModElt*⟩... endth

⟨*Interface*⟩ ::= ⟨*ModId*⟩ [[⟨*ModId*⟩... :: ⟨*ModExp*⟩
                                 {, ⟨*ModId*⟩... :: ⟨*ModExp*⟩}...]]

⟨*ModElt*⟩ ::=
     {protecting | extending | including | using} ⟨*ModExp*⟩ . |
     using ⟨*ModExp*⟩ with ⟨*ModExp*⟩ {and ⟨*ModExp*⟩}... |
     define ⟨*SortId*⟩ is ⟨*ModExp*⟩ . |
     principal-sort ⟨*Sort*⟩ . |
     sort ⟨*SortId*⟩... . |
     subsort ⟨*Sort*⟩... { < ⟨*Sort*⟩... }... . |
     as ⟨*Sort*⟩ : ⟨*Term*⟩ if ⟨*Term*⟩ . |
     op ⟨*OpForm*⟩ : ⟨*Sort*⟩... -> ⟨*Sort*⟩ [⟨*Attr*⟩] . |
     ops {⟨*Sym*⟩ |
          (⟨*OpForm*⟩)}... : ⟨*Sort*⟩... -> ⟨*Sort*⟩ [⟨*Attr*⟩] . |
     op-as ⟨*OpForm*⟩ : ⟨*Sort*⟩... -> ⟨*Sort*⟩
          for ⟨*Term*⟩ if ⟨*Term*⟩ [⟨*Attr*⟩] . |
     [⟨*RuleLabel*⟩] let ⟨*Sym*⟩ [: ⟨*Sort*⟩] = ⟨*Term*⟩ . |
     var ⟨*VarId*⟩... : ⟨*Sort*⟩ . |
     vars-of [⟨*ModExp*⟩] . |
     [⟨*RuleLabel*⟩] eq ⟨*Term*⟩ = ⟨*Term*⟩ . |
     [⟨*RuleLabel*⟩] cq ⟨*Term*⟩ = ⟨*Term*⟩ if ⟨*Term*⟩ . |
     ⟨*Misc*⟩

⟨*Attr*⟩ ::= [{assoc | comm | {id: | idr:} ⟨*Term*⟩ | idem |
     memo | strat (⟨*Int*⟩...) | prec ⟨*Nat*⟩ |
     gather ({e | E | &}...) | poly ⟨*Lisp*⟩ | intrinsic}...]

⟨*RuleLabel*⟩ ::= ⟨*Id*⟩... {, ⟨*Id*⟩... }...

⟨*ModId*⟩ --- simple identifier, by convention all caps
⟨*SortId*⟩ --- simple identifier, by convention capitalized
⟨*VarId*⟩ --- simple identifier, typically capitalized
⟨*OpName*⟩ ::= ⟨*Sym*⟩ {"_" | " " | ⟨*Sym*⟩}...
⟨*Sym*⟩ --- any operator syntax symbol (blank delimited)
⟨*OpForm*⟩ ::= ⟨*OpName*⟩ | (⟨*OpName*⟩)
⟨*Sort*⟩ ::= ⟨*SortId*⟩ | ⟨*SortId*⟩.⟨*SortQual*⟩
⟨*SortQual*⟩ ::= ⟨*ModId*⟩ | (⟨*ModExp*⟩)
⟨*Lisp*⟩ --- a Lisp expression
⟨*Nat*⟩ --- a natural number
⟨*Int*⟩ --- an integer

⟨*Builtins*⟩ ::=
    bsort ⟨*SortId*⟩ ⟨*Lisp*⟩ . |
    [⟨*RuleLabel*⟩] bq ⟨*Term*⟩ = ⟨*Lisp*⟩ . |
    [⟨*RuleLabel*⟩] beq ⟨*Term*⟩ = ⟨*Lisp*⟩ . |
    [⟨*RuleLabel*⟩] cbeq ⟨*Term*⟩ = ⟨*Lisp*⟩ if ⟨*BoolTerm*⟩ . |
    [⟨*RuleLabel*⟩] cbq ⟨*Term*⟩ = ⟨*Lisp*⟩ if ⟨*BoolTerm*⟩ .

--- views ---

⟨*View*⟩ ::=
    view [⟨*ModId*⟩] from ⟨*ModExp*⟩ to ⟨*ModExp*⟩ is
        ⟨*ViewElt*⟩... endv |
    view ⟨*ModId*⟩ of ⟨*ModExp*⟩ as ⟨*ModExp*⟩ is
        ⟨*ViewElt*⟩... endv

--- terms ---

⟨*Term*⟩ ::= ⟨*Mixfix*⟩ | ⟨*VarId*⟩ | (⟨*Term*⟩) |
    ⟨*OpName*⟩ (⟨*Term*⟩ {, ⟨*Term*⟩}...) | (⟨*Term*⟩).⟨*OpQual*⟩
  --- precedence and gathering rules
  --- used to eliminate ambiguity

⟨*OpQual*⟩ ::= ⟨*Sort*⟩ | ⟨*ModId*⟩ | (⟨*ModExp*⟩)
⟨*Mixfix*⟩ --- mixfix operator applied to arguments

--- module expressions ---

⟨*ModExp*⟩ ::= ⟨*ModId*⟩ | ⟨*ModId*⟩ is ⟨*ModExpRenm*⟩ |
    ⟨*ModExpRenm*⟩ + ⟨*ModExp*⟩ | ⟨*ModExpRenm*⟩

⟨*ModExpRenm*⟩ ::=
    ⟨*ModExpInst*⟩ * (⟨*RenameElt*⟩ {, ⟨*RenameElt*⟩}...) |
    ⟨*ModExpInst*⟩

⟨*ModExpInst*⟩ ::=
    ⟨*ParamModExp*⟩[⟨*Arg*⟩ {,⟨*Arg*⟩}...] | (⟨*ModExp*⟩)

⟨*ParamModExp*⟩ ::=
    ⟨*ModId*⟩ | (⟨*ModId*⟩ * (⟨*RenameElt*⟩ {, ⟨*RenameElt*⟩}...))

⟨*RenameElt*⟩ ::=
    sort ⟨*SortRef*⟩ to ⟨*SortId*⟩ | op ⟨*OpRef*⟩ to ⟨*OpForm*⟩

⟨*Arg*⟩ ::= ⟨*ViewArg*⟩ | ⟨*ModExp*⟩ | [sort] ⟨*SortRef*⟩ | [op] ⟨*OpRef*⟩
--- may need to precede ⟨*SortRef*⟩ by "sort" and
--- ⟨*OpRef*⟩ by "op" to distinguish from general case
--- (i.e., from a module name)

⟨*ViewArg*⟩ ::=
    view [from ⟨*ModExp*⟩] to ⟨*ModExp*⟩ is ⟨*ViewElt*⟩... endv

⟨*ViewElt*⟩ ::=
    sort ⟨*SortRef*⟩ to ⟨*SortRef*⟩ . | var ⟨*VarId*⟩... : ⟨*Sort*⟩ . |
    op ⟨*OpExpr*⟩ to ⟨*Term*⟩ . | op ⟨*OpRef*⟩ to ⟨*OpRef*⟩ .
 --- priority given to ⟨*OpExpr*⟩ case
 --- vars are declared with sorts from source of view

⟨*SortRef*⟩ ::= ⟨*Sort*⟩ | (⟨*Sort*⟩)
⟨*OpRef*⟩ ::= ⟨*OpSpec*⟩ | (⟨*OpSpec*⟩) | (⟨*OpSpec*⟩).⟨*OpQual*⟩ |
    ((⟨*OpSpec*⟩).⟨*OpQual*⟩)
 --- in views (op).(M) must be enclosed in (),
 --- i.e., ((op).(M))
⟨*OpSpec*⟩ ::= ⟨*OpName*⟩ | ⟨*OpName*⟩ : ⟨*SortId*⟩... -> ⟨*SortId*⟩
⟨*OpExpr*⟩ --- a ⟨*Term*⟩ consisting of a single operator
              --- applied to variables

--- equivalent forms ---

assoc = associative	comm = commutative
cq = ceq	dfn = define
ev = eval	evq = eval-quiet
jbo = endo	ht = endth
endv = weiv = endview	ex = extending
gather = gathering	id: = identity:
idem = idempotent	idr: = identity-rules:
in = input	inc = including
obj = object	poly = polymorphic
prec = precedence	psort = principal-sort
pr = protecting	q = quit
red = reduce	rl = red-loop
sh = show	sorts = sort
strat = strategy	subsorts = subsort
th = theory	us = using
vars = var	*** = ---
***> = --->	

```
--- Lexical analysis ---

--- Tokens are sequences of characters delimited by blanks
--- "(", ")", and "," are always treated as
---    single character symbols
--- Tabs and returns are equivalent to blanks
---    (except inside comments)
--- Normally, "[", "]", "_", ",", "{", and "}"
--- are also treated as single character symbols.
```

Appendix C : More Examples

This appendix contains a number of examples that illustrate the power and flexibility of OBJ's unusual features, including hierarchical parameterized modules, subsorts, and rewriting modulo attributes.

C.1   SOME SET THEORY

The following two objects define some constructions on sets that may be useful in other examples, such as the category theory example in Appendix C.8. The use of memo has quite a significant effect on the test cases.

Warning: These particular definitions are very inefficient.   The example set2.obj distributed with OBJ3 provides a more efficient alternative.

```
obj BSET[X :: TRIV] is
  sort Set .
  pr IDENTICAL .
  ops ({}) omega : -> Set .
  op {_} : Elt -> Set .
  op _+_ : Set Set -> Set [assoc comm id: ({})] .
    *** exclusive or
  op _&_ : Set Set -> Set [assoc comm idem id: omega] .
    *** intersection
  vars S S' S'' : Set .    vars E E' : Elt .
  eq S + S = {} .
  cq { E } & { E' } = {} if E =/= E' .
  eq S & {} = {} .
  cq S & (S' + S'') = (S & S') + (S & S'')
      if (S' =/== {}) and (S'' =/== {}) .
    *** made conditional as an example of how to avoid
    *** non-termination from identity completion
    *** (in fact, not required)
endo
```

```
obj SET[X :: TRIV] is
  protecting BSET[X] .
  protecting INT .
  op _U_ : Set Set -> Set [assoc comm id: ({})] .
  op _-_ : Set Set -> Set .
  op #_ : Set -> Int [prec 0] .
  op _in_ : Elt Set -> Bool .
  op _in_ : Set Set -> Bool .
  op empty?_ : Set -> Bool .
  var X : Elt .    vars S S' S'' : Set .
  eq S U S' = (S & S') + S + S' .
  eq S - S' = S + (S & S') .
  eq empty? S = S == {} .
  eq X in S = { X } & S =/= {} .
  eq S in S' = S U S' == S' .
  eq # {} = 0 .
  cq #({ X } + S) = # S if X in S .
  cq #({ X } + S) = 1 + # S if not X in S .
endo

*** test cases
obj SET-OF-INT is
  protecting SET[INT] .
  ops s1 s2 s3 : -> Set [memo] .
  eq s1 = { 1 } .
  eq s2 = s1 U { 2 } .
  eq s3 = s2 U { 3 } .
endo
reduce s3 .                 ***> should be: {1,2,3}
reduce # s3 .               ***> should be: 3
reduce (s2 U s1) .          ***> should be: {1,2}
reduce #(s3 U s1) .         ***> should be: 3
reduce empty?(s3 + s3) .    ***> should be: true
reduce empty?(s1 + s3) .    ***> should be: false
reduce 3 in s2 .            ***> should be: false
reduce s1 in s3 .           ***> should be: true
reduce s1 - s3 .            ***> should be: {}
reduce s3 - s2 .            ***> should be: {3}
reduce s3 & s1 .            ***> should be: {1}
reduce s3 & s2 .            ***> should be: {1,2}
reduce omega U s2 .         ***> should be: omega
```

C.2   A SIMPLE PROGRAMMING LANGUAGE

It is generally rather straightforward to write specifications of programming languages in OBJ, as we hope the following example shows. (This example has been adapted from [69]; the first such use of OBJ occurs in [79].) This example is preceded by two standard generic modules, which are also used in some other examples below.

```
obj LIST[X :: TRIV] is
  sorts List NeList .
  op nil : -> List .
  subsorts Elt < NeList < List .
  op __ : List List -> List [assoc id: nil] .
  op __ : NeList List -> NeList .
  op __ : NeList NeList -> NeList .
  protecting NAT .
  op |_| : List -> Nat .
  eq | nil | = 0 .
  var E : Elt .   var L : List .
  eq | E L | = 1 + | L | .
  op tail_ : NeList -> List [prec 120] .
  var E : Elt .   var L : List .
  eq tail E L = L .
endo

obj ARRAY[INDEX VALUE :: TRIV] is
  sort Array .
  op nilArr : -> Array .
  op put : Elt.INDEX Elt.VALUE Array -> Array .
  op _[_] : Array Elt.INDEX -> Elt.VALUE .
  op _in_ : Elt.INDEX Array -> Bool .
  op undef : Elt.INDEX -> Elt.VALUE .   *** err-op
  var A : Array .
  var I I' : Elt.INDEX .   var E : Elt.VALUE .
  eq put(I,E,A)[ I ] = E .
  ceq put(I,E,A)[ I' ] = A [ I' ] if I =/= I' .
  eq I in nilArr = false .
  eq I in put(I',E,A) = I == I' or I in A .
  ceq A [ I ] = undef(I) if not I in A .   *** err-eqn
endo

*** the expressions of Fun
obj EXP is
  dfn Env is ARRAY[QID,INT] .
  sorts IntExp BoolExp .
  subsorts Int Id < IntExp .
  subsorts Bool < BoolExp .
  ops (_and_) (_or_) : BoolExp BoolExp -> BoolExp .
  op not_ : BoolExp -> BoolExp .
  op _<_ : IntExp IntExp -> BoolExp .
  op _=_ : IntExp IntExp -> BoolExp .
  op if_then_else_fi : BoolExp IntExp IntExp -> IntExp .
  ops (_+_) (_-_) (_*_) : IntExp IntExp -> IntExp .
  op [[_]]_ : IntExp Env -> Int .
  op [[_]]_ : BoolExp Env -> Bool .
```

```
    var N : Int .           var T : Bool .
    vars E E' : IntExp .   vars B B' : BoolExp .
    var I : Id .            var V : Env .
    eq [[ N ]] V = N .
    eq [[ I ]] V  = V [ I ] .
    eq [[ E + E' ]] V = ([[ E ]] V) + ([[ E' ]] V) .
    eq [[ E - E' ]] V = ([[ E ]] V) - ([[ E' ]] V) .
    eq [[ E * E' ]] V = ([[ E ]] V) * ([[ E' ]] V) .
    eq [[ T ]] V = T .
    eq [[ E < E' ]] V = ([[ E ]] V) < ([[ E' ]] V) .
    eq [[(E = E')]] V = ([[ E ]] V) == ([[ E' ]] V) .
    eq [[ B and B' ]] V = ([[ B ]] V) and ([[ B' ]] V) .
    eq [[ B or  B' ]] V = ([[ B ]] V) or  ([[ B' ]] V) .
    eq [[ not B ]] V = not([[ B ]] V) .
    eq [[ if B then E else E' fi ]] V =
        if [[ B ]] V then [[ E ]] V else [[ E' ]] V fi .
endo


*** the statements of Fun
obj STMT is
    sort Stmt .
    protecting EXP .
    op _;_ : Stmt Stmt -> Stmt [assoc] .
    op _:=_ : Id IntExp -> Stmt .
    op while_do_od : BoolExp Stmt -> Stmt .
    op [[_]]_ : Stmt Env -> Env .
    vars S S' : Stmt .     var V : Env .
    var E : IntExp .       var B : BoolExp .
    var I : Id .
    eq [[ I := E ]] V = put(I,[[ E ]] V, V) .
    eq [[ S ; S' ]] V = [[ S' ]] [[ S ]] V .
    eq [[ while B do S od ]] V = if [[ B ]] V then
        [[ while B do S od ]] [[ S ]] V else V fi .
endo


*** evaluation of Fun programs
obj FUN is
    sorts Fun Init .
    protecting STMT .
    dfn IdList is LIST[QID] .
    dfn IntList is LIST[INT] .
    dfn InitList is
        (LIST *(op nil to nil-init, op (__) to (_;_)))[Init] .
    op _initially_ : Id IntExp -> Init [prec 1].
    op fun _ _ is vars _ body: _ : Id IdList InitList Stmt -> Fun .
    op [[_:=_]]_ : IdList IntList Env -> Env .
    op [[_]]_ : InitList Env -> Env .
    op [[_]][_]_ : Fun Env IntList -> Env .
    op [[_]]_ : Fun IntList -> Int .
    op wrong#args : -> Env .   *** err-op
```

```
        vars I F : Id .     var Is : IdList .
        var N : Int .       var Ns : IntList .
        var E : IntExp .    var INs : InitList .
        var S : Stmt .      var V : Env .
        eq [[ nil-init ]] V = V .
        eq [[(I initially E); INs ]] V = [[ INs ]] [[ I := E ]] V .
        eq [[ I Is := N Ns ]] V =
            ([[ I := N ]] ([[ Is := Ns ]] V)).STMT .
        eq [[(nil).IdList := (nil).IntList ]] V = V .
        eq [[ fun F(Is) is vars nil-init body: S ]][ V ](Ns) =
            [[ S ]] V .
        eq [[ fun F(Is) is vars INs body: S ]][ V ](Ns) =
            [[ S ]] [[ INs ]] [[ Is := Ns ]] V .
        eq [[ fun F(Is) is vars INs body: S ]](Ns) =
            [[ fun F(Is) is vars INs body: S ]][ nilArr ](Ns) [ F ] .
        cq [[ Is := Ns ]] V = wrong#args if | Is | =/= | Ns | .
            *** err-qn
endo

*** pow(n m) finds the nth power of m for positive n or 0
reduce [[ fun 'pow('n 'm) is vars 'pow initially 1 body:
            while 0 < 'n
            do ('pow := 'pow * 'm);('n := 'n - 1) od ]](4 2) .
***> should be: 16

*** factorial of n
reduce [[ fun 'fac('n)
            is vars ('fac initially 1);('i initially 0)
            body: while 'i < 'n
                do ('i := 'i + 1); ('fac := 'i * 'fac) od ]](5) .
***> should be: 120

*** max finds the maximum of a list of three numbers
reduce [[ fun 'max('a 'b 'c) is vars 'n initially 2 body:
            ('max := 'a); while 0 < 'n do
            ('n := 'n - 1); ('x := 'b); ('b := 'c);
            ('max := if 'x < 'max then 'max else 'x fi) od
        ]](3 123 32) .
***> should be: 123
```

C.3   UNIFICATION

The use of associative and/or commutative matching allows writing a simple and elegant unification algorithm in OBJ3. A more efficient version of this algorithm can be used to implement logic (i.e., relational) programming on the Rewrite Rule Machine; see [75, 107] for more detail.

In this code, a term is either a variable (such as 'X) or else is of the form F[T], where F is an operator symbol (such as 'F) and T is a list of terms;

a constant is of the form F[nil]. An equation is a pair of terms separated by =, and a system of equations is a list of equations, separated by & signs. The symbols { and } are used to delimit subsystems of equations. The form let X be T1 in T2 indicates the substitution of T1 for X in T2; this operator extends to term lists, equations and systems. A system to be unified, presented in the form {{ S }}, is reduced to another system { S' } in "solved form", by progressively moving solved equations out of the inner brackets, so that in {S1 & {S2}}, the equations in S1 are solved, while those in S2 are not.

```
obj SUBST is
   sorts Eqn Term .
   protecting QID .
   subsort Id < Term .
   pr TERMS is (LIST *(sort List to TermList,
                       sort NeList to NeTermList))[Term].
   dfn Op is QID .
   op _[_] : Op TermList -> Term [prec 1] .
   op _=_ : Term Term -> Eqn [comm prec 120] .
   pr SYSTEM is (LIST *(sort List to System,
                        sort NeList to NeSystem,
                        op nil to null,
                        op (__) to (_&_)))[Eqn].
   op {_} : System -> System .    *** scope delimiter
   op _=_ : TermList TermList -> System [comm prec 120] .
   vars T U V : Term .    var Us : NeTermList .
   var S : NeSystem .    var Ts : TermList .
   eq (T Ts = U Us) = (T = U) & (Ts = Us).
   op let_be_in_ : Id Term Term -> Term .
   op let_be_in_ : Id Term TermList -> TermList .
   op let_be_in_ : Id Term Eqn -> Eqn .
   op let_be_in_ : Id Term System -> System .
   vars X Y : Id .    var F : Op .
   eq let X be T in nil = nil .
   eq let X be T in Y = if X == Y then T else Y fi .
   eq let X be T in F[Ts] = F[let X be T in Ts].
   eq let X be T in (U Us) = (let X be T in U) (let X be T in Us).
   eq let X be T in (U = V) =
       (let X be T in U) = (let X be T in V) .
   eq let X be T in null = null .
   eq let X be T in ((U = V) & S) =
       (let X be T in (U = V)) & (let X be T in S).
endo
```

```
***> first without occur check
obj UNIFY is
using SUBST with SYSTEM and TERMS .
op unify_ : System -> System [prec 120].
op fail : -> Eqn .
var T : Term .              vars Ts Us : NeTermList .
vars S S' S'' : System .  var X : Id .
eq unify S = {{S}} .
eq S & (T = T) & S' = S & S' .
eq S & fail & S' = fail .
eq let X be T in fail = fail .
eq {null} = null .
eq {fail} = fail .
vars F G : Op .    vars X : Id .
eq {S & (F[Ts] = G[Us]) & S'} = if F == G and | Ts | == | Us |
   then {S & (Ts = Us) & S'} else fail fi .
eq {S & {S' & (X = T) & S''}} =
   if X == T then {S & {S' & S''}} else
   {(X = T) & (let X be T in S) & {let X be T in S' & S''}} fi .
endo

reduce unify 'f['g['X] 'Y] = 'f['g['h['Y]] 'h['Z]].
reduce unify 'f['X 'Y] = 'f['Y 'g['Y]].
reduce unify ('f['g['X] 'Y] = 'f['g['h['Y]] 'h['Z]])
             & ('h['X] = 'Z).
reduce unify 'f['X 'g['Y]] = 'f['Z 'Z].
reduce unify 'f['X 'g['Y]] = 'f['Z].
reduce unify 'f['Y 'g['Y]] = 'f['h['Z] 'Z].
reduce unify 'f['Y 'a[nil]] = 'f['g['a[nil]] 'Z].

***> now add occur check
obj UNIFY-OCH is using UNIFY .
  op _in_ : Id TermList -> Bool .
  vars X Y : Id .    var F : Op .
  var T : Term .     var Ts : NeTermList .
  eq X in Y = X == Y .
  eq X in F[Ts] = X in Ts .
  eq X in T Ts = X in T or X in Ts .
  cq (X = T) = fail if X in T .
endo

reduce unify 'f['g['X] 'Y] = 'f['g['h['Y]] 'h['Z]].
reduce unify 'f['X 'Y] = 'f['Y 'g['Y]].
reduce unify ('f['g['X] 'Y] = 'f['g['h['Y]] 'h['Z]])
             & ('h['X] = 'Z).
reduce unify 'f['X 'g['Y]] = 'f['Z 'Z].
reduce unify 'f['X 'g['Y]] = 'f['Z].
reduce unify 'f['Y 'g['Y]] = 'f['h['Z] 'Z].
reduce unify 'f['Y 'a[nil]] = 'f['g['a[nil]] 'Z].
```

C.4   SOME THEOREM PROVING

Because OBJ3 is rigorously based upon order sorted equational logic, every OBJ3 computation proves some theorem. By choosing the right specification and the right term, these computations can be made to prove interesting theorems, as the following examples demonstrate. It is not enough just to give the OBJ code for a proof – called its *proof score* – and then do the computation; it is also necessary to show that if all reductions in the proof score evaluate to true, then the theorem really has been proved. Many such justifications are given in [51], from which the proof scores in this section were taken. Further justifications, and some more complex proofs, including the verification of parameterized modules, and some hardware circuits, may be found in [59]; see also [66]. Such proof scores are generated and checked by Kumo [65, 64, 78, 60].

The following simple specification of the natural numbers is used in several examples below.

```
obj NAT is
  sort Nat .
  op 0 : -> Nat .
  op s_ : Nat -> Nat [prec 1] .
  op _+_ : Nat Nat -> Nat .
  vars L M N : Nat .
  eq M + 0 = M .
  eq M + s N = s(M + N) .
endo
```

C.4.1   Associativity of Addition.   The following proves that addition of natural numbers is associative.

```
open .
ops l m n : -> Nat .

*** base case, n=0: 1+(m+0)=(1+m)+0
reduce 1 + (m + 0) == (1 + m) + 0 .

*** induction step
eq 1 + (m + n) = (1 + m) + n .
reduce 1 + (m + s n) == (1 + m) + s n .
close

*** thus we can assert
obj ASSOC is
  protecting NAT .
  vars-of NAT .
  eq L + (M + N) = (L + M) + N .
endo
```

C.4.2   Commutativity of Addition.   The following proves that addition of natural numbers is commutative.

```
open .
vars-of NAT .
ops m n : -> Nat .

*** show lemma0: 0 + n = n, by induction on n
*** base for lemma0, n=0
reduce 0 + 0 == 0 .
*** induction step
eq 0 + n = n .
reduce 0 + (s n) == s n .
*** thus we can assert
eq 0 + N = N .

*** show lemma1: (s m) + n = s(m + n), again by induction on n
*** base for lemma1, n=0
reduce (s m)+ 0 == s(m + 0) .
*** induction step
eq (s m)+ n = s(m + n) .
reduce (s m) + (s n) == s(m + s n) .
*** thus we can assert
eq (s M)+ N = s(M + N).

*** show m + n = n + m, again by induction on n
*** the base case, n=0
reduce m + 0 == 0 + m .
*** induction step
eq m + n = n + m .
reduce m + (s n) == (s n) + m .
close
```

Of course, we must not assert commutativity as a rewrite rule, or we would get non-terminating reductions. The above two proofs show that we are entitled to use associative-commutative rewriting for +, and we do so below.

It is interesting to contrast the above proofs with corresponding proofs due to Paulson in Cambridge LCF [129]. The LCF proofs are much more complex, in part because LCF functions are partial, and therefore must be proved total, whereas functions are automatically total (on their domain) in equational logic.

C.4.3   Formula for $1 + \ldots + n$.   We now give a standard inductive proof over the natural numbers, the formula for the sum of the first n positive natural numbers,

$$1 + 2 + \ldots + n = n(n + 1)/2.$$

Here we take advantage of the two results proven above by giving + the attributes assoc and comm; the score, as given, will not work if either (or both) of these attributes are deleted. This application of associative/commutative rewriting saves the user from having to worry about the ordering and grouping of subterms within terms headed by +.

```
obj NAT is
  sort Nat .
  op 0 : -> Nat .
  op s_ : Nat -> Nat [prec 1] .
  op _+_ : Nat Nat -> Nat [assoc comm] .
  vars M N : Nat .
  eq M + 0 = M .
  eq M + s N = s(M + N).
  op _*_ : Nat Nat -> Nat .
  eq M * 0 = 0 .
  eq M * s N = (M * N)+ M .
endo

open .
vars-of NAT .
ops m n : -> Nat .

*** first show two lemmas, 0*n=0 and (sm)*n=(m*n)+n
*** base for first lemma
reduce 0 * 0 == 0 .
*** induction step for first lemma
eq 0 * n = 0 .
reduce 0 * s n == 0 .
*** thus we can assert
eq 0 * N = 0 .

*** base for second lemma
reduce (s n)* 0 == (n * 0) + 0 .
*** induction step for second lemma
eq (s m) * n = (m * n)+ n .
reduce (s m)*(s n) == (m * s n)+ s n .
*** thus
eq (s M)* N = (M * N)+ N .

*** now define
op sum : Nat -> Nat .
eq sum(0) = 0 .
eq sum(s N) = (s N)+ sum(N) .

*** show sum(n)+sum(n)=n*sn
*** base case
reduce sum(0) + sum(0) == 0 * s 0 .
*** induction step
eq sum(n) + sum(n) = n * s n .
reduce sum(s n) + sum(s n) == (s n)*(s s n) .
close
```

C.4.4   Fermat's Little Theorem for $p = 3$.   The so-called "little Fermat theorem" says that

$$x^p \equiv x \pmod p$$

for any prime p, i.e., that the remainder of x^p by p equals the remainder of x by p. The following OBJ3 proof score for the case $p = 3$ needs a slightly more sophisticated natural number object which assumes that we have already proven that multiplication is associative and commutative. This is a nice example of an inductive proof where there are non-trivial relations among the constructors. (We thank Dr. Emmanuel Kounalis for doubting that OBJ3 could handle non-trivial relations on constructors, and then presenting the challenge to prove this result.)

```
obj NAT is
  sort Nat .
  op 0 : -> Nat .
  op s_ : Nat -> Nat [prec 1] .
  op _+_ : Nat Nat -> Nat [assoc comm] .
  vars L M N : Nat .
  eq M + 0 = M .
  eq M + s N = s(M + N) .
  op _*_ : Nat Nat -> Nat [assoc comm] .
  eq M * 0 = 0 .
  eq M * s N = (M * N)+ M .
  eq L * (M + N) = (L * M) + (L * N) .
  eq M + M + M = 0 .
endo

*** base case, x = 0
reduce 0 * 0 * 0 == 0 .
*** induction step
open .
op x : -> Nat .
eq x * x * x = x .
reduce (s x)*(s x)*(s x) == s x .
close
```

The same technique can be used for $p = 5$, $p = 7$, etc., but something more sophisticated is needed to get the result for all primes.

C.4.5   Left and Right Group Axioms.   A standard example in group theory is to prove that the right handed versions of the axioms follow from the left handed versions. It is straightforward to do this example using OBJ's apply feature. The terms following the numbers in square brackets (e.g., [0]) show what the result should be.

```
th GROUPL is
  sort Elt .
  op _*_ : Elt Elt -> Elt .
  op e : -> Elt .
  op _-1 : Elt -> Elt [prec 2] .
  var A B C : Elt .
  [lid] eq e * A = A .
  [lnv] eq A -1 * A = e .
  [las] eq A * (B * C) = (A * B) * C .
endth


open .
op a : -> Elt .

*** first, prove the right inverse law:
start a * a -1 .
 ***> [0] (a * a -1)
apply -.lid at term .
 ***> [1] e * (a * a -1)
apply -.lnv with A = (a -1) within term .
 ***> [2] ((a -1) -1 * a -1) * (a * a -1)
apply .las at term .
 ***> [3] ((a -1 -1 * a -1)* a)* a -1
apply -.las with A = (a -1 -1) within term .
 ***> [4] ((a -1 -1 * (a -1 * a)) * a -1
apply .lnv within term .
 ***> [5] (a -1 -1 * e) * a -1
apply -.las at term .
 ***> [6] a -1 -1 * (e * a -1)
apply .lid within term .
 ***> [7] a -1 -1 * a -1
apply .lnv at term .
 ***> [8] e

*** we can now add the proven equation
  [rnv] eq (A * (A -1)) = e .

*** next, we prove the right identity law:
start a * e .
 ***> [0] a * e
apply -.lnv with A = a within term .
 ***> [1] a *(a -1 * a)
apply .las at term .
 ***> [2] (a * a -1)* a
apply .rnv within term .
 ***> [3] e * a
apply .lid at term .
 ***> [4] a
```

```
***> we can add the proven equation
 [rid] eq A * e = A .
close
```

This example can be simplified by assuming associativity of the group multiplication as an attribute:

```
th GROUPLA is
  sort Elt .
  op _*_ : Elt Elt -> Elt [assoc] .
  op e : -> Elt .
  op _-1 : Elt -> Elt [prec 2] .
  var A : Elt .
  [lid]  eq e * A = A .
  [linv] eq A -1 * A = e .
endth


open .
op a : -> Elt .

*** first, prove the right inverse law:
start a * a -1 .
apply -.lid at term .
  ***> should be: e * a * a -1
apply -.linv with A = (a -1) within term .
  ***> should be: a -1 -1 * a -1 * a * a -1
apply .linv at [2 .. 3] of term .
  ***> should be: a -1 -1 * e * a -1
apply reduction at term .
  ***> should be: e

*** add the proven equation:
 [rinv] eq A * A -1 = e .

*** second prove the right identity law:
start a * e .
apply -.linv with A = a within term .
  ***> should be: a * a -1 * a
apply .rinv at [1 .. 2] .
  ***> should be: e * a
apply reduction at term .
  ***> should be: a

*** add the proven equation:
 [rid] eq A * e = A .
close
```

C.4.6   Injective Functions.   Proving that an injective function with a right inverse is an isomorphism gives a good illustration of `apply` when there are conditional equations.

```
th INJ is
  sorts A B .
  op f_ : A -> B .
  op g_ : B -> A .
  var A : A . vars B B' : B .
  [Inv] eq g f A = A .
  [inj] cq B = B' if g B == g B' .
endth

open .
op b : -> B .

start f g b .
apply .inj with B' = b at term .
apply red at term .
***> should be: b
close
```

What happens here is that, in order to apply the rule `.inj` to `f g b` with `B'` = b, we must first prove that the condition is true, which in this case is that `g f g b == g b`. Therefore, OBJ3 shifts its focus from the original term for reduction, to the condition, so that `red` (i.e., reduction) is actually applied to `g f g b == g b`. In fact, the rule `.Inv` applies, to give `g b == g b`, which reduces to `true` by a built in rule for `==`. Therefore the given term, `f g b` is rewritten to b. This establishes the equation

```
eq f g b = b .
```

and hence that

```
eq f g b = b .
```

so that g is indeed as isomorphism.

C.5   LAZY EVALUATION

This subsection gives the famous Sieve of Erastosthenes, which finds all the prime numbers. Since this is an infinite structure, laziness is needed to actually run it.

```
obj LAZYLIST[X :: TRIV] is
  sort List .
  subsort Elt < List .
  op nil : -> List .
  op __ : List List -> List [assoc idr: nil strat (0)] .
endo
```

```
obj SIEVE is
  protecting LAZYLIST[INT] .
  op force : List List -> List [strat (1 2 0)] .
  op show_upto_ : List Int -> List .
  op filter_with_ : List Int -> List .
  op ints-from_ : Int -> List .
  op sieve_ : List -> List .
  op primes : -> List .
  var P I E : Int .
  var S L : List .
  eq force(L,S) = L S .
  eq show nil upto I = nil .
  eq show E S upto I = if I == 0 then nil
    else force(E,show S upto (I - 1)) fi .
  eq filter nil with P = nil .
  eq filter I S with P = if (I rem P) == 0 then filter S with P
    else I (filter S with P) fi .
  eq ints-from I = I (ints-from (I + 1)) .
  eq sieve nil = nil .
  eq sieve (I S) = I (sieve (filter S with I)) .
  eq primes = sieve (ints-from 2) .
endo

reduce show primes upto 10 .
***> should be: 2 3 5 7 11 13 17 19 23 29
```

C.6   COMBINATORS

The convention for terms in combinatory algebra requires the use of gathering attributes. Some rather nice calculations can then be done, in exactly the usual notation. Here is the basic object:

```
obj COMBINATORS is
  sort T .
  op __ : T T -> T [gather (E e)]. *** forces left association
  ops S K I : -> T .
  vars M N P : T .
  eq K M N = M .
  eq I M = M .
  eq S M N P = (M P) (N P).
endo
```

Now the reductions, all of which should evaluate to `true`, because all of them correspond to identities of combinatory algebra:

```
open .
ops m n p : -> T .

red S K K m == I m .
red S K S m == I m .
red S I I I m == I m .

red K m n == S(S(K S)(S(K K)K))(K(S K K))m n .
red S m n p ==
     S(S(K S)(S(K(S(K S)))(S(K(S(K K)))S)))(K(K(S K K)))m n p .
red S(K K) m n p == S(S(K S)(S(K K)(S(K S)K)))(K K) m n p .

let X = S I .
red X X X X m == X(X(X X)) m .

close
```

The last of these takes 27 rewrites, and is not the sort of thing that one would like to do by hand!

C.7   A NUMBER HIERARCHY

The various number systems used in modern mathematics exhibit a very rich hierarchy of sorts and subsorts, from the nonzero natural numbers up to the quarternions. The way this example avoids division by zero is also a nice illustration of using order sorted algebra to define functions on subsorts. (Most of the work on this example was done by Dr. José Meseguer.)

```
obj NAT is
  sorts Nat NzNat Zero .
  subsorts Zero NzNat < Nat .
  op 0 : -> Zero .
  op s_ : Nat -> NzNat .
  op p_ : NzNat -> Nat .
  op _+_ : Nat Nat -> Nat [assoc comm] .
  op _*_ : Nat Nat -> Nat .
  op _*_ : NzNat NzNat -> NzNat .
  op _>_ : Nat Nat -> Bool .
  op d : Nat Nat -> Nat [comm] .
  op quot : Nat NzNat -> Nat .
  op gcd : NzNat NzNat -> NzNat [comm] .
  vars N M : Nat .    vars N' M' : NzNat .
  eq p s N = N .
  eq N + 0 = N .
  eq (s N) + (s M) = s s (N + M) .
  eq N * 0 = 0 .
  eq 0 * N = 0 .
```

```
    eq (s N) * (s M) = s (N + (M + (N * M))) .
    eq 0 > M = false .
    eq N' > 0 = true .
    eq s N > s M = N > M .
    eq d(0,N) = N .
    eq d(s N, s M) = d(N,M) .
    eq quot(N,M') = if ((N > M') or (N == M'))
                    then s quot(d(N,M'),M') else 0 fi .
    eq gcd(N',M') = if N' == M' then N' else (if N' > M' then
        gcd(d(N',M'),M') else gcd(N',d(N',M')) fi) fi .
endo

obj INT is
    sorts Int NzInt .
    protecting NAT .
    subsort Nat < Int .
    subsorts NzNat < NzInt < Int .
    op -_ : Int -> Int .
    op -_ : NzInt -> NzInt .
    op _+_ : Int Int -> Int [assoc comm] .
    op _*_ : Int Int -> Int .
    op _*_ : NzInt NzInt -> NzInt .
    op quot : Int NzInt -> Int .
    op gcd : NzInt NzInt -> NzNat [comm] .
    vars I J : Int .    vars I' J' : NzInt .
    vars N' M' : NzNat .
    eq - - I = I .
    eq - 0 = 0 .
    eq I + 0 = I .
    eq M' + (- N') = if N' == M' then 0 else
        (if N' > M' then - d(N',M') else d(N',M') fi) fi .
    eq (- I) + (- J) = - (I + J) .
    eq I * 0 = 0 .
    eq 0 * I = 0 .
    eq I * (- J) = - (I * J) .
    eq (- J) * I = - (I * J) .
    eq quot(0,I') = 0 .
    eq quot(- I',J') = - quot(I',J') .
    eq quot(I',- J') = - quot(I',J') .
    eq gcd(- I',J') = gcd(I',J') .
endo
```

```
obj RAT is
  sorts Rat NzRat .
  protecting INT .
  subsort Int < Rat .
  subsorts NzInt < NzRat < Rat .
  op _/_ : Rat NzRat -> Rat .
  op _/_ : NzRat NzRat -> NzRat .
  op -_  : Rat -> Rat .
  op -_  : NzRat -> NzRat .
  op _+_ : Rat Rat -> Rat [assoc comm] .
  op _*_ : Rat Rat -> Rat .
  op _*_ : NzRat NzRat -> NzRat .
  vars I' J' : NzInt .    vars R S : Rat .
  vars R' S' : NzRat .
  eq R / (R' / S') = (R * S') / R' .
  eq (R / R') / S' = R / (R' * S') .
  cq J' / I' = quot(J',gcd(J',I')) / quot(I',gcd(J',I'))
     if gcd(J',I') =/= s 0 .
  eq R / s 0 = R .
  eq 0 / R' = 0 .
  eq R / (- R') = (- R) / R' .
  eq - (R / R') = (- R) / R' .
  eq R + (S / R') = ((R * R') + S) / R' .
  eq R * (S / R') = (R * S) / R' .
  eq (S / R') * R = (R * S) / R' .
endo

obj CPX-RAT is
  sorts Cpx Imag NzImag NzCpx .
  protecting RAT .
  subsort Rat < Cpx .
  subsort NzRat < NzCpx .
  subsorts NzImag < NzCpx Imag < Cpx .
  subsorts Zero < Imag .
  op _i : Rat -> Imag .
  op _i : NzRat -> NzImag .
  op -_ : Cpx -> Cpx .
  op -_ : NzCpx -> NzCpx .
  op _+_ : Cpx Cpx -> Cpx [assoc comm] .
  op _+_ : NzRat NzImag -> NzCpx [assoc comm] .
  op _*_ : Cpx Cpx -> Cpx .
  op _*_ : NzCpx NzCpx -> NzCpx .
  op _/_ : Cpx NzCpx -> Cpx .
  op _# : Cpx -> Cpx .
  op |_|^2 : Cpx -> Rat .
  op |_|^2 : NzCpx -> NzRat .
  vars R S : Rat .    vars R' R'' S' S'' : NzRat .
  vars A B C : Cpx .
  eq 0 i = 0 .
```

```
  eq C + 0 = C .
  eq (R i) + (S i) = (R + S) i .
  eq -(R' + (S' i)) = (- R') + ((- S') i ) .
  eq -(S' i) = (- S') i .
  eq R * (S i) = (R * S) i .
  eq (S i) * R = (R * S) i .
  eq (R i) * (S i) = - (R * S) .
  eq C * (A + B) = (C * A) + (C * B) .
  eq (A + B) * C = (C * A) + (C * B) .
  eq R # = R .
  eq (R' + (S' i))# = R' + ((- S') i) .
  eq (S' i) # = ((- S') i) .
  eq | C |^2 = C * (C #) .
  eq (S' i) / R'' = (S' / R'') i .
  eq (R' + (S' i)) / R'' = (R' / R'') + ((S' / R'') i) .
  eq A / (R' i) = A * (((- s 0) /  R') i) .
  eq A / (R'' + (R' i)) =
     A *((R'' / |(R'' + (R' i))|^2)
        + (((- R') / |(R'' + (R' i))|^2) i)).
endo

obj QUAT-RAT is
  sorts Quat NzQuat J NzJ .
  protecting CPX-RAT .
  subsorts NzJ Zero < J < Quat .
  subsorts NzCpx < NzQuat Cpx < Quat .
  subsort NzJ < NzQuat .
  op _j : Cpx -> J .
  op _j : NzCpx -> NzJ .
  op -_ : Quat -> Quat .
  op _+_ : Quat Quat -> Quat [assoc comm] .
  op _+_ : Cpx NzJ -> NzQuat [assoc comm] .
  op _*_ : Quat Quat -> Quat .
  op _*_ : NzQuat NzQuat -> NzQuat .
  op _/_ : Quat NzQuat -> Quat .
  op _# : Quat -> Quat .
  op |_|^2 : Quat -> Rat .
  op |_|^2 : NzQuat -> NzRat .
  vars O P Q : Quat .    vars B C : Cpx .
  vars C' : NzCpx .
  eq 0 j = 0 .
  eq Q + 0 = Q .
  eq -(C + (B j)) = (- C) + ((- B) j ) .
  eq (C j) + (B j) = (C + B) j .
  eq C * (B j) = (C * B) j .
  eq (B j) * C = (B * (C #)) j .
  eq (C j) * (B j) = - (C * (B #)) .
  eq Q * (O + P) = (Q * O) + (Q * P) .
  eq (O + P) * Q = (O * Q) + (P * Q) .
  eq (P + Q) # = (P #) + (Q #) .
```

```
    eq (C j) # = (- C) j .
    eq | Q |^2 = Q * (Q #) .
    eq Q / (C' j) = Q * ((s 0 / (- C')) j) .
    eq Q / (C + (C' j)) = Q * (((C #) / |(C + (C' j))|^2) +
        (((- C') / |(C + (C' j))|^2) j)) .
endo

obj TST is
    protecting QUAT-RAT .
    ops 1 2 3 4 5 6 7 8 9 : -> NzNat [memo] .
    eq 1 = s 0 .  eq 2 = s 1 .  eq 3 = s 2 .
    eq 4 = s 3 .  eq 5 = s 4 .  eq 6 = s 5 .
    eq 7 = s 6 .  eq 8 = s 7 .  eq 9 = s 8 .
endo
reduce 3 + 2 .
reduce 3 * 2 .
reduce p p 3 .
reduce 4 > 8 .
reduce d(2,8) .
reduce quot(7,2) .
reduce gcd(9,6) .
reduce (- 4) + 8 .
reduce (- 4) * 2 .
reduce 8 / (- 2) .
reduce (1 / 3) + (4 / 6) .
reduce | 1 + (2 i) |^2 .
reduce | (1 + (3 i)) + (1 + ((- 2) i)) |^2 .
reduce (3 + ((3 i) + ((- 2) i))) / ((2 i) + 2) .
reduce (2 + ((3 i) j)) * ((5 i) + (7 j)) .
reduce (1 + ((1 i) j)) / (2 j) .
```

C.8   CATEGORIES AND COPRODUCTS

This subsection specifies categories and coproducts. Some familiarity with category theory may be needed (e.g., sections 2.3 and 3.9 of [88]); on the other hand, the code may also provide a more concrete understanding of the categorical concepts; see also [136]. Note how universal morphisms are defined as a subsort, and also the use of sort constraints. (Recall that the semantics of op-as is not yet implemented.) The use of memo has quite a significant effect on performance in this example.

```
*** theory of categories
th CAT-TH is
  sorts Mor Obj .
  ops (d0_) (d1_) : Mor -> Obj .
  op-as _;_ : Mor Mor -> Mor
      for M1 ; M2 if d1 M1 == d0 M2 [assoc] .
  op id_ : Obj -> Mor .
  var O : Obj .
  vars M M0 M1 : Mor .
  eq d0 id O = O .
  eq d1 id O = O .
  eq d0 (M0 ; M1) = d0 M0 .
  eq d1 (M0 ; M1) = d1 M1 .
  eq (id d0 M); M = M .
  eq M ; id d1 M = M .
endth

*** generic category of sets
obj CAT-SET[X :: TRIV] is
  sort Fn .
  protecting SET[X] .
  ops (d0_) (d1_) : Fn -> Set .
  op-as _;_ : Fn Fn -> Fn for F1 ; F2 if d1 F1 == d0 F2 [assoc] .
  op id_ : Set -> Fn .
  op-as _of_ : Fn Elt -> Elt
      for F of X if (X in d0 F) and (F of X in d1 F) .
  var O : Set .
  vars F F0 F1 : Fn .
  var E : Elt .
  eq d0 id O = O .
  eq d1 id O = O .
  eq d0 (F0 ; F1) = d0 F0 .
  eq d1 (F0 ; F1) = d1 F1 .
  eq (id d0 F) ; F = F .
  eq F ; id d1 F = F .
  eq (F0 ; F1) of E = F0 of (F1 of E) .
  eq (id O) of E = E .
endo

*** CAT-SET always gives a category
view CAT-SET-AS-CAT from CAT-TH to CAT-SET is
  sort Obj to Set .
  sort Mor to Fn .
endv
```

```
*** 2-cones in C
obj CO2CONE[C :: CAT-TH] is
  sort Co2cone .
  define Base is 2TUPLE[Obj,Obj] .
  op-as cone : Mor Mor -> Co2cone
     for cone(M1,M2) if d1 M1 == d1 M2 .
  ops j1 j2 : Co2cone -> Mor .
  op apex : Co2cone -> Obj .
  op base : Co2cone -> Base .
  vars M1 M2 : Mor .
  eq j1(cone(M1,M2)) = M1 .
  eq j2(cone(M1,M2)) = M2 .
  eq apex(cone(M1,M2)) = d1 M1 .
  eq base(cone(M1,M2)) = << d0 M1 ; d0 M2 >> .
endo

*** theory of coproduct in C
th CO2PROD-TH[C :: CAT-TH] is
  sort Uco2cone .
  protecting CO2CONE[C] .
  subsort Uco2cone < Co2cone .      *** a very nice subsort!
  op ucone : Obj Obj -> Uco2cone .  *** coproduct cone
  op _++_ : Obj Obj -> Obj .        *** coproduct object
  op-as umor : Uco2cone Co2cone -> Mor
     for umor(U,C) if base(U) == base(C) .
  vars A B : Obj .
  vars F G H : Mor .
  eq apex(ucone(A,B)) = A ++ B .
  eq base(ucone(A,B)) = << A ; B >> .
  eq (j1(ucone(A,B))); umor(ucone(A,B),cone(F,G)) = F .
  eq (j2(ucone(A,B))); umor(ucone(A,B),cone(F,G)) = G .
  cq H = umor(ucone(A,B),cone(F,G))
     if (j1(ucone(A,B)); H == F) and (j2(ucone(A,B)); H == G) .
endth

*** theory of injections for building a coproduct
th 2INJ-TH is
  sort Elt .
  ops i0 i1 i0inv i1inv : Elt -> Elt .
  ops i0pred i1pred : Elt -> Bool .
  var E : Elt .
  eq i0inv(i0(E)) = E .
  eq i1inv(i1(E)) = E .
  eq i0pred(i0(E)) = true .
  eq i0pred(i1(E)) = false .
  eq i1pred(i1(E)) = true .
  eq i1pred(i0(E)) = false .
endth
```

```
*** coproduct in a category of sets, given injections for it
obj CO2PROD-CAT-SET[J :: 2INJ-TH] is
  sort Uco2cone .
  extending CO2CONE[view to CAT-SET[J] is
      sort Obj to Set .
      sort Mor to Fn .
    endv] .
  subsort Uco2cone < Co2cone .
  op ucone : Set Set -> Uco2cone .
  op-as umor : Uco2cone Co2cone -> Fn
    for umor(U,C) if base(U) == base(C) .
  ops I0 I1 : Set -> Set .
  op _++_ : Set Set -> Set [memo] .
  vars A B S : Set .
  vars F G : Fn .
  var E : Elt .
  eq I0({}) = {} .
  eq I0({ E } + S) = { i0(E) } + I0(S) .
  eq I1({}) = {} .
  eq I1({ E } + S) = { i1(E) } + I1(S) .
  eq A ++ B = I0(A) U I1(B) .
  eq apex(ucone(A,B)) = A ++ B .
  eq base(ucone(A,B)) = << A ; B >> .
  cq j1(ucone(A,B)) of E = i0(E) if E in A .
  cq j2(ucone(A,B)) of E = i1(E) if E in B .
  cq umor(ucone(A,B),cone(F,G)) of E = F of i0inv(E)
      if i0pred(E) .
  cq umor(ucone(A,B),cone(F,G)) of E = G of i1inv(E)
      if i1pred(E) .
endo

*** CO2PROD-CAT-SET gives a coproduct
*** view CO2PROD-CAT-SET-AS-CO2PROD-TH[J :: 2INJ-TH]
***     from CO2PROD-TH[CAT-SET[J]] to CO2PROD-CAT-SET[J] endv
*** don't have parameterized views yet

*** constructions for the category of sets of integers
make CAT-SET-INT is CAT-SET[INT]*(op omega to ints) endm
```

```
*** coproduct in the category of sets of integers
make CO2PROD-CAT-SET-INT is
  CO2PROD-CAT-SET[view to INT is
      var I : Elt .
      op i0(I) to (2 * I) .
      op i0inv(I) to (I quo 2) .
      op i0pred(I) to (I rem 2 == 0) .
      op i1(I) to 1 + (2 * I) .
      op i1inv(I) to ((I - 1) quo 2) .
      op i1pred(I) to (I rem 2 == 1) .
    endv]
endm

*** this says the above really is a coproduct
view CO2PROD-CAT-SET-INT-VIEW
    from CO2PROD-TH[view to CAT-SET[INT] is
                        sort Obj to Set .
                        sort Mor to Fn .  endv]
    to CO2PROD-CAT-SET-INT is endv
*** note the view within view and empty body of outermost view

*** some test cases
obj CO2PROD-TEST is
  protecting CO2PROD-CAT-SET-INT .
  ops s1 s2 s3 s4 : -> Set [memo] .
  eq s1 = { 1 } .
  eq s2 = s1 U { 2 } .
  eq s3 = s2 U { 3 } .
  eq s4 = { 2 } U { 3 } .
  op g : -> Fn .
  eq g of 3 = 2 .
  eq g of 2 = 1 .
  eq d0 g = s4 .
  eq d1 g = s3 .
endo

reduce base(ucone(s1,s1)) .        ***> should be: <<{1};{1}>>
reduce apex(ucone(s1,s1)) .        ***> should be: {2,3}
reduce umor(ucone(s1,s1),cone(id s1,id s1)) of 2 .
  ***> should be: 1
reduce umor(ucone(s1,s1),cone(id s1,id s1)) of 3 .
  ***> should be: 1

reduce base(ucone(s2,s3)) .
  ***> should be: <<{1,2};{1,2,3}>>
reduce apex(ucone(s2,s3)) .
  ***> should be: {2,4,3,5,7}
reduce umor(ucone(s2,s3),cone(id s2,id s3)) of 2 .
  ***> should be: 1
```

```
reduce umor(ucone(s2,s3),cone(id s2,id s3)) of 4 .
  ***> should be: 2
reduce umor(ucone(s2,s3),cone(id s2,id s3)) of 3 .
  ***> should be: 1
reduce umor(ucone(s2,s3),cone(id s2,id s3)) of 5 .
  ***> should be: 2
reduce umor(ucone(s2,s3),cone(id s2,id s3)) of 7 .
  ***> should be: 3

reduce base(ucone(s4 ,s3)) .
  ***> should be: <<{2,3};{1,2,3}>>
reduce apex(ucone(s4,s3)) .
  ***> should be: {4,6,3,5,7}
reduce umor(ucone(s4,s3),cone(g,id s3)) of 4 .
  ***> should be: 1
reduce umor(ucone(s4,s3),cone(g,id s3)) of 6 .
  ***> should be: 2
reduce umor(ucone(s4,s3),cone(g,id s3)) of 3 .
  ***> should be: 1
reduce umor(ucone(s4,s3),cone(g,id s3)) of 5 .
  ***> should be: 2
reduce umor(ucone(s4,s3),cone(g,id s3)) of 7 .
  ***> should be: 3
```

Appendix D : Built-ins and the Standard Prelude

This Appendix gives details of how Lisp can be called from within OBJ3 programs, with a number of examples, including the complete OBJ3 standard prelude.

D.1   THE LISP INTERFACE

OBJ3 provides two ways to take advantage of the (Common-)Lisp underlying its implementation: *built-in sorts* and *built-in righthand sides* for rules; we call rules with such built-in righthand sides *built-in rules*.

Built-in sorts are sorts whose elements are constants represented by Lisp values. General mechanisms are provided for reading, printing, creating Lisp representations for, and testing sort membership for constants of these sorts. In general, built-in sorts can be used in any context where a non-built-in sort can be used, although a constant of a built-in sort cannot be the lefthand side of a rule.

The built-in rules come in two varieties, a simplified version that makes writing rules for operators defined on built-in sorts easy, and a general kind that allows arbitrary actions on the redex to be specified. However, to take full advantage of this latter type of rule, one must be familiar with the internal term representation of OBJ3 and the implementation functions for manipulating this representation. Built-in rules can be used wherever an ordinary rule can be.

D.1.1   Built-in Sorts.   Built-in sorts may contain any (countable) number of constants. For example, a version of NATS with a built-in sort Nat is equivalent to an idealized non-built-in version of the form

```
obj NATS is
  sort Nat .
  ops 0 1 2 3 4 5 6 7 8 9 10 11 12 13 ... : -> Nat .
  op _+_ : Nat Nat -> Nat .
  *** etc.
endo
```

with an infinite number of constants. (The name NATS is chosen to avoid clashing with the predefined object NAT.) Some other useful built-in sorts are floating-point numbers, identifiers, strings, and arrays.

Constants in a built-in sort have an associated Lisp representation. Such a built-in sort is introduced by a declaration of the form

> bsort ⟨*SortId*⟩
> (⟨*Token-Predicate*⟩ ⟨*Creator*⟩ ⟨*Printer*⟩ ⟨*Sort-Predicate*⟩) .

which gives the name of the sort, two Lisp functions for reading, a function for printing constants of the sort, and a predicate that can be used to test whether a Lisp value represents a constant of the given sort. A sort declaration of this kind can occur wherever an ordinary sort declaration can occur.

When an OBJ expression is read, it is first lexically analyzed into a sequence of tokens that are either special single character symbols, such as "(" and "]", or else are sequences of characters delimited by these special single character symbols or spaces. Internally, such tokens are represented by Lisp strings. For example, the representation of the token "37" is the Lisp string "37" of length two.

In more detail now:

- ⟨*Token-Predicate*⟩ is a Lisp predicate that can be applied to an input token (a Lisp string) to determine if the token is a representation of a value in the built-in sort (it is applied by funcall); for example, "37" from NATS should result in true and "A+B" in false. With this mechanism, the syntactic representation of a built-in constant can only be a single token.

- ⟨*Creator*⟩ is a Lisp function that will map a token (a Lisp string) to a Lisp representation for that token as a built-in constant. The Lisp function `read-from-string` is very useful as a creator function for built-in sorts that correspond directly to Lisp types. For example, "37" should be mapped to the Lisp value 37.

- ⟨*Printer*⟩ is a Lisp function that will print out the desired external representation of the internal Lisp value representing one of the built-in sort constants. The Lisp function `prin1` is very useful as a ⟨*Printer*⟩ function for printing out values that correspond directly to Lisp types. For example, 37 should be printed by printing the digit 3 followed by the digit 7. Because the user can define the printer function to meet particular needs, there is no assumption that this function is an inverse to the ⟨*Creator*⟩ function. Indeed, the syntactic representation of a built-in constant may involve many tokens, but then this representation cannot be read in as a built-in constant.

- ⟨*Sort-Predicate*⟩ is a Lisp predicate that is true only for Lisp values that are representations of constants in the built-in sort. For example, 3 should be considered to be in sort `Nat`, and -3 should not. The purpose and use of this predicate are discussed further below.

For example, to define `NATS` we might first define some Lisp functions, with

```
ev (progn
(defun obj_NATS$is_Nat_token (token)
  (every #'digit-char-p token))
(defun obj_NATS$create_Nat (token)
  (read-from-string token))
(defun obj_NATS$print_Nat (x) (prin1 x))
(defun obj_NATS$is_Nat (x)
  (and (integerp x) (<= 0 x))))
```

Then we can define

```
obj NATS is
  bsort Nat (obj_NATS$is_Nat_token obj_NATS$create_Nat
             obj_NATS$print_Nat obj_NATS$is_Nat) .
endo
```

which supports the natural number constants, as in

```
OBJ> red 100 .
reduce in NATS : 100
rewrites: 0
result Nat: 100
```

However, this object is not very useful, because no operators have been associated to the built-in sort.

Warning: A current implementation restriction does not allow a built-in constant to be the lefthand side of a rule. Built-in constants are always considered to be in reduced form, so that rule applications are never attempted on them.

D.1.2 Subsorts of Built-in Sorts. It is possible for a built-in sort to be a subsort of another built-in sort, but a non-built-in sort cannot be a subsort of a built-in sort. However, a non-built-in sort can be a supersort of a built-in sort. For the sort of newly created built-in constants to be properly assigned, a sort predicate must be provided for each built-in sort. An example of this will later be seen in a version of the rational numbers using Common Lisp rationals.

When there are built-in subsorts of the sort of a newly created built-in constant, then the sort that is assigned to the constant is determined by scanning the list of subsorts, applying the sort predicates to the Lisp value to determine if it lies in the corresponding subsort, and choosing the lowest acceptable sort as the sort of the constant. It is assumed that there is always a unique lowest sort. It is critical only that the sort predicate for a built-in sort should be false for values that are in supersorts of the built in sort. It is not necessary for it to be false for constants in subsorts of the given sort.

If there is no enclosing built-in supersort, then it can be the constant true, and have a definition like

```
(defun obj_NATS$is_Nat (x) t)
```

because the ⟨*Sort-Predicate*⟩ function will only be called for built-in constants of that sort (if it is called at all). This will not affect the operational behavior of OBJ in this case. However, it is better for the predicate to be exact in order to allow the easy incorporation of new supersorts.

D.1.3 Built-in Rules. Built-in rules provide a way of using Lisp expressions to perform computations. These are essential for the usefulness of built-in sorts, but they can also be used for non-built-in data. Built-in rules are either of a special *simple* form or else are *general*.

Simple built-in rules can be unconditional or conditional, with the syntax

```
bq ⟨Term⟩ = ⟨Lisp Expression⟩ . |
cbq ⟨Term⟩ = ⟨Lisp Expression⟩ if ⟨BoolTerm⟩ .
```

The key restriction on simple built-in rules is that *the sort of each variable appearing in the lefthand side must be a built-in sort.*

The lefthand side of these rule is matched against terms in exactly the usual fashion; also, in the conditional case, the condition is just an OBJ term, and it is treated in exactly the same way as a condition in a non-built-in rule. If a match is found for the variables in the lefthand side such that each variable matches a built-in constant (and the condition is satisfied if the built-in rule is conditional), then the righthand side is evaluated in a Lisp environment with Lisp variables having names corresponding to the OBJ variables (as usual in Common Lisp, the case, upper or lower, of variables in the Lisp expression is ignored) bound to the Lisp value of the built-in constants to which they were matched. Because the variables must match constants of the corresponding built-in sorts, a bottom-up evaluation strategy is necessary, regardless of the strategy specified for the operator. The sort of the lefthand side is usually a built-in sort, and in this case the Lisp value of the righthand side of the rule is automatically converted to a built-in constant of that sort. If the sort of the lefthand side is not a built-in sort, then, with one exception that will be mentioned next, the value of the righthand side should be a Lisp representation of a term of that sort (or a subsort of that sort). A special case is that, if the sort of the lefthand side is Bool, then the value of the righthand side Lisp expression can be any Lisp value that will be converted to a Boolean value by mapping nil to false and all other Lisp values to true. For this case, a special conversion is performed; this makes it very easy to define predicates.

As an example, consider

```
obj NATS is
  bsort Nat (obj_NATS$is_Nat_token obj_NATS$create_Nat
                obj_NATS$print_Nat obj_NATS$is_Nat) .
  op _+_ : Nat Nat -> Nat .
  vars M N : Nat .
  bq M + N = (+ M N) .
endo
```

We can then do the following reduction.

```
OBJ> red 123 + 321 .
reduce in NATS : 123 + 321
rewrites: 1
result Nat: 444
```

Because the matching of the lefthand side is done in the usual fashion, the operators appearing in the lefthand side can even be associative and commutative.

The *general* form of a built-in rule has the following syntax

```
bq ⟨Term⟩ = ⟨Lisp Expression⟩ . |
cbq ⟨Term⟩ = ⟨Lisp Expression⟩ if ⟨BoolTerm⟩ .
```

where now the variables in the lefthand side can have arbitrary sorts. The lefthand side and condition are treated as usual.

The process of applying the rule is a bit different in this case. The lefthand side is matched as usual creating the correspondence between variables in the lefthand side and subterms of the term being rewritten. The righthand side is evaluated in an environment where Lisp variables with names corresponding to the OBJ variables (case is ignored) are bound to the internal OBJ3 representation of the terms matched by the variables. The Lisp value of the righthand side is expected to be an internal OBJ3 representation of a term that then destructively replaces the top-level structure of the term matched. An exception is that, if the Lisp code evaluates the expression (obj$rewrite_fail), then the rewrite is aborted and the term is left unchanged. (This has the effect of making the rule conditional in an implicit way; the condition is checked in the Lisp code for the righthand side.) An additional feature is that the righthand side is evaluated in an environment where module is bound to the module that the rule comes from; this feature is necessary to correctly treat general built-in rules in instances of parameterized modules.

The following is a simple example:

```
obj NATS is
   bsort Nat (obj_NATS$is_Nat_token obj_NATS$create_Nat
                   obj_NATS$print_Nat obj_NATS$is_Nat) .
   op _+_ : Nat Nat -> Nat .
   vars M N : Nat .
   bq M + N = (+ M N) .
   op print _ : Nat -> Nat .
   bq print M =
       (progn (princ " = ") (term$print M) (terpri) M) .
endo
```

The operator print returns just its argument, but has the side-effect of printing the term resulting from evaluating its argument preceded by the "=" sign. For example,

```
red (print (3 + 2)) + 4 .
```

produces the following output from OBJ3:

```
==============================================
reduce in NATS : print (3 + 2) + 4
= 5
rewrites: 3
result Nat: 9
==============================================
```

The line containing "= 5" is the output produced by the use of `print`. Such print operators can be very useful; in many cases, one may want to add an extra argument that provides an output label. General built-in rules can be written to perform arbitrary transformations on a term using any of the functions defined in the OBJ3 implementation. Thus it is useful to be familiar with the functions provided by the implementation when writing such general built-in rules. Some basic functions are discussed below.

It is often useful to initialize some Lisp variables after certain OBJ objects are created. This can be done using `eval` or `ev`. There are examples of this in the OBJ3 standard prelude.

In general, the module that the rules are associated with may be an instance of a parameterized module. In this case, it is necessary to write the rules so that the extra parameter `module` is used to create structures within that module. When locating the correct instance of an operator one must first determine its module, then the sorts of its arguments and result, and then its name. In the case where there are no ambiguities, some simpler functions can be used, e.g., to find an operator based only on its name.

Functions that are useful for the general built-in rules are given below (note that these are all Lisp functions from the OBJ3 implementation). The Lisp functions will be described, in part, by giving declarations similar to OBJ operator declarations. Of course these need to be interpreted as informal descriptions of Lisp functions that may have side-effects and that manipulate particular Lisp representations of the values given as arguments.

The sorts that will be referred to are:

- `Bool, NzNat, Lisp-Value`
  `Bool`, `NzNat`, and `Lisp-Value` are OBJ sort names for the related standard Lisp types.

- `Sort-Name`
  A `Sort-Name` is a Lisp string naming a sort.

- `Op-Name`
  An `Op-Name` is a Lisp list of the tokens, represented as Lisp strings, that constitute the name of the operator. For example, the name of `_+_ : Nat Nat -> Nat` is `("_" "+" "_")`.

- Sort-Order
  A `Sort-Order` is a representation of a partial order on the sorts.

- `Sort, Operator, Term, Module, Module-Expression`
  `Sort, Operator, Term, Module,` and `Module-Expression` correspond to the Lisp representations of these sorts. Values of the sorts `Sort`, `Operator`, `Term`, and `Module` are composite objects with many components, some of which are likely not to be of interest here. For these

sorts, functions selecting the interesting features of the values are given below.

- `SortSet`
  SortSet is a set of sorts represented by a list.

- `LIST[Term], LIST[Sort]`
  LIST[–] indicates that the values so described will be Lisp lists of the specified sort.

The following functions are useful for term manipulation:

- `modexp_eval$eval : Module-Expression → Module`
  The argument can be the name of a specific named module, such as "INT". This can be used to find specific named modules.

- `sort$is_built_in : Sort → Bool`
  This predicate decides whether the sort given is a built-in sort.

- `module$sort_order : Module → Sort-Order`
  This selector provides access to the sort order for the given module, i.e., the representation of the sort structure.

- `sort_order$is_included_in : Sort-Order Sort Sort → Bool`
  This predicate decides if the first sort is a subsort of the second in the given sort order.

- `sort_order$is_strictly_included_in : Sort-Order Sort Sort → Bool`
  Same as above but excludes the case when two sorts are equal.

- `sort_order$lower_sorts : Sort-Order Sort → SortSet`
  This function produces a list of the sorts lower than a given sort in the given sort order.

- `mod_eval$$find_sort_in : Module Sort-Name → Sort`
  This function can be used to find the named sort in the given module. A typical sort name is `"'Int'"`.

- `sort$name : Sort → Sort-Name`
  This selector provides the name of a given sort.

- `operator$name : Operator → Op-Name`
  This selector provides the name of the given operator.

- `operator$is_same_operator : Operator Operator → Bool`
  This predicate decides if the two operators are the same operator.

- `operator$arity` : `Operator → LIST[Sort]`
  This selector provides the arity of the given operator as a list of sorts, which may be `nil`.

- `operator$coarity` : `Operator → Sort`
  This selector provides the co-arity of the given operator.

- `mod_eval$$find_operator_in` :
  `Module Op-Name LIST[Sort] Sort → Operator`
  This function locates the operator with the given name, arity (list of sorts) and coarity (value sort), or returns `nil` if there is none such.

- `mod_eval$$find_operator_named_in` :
  `Module Op-Name → Operator`
  This function attempts to locate an operator purely based on its name.

- `term$is_var` : `Term → Bool`
  This predicate decides if a term is a variable. It may be that the terms that you are manipulating are primarily be ground terms, but, in general, it is preferable to consider the case of variables in the definitions of functions.

- `term$is_constant` : `Term → Bool`
  This predicate decides if a term is a constant.

- `term$head` : `Term → Operator`
  This function produces the operator that is the head operator of a non-variable term. It is an error to apply this function to a term that is a variable.

- `term$subterms` : `Term → LIST[Term]`
  This function produces the list of top-level subterms of the given term.

- `term$make_term` : `Operator LIST[Term] → Term`
  This function creates a new term with the given head operator and list of arguments.

- `term$make_term_with_sort_check` :
  `Operator LIST[Term] → Term`
  This function is similar to the last, but may replace the operator with a lower operator in the case of overloading. If there is a lower overloaded operator whose arity fits the sorts of the given arguments, then this operator will be used instead of the given operator.

- `term$arg_n` : `Term NzNat → Term`
  This function gives easy access to the n-th (counting from 1) top-level argument of the given term.

■ `term$sort : Term → Sort`
This function computes the sort of a term whether or not it is a variable.

■ `term$is_reduced : Term → Bool`
This function checks whether or not the term has been marked as fully reduced. This flag is updated by side-effect.

■ `term$!replace : Term Term → Term`
The Lisp representation for the first argument term is destructively altered in such a way that it will appear to have the same term structure as the second term argument. The altered representation of the first term is returned.

■ `term$!update_lowest_parse_on_top : Term → Term`
This will update the sort of the term, for example, when a subterm has been altered so that it now has a lower sort.

■ `term$retract_if_needed : Sort-Order Term Sort → Term`
This function either returns the term, or a retract applied to the term depending on whether or not the sort of the term is included in the given sort.

■ `term$is_built_in_constant : Term → Bool`
This predicate decides if the term is a built-in constant or not.

■ `term$similar : Term Term → Bool`
Tests if the two terms have the same term structure without taking attributes into account.

■ `term$equational_equal : Term → Bool`
Tests if the terms have the equivalent structure taking attributes into account.

■ `term$make_built_in_constant : Sort Lisp-Value → Term`
This function creates a *term* which is a built-in constant for the given built-in sort and Lisp value. The sort predicate for the built-in sort is not applied.

■ `term$make_built_in_constant_with_sort_check :`
`Sort Lisp-Value → Term`
Similar to above, but may replace the given sort by a lower sort.

■ `term$built_in_value : Term → Lisp-Value`
This function produces the Lisp value from a built-in constant.

- `obj_BOOL$is_true : Term → Bool`
  This function tests whether the term given as its argument is the constant `true`. The value is a Lisp boolean, i.e. `T` for `true` and `NIL` for `false`.

- `rew$!normalize : Term → Term`
  This is the OBJ evaluation function. The term given as an argument is reduced and is updated by side-effect as well as being returned as the value of the function.

The following functions are specific to terms where the top operator is associative (A) or associative-commutative (AC):

- `term$list_assoc_subterms : Term Operator → LIST[Term]`
  This function computes the list of subterms of the given term that are on the fringe of the tree at the top of the term the nodes of which are all terms headed with the given associative operator or operators overloaded by this operator. This can be the whole term.

- `term$list_AC_subterms : Term Operator → LIST[Term]`
  Similar to the above, but for associative-commutative (AC) operators.

- `term$make_right_assoc_normal_form :`
  `Operator LIST[Term] → Term`
  This function builds a term from the given associative operator and the list of terms by building a right-associated binary tree.

- `term$make_right_assoc_normal_form_with_sort_check :`
  `Operator LIST[Term] → Term`
  Similar to the above, but may replace the operator by lower operators.

The predefined object `BUILT-IN` (see Section D.3) allows the creation of built-in subterms of righthand sides of rules. The default syntax is "`built-in:` ⟨*Lisp*⟩", where the Lisp expression represents a function, to be `funcall`-ed, that takes one argument, which is a substitution, and produces two values, a term which is the intended instantiation for this subterm, and a success indicator . In general, it will be necessary to deal with the incompatibility of the sort `Built-in` with the sorts of other operators in the righthand side. Here is a sketch of a use of this feature:

```
op r : Universal -> A .
var X : A .
eq f(X) = X + r(built-in:
                (lambda (u) (create-term u))) .
eq r(X) = X .
```

Note that "`built-in:`" is now a very special keyword, and cannot be used in any other context, though this can be disabled by

```
ev (setq obj_BUILT-IN$keyword nil) .
```

D.2   EXAMPLES

We now give a number of somewhat larger examples, including cells (which have internal memory), arrays of integers, and an efficient sorting program. Other examples appear in the standard prelude, although the Lisp code used in the standard prelude is not given in this paper.

D.2.1   Cells.   The basic idea of this example is very simple, namely to provide a parameterized object that creates *cells* containing values of a given sort. Such cells are an abstract version of procedural variables that can be modified by side-effects or destructive assignments. Of course, this module is not functional.

```
*** obj code for cells

ev (defun set-cell-rule (i x) (setf (cadr i) x) i)

obj CELL[X :: TRIV] is
  sort Cell .
  op cell _ : Elt -> Cell .
  op new-cell _ : Elt -> Cell .
  op val _ : Cell -> Elt .
  op set _ _ : Cell Elt -> Cell .
  var I : Cell .
  var X : Elt .
  eq new-cell X = cell X .
  eq val (cell  X) = X .
  beq set I X = (set-cell-rule I X) .
endo

*** sample program using this
obj TEST is
  pr CELL[INT] .

  sort A .
  subsort Int Cell < A .
  op _|_ : A A -> A .

  op dbl _ : A -> A .
  op incr _ : A -> A .
```

```
    var U V : A .
    var C : Cell .

    eq dbl U = U | U .
    eq incr (U | V) = (incr U) | (incr V) .
    eq incr C = val (set C (1 + (val C))) .
  endo

  red incr (dbl (dbl (dbl (new-cell 0)))) .
  *** result A: ((1 | 2) | (3 | 4)) | ((5 | 6) | (7 | 8))
```

D.2.2   Arrays of Integers.   The following code provides arrays of integers that can be modified by side-effect. This might be useful for a functional program for table-lookup (side-effects would only be used for building the table).

```
    ev
    (defun arrayint$print (x)
      (princ "[")
      (dotimes (i (length x))
        (when (< 0 i) (princ ",")) (print$check)
        (prin1 (aref x i)))
      (princ "]"))

    obj ARRAYINT is
      pr INT .
      bsort ArrayInt ((lambda (x) nil) (lambda (x) (break))
                      arrayint$print (lambda (x) t)) .

      op make-array : Nat Int -> ArrayInt .
      op length _ : ArrayInt -> Nat .
      op _[_] : ArrayInt Nat -> Int .
      op _[_] := _ : ArrayInt Nat Int -> ArrayInt .

      var A : ArrayInt .
      var I : Int .
      var N : Nat .
      bq make-array(N,I) =
           (make-array (list N) :initial-element I) .
      bq length(A) = (length A) .
      bq A[N] = (aref A N) .
      bq A[N] := I = (progn (setf (aref A N) I) A) .
    endo
```

The commands

```
red make-array(10,1) .
red (make-array(10,1))[5] .
red (make-array(10,1))[5] := 33 .
```

produce the following output:

```
============================================
reduce in ARRAYINT : make-array(10,1)
rewrites: 1
result ArrayInt: [1,1,1,1,1,1,1,1,1,1]
============================================
reduce in ARRAYINT : make-array(10,1)[5]
rewrites: 2
result NzNat: 1
============================================
reduce in ARRAYINT : make-array(10,1)[5]:= 33
rewrites: 2
result ArrayInt: [1,1,1,1,1,33,1,1,1,1]
============================================
```

D.2.3   Sorting. This example defines a parameterized sorting module. The parameter provides the partial order used and the sorting is done using the Lisp function `sort`. A small point of some interest is that an operator named `_<<_` is introduced as an alias for the parameter operator `_ < _` simply to provide an easy way to locate the parameter operator after instantiation. This is needed because the name of a parameter operator cannot be known for an instance of the parameterized module, where such a parameter may have been mapped to an arbitrary term by the view defining the instantiation. For similar reasons, the operator `_<<_` as well as the other operators `_,_` and `empty` appearing in the parameterized SORT module below should not be renamed by a module renaming.

   As usual, the parameter of our sorting module is the theory of partially ordered sets:

```
th POSET is
  sort Elt .
  op _<_ : Elt Elt -> Bool .
  vars E1 E2 E3 : Elt .
  eq E1 < E1 = false .
  cq E1 < E3 = true if E1 < E2 and E2 < E3 .
endth
```

The Lisp function `sort-list` used in the SORT module below has two arguments, a module (namely the given instantiation of the parameterized module SORT) and a list to be sorted. Its definition is as follows:

```
ev
; NOTE: sort-list will not work if any of the operators
; found by name, i.e. _<<_, empty, and _,_, below are
; renamed in a module renaming.

(defun sort-list (mod l)
  (let ((test (mod_eval$$find_operator_named_in
                mod '("_" "<<" "_")))
        (empty (mod_eval$$find_operator_named_in
                 mod '("empty")))
        (conc (mod_eval$$find_operator_named_in
                mod '("_" "," "_"))))
    (if (eq empty (term$head l))
        l
      (let ((sorted (sort
                      (term$list_assoc_subterms l conc)
                      #'(lambda (x y)
                          (obj_BOOL$is_true
                           (rew$!normalize
                            (term$make_term test
                             (list x y)))))
                      )))
        (term$make_right_assoc_normal_form_with_sort_check
         conc sorted)
        ))
    ))
```

We are now ready to define a parameterized sorting module with a built-in equation involving the `sort-list` function:

```
obj SORT[ORDER :: POSET] is
  sort List .
  subsort Elt < List .
  op empty : -> List .
  op _,_ : List List -> List [assoc idr: empty] .
  op sort _ : List -> List .
  op _<<_ : Elt Elt -> Bool .
  vars E1 E2 : Elt .
  eq E1 << E2 = E1 < E2 .
  var L : List .
  beq sort L = (sort-list module L) .
endo
```

Here is a sample reduction for sorting lists of integers.

```
obj TEST is pr SORT[INT] . endo
```

```
red sort (9, 8, 7, 6, 5, 4, 3, 2, 1, 0) .
***> result List: 0,1,2,3,4,5,6,7,8,9
```

D.3   THE STANDARD PRELUDE

Before giving the prelude, we comment on some changes since Release 1
ıf OBJ3:

- The module THAT has been renamed to LAST-TERM, and the operator
  [that] has been renamed to [term].

- The module RAT has been slightly changed so that the built-in constant
  values are printed like 1/2, rather than 1 / 2, and the same syntax (1/2)
  can be used for the input of these constants. (Previously, there was no
  syntax for the input of these constants.)

- The object BUILT-IN has been modified to allow the creation of built-in
  subterms of right sides of rules, as discussed in Section D.1.

- A object LISP has been added. It provides a built-in Lisp sort. The
  default syntax is "lisp: ⟨*Lisp*⟩". This can be used to allow the use of
  string data with Lisp syntax for the strings. The keyword that introduces
  the data (above "lisp:") can be changed to be some other symbol
  by setq-ing the variable obj_LISP$keyword to that other token (e.g.
  "string:"). Note that "lisp:" is now a very special keyword, and
  ·annot be used in any other context (this can be disabled by "ev (setq
     ·ᵀᶜᴾ$keyword nil)").

What follows is the exact text of the standard prelude that is used to build OBJ3; it uses many Lisp functions that are not defined here, but rather in another file.

```
--- OBJ standard prelude

ev (setq *obj$include_BOOL* nil)

obj UNIVERSAL is
  sort Universal .
endo

ev (progn (obj_UNIVERSAL$install) 'done)

obj ERR is
 bsort Err
   (obj_ERR$is_Err_token
    obj_ERR$create_Err
    obj_ERR$print_Err
    obj_ERR$is_Err) .
endo

ev (progn (obj_ERR$install) 'done)

obj BUILT-IN is
 bsort Built-in
   (obj_BUILT-IN$is_Built-in_token
    obj_BUILT-IN$create_Built-in
    obj_BUILT-IN$print_Built-in
    obj_BUILT-IN$is_Built-in) .
endo

ev (progn (obj_BUILT-IN$install) 'done)

obj LISP is
 bsort Lisp
   (obj_LISP$is_Lisp_token
    obj_LISP$create_Lisp
    obj_LISP$print_Lisp
    obj_LISP$is_Lisp) .
endo
```

```
obj TRUTH-VALUE is
  sort Bool .
  op false : -> Bool .
  op true : -> Bool .
endo

obj TRUTH is
  pr TRUTH-VALUE .
  pr UNIVERSAL .
  op if_then_else_fi :
      Bool Universal Universal -> Universal
      [polymorphic obj_BOOL$if_resolver
        intrinsic strategy (1 0)
        gather (& & &) prec 0] .
  op _==_ : Universal Universal -> Bool
      [polymorphic obj_BOOL$eqeq_resolver
        strategy (1 2 0) prec 51] .
  op _=/=_ : Universal Universal -> Bool
      [polymorphic obj_BOOL$non-eqeq_resolver
        strategy (1 2 0) prec 51] .
  ev (obj_TRUTH$setup)
  var XU YU : Universal .
  eq if true then XU else YU fi = XU .
  eq if false then XU else YU fi = YU .
  ev (obj_TRUTH$install)
  beq XU == YU =
      (obj_BOOL$coerce_to_Bool
        (term$equational_equal XU YU)) .
  beq XU =/= YU =
      (obj_BOOL$coerce_to_Bool
        (not (term$equational_equal XU YU))) .
  ev (obj_TRUTH$install)
endo

obj BOOL is
  pr TRUTH .
  op _and_ : Bool Bool -> Bool [assoc comm idr: true
strat (1 2 0)
gather (e E) prec 55] .
  op _or_ : Bool Bool -> Bool [assoc comm idr: false
strat (1 2 0)
gather (e E) prec 59] .
```

```
  op _xor_ : Bool Bool -> Bool [assoc comm idr: false
strat (1 2 0)
gather (e E) prec 57] .
  op not_ : Bool -> Bool [prec 53] .
  op _implies_ : Bool Bool -> Bool [gather (e E) prec 61] .
  ev (obj_BOOL$setup)
  vars A B : Bool .
  eq not true = false .
  eq not false = true .
  eq false and A = false .
  eq true or A = true .
  eq A implies B = (not A) or B .
  eq true xor true = false .
endo

obj IDENTICAL is
  pr BOOL .
  op _===_ : Universal Universal -> Bool
       [strategy (0) prec 51] .
  op _=/==_ : Universal Universal -> Bool
       [strategy (0) prec 51] .
  var XU YU : Universal .
  bq XU === YU =
     (obj_BOOL$coerce_to_Bool (term$similar XU YU)) .
  bq XU =/== YU =
     (obj_BOOL$coerce_to_Bool (not (term$similar XU YU))) .
endo

ev (progn (obj_IDENTICAL$setup) 'done)

obj LAST-TERM is
  protecting UNIVERSAL .
  protecting TRUTH-VALUE .
  op last-term-undefined : -> Universal .
  op [term] : -> Universal .
  eq [term] = last-term-undefined .
endo

ev (progn (obj_LAST-TERM$install) 'done)
```

```
obj NZNAT is
  bsort NzNat
    (obj_NZNAT$is_NzNat_token obj_NZNAT$create_NzNat prin1
     obj_NZNAT$is_NzNat) .
  protecting BOOL .
  op _+_ : NzNat NzNat -> NzNat [assoc comm prec 33] .
  op d : NzNat NzNat -> NzNat [comm] .
  op _*_ : NzNat NzNat -> NzNat
     [assoc comm idr: 1 prec 31] .
  op quot : NzNat NzNat -> NzNat [gather (E e) prec 31] .
  op _<_ : NzNat NzNat -> Bool [prec 51] .
  op _<=_ : NzNat NzNat -> Bool [prec 51] .
  op _>_ : NzNat NzNat -> Bool [prec 51] .
  op _>=_ : NzNat NzNat -> Bool [prec 51] .
  op s_ : NzNat -> NzNat [prec 15] .
  vars NN NM : NzNat .
  bq NN + NM = (+ NN NM) .
  bq d(NN,NM) = (if (= NN NM) 1 (abs (- NN NM))) .
  bq NN * NM = (* NN NM) .
  bq quot(NN,NM) = (if (> NN NM) (truncate NN NM) 1) .
  bq NN < NM = (< NN NM) .
  bq NN <= NM = (<= NN NM) .
  bq NN > NM = (> NN NM) .
  bq NN >= NM = (>= NN NM) .
  bq s NN = (1+ NN) .
jbo

obj NAT is
  bsort Nat
    (obj_NAT$is_Nat_token obj_NAT$create_Nat prin1
     obj_NAT$is_Nat) .
  protecting NZNAT .
  bsort Zero
    (obj_NAT$is_Zero_token obj_NAT$create_Zero prin1
     obj_NAT$is_Zero) .
  subsorts NzNat < Nat .
  subsorts Zero < Nat .
  op _+_ : Nat Nat -> Nat [assoc comm idr: 0 prec 33] .
  op sd : Nat Nat -> Nat [comm] .
  op _*_ : Nat Nat -> Nat [assoc comm idr: 1 prec 31] .
  op _quo_ : Nat NzNat -> Nat [gather (E e) prec 31] .
  op _rem_ : Nat NzNat -> Nat [gather (E e) prec 31] .
```

```
    op _divides_ : NzNat Nat -> Bool [prec 51] .
    op _<_ : Nat Nat -> Bool [prec 51] .
    op _<=_ : Nat Nat -> Bool [prec 51] .
    op _>_ : Nat Nat -> Bool [prec 51] .
    op _>=_ : Nat Nat -> Bool [prec 51] .
    op s_ : Nat -> NzNat [prec 15] .
    op p_ : NzNat -> Nat [prec 15] .
    var M N : Nat .
    var NN : NzNat .
*** eq N + 0 = N .
  bq sd(M,N) = (abs (- M N)) .
  eq N * 0 = 0 .
  bq M quo NN = (truncate M NN) .
  bq M rem NN = (rem M NN) .
  bq NN divides M = (= 0 (rem M NN)) .
  eq N < 0 = false .
  eq 0 < NN = true .
  eq NN <= 0 = false .
  eq 0 <= N = true .
  eq 0 > N = false .
  eq NN > 0 = true .
  eq 0 >= NN = false .
  eq N >= 0 = true .
  eq s 0 = 1 .
  bq p NN = (- NN 1) .
jbo

obj INT is
  bsort Int
    (obj_INT$is_Int_token obj_INT$create_Int prin1
     obj_INT$is_Int) .
  bsort NzInt
    (obj_INT$is_NzInt_token obj_INT$create_NzInt prin1
     obj_INT$is_NzInt) .
  protecting NAT .
  subsorts Nat < Int .
  subsorts NzNat < NzInt < Int .
  op -_ : Int -> Int [prec 15] .
  op -_ : NzInt -> NzInt [prec 15] .
  op _+_ : Int Int -> Int [assoc comm idr: 0 prec 33] .
  op _-_ : Int Int -> Int [gather (E e) prec 33] .
  op _*_ : Int Int -> Int [assoc comm idr: 1 prec 31] .
```

```
 op _*_ : NzInt NzInt -> NzInt
    [assoc comm idr: 1 prec 31] .
 op _quo_ : Int NzInt -> Int [gather (E e) prec 31] .
 op _rem_ : Int NzInt -> Int [gather (E e) prec 31].
 op _divides_ : NzInt Int -> Bool [prec 51] .
 op _<_ : Int Int -> Bool [prec 51] .
 op _<=_ : Int Int -> Bool [prec 51] .
 op _>_ : Int Int -> Bool [prec 51] .
 op _>=_ : Int Int -> Bool [prec 51] .
 op s_ : Int -> Int [prec 15] .
 vars I J : Int .
 var NJ : NzInt .
 bq - I = (- I) .
 bq I + J = (+ I J) .
*** bq I - J = (- I J) .
 eq I - J = I + (- J) .
 bq I * J = (* I J) .
 bq I quo NJ = (truncate I NJ) .
 bq I rem NJ = (rem I NJ) .
 bq NJ divides I = (= 0 (rem I NJ)) .
 bq I < J = (< I J) .
 bq I <= J = (<= I J) .
 bq I > J = (> I J) .
 bq I >= J = (>= I J) .
 eq s I = 1 + I .
jbo

obj RAT is
  bsort Rat
    (obj_RAT$is_Rat_token obj_RAT$create_Rat obj_RAT$print
    rationalp) .
  bsort NzRat
    (obj_RAT$is_NzRat_token obj_RAT$create_NzRat
    obj_RAT$print obj_RAT$is_NzRat) .
  protecting INT .
  subsorts Int < Rat .
  subsorts NzInt < NzRat < Rat .
  op -_ : Rat -> Rat [prec 15] .
  op -_ : NzRat -> NzRat [prec 15] .
  op _+_ : Rat Rat -> Rat [assoc comm idr: 0 prec 33] .
  op _-_ : Rat Rat -> Rat [gather (E e) prec 33] .
  op _*_ : Rat Rat -> Rat [assoc comm idr: 1 prec 31] .
```

```
  op _*_ : NzRat NzRat -> NzRat
    [assoc comm idr: 1 prec 31] .
  op _/_ : Rat NzRat -> Rat [gather (E e) prec 31] .
  op _/_ : NzRat NzRat -> NzRat [gather (E e) prec 31] .
  op _rem_ : Rat NzRat -> Rat [gather (E e) prec 31] .
  op _<_ : Rat Rat -> Bool [prec 51] .
  op _<=_ : Rat Rat -> Bool [prec 51] .
  op _>_ : Rat Rat -> Bool [prec 51] .
  op _>=_ : Rat Rat -> Bool [prec 51] .
  vars R S : Rat .
  vars NS : NzRat .
  bq - R = (- R) .
  bq R + S = (+ R S) .
*** bq R - S = (- R S) .
  eq R - S = R + (- S) .
  bq R * S = (* R S) .
  bq R / NS = (/ R NS) .
  bq R rem NS = (rem R NS) .
  bq R < S = (< R S) .
  bq R <= S = (<= R S) .
  bq R > S = (> R S) .
  bq R >= S = (>= R S) .
jbo

obj ID is
 bsort Id (obj_ID$is_Id_token obj_ID$create_Id
           obj_ID$print_Id obj_ID$is_Id) .
 pr BOOL .
 op _<_ : Id Id -> Bool [prec 51] .
 var !X !Y : Id .
 --- the variable names have been chosen so that
 --- they are not Id's
 bq !X < !Y = (string< !X !Y) .
endo

obj QID is
 --- Quoted IDentifier
 --- symbols starting with ' character
 bsort Id (obj_QID$is_Id_token obj_QID$create_Id
           obj_QID$print_Id obj_QID$is_Id) .
endo
```

```
obj QIDL is
 protecting QID .
 pr BOOL .
 op _<_ : Id Id -> Bool [prec 51] .
 var X Y : Id .
 bq X < Y = (string< X Y) .
endo

th TRIV is
  sort Elt .
endth

obj FLOAT is
 bsort Float
   (obj_FLOAT$is_Float_token obj_FLOAT$create_Float
    obj_FLOAT$print_Float obj_FLOAT$is_Float) .
 pr BOOL .

 op -_ : Float -> Float [prec 15] .
 op _+_ : Float Float -> Float [assoc comm prec 33] .
 op _-_ : Float Float -> Float [gather (E e) prec 33] .
 op _*_ : Float Float -> Float [assoc comm prec 31] .
 op _/_ : Float Float -> Float [gather (E e) prec 31] .
 op _rem_ : Float Float -> Float [gather (E e) prec 31] .
 op exp : Float -> Float .
 op log : Float -> Float .
 op sqrt : Float -> Float .
 op abs : Float -> Float .
 op sin : Float -> Float .
 op cos : Float -> Float .
 op atan : Float -> Float .
 op pi : -> Float .
 op _<_ : Float Float -> Bool [prec 51] .
 op _<=_ : Float Float -> Bool [prec 51] .
 op _>_ : Float Float -> Bool [prec 51] .
 op _>=_ : Float Float -> Bool [prec 51] .
 op _=[_]_ : Float Float Float -> Bool [prec 51] .

 vars X Y Z : Float .
 bq X + Y = (+ X Y) .
 bq - X = (- X) .
 bq X - Y = (- X Y) .
```

```
 bq X * Y = (* X Y) .
 bq X / Y = (/ X Y) .
 bq X rem Y = (rem X Y) .
 bq exp(X) = (exp X) .
 bq log(X) = (log X) .
 bq sqrt(X) = (sqrt X) .
 bq abs(X) = (abs X) .
 bq sin(X) = (sin X) .
 bq cos(X) = (cos X) .
 bq atan(X) = (atan X) .
 bq pi = pi .
 bq X < Y = (< X Y) .
 bq X <= Y = (<= X Y) .
 bq X > Y = (> X Y) .
 bq X >= Y = (>= X Y) .
 bq (X =[ Z ] Y) = (< (abs (- X Y)) Z) .
endo

obj 2TUPLE[C1 :: TRIV, C2 :: TRIV] is
  sort 2Tuple .
  op <<_;_>> : Elt.C1 Elt.C2 -> 2Tuple .
  op 1*_ : 2Tuple -> Elt.C1 .
  op 2*_ : 2Tuple -> Elt.C2 .
  var e1 : Elt.C1 .
  var e2 : Elt.C2 .
  eq 1* << e1 ; e2 >> = e1 .
  eq 2* << e1 ; e2 >> = e2 .
endo

obj 3TUPLE[C1 :: TRIV, C2 :: TRIV, C3 :: TRIV] is
  sort 3Tuple .
  op <<_;_;_>> : Elt.C1 Elt.C2 Elt.C3 -> 3Tuple .
  op 1*_ : 3Tuple -> Elt.C1 .
  op 2*_ : 3Tuple -> Elt.C2 .
  op 3*_ : 3Tuple -> Elt.C3 .
  var e1 : Elt.C1 .
  var e2 : Elt.C2 .
  var e3 : Elt.C3 .
  eq 1* << e1 ; e2 ; e3 >> = e1 .
  eq 2* << e1 ; e2 ; e3 >> = e2 .
  eq 3* << e1 ; e2 ; e3 >> = e3 .
endo
```

```
obj 4TUPLE[C1 :: TRIV, C2 :: TRIV,
          C3 :: TRIV, C4 :: TRIV] is
  sort 4Tuple .
  op <<_;_;_;_>> : Elt.C1 Elt.C2 Elt.C3 Elt.C4 -> 4Tuple .
  op 1*_ : 4Tuple -> Elt.C1 .
  op 2*_ : 4Tuple -> Elt.C2 .
  op 3*_ : 4Tuple -> Elt.C3 .
  op 4*_ : 4Tuple -> Elt.C4 .
  var e1 : Elt.C1 .
  var e2 : Elt.C2 .
  var e3 : Elt.C3 .
  var e4 : Elt.C4 .
  eq 1* << e1 ; e2 ; e3 ; e4 >> = e1 .
  eq 2* << e1 ; e2 ; e3 ; e4 >> = e2 .
  eq 3* << e1 ; e2 ; e3 ; e4 >> = e3 .
  eq 4* << e1 ; e2 ; e3 ; e4 >> = e4 .
endo

ev (setq *obj$include_BOOL* t)
ev (progn (obj$prelude_install) 'done)
```

References

[1]   Hitoshi Aida, Joseph Goguen, Sany Leinwand, Patrick Lincoln, José Meseguer, Babak Taheri, and Timothy Winkler. Simulation and performance estimation for the Rewrite Rule Machine. In *Proceedings, Fourth Symposium on the Frontiers of Massively Parallel Computation*, pages 336–344. IEEE, October 1992.

[2]   Hitoshi Aida, Joseph Goguen, and José Meseguer. Compiling concurrent rewriting onto the rewrite rule machine. In Stéphane Kaplan and Misuhiro Okada, editors, *Conditional and Typed Rewriting Systems*, pages 320–332. Springer, 1991. Lecture Notes in Computer Science, Volume 516; also, Technical Report SRI-CSL-90-03, Computer Science Lab, SRI International, February, 1990.

[3]   Antonio Alencar and Joseph Goguen. OOZE: An object-oriented Z environment. In Pierre America, editor, *European Conference on Object Oriented Programming*. Springer, 1991. Lecture Notes in Computer Science, Volume 512.

[4]   Franz Baader and Tobias Nipkow. *Term Rewriting and All That*. Cambridge, 1998.

[5]   Eugenio Battiston, Fiorella De Cindio, and Giancarlo Mauri. OBJSA net systems: a class of high-level nets having objects as domains. In Joseph Goguen and Grant Malcolm, editors, *Software Engineering with OBJ: Algebraic Specification in Action*. Kluwer, to appear.

[6]   Jan Bergstra and John Tucker. Characterization of computable data types by means of a finite equational specification method. In Jaco de Bakker and Jan van Leeuwen, editors, *Automata, Languages and Programming, Seventh Colloquium*, pages 76–90. Springer, 1980. Lecture Notes in Computer Science, Volume 81.

[7]   Rod Burstall. Programming with modules as typed functional programming. *Proceedings, International Conference on Fifth Generation Computing Systems*, 1985.

[8]   Rod Burstall and Joseph Goguen. Putting theories together to make specifications. In Raj Reddy, editor, *Proceedings, Fifth International Joint Conference on Artificial Intelligence*, pages 1045–1058. Department of Computer Science, Carnegie-Mellon University, 1977.

[9]   Rod Burstall and Joseph Goguen. The semantics of Clear, a specification language. In Dines Bjorner, editor, *Proceedings, 1979 Copenhagen Winter School on Abstract Software Specification*, pages 292–332. Springer, 1980. Lecture Notes in Computer Science, Volume 86; based on unpublished notes handed out at the Symposium on Algebra and Applications, Stefan Banach Center, Warsaw, Poland, 1978.

[10]   Rod Burstall and Joseph Goguen. An informal introduction to specifications using Clear. In Robert Boyer and J Moore, editors, *The Correctness Problem in Computer Science*, pages 185–213. Academic, 1981. Reprinted in *Software Specification Techniques*, Narain Gehani and Andrew McGettrick, editors, Addison-Wesley, 1985, pages 363–390.

[11]   Rod Burstall and Joseph Goguen. Algebras, theories and freeness: An introduction for computer scientists. In Martin Wirsing and Gunther Schmidt, editors, *Theoretical Foundations of Programming Methodology*, pages 329–350. Reidel, 1982. Proceedings, 1981 Marktoberdorf NATO Summer School, NATO Advanced Study Institute Series, Volume C91.

[12]   Rod Burstall and Butler Lampson. A kernel language for abstract data types and modules. In Giles Kahn, David MacQueen, and Gordon Plotkin, editors, *Proceedings, International Symposium on the Semantics of Data Types*, volume 173 of *Lecture Notes in Computer Science*, pages 1–50. Springer, 1984.

[13] Rod Burstall, David MacQueen, and Donald Sannella. Hope: an experimental applicative language. In *Proceedings, First LISP Conference*, volume 1, pages 136–143. Stanford University, 1980.

[14] Carlo Cavenathi, Marco De Zanet, and Giancarlo Mauri. MC-OBJ: a C interpreter for OBJ. *Note di Software*, 36/37:16–26, October 1988. In Italian.

[15] Thomas Cheatham. The introduction of definitional facilities into higher level programming languages. In *Proceedings, AFIPS Fall Joint Computer Conference*, pages 623–637. Spartan Books, 1966.

[16] Manuel Clavel, Steven Eker, Patrick Lincoln, and José Meseguer. Principles of Maude. In José Meseguer, editor, *Proceedings, First International Workshop on Rewriting Logic and its Applications*. Elsevier Science, 1996. Volume 4, *Electronic Notes in Theoretical Computer Science*.

[17] Manuel Clavel, Steven Eker, and José Meseguer. Current design and implementation of the Cafe prover and Knuth-Bendix tools, 1997. Presented at CafeOBJ Workshop, Kanazawa, October 1997.

[18] Manuel Clavel and José Meseguer. Reflection and strategies in rewriting logic. In José Meseguer, editor, *Proceedings, First International Workshop on Rewriting Logic and its Applications*. Elsevier Science, 1996. Volume 4, *Electronic Notes in Theoretical Computer Science*.

[19] CoFI.   CASL   summary,   1999.
      http://www.brics.dk/Projects/CoFi/.

[20] Derek Coleman, Robin Gallimore, and Victoria Stavridou. The design of a rewrite rule interpreter from algebraic specifications. *IEE Software Engineering Journal*, July:95–104, 1987.

[21] Hubert Comon. *Unification et Disunification: Théories et Applications*. PhD thesis, Université de l'Institut Polytechnique de Grenoble, 1988.

[22] Department of Defense. Reference manual for the Ada programming language. United States Government, Report ANSI/MIL-STD-1815A, 1983.

[23] Nachum Dershowitz and Jean-Pierre Jouannaud. Notations for rewriting. *Bulletin of the European Association for Theoretical Computer Science*, 43:162–172, 1990.

[24] Nachum Dershowitz and Jean-Pierre Jouannaud. Rewriting systems. In Jan van Leeuwen, editor, *Handbook of Theoretical Computer Science, Volume B: Formal Methods and Semantics*, pages 243–320. North-Holland, 1990.

[25]   Răzvan Diaconescu. *Category-based Semantics for Equational and Constraint Logic Programming*. PhD thesis, Programming Research Group, Oxford University, 1994.

[26]   Răzvan Diaconescu and Kokichi Futatsugi. *CafeOBJ Report: The Language, Proof Techniques, and Methodologies for Object-Oriented Algebraic Specification*. World Scientific, 1998. AMAST Series in Computing, Volume 6.

[27]   Răzvan Diaconescu and Kokichi Futatsugi. Logical foundations of CafeOBJ, 1999. Submitted for publication.

[28]   David Duce. Concerning the compatibility of PHIGS and GKS. In Joseph Goguen and Grant Malcolm, editors, *Software Engineering with OBJ: Algebraic Specification in Action*. Kluwer, to appear.

[29]   Hartmut Ehrig and Bernd Mahr. *Fundamentals of Algebraic Specification 1: Equations and Initial Semantics*. Springer, 1985. EATCS Monographs on Theoretical Computer Science, Volume 6.

[30]   Kokichi Futatsugi. Hierarchical software development in HISP. In T. Kitagawa, editor, *Computer Science and Technologies 1982*, pages 151–174. OHMSA/North Holland, 1982. Japan Annual Review in Electronics, Computer and Telecommunications Series.

[31]   Kokichi Futatsugi. An overview of OBJ2. In Kazuhiru Fuchi and Maurice Nivat, editors, *Proceedings, France-Japan AI and CS Symposium*. ICOT, 1986. Also Information Processing Society of Japan, Technical Memorandum PL-86-6.

[32]   Kokichi Futatsugi. Trends in formal specification methods based on algebraic specification techniques — from abstract data types to software processes: A personal perspective. In *Proceedings, International Conference Commemorating the 30th Anniversary of the Information Processing Society of Japan*, pages 59–66. Information Processing Society of Japan, 1990.

[33]   Kokichi Futatsugi. Product-centered process description = algebraic specification of environment + SCRIPT. In *Proceedings, 6th International Software Process Workshop*, pages 95–97. IEEE, 1991.

[34]   Kokichi Futatsugi. Structuring and derivation in algebraic specification/programming languages. *Journal of Information Processing Society of Japan*, 14(2):153–163, 1991.

[35]   Kokichi Futatsugi, Joseph Goguen, Jean-Pierre Jouannaud, and José Meseguer. Principles of OBJ2. In Brian Reid, editor, *Proceedings, Twelfth ACM Symposium on Principles of Programming Languages*, pages 52–66. Association for Computing Machinery, 1985.

[36] Kokichi Futatsugi, Joseph Goguen, José Meseguer, and Koji Okada. Parameterized programming in OBJ2. In Robert Balzer, editor, *Proceedings, Ninth International Conference on Software Engineering*, pages 51–60. IEEE Computer Society, March 1987.

[37] Kokichi Futatsugi, Joseph Goguen, José Meseguer, and Koji Okada. Parameterized programming and its application to rapid prototyping in OBJ2. In Yoshihiro Matsumoto and Yutaka Ohno, editors, *Japanese Perspectives on Software Engineering*, pages 77–102. Addison Wesley, 1989.

[38] Kokichi Futatsugi and Koji Okada. Specification writing as construction of hierarchically structured clusters of operators. In *Proceedings, 1980 IFIP Congress*, pages 287–292. IFIP, 1980.

[39] Kokichi Futatsugi and Koji Okada. A hierarchical structurting method for functional software systems. In *Proceedings, 6th International Conference on Software Engineering*, pages 393–402. IEEE, 1982.

[40] Christopher Paul Gerrard. The specification and controlled implementation of a configuration management tool using OBJ and Ada, 1988. Gerrard Software Limited.

[41] Martin Gogolla. Partially ordered sorts in algebraic specifications. In Bruno Courcelle, editor, *Proceedings, Ninth CAAP (Bordeaux)*, pages 139–153. Cambridge, 1984. Also Forschungsbericht Nr. 169, Universität Dortmund, Abteilung Informatik, 1983.

[42] Martin Gogolla. A final algebra semantics for errors and exceptions. In Hans-Jörg Kreowski, editor, *Recent Trends in Data Type Specification*, volume Informatik-Fachberichte 116, pages 89–103. Springer, 1985. Selected papers from the Third Workshop on Theory and Applications of Abstract Data Types.

[43] Joseph Goguen. Abstract errors for abstract data types. In Eric Neuhold, editor, *Proceedings, First IFIP Working Conference on Formal Description of Programming Concepts*, pages 21.1–21.32. MIT, 1977. Also in *Formal Description of Programming Concepts*, Peter Neuhold, Ed., North-Holland, pages 491–522, 1979.

[44] Joseph Goguen. Order sorted algebra. Technical Report 14, UCLA Computer Science Department, 1978. Semantics and Theory of Computation Series.

[45] Joseph Goguen. Some design principles and theory for OBJ-0, a language for expressing and executing algebraic specifications of programs. In Edward Blum, Manfred Paul, and Satsoru Takasu, editors, *Proceedings, Conference on Mathematical Studies of Information Processing*, pages 425–473. Springer, 1979. Lecture Notes in Computer Science, Volume 75.

[46]   Joseph Goguen. How to prove algebraic inductive hypotheses without induction, with applications to the correctness of data type representations. In Wolfgang Bibel and Robert Kowalski, editors, *Proceedings, Fifth Conference on Automated Deduction*, pages 356–373. Springer, 1980. Lecture Notes in Computer Science, Volume 87.

[47]   Joseph Goguen. Parameterized programming. *Transactions on Software Engineering*, SE–10(5):528–543, September 1984.

[48]   Joseph Goguen. Merged views, closed worlds and ordered sorts: Some novel database features in OBJ. In Alex Borgida and Peter Buneman, editors, *Workshop on Database Interfaces*, pages 38–47. University of Pennsylvania, Computer Science Department, 1985. This workshop took place in October, 1982.

[49]   Joseph Goguen. Reusing and interconnecting software components. *Computer*, 19(2):16–28, February 1986. Reprinted in *Tutorial: Software Reusability*, Peter Freeman, editor, IEEE Computer Society, 1987, pages 251–263, and in *Domain Analysis and Software Systems Modelling*, Rubén Prieto-Díaz and Guillermo Arango, editors, IEEE Computer Society, 1991, pages 125–137.

[50]   Joseph Goguen. Modular algebraic specification of some basic geometrical constructions. *Artificial Intelligence*, pages 123–153, 1988. Special Issue on Computational Geometry, edited by Deepak Kapur and Joseph Mundy; also, Report CSLI-87-87, Center for the Study of Language and Information at Stanford University, March 1987.

[51]   Joseph Goguen. OBJ as a theorem prover, with application to hardware verification. In V.P. Subramanyan and Graham Birtwhistle, editors, *Current Trends in Hardware Verification and Automated Theorem Proving*, pages 218–267. Springer, 1989.

[52]   Joseph Goguen. Principles of parameterized programming. In Ted Biggerstaff and Alan Perlis, editors, *Software Reusability, Volume I: Concepts and Models*, pages 159–225. Addison Wesley, 1989.

[53]   Joseph Goguen. Proving and rewriting. In Hélène Kirchner and Wolfgang Wechler, editors, *Proceedings, Second International Conference on Algebraic and Logic Programming*, pages 1–24. Springer, 1990. Lecture Notes in Computer Science, Volume 463.

[54]   Joseph Goguen. Semantic specifications for the Rewrite Rule Machine. In Aki Yonezawa and Takayasu Ito, editors, *Concurrency: Theory, Language and Architecture*, pages 216–234, 1991. Proceedings of a U.K.–Japan Workshop; Springer, Lecture Notes in Computer Science, Volume 491.

[55]   Joseph Goguen. Types as theories. In George Michael Reed, Andrew William Roscoe, and Ralph F. Wachter, editors, *Topology and*

Category Theory in Computer Science, pages 357–390. Oxford, 1991. Proceedings of a Conference held at Oxford, June 1989.

[56] Joseph Goguen. Stretching first order equational logic: Proofs with partiality, subtypes and retracts. In Maria Paola Bonacina and Ulrich Furbach, editors, *Proceedings, Workshop on First Order Theorem Proving*, pages 78–85. Johannes Kepler Univ. Linz, 1997. Schloss Hagenberg, Austria, October 1997; RISC-Linz Report No. 95–50; revised version to appear in *Journal of Symbolic Computation*.

[57] Joseph Goguen. Cse 230 homepage, 1999. Available at http://www.cs.ucsd.edu/users/goguen/courses/230.

[58] Joseph Goguen. An introduction to algebraic semiotics, with applications to user interface design. In Chrystopher Nehaniv, editor, *Computation for Metaphors, Analogy and Agents*, pages 242–291. Springer, 1999. Lecture Notes in Artificial Intelligence, Volume 1562.

[59] Joseph Goguen. *Theorem Proving and Algebra*. MIT, to appear.

[60] Joseph Goguen. Social and semiotic analyses for theorem prover user interface design, to appear, 2000. Special issue on user interfaces for theorem provers.

[61] Joseph Goguen and Răzvan Diaconescu. An Oxford survey of order sorted algebra. *Mathematical Structures in Computer Science*, 4:363–392, 1994.

[62] Joseph Goguen, Jean-Pierre Jouannaud, and José Meseguer. Operational semantics of order-sorted algebra. In Wilfried Brauer, editor, *Proceedings, 1985 International Conference on Automata, Languages and Programming*. Springer, 1985. Lecture Notes in Computer Science, Volume 194.

[63] Joseph Goguen, Claude Kirchner, José Meseguer, and Timothy Winkler. OBJ as a language for concurrent programming. In Steven Kartashev and Svetlana Kartashev, editors, *Proceedings, Second International Supercomputing Conference, Volume I*, pages 195–198. International Supercomputing Institute Inc. (St. Petersburg FL), 1987.

[64] Joseph Goguen, Kai Lin, Akira Mori, Grigore Roşu, and Akiyoshi Sato. Distributed cooperative formal methods tools. In Michael Lowry, editor, *Proceedings, Automated Software Engineering*, pages 55–62. IEEE, 1997.

[65] Joseph Goguen, Kai Lin, Akira Mori, Grigore Roşu, and Akiyoshi Sato. Tools for distributed cooperative design and validation. In *Proceedings, CafeOBJ Symposium*. Japan Advanced Institute for Science and Technology, 1998. Namazu, Japan, April 1998.

[66]   Joseph Goguen and Grant Malcolm. *Algebraic Semantics of Imperative Programs*. MIT, 1996.

[67]   Joseph Goguen and Grant Malcolm. A hidden agenda. Technical Report CS97–538, UCSD, Dept. Computer Science & Eng., May 1997. To appear in special issue of *Theoretical Computer Science* on Algebraic Engineering, edited by Chrystopher Nehaniv and Masamo Ito. Extended abstract in *Proc., Conf. Intelligent Systems: A Semiotic Perspective, Vol. I*, ed. J. Albus, A. Meystel and R. Quintero, Nat. Inst. Science & Technology (Gaithersberg MD, 20–23 October 1996), pages 159–167.

[68]   Joseph Goguen and Grant Malcolm. Hidden coinduction: Behavioral correctness proofs for objects. *Mathematical Structures in Computer Science*, 9(3):287–319, June 1999.

[69]   Joseph Goguen and José Meseguer. Rapid prototyping in the OBJ executable specification language. *Software Engineering Notes*, 7(5):75–84, December 1982. Proceedings of Rapid Prototyping Workshop.

[70]   Joseph Goguen and José Meseguer. Universal realization, persistent interconnection and implementation of abstract modules. In M. Nielsen and E.M. Schmidt, editors, *Proceedings, 9th International Conference on Automata, Languages and Programming*, pages 265–281. Springer, 1982. Lecture Notes in Computer Science, Volume 140.

[71]   Joseph Goguen and José Meseguer. Eqlog: Equality, types, and generic modules for logic programming. In Douglas DeGroot and Gary Lindstrom, editors, *Logic Programming: Functions, Relations and Equations*, pages 295–363. Prentice-Hall, 1986. An earlier version appears in *Journal of Logic Programming*, Volume 1, Number 2, pages 179–210, September 1984.

[72]   Joseph Goguen and José Meseguer. Models and equality for logical programming. In Hartmut Ehrig, Giorgio Levi, Robert Kowalski, and Ugo Montanari, editors, *Proceedings, 1987 TAPSOFT*, pages 1–22. Springer, 1987. Lecture Notes in Computer Science, Volume 250.

[73]   Joseph Goguen and José Meseguer. Order-sorted algebra solves the constructor selector, multiple representation and coercion problems. In *Proceedings, Second Symposium on Logic in Computer Science*, pages 18–29. IEEE Computer Society, 1987. Also Report CSLI-87-92, Center for the Study of Language and Information, Stanford University, March 1987; revised version in *Information and Computation, 103*, 1993.

[74]   Joseph Goguen and José Meseguer. Unifying functional, object-oriented and relational programming, with logical semantics. In Bruce Shriver and Peter Wegner, editors, *Research Directions in Object-Oriented Programming*, pages 417–477. MIT, 1987. Preliminary version in *SIGPLAN Notices*, Volume 21, Number 10, pages 153–162, October 1986.

[75] Joseph Goguen and José Meseguer. Software for the Rewrite Rule Machine. In Hideo Aiso and Kazuhiro Fuchi, editors, *Proceedings, International Conference on Fifth Generation Computer Systems 1988*, pages 628–637. Institute for New Generation Computer Technology (ICOT), 1988.

[76] Joseph Goguen and José Meseguer. Order-sorted algebra I: Equational deduction for multiple inheritance, overloading, exceptions and partial operations. *Theoretical Computer Science*, 105(2):217–273, 1992. Also Programming Research Group Technical Monograph PRG–80, Oxford University, December 1989, and Technical Report SRI-CSL-89-10, SRI International, Computer Science Lab, July 1989; originally given as lecture at *Seminar on Types*, Carnegie-Mellon University, June 1983; many draft versions exist, from as early as 1985.

[77] Joseph Goguen, José Meseguer, and David Plaisted. Programming with parameterized abstract objects in OBJ. In Domenico Ferrari, Mario Bolognani, and Joseph Goguen, editors, *Theory and Practice of Software Technology*, pages 163–193. North-Holland, 1983.

[78] Joseph Goguen, Akira Mori, and Kai Lin. Algebraic semiotics, ProofWebs and distributed cooperative proving. In Yves Bartot, editor, *Proceedings, User Interfaces for Theorem Provers*, pages 25–34. INRIA, 1997. (Sophia Antipolis, 1–2 September 1997).

[79] Joseph Goguen and Kamran Parsaye-Ghomi. Algebraic denotational semantics using parameterized abstract modules. In J. Diaz and I. Ramos, editors, *Formalizing Programming Concepts*, pages 292–309. Springer, 1981. Lecture Notes in Computer Science, Volume 107.

[80] Joseph Goguen and Grigore Roşu. Hiding more of hidden algebra. In *Proceedings, World Congress on Formal Methods, 1999*. Springer, to appear 1999. Toulouse, France.

[81] Joseph Goguen, Andrew Stevens, Keith Hobley, and Hendrik Hilberdink. 2OBJ, a metalogical framework based on equational logic. *Philosophical Transactions of the Royal Society, Series A*, 339:69–86, 1992. Also in *Mechanized Reasoning and Hardware Design*, edited by C.A.R. Hoare and Michael J.C. Gordon, Prentice-Hall, 1992, pages 69–86.

[82] Joseph Goguen and Joseph Tardo. An introduction to OBJ: A language for writing and testing software specifications. In Marvin Zelkowitz, editor, *Specification of Reliable Software*, pages 170–189. IEEE, 1979. Reprinted in *Software Specification Techniques*, Nehan Gehani and Andrew McGettrick, editors, Addison Wesley, 1985, pages 391–420.

[83] Joseph Goguen, James Thatcher, and Eric Wagner. An initial algebra approach to the specification, correctness and implementation of abstract

data types. In Raymond Yeh, editor, *Current Trends in Programming Methodology, IV*, pages 80–149. Prentice-Hall, 1978.

[84]   Joseph Goguen, James Thatcher, Eric Wagner, and Jesse Wright. Abstract data types as initial algebras and the correctness of data representations. In Alan Klinger, editor, *Computer Graphics, Pattern Recognition and Data Structure*, pages 89–93. IEEE, 1975.

[85]   Joseph Goguen and William Tracz. An implementation-oriented semantics for module composition. In Gary Leavens and Murali Sitaraman, editors, *Foundations of Component-based Systems*. Cambridge, 1999. To appear.

[86]   Joseph Goguen and Timothy Winkler. Introducing OBJ3. Technical report, SRI International, Computer Science Lab, 1988.

[87]   Joseph Goguen and David Wolfram. On types and FOOPS. In Robert Meersman, William Kent, and Samit Khosla, editors, *Object Oriented Databases: Analysis, Design and Construction*, pages 1–22. North Holland, 1991. Proceedings, IFIP TC2 Conference, Windermere, UK, 2–6 July 1990.

[88]   Robert Goldblatt. *Topoi, the Categorial Analysis of Logic*. North-Holland, 1979.

[89]   Michael J.C. Gordon, Robin Milner, and Christopher Wadsworth. *Edinburgh LCF*. Springer, 1979. Lecture Notes in Computer Science, Volume 78.

[90]   John Guttag. *The Specification and Application to Programming of Abstract Data Types*. PhD thesis, University of Toronto, 1975. Computer Science Department, Report CSRG–59.

[91]   Robert Harper, David MacQueen, and Robin Milner. Standard ML. Technical Report ECS-LFCS-86-2, Department of Computer Science, University of Edinburgh, 1986.

[92]   Jieh Hsiang. *Refutational Theorem Proving using Term Rewriting Systems*. PhD thesis, University of Illinois at Champaign-Urbana, 1981.

[93]   Gérard Huet and Derek Oppen. Equations and rewrite rules: A survey. In Ron Book, editor, *Formal Language Theory: Perspectives and Open Problems*, pages 349–405. Academic, 1980.

[94]   John Hughes. Why functional programming matters. Technical Report 16, Programming Methodology Group, University of Goteborg, November 1984.

[95]   John Hughes. Abstract interpretations of first order polymorphic functions. In Cordelia Hall, John Hughes, and John O'Donnell, editors, *Proceedings of the 1988 Glasgow Workshop on Functional Programming*,

pages 68–86. Computing Science Department, University of Glasgow, 1989.

[96] Jean-Pierre Jouannaud and Claude Marché. Completion modulo associativity, commutativity and identity. In Alfonso Miola, editor, *Proceedings, DISCO '90*, pages 111–120. Springer, 1991. Lecture Notes in Computer Science, Volume 429; to appear in *Theoretical Computer Science*.

[97] Jean-Pierre Jouannaud and Mitsuhiro Okada. Executable higher-order algebraic specification languages. In *Proceedings, 6th Symposium on Logic in Computer Science*, pages 350–361. IEEE, 1991.

[98] Heinz Kaphengst and Horst Reichel. Initial algebraic semantics for non-context-free languages. In Marek Karpinski, editor, *Fundamentals of Computation Theory*, pages 120–126. Springer, 1977. Lecture Notes in Computer Science, Volume 56.

[99] Claude Kirchner. Order sorted equational matching, 1988.

[100] Claude Kirchner, Hélène Kirchner, and Aristide Mégrelis. OBJ for OBJ. In Joseph Goguen and Grant Malcolm, editors, *Software Engineering with OBJ: Algebraic Specification in Action*. Kluwer, to appear.

[101] Claude Kirchner, Hélène Kirchner, and José Meseguer. Operational semantics of OBJ3. In T. Lepistö and Aarturo Salomaa, editors, *Proceedings, 15th International Colloquium on Automata, Languages and Programming*, pages 287–301. Springer, 1988. (Tampere, Finland, 11–15 July 1988.) Lecture Notes in Computer Science, Volume 317.

[102] Jan Willem Klop. Term rewriting systems: A tutorial. *Bulletin of the European Association for Theoretical Computer Science*, 32:143–182, June 1987.

[103] Jan Willem Klop. Term rewriting systems: from Church-Rosser to Knuth-Bendix and beyond. In Samson Abramsky, Dov Gabbay, and Tom Maibaum, editors, *Handbook of Logic in Computer Science*, pages 1–117. Oxford, 1992.

[104] Donald Knuth and Peter Bendix. Simple word problems in universal algebra. In J. Leech, editor, *Computational Problems in Abstract Algebra*. Pergamon, 1970.

[105] John T. Latham. Abstract Pascal: A tutorial introduction. Technical Report Version 2.1, University of Manchester, Department of Computer Science, 1987.

[106] Sany Leinwand and Joseph Goguen. Architectural options for the Rewrite Rule Machine. In Steven Kartashev and Svetlana Kartashev, editors, *Proceedings, Second International Supercomputing Conference,*

Volume 1, pages 63–70. International Supercomputing Institute Inc. (St. Petersburg FL), 1987.

[107] Sany Leinwand, Joseph Goguen, and Timothy Winkler. Cell and ensemble architecture of the Rewrite Rule Machine. In Hideo Aiso and Kazuhiro Fuchi, editors, *Proceedings, International Conference on Fifth Generation Computer Systems 1988*, pages 869–878. Institute for New Generation Computer Technology (ICOT), 1988.

[108] Patrick Lincoln and Jim Christian. Adventures in associative-commutative unification. *Journal of Symbolic Computation*, 8:217–240, 1989. Also appears in *Unification*, edited by Claude Kirchner (Academic, 1990), pages 393–416.

[109] Grant Malcolm and Joseph Goguen. An executable course on the algebraic semantics of imperative programs. In Michael Hinchey and C. Neville Dean, editors, *Teaching and Learning Formal Methods*, pages 161–179. Academic, 1996.

[110] Narciso Martí-Oliet and José Meseguer. Inclusions and subtypes. Technical Report SRI-CSL-90-16, SRI International, Computer Science Lab, December 1990.

[111] Per Martin-Löf. Constructive mathematics and computer programming. In *Logic, Methodology and Philosophy of Science VI*, pages 153–175. North-Holand, 1982.

[112] José Meseguer. A logical theory of concurrent objects. In *ECOOP-OOPSLA'90 Conference on Object-Oriented Programming, Ottawa, Canada, October 1990*, pages 101–115. ACM, 1990.

[113] José Meseguer. Conditional rewriting logic: Deduction, models and concurrency. In Stéphane Kaplan and Misuhiro Okada, editors, *Conditional and Typed Rewriting Systems*, pages 64–91. Springer, 1991. Lecture Notes in Computer Science, Volume 516.

[114] José Meseguer. Conditional rewriting logic as a unified model of concurrency. *Theoretical Computer Science*, 96(1):73–155, 1992.

[115] José Meseguer. Membership algebra as a logical framework for equational specification, 1997. Draft manuscript. Computer Science Lab, SRI International.

[116] José Meseguer and Joseph Goguen. Initiality, induction and computability. In Maurice Nivat and John Reynolds, editors, *Algebraic Methods in Semantics*, pages 459–541. Cambridge, 1985.

[117] José Meseguer, Joseph Goguen, and Gert Smolka. Order-sorted unification. *Journal of Symbolic Computation*, 8:383–413, 1989.

[118] Donald Michie. 'Memo' functions and machine learning. *Nature*, 218:19–22, April 1968.

[119] Robin Milner. A theory of type polymorphism in programming. *Journal of Computer and System Sciences*, 17(3):348–375, 1978.

[120] Peter Mosses. Abstract semantic algebras! In Dines Bjorner, editor, *Formal Description of Programming Concepts II*, pages 45–70. IFIP, 1983.

[121] Peter Mosses. A basic semantic algebra. In Giles Kahn, David Mac-Queen, and Gordon Plotkin, editors, *Proceedings, International Symposium on the Semantics of Data Types*, pages 87–107. Springer, 1985. Lecture Notes in Computer Science, Volume 173.

[122] Peter Mosses. Unified algebras and institutions. In *Proceedings, Fourth Annual Conference on Logic in Computer Science*, pages 304–312. IEEE, 1989.

[123] Alan Mycroft. *Abstract Interpretation and Optimising Transformations for Applicative Programs*. PhD thesis, University of Edingurgh, 1981.

[124] Ataru Nakagawa and Kokichi Futatsugi. Stepwise refinement process with modularity: An algebraic approach. In *Proceedings, 11th International Conference on Software Engineering*, pages 166–177. IEEE, 1989.

[125] Ataru Nakagawa and Kokichi Futatsugi. Software process *a la* algebra: OBJ for OBJ. In *Proceedings, 12th International Conference on Software Engineering*, pages 12–32. IEEE, 1990.

[126] Ataru Nakagawa, Kokichi Futatsugi, S. Tomura, and T. Shimizu. Algebraic specification of MacIntosh's QuickDraw using OBJ2. Technical Report Draft, ElectroTechnical Laboratory, Tsukuba Science City, Japan, 1987. In *Proceedings*, Tenth International Conference on Software Engineering, Singapore, April 1988.

[127] Kazuhito Ohmaki, Kokichi Futatsugi, and Koichi Takahashi. A basic LOTOS simulator in OBJ. In *Proceedings, International Conference Commemorating the 30th Anniversary of the Information Processing Society of Japan*, pages 497–504. Information Processing Society of Japan, 1990.

[128] Kazuhito Ohmaki, Koichi Takahashi, and Kokichi Futatsugi. A LOTOS simulator in OBJ. In *Proceedings, FORTE'90: Third International Conference on Formal Description Techniques*, November 1990.

[129] Lawrence Paulson. *Logic and Computation: Interactive Proof with Cambridge LCF*. Cambridge, 1987. Cambridge Tracts in Theoretical Computer Science, Volume 2.

[130] Francisco Pinheiro and Joseph Goguen. An object-oriented tool for tracing requirements. *IEEE Software*, pages 52–64, March 1996. Special issue of papers from ICRE'96.

[131] David Plaisted. An initial algebra semantics for error presentations. SRI International, Computer Science Laboratory, 1982.

[132] Axel Poigné. On semantic algebras: Higher order structures. Informatik II, Universität Dortmund, 1983.

[133] Axel Poigné. Once more on order-sorted algebra. Technical Report Draft, GMD, 1990.

[134] Axel Poigné. Parameterization for order-sorted algebraic specification. *Journal of Computer and System Sciences*, 40(3):229–268, 1990.

[135] John Reynolds. Using category theory to design implicit conversions and generic operators. In Neal Jones, editor, *Semantics Directed Compiler Generation*, pages 211–258. Springer, 1980. Lecture Notes in Computer Science, Volume 94.

[136] David Rydeheard and Rod Burstall. *Computational Category Theory*. Prentice-Hall, 1988.

[137] Augusto Sampaio. A comparative study of theorem provers: Proving correctness of compiling specifications. Technical Report PRG-TR-20-90, Oxford University Computing Laboratory, 1990.

[138] Augusto Sampaio. *An Algebraic Approach to Compiler Design*, volume 4. World Scientific, 1998.

[139] Dana Scott and Christopher Strachey. Towards a mathematical semantics for computer languages. In *Proceedings, 21st Symposium on Computers and Automata*, pages 19–46. Polytechnic Institute of Brooklyn, 1971. Also Programming Research Group Technical Monograph PRG–6, Oxford.

[140] Gert Smolka and Hassan Aït-Kaci. Inheritance hierarchies: Semantics and unification. Technical Report Report AI-057-87, MCC, 1987. In *Journal of Symbolic Computation*, 1988.

[141] Gert Smolka, Werner Nutt, Joseph Goguen, and José Meseguer. Order-sorted equational computation. In Maurice Nivat and Hassan Aït-Kaci, editors, *Resolution of Equations in Algebraic Structures, Volume 2: Rewriting Techniques*, pages 299–367. Academic, 1989. Preliminary version in *Proceedings*, Colloquium on the Resolution of Equations in Algebraic Structures, held in Lakeway, Texas, May 1987, and SEKI Report SR-87-14, Universität Kaiserslautern, December 1987.

[142] J. Michael Spivey. *The Z Notation: A Reference Manual*. Prentice-Hall, 1989.

[143] S. Sridhar. An implementation of OBJ2: An object-oriented language for abstract program specification. In K.V. Nori, editor, *Proceedings, Sixth Conference on Foundations of Software Technology and Theoretical*

Computer Science, pages 81–95. Springer, 1986. Lecture Notes in Computer Science, Volume 241.

[144] Victoria Stavridou. Specifying in OBJ, verifying in REVE, and some ideas about time. Technical report, Department of Computer Science, University of Manchester, 1987.

[145] Victoria Stavridou, Joseph Goguen, Steven Eker, and Serge Aloneftis. FUNNEL: A CHDL with formal semantics. In *Proceedings, Advanced Research Workshop on Correct Hardware Design Methodologies*, pages 117–144. IEEE, 1991.

[146] Victoria Stavridou, Joseph Goguen, Andrew Stevens, Steven Eker, Serge Aloneftis, and Keith Hobley. FUNNEL and 2OBJ: towards an integrated hardware design environment. In *Theorem Provers in Circuit Design*, volume IFIP Transactions, A-10, pages 197–223. North-Holland, 1992.

[147] Christopher Strachey. Fundamental concepts in programming languages. Lecture Notes from International Summer School in Computer Programming, Copenhagen, 1967.

[148] Joseph Tardo. *The Design, Specification and Implementation of OBJT: A Language for Writing and Testing Abstract Algebraic Program Specifications*. PhD thesis, UCLA, Computer Science Department, 1981.

[149] David Turner. Miranda: A non-strict functional language with polymorphic types. In Jean-Pierre Jouannaud, editor, *Functional Programming Languages and Computer Architectures*, pages 1–16. Springer, 1985. Lecture Notes in Computer Science, Volume 201.

[150] William Wadge. Classified algebras. Technical Report 46, University of Warwick, October 1982.

[151] Mitchell Wand. First-order identities as a defining language. *Acta Informatica*, 14:337–357, 1980. Originally Report 29, Computer Science Deptartment, Indiana University, 1977.

[152] Timothy Winkler, Sany Leinwand, and Joseph Goguen. Simulation of concurrent term rewriting. In Steven Kartashev and Svetlana Kartashev, editors, *Proceedings, Second International Supercomputing Conference, Volume I*, pages 199–208. International Supercomputing Institute Inc. (St. Petersburg FL), 1987.

[153] Steven Zilles. Abstract specification of data types. Technical Report 119, Computation Structures Group, Massachusetts Institute of Technology, 1974.

II
OBJ SPECIFICATIONS

Chapter 2

SPECIFYING IN OBJ, VERIFYING IN REVE AND SOME IDEAS ABOUT TIME

Victoria Stavridou

SRI International, Menlo Park CA 94025, USA

Abstract

It is widely recognised that formal specification and verification plays an important role in the design and construction of both software and hardware systems. In this paper we investigate the applicability of the OBJ specification language and the REVE theorem prover, both of which have been traditionally used in connection with software development, as tools for the specification and verification of digital systems. We therefore identify the aspects of these systems which are relevant to hardware development. In particular, we are concerned with optimising proofs in REVE and specifying behaviour of circuits through time.

1   INTRODUCTION

Formal specification and verification of digital systems have been gathering momentum for some time. In common with software development, formal methods in hardware aim to provide rigorous design methodologies and "error-free" systems. The significance of the latter is all too obvious in high integrity applications.

The HArdware VErification project in the Computer Science Department at the University of Manchester aims at producing a development methodology for digital systems based on formal techniques. To this end, we conduct a series of controlled experiments using different formalisms and associated tools on a set of incrementally complex examples. In particular, we are investigating pairs (*Specification Language, Theorem Prover*). Our specifications serve a dual purpose, in that they are used both for simulating a circuit and performing formal checks on its behaviour. In this context, we have used UMIST OBJ [21] as the specification and simulation language and REVE [15] as the theorem prover supporting formal reasoning about the OBJ specifications. In this paper we report on our experiences with this particular pair. Work on other such pairs is reported in [19], which also contains details of the HAVE project.

The first phase of HAVE involves the use of a n-bit wide parallel binary adder as a test case. The adder will be formally specified, simulated and we will attempt to prove that it does indeed produce the mathematical sum of its inputs. We chose this example for the following reasons.

- The circuit is combinational, hence timing issues do not have to be considered, thus simplifying the exercise.

- The circuit displays a hierarchical structure thus exploring the composition/decomposition support provided by the various formalisms.

- The proof of the desired property requires inductive arguments.

This paper is practical in content and is organised as follows. Section 2 presents the specification of the adder in UMIST OBJ and examines the associated issues. The proof about the behaviour of the adder is discussed in Section 3 which also underlines the practical problems involved in performing proofs about OBJ specifications using REVE. Section 4 presents two alternative techniques for specifying behaviours of circuits through time. Finally Section 5 outlines relevant work in this area and our experience with OBJ and REVE is summarised in Section 6.

2   SPECIFYING THE ADDER

The n-bit wide parallel binary adder is a purely combinational device. As outlined in the previous section, the specification will be used for both simulation and verification. The aim is to prove that the circuit produces the mathematical sum of its inputs.

2.1   OBJ AS A FORMALISM FOR HARDWARE DESCRIPTION

Although OBJ has traditionally been used for writing and executing algebraic specifications of programs, in common with other declarative languages, it also provides a convenient notation for expressing circuit behaviour. Hardware components can be modelled as functions from inputs to outputs and are thus readily expressible in notations supporting functional definitions. In OBJ devices are modelled as abstract data types. Additionally, OBJ has a number of features which are helpful when specifying hardware.

- Specifications must be readable and easily understood in order to be used effectively by hardware designers. Mixfix syntax enhances readability and the ability to define functions through case analysis eliminates the need for selector operations which give rise to strange encodings (e.g., car and cdr combinations in Lisp).

- A notation used for hardware specification must support composition and decomposition since these are very important concepts in system design. OBJ supports these through its modular structure and abstraction mechanisms.

- Specifying behaviour through time requires higher order functions. As will be discussed later, OBJ's powerful parameterisation facilities provide implicit support for defining higher order functions.

- By encoding the basic Boolean algebra rules in an OBJ program, the term rewriting semantics of the language can be used for circuit optimisation. Due to the inaccuracy of hardware models currently in use, there are a number of difficulties involved in this process. [3] further discusses circuit optimisation using reduction techniques and identifies particular problems.

2.2 THE SPECIFICATION

Since the length of the adder is not specified, the inputs and the output are modelled using vectors of bits. To eliminate the need for traversing the vectors before additions, the least significant bit is held at the head of the vector.

```
OBJ Vector
SORTS vector
OPS nil : -> vector
    _._ : BOOL vector -> vector
JBO
```

This object can be enriched with the following operations which implement mappings from vectors of bits onto natural numbers and vice versa. These operations are used for simulation and for formulating the adder theorem later on.

```
bin-to-nat : vector -> nat

( bin-to-nat(nil) = 0 )
( bin-to-nat(b . v) = bit(b) + (2 * bin-to-nat(v)) )
```

where operator bit provides a mapping from bits to natural numbers:

```
bit : BOOL -> nat
```

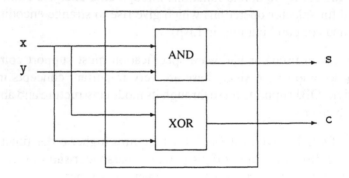

Figure 2.1   The half adder

```
( bit(T) = 1 )
( bit(F) = 0 )
```

nat-to-bin maps natural numbers onto vectors of bits:

```
nat-to-bin : nat -> vector

( nat-to-bin(0) = nil )
( nat-to-bin(succ(n)) = not(even(succ(n))) .
                        nat-to-bin(succ(n) div 2) )
```

Finally, the operator inc adjusts the input bit vector so that its natural number representation is incremented by 1:

```
inc : vector -> vector

( inc(nil) = T . nil )
( inc(T . v) = F . (inc(v)) )
( inc(F . v) = T . v )
```

The basic building block of the n-bit adder is the half adder (Figure 2.1) which consists of an AND and an XOR gate. The circuit produces a sum and a carry output which are paired using sort pair with selectors sum and carry.

```
OBJ Half-Adder
SORTS pair
OPS mkpair : BOOL BOOL -> pair
    halfadder : BOOL BOOL -> pair
    sum : pair -> BOOL
```

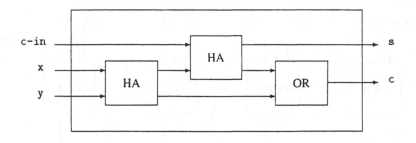

Figure 2.2   The full adder

```
      carry : pair -> BOOL
VARS x,y,s,c : BOOL
EQNS ( halfadder(x,y) = mkpair(x xor y, x and y) )
     ( sum(mkpair(s,c)) = s )
     ( carry(mkpair(s,c)) = c )
JBO
```

where the _xor_ operator is trivially defined as

```
_xor_ : BOOL BOOL -> BOOL (COMM)

( F xor x = x )
( T xor x = not(x) )
```

The full adder (Figure 2.2) is made up of two half adders and an OR gate.

```
OBJ Full-Adder / Half-Adder
OPS fulladder : BOOL BOOL BOOL -> pair
VARS x,y,c-in : BOOL
EQNS ( fulladder(x,y,c-in) =
        mkpair(sum(halfadder(sum(halfadder(x,y)),c-in)),
           carry(halfadder(x,y)) or
           carry(halfadder(sum(halfadder(x,y)),c-in))) )
JBO
```

The n-bit adder consists of a cascade of *n* full adders with the output carry of the $(i - 1)^{th}$ unit connected to the input carry of the ith unit as shown in Figure 2.3.

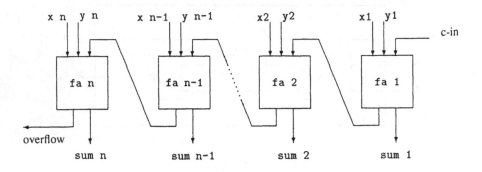

Figure 2.3   N-bit wide parallel binary adder

```
OBJ Adder / Full-Adder Vector
OPS adder : BOOL vector vector -> vector
VARS bit1,bit2,c-in : BOOL
     v1,v2 : vector
EQNS ( adder(F,nil,v2) = v2 )
     ( adder(T,nil,v2) = inc(v2) )
     ( adder(F,v1,nil) = v1 )
     ( adder(T,v1,nil) = inc(v1) )
     ( adder(c-in, bit1 . v1, bit2 . v2) =
       sum(fulladder(bit1,bit2,c-in)) .
       adder(carry(fulladder(bit1,bit2,c-in)),v1,v2) )
JBO
```

This specification of the adder can be used to perform simulation. The tests are carried out using the auxillary operator `test`.

```
test : nat nat -> nat

( test(n1,n2) =
bin-to-nat(adder(F,nat-to-bin(n1),nat-to-bin(n2))) )
```

The input carry `c-in` is set to F to indicate that an addition is about to take place. A typical test and result are shown below.

```
run test(2345,456) nur

AS nat : 2801
```

3 VERIFICATION

OBJ equations are sentences in many sorted equational logic. It is therefore possible to reason about the adder specifications formally. In order to use term rewriting as a decision procedure for the equational theory defined by a specification, the corresponding term rewriting system must be shown to be canonical or complete. A term rewriting system is canonical iff it has the Church-Rosser property and is finitely terminating [10]. OBJ specifications, however, are not subject to such completion checks. Consequently, before the OBJ specification can be used for formal reasoning, a canonical term rewriting system must be constructed from the equations in the specification. Practically this means that we must use a completion procedure such as the Knuth-Bendix algorithm [12]. Knuth-Bendix is supported by the REVE theorem prover. In particular, the version used here (2.4) supports completion of equational theories modulo associative-commutative operators but does not allow conditional equations or rules.

The semantics of OBJ specifications are given by initial algebras defined by the set of equations. Using just the initial model compromises the completeness property of equational logic and thus, we can no longer prove an equation valid (or invalid) in the initial algebra by mere reasoning; some kind of induction is necessary. REVE supports *proof by consistency* or *inductionless induction* [6], in particular the Huet-Hullot flavour [9]. This permits proofs of equations without explicit induction. The principle is that

> if a set of equations contains the axiomatisation of an equality predicate, then an equation is valid in the initial algebra iff adding it as an axiom does not make the theory inconsistent (in the sense that `true=false` is derivable).[1]

3.1 OBJ SPECIFICATIONS AS INPUT TO REVE

The OBJ specifications cannot be fed directly into REVE for completion. The following amendments are required:

1. OBJ's = must be replaced by REVE's ==;

2. Variable names must be changed to begin with the letters x,y,z,w to conform with REVE's naming conventions;

3. Outer parentheses must be stripped from OBJ equations;

4. Sorting information, signatures and variable declarations must be removed from the OBJ text;

---

[1] quote from [9]

5. Conditional equations must either be removed or replaced by a set of unconditional ones.

Items 2 and 4 above underline the fact that REVE is not many sorted whereas OBJ is. A dangerous consequence of this is that REVE will accept and will attempt to work with ill-defined terms. Item 5 is even more important. Most specifications contain conditional rules and it is not always straightforward or even possible to replace these by unconditional ones. Introducing an if_then_else operator does not solve the problem because no suitable reduction ordering on the terms can be found. Hence, the absence of a completion procedure for conditional equations in the version of REVE used here, was a serious obstacle in proving the correctness of the adder circuit.

3.2   A PRACTICAL VIEW OF THE DECISION PROCEDURE

The text of the OBJ specification is shown below after having been changed to conform with constraints of the previous section.

```
1.  and(x, F) == F
2.  and(x, T) == x
3.  xor(x, x) == F
4.  xor(x, F) == x
5.  or(x,T) == T
6.  or(x,F) == x
7.  1 == succ(0)
8.  2 == succ(succ(0))
9.  x + 0 == x
10. x + succ(y) == succ(x + y)
11. x * 0 == 0
12. bin-to-nat(nil) == 0
13. bin-to-nat(x.y) == bit(x) + 2 * bin-to-nat(y)
14. carry(mkpair(x, y)) == x
15. sum(mkpair(x, y)) == x
16. x * succ(y) == (x * y) + x
17. (x+y)*z ==   (x*z) + (y*z)
18. inc(nil) ==   T.nil
19. inc(F.x) == T.x
20. inc(T.x) == F.inc(x)
21. halfadder(x, y) == mkpair(xor(x,y),and(x, y))
22. adder(F,x,nil) == x
23. adder(T,x,nil) == inc(x)
24. adder(F,nil,x) == x
```

```
25. adder(T,nil,x) == inc(x)
26. adder(z, x . xva, y . yvb) ==
        sum(fulladder(x,y,z,)) .
            adder(carry(fulladder(x,y,z)),xva,yvb)
27. fulladder(x,y,z) ==
        mkpair(sum(halfadder(sum(halfadder(x,y)),z)),
        or(carry(halfadder(x,y)),
            carry(halfadder(sum(halfadder(x,y)),z)))))
28. bit(F) == 0
29. bit(T) == succ(0)
```

Deciding whether an arbitrary term rewriting system is canonical is undecidable (because the finite termination of such a system is undecidable) [10]. Therefore, the Knuth-Bendix procedure might loop forever when attempting to complete a system which has no equivalent terminating and Church-Rosser system. Knuth-Bendix is used both for deciding whether a system is canonical and whether an equation (proposition) is valid in an equational theory (by using the inductive extension of the algorithm as presented in [9]). However, the Knuth-Bendix procedure is a computationally intensive process. When the equational theory contains associative-commutative operators (+, *, and and or in this particular system), the algorithm is even more inefficient. The situation is made worse because the user has no control over the search strategy that REVE uses. Undecidability coupled with inefficiency mean that, in practice, once the algorithm has been running for some time, the user cannot tell whether the set of rewrite rules is genuinely not canonical and Knuth-Bendix is looping forever or the algorithm is just taking a long time in discovering the equivalent canonical system. This then means, that although the algorithm might eventually terminate for complete systems and valid equations (if that is, the correct reduction ordering has been found), its use is not practical for a large class of problems in the hardware verification domain.

A way of overcoming the problem is to construct alternative but *equivalent* sets of rules to the original one. Then completion and proof of properties can be attempted again on a new system. These systems must be simpler than the original one in the sense that Knuth-Bendix is presented with a simpler task. The process of finding such systems amounts to performing some of the steps of the decision procedure manually. Furthermore, if the notion of completion is formalised within the framework of a proof theory [2], then these steps can be regarded as applications of the following inference rules:

- Orienting an equation.

$$\frac{(\mathcal{E} \cup \{s = t\}, \mathcal{R})}{(\mathcal{E}, \mathcal{R} \cup \{s \to t\})} \quad if \quad s > t$$

- Adding an equational consequence.

$$\frac{(\mathcal{E},\mathcal{R})}{(\mathcal{E}\cup\{s=t\},\mathcal{R})} \quad if \quad s \leftarrow_{\mathcal{R}} u \rightarrow_{\mathcal{R}} t$$

- Simplifying an equation.

$$\frac{(\mathcal{E}\cup\{s=t\},\mathcal{R})}{(\mathcal{E}\cup\{u=t\},\mathcal{R})} \quad if \quad s \rightarrow_{\mathcal{R}} u$$

where $\mathcal{E}$ is a set of equations, $\mathcal{R}$ is a set of rewrite rules, $>$ is a reduction ordering, $\rightarrow_{\mathcal{R}}$ is the reduction relation and $\leftarrow_{\mathcal{R}}$ is the inverse of the reduction relation as defined in [2].

Here are some examples of applying these inference rules. Multiplication in the above system is redundant since it is defined in terms of addition. The equations defining multiplication (11, 16 and 17) can be removed and all occurrences of * replaced by + terms. This is achieved by orienting the equations defining multiplication and using the resulting rewrite rules to simplify equation 13 yielding equation 12 below.

```
1.  and(x, F) == F
2.  and(x, T) == x
3.  xor(x, x) == F
4.  xor(x, F) == x
5.  or(x,T) == T
6.  or(x,F) == x
7.  1 == succ(0)
8.  2 == succ(succ(0))
9.  x + 0 == x
10. x = succ(y) == succ(x + y)
11. bin-to-nat(nil) == 0
12. bin-to-nat(x.y) ==
        bit(x) + bin-to-nat(y) = bin-to-nat(y)
13. carry(mkpair(x, y)) == y
14. sum(mkpair(x, y)) == x
15. inc(nil) == T.nil
16. inc(F.x) == T.x
17. inc(T.x) == F.inc(x)
18. halfadder(x, y) == mkpair(xor(x,y),and(x, y))
19. adder(F,x,nil) == x
20. adder(T,x,nil) == inc(x)
21. adder(F,nil,x) == x
```

```
22. adder(T,nil,x) == inc(x)
23. adder(z, x . xva, y . yvb) ==
        sum(fulladder(x,y,z)) .
          adder(carry(fulladder(x,y,z)),xva,yvb)
24. fulladder(x,y,z) ==
        mkpair(sum(halfadder(sum(halfadder(x,y)),z)),
        or(carry(halfadder(x,y)),
          carry(halfadder(sum(halfadder(x,y)),z)))))
25. bit(F) == 0
26. bit(T) ==  succ(0)
```

The task of the completion procedure can be further simplified by enhancing the set of equations with some of the critical pairs that the algorithm would otherwise have to produce itself. Note that since REVE is unsorted, Knuth-Bendix cannot use equations for generating critical pairs selectively, on the basis of typing information available in the OBJ specification. The completion procedure is, therefore, unnecessarily time consuming. Manual generation of critical pairs also allows removing these equations from the system, whose consequences have been replaced by the equations generated from the appropriate critical pairs. Therefore, equations 18 and 24 defining the behaviour of the half and full adder respectively, can be replaced by their consequences as shown in equations 10 to 13 and 14 to 21 below. An example of deriving such a critical pair equation is shown below, where equation 10 is derived in 6 steps as follows:

1. Unifying the left hand sides of equations 1 and 18 produces the critical pair

   ```
   halfadder(and(x,F),y)
   mkpair(xor(and(x,F),y)and(and(x,F),y))
   ```

2. Orienting equation 1 and using it to simplify the critical pair

   ```
   halfadder(F,y)
   mkpair(xor(F,y),F)
   ```

3. Adding the critical pair equation to the system

   ```
   halfadder(F,y) == mkpair(xor(F,y),F)
   ```

4. Unifying the critical pair equation with equation 3 produces another critical pair

```
halfadder(F,xor(x,x))
mkpair(xor(x,x),F)
```

5. Orienting equation 3 and using it to simplify the critical pair

```
halfadder(F,F)
mkpair(F,F)
```

6. Adding the new critical pair equation to the system

```
halfadder(F,F) == mkpair(F,F)
```

The rest of the equations are derived in a similar way. The system below shows the simplified equations for the halfadder and the fulladder. Note also that since and, or, xor are no longer required their definitions can be removed from the system.

```
1.  x + 0 == x
2.  x + succ(y) == succ(x + y)
3.  bin-to-nat(nil) == 0
4.  bin-to-nat(x.y) ==
          bit(x) + bin-to-nat(y) + bin-to-nat(y)
5.  carry(mkpair(x, y)) == y
6.  sum(mkpair(x, y)) == x
7.  inc(nil) == T.nil
8.  inc(F.x) == T.x
9.  inc(T.x) == F.inc(x)
10.  halfadder(F,F) == mkpair(F,F)
11.  halfadder(F,T) == mkpair(T,F)
12.  halfadder(T,F) == mkpair(T,F)
13.  halfadder(T,T) == mkpair(F,T)
14.  fulladder(F,F,F) == mkpair(F,F)
15.  fulladder(F,F,T) == mkpair(T,F)
16.  fulladder(F,T,F) == mkpair(T,F)
17.  fulladder(F,T,T) == mkpair(F,T)
18.  fulladder(T,F,F) == mkpair(T,F)
19.  fulladder(T,F,T) == mkpair(F,T)
20.  fulladder(T,T,F) == mkpair(F,T)
21.  fulladder(T,T,T) == mkpair(T,T)
22.  adder(F,x,nil) == x
```

```
23. adder(T,x,nil) == inc(x)
24. adder(F,nil,x) == x
25. adder(T,nil,x) == inc(x)
26. adder(z, x . xva, y . yvb) ==
            sum(fulladder(x,y,z)) .
                adder(carry(fulladder(x,y,z)),xva,yvb)
27. bit(F) == 0
28. bit(T) == succ(0)
```

In fact, this last system is one that can be successfully used to prove the theorem about the correctness of the adder, which can be formulated as follows:

```
bin-to-nat(adder(x,y,z)) ==
    bin-to-nat(y) + bin-to-nat(z) = bit(x)
```

where + is associative-communicative. The completed set of rules below shows the proved theorem as rule 29:

```
1.   0 + x  ⟹ x
2.   bin-to-nat(nil) ⟹ 0
3.   carry(mkpair(x, y)) ⟹ y
4.   sum(mkpair(x, y)) ⟹ x
5.   inc(nil) ⟹ T . nil
6.   inc(F . x) ⟹ T . x
7.   inc(T . x) ⟹ F . inc(x)
8.   halfadder(F, F) ⟹ mkpair(F, F)
9.   halfadder(F, T) ⟹ mkpair(T, F)
10.  halfadder(T, F) ⟹ mkpair(T, F)
11.  halfadder(T, T) ⟹ mkpair(F, T)
12.  fulladder(F, F, F) ⟹ mkpair(F, F)
13.  fulladder(F, F, T) ⟹ mkpair(T, F)
14.  fulladder(F, T, F) ⟹ mkpair(T, F)
15.  fulladder(F, T, T) ⟹ mkpair(F, T)
16.  fulladder(T, F, F) ⟹ mkpair(T, F)
17.  fulladder(T, F, T) ⟹ mkpair(F, T)
18.  fulladder(T, T, F) ⟹ mkpair(F, T)
19.  fulladder(T, T, T) ⟹ mkpair(T, T)
20.  adder(F, x, nil) ⟹ x
21.  adder(F, nil, x) ⟹ x
22.  bit(F) ⟹ 0
23.  bit(T) ⟹ succ(0)
24.  adder(T, x, nil) ⟹ inc(x)
25.  adder(T, nil, x) ⟹ inc(x)
```

```
26. succ(y) + x ⟹ succ(x + y)
27. bin-to-nat(x . y) ⟹
        bin-to-nat(y) + bin-to-nat(y) + bit(x)
28. adder(z, x . xva, y . yvb) ⟹
        sum(fulladder(x, y, z)) .
        adder(carry(fulladder(x, y, z)), xva, yvb)
29. bin-to-nat(adder(x, y, z)) ⟹
        bin-to-nat(y) + bin-to-nat(z) + bit(x)
30. bin-to-nat(inc(y)) ⟹ succ(bin-to-nat(y))
31. bit(carry(fulladder(x, y, x1))) +
    bit(carry(fulladder(x, y, x1))) +
    bit(sum(fulladder(x, y, x1))) ⟹
        bit(x) + bit(x1) + bit(y)
```

Note, that REVE has discovered two lemmas required for this proof. These are shown as rules 30 and 31.

3.3   PROVING EQUIVALENCE OF TWO SETS OF EQUATIONS

Although manual application of the inference rules, as discussed above, facilitates proofs which cannot be obtained automatically within realistic time limits, it does nonetheless introduce a potential source of errors in the proving process. These rules can be applied incorrectly as well as correctly. The problem can be solved by formally showing that the succesion of equation sets generated by the application of the inference rules have *equivalent* initial models.

Given two sets of equations S_1 and S_2, then in order to prove that $S_1 \cong S_2$, we must show that:

$$\forall e \in S. \ S_1 \models e \ \text{and} \ \forall e'. \ S_2 \models e'$$

where $S = S_2 - S_1$ and $S' = S_1 - S_2$. Practically, this means that both sets must be completed and then each equation in one system must be shown to be a consequence of the other. Since equivalence is transitive, if we prove each transformation during the refinement, then the most complex system is equivalent to the simplest one, and thus the theorem is valid in the system we started with.

In general, if S_1 is simpler than S_2, then to prove that $S_2 \implies S_1$, standard equational reasoning suffices, whereas to prove that $S_1 \implies S_2$, we need an inductive argument. Both these proofs have been done for the three systems of the previous section using REVE itself.

4   SPECIFYING BEHAVIOUR IN TIME

Being able to talk about time is essential for specifying the behaviour of sequential devices. Specifying such devices or systems usually involves higher order functions, since input and output lines are modelled as mappings from times to values. For instance the specification of a unit delay in HOL [8] is given by the predicate

$$\mathrm{Del}(i,o) = !t.o(t+1) = i(t)$$

where ! is the universal quantifier. OBJ does not support higher order functions. Therefore, we need an alternative way of expressing properties involving time. Below we discuss two such different techniques.

4.1   HISTORIES

The basic idea here is that a line can be modelled by its *history*. Such a history is simply a sequence of *instances*. Every time the clock ticks, the next instance in the history of the line is generated. An instance can be defined as 3-tuple (*name, value, time*). This concept of history is similar to Lucid histories [1]. In OBJ we have:

```
OBJ Name
SORTS name
OPS 11,12 : -> name
JBO
```

which generates some names for lines. Instances are defined as follows:

```
OBJ Instance / Name
SORTS instance
OPS
    mkinstance : name BOOL nat -> instance
    name? : instance -> name
    value : instance -> BOOL
    time  : instance -> nat
VARS
    1 : name
    val : BOOL
    t : nat
EQNS
    ( name?(mkinstance(1,val,t)) = 1 )
    ( value(mkinstance(1,val,t)) - val )
    ( time(mkinstance(1,val,t)) = t )
JBO
```

Thus time is modelled with natural numbers.

```
OBJ History / Instance
SORTS history
OPS
    empty : -> history
    _._   : instance history -> history
JBO
```

Now we can define operations that look into the history of a line and retrieve some information:

```
OBJ Operations / History
OPS
    last : history -> BOOL
    nth  : nat history -> BOOL
VARS
    l : name
    val : BOOL
    t,n : nat
    h : history
EQNS
    ( last(mkinstance(l,val,t) . h ) = value(head(h))
        IF not(h==empty) )

    ( nth(succ(n),mkinstance(l,val,t) . h) = val
        IF succ(n) == t )
    ( nth(succ(n),mkinstance(l,val,t) . h) = nth(n,h)
        IF (succ(n) < t) and not(h==empty) )
JBO
```

where last returns the value of the line at time $(t - 1)$ and nth returns the value at time $(t - n)$. Note that the definitions are partial. The register can now be specified as

```
OBJ Delay / History
OPS
    delay : history history -> history
VARS
    l : name
    val : BOOL
    t,n : nat
    h,h' : history
```

```
EQNS
  ( delay(mkinstance(1,val,t) . h, h') =
      mkinstance(1,val,t+1) . h' )
JBO
```

Effectively a hardware device is modelled through the instances it causes to the history of its i/o lines. Although this approach is adequate for defining simple circuits, descriptions of more complex systems are very complicated and riddled with detail. More fundamentally, it is not clear how to compose primitive components into larger ones without the ability to define higher order functions. We therefore feel that histories in the context of OBJ do not provide an effective way of specifying behaviour through time.

4.2   MODULE EXPRESSIONS

OBJ3 [7] has a comprehensive set of parameterisation facilities. Apart from the obvious benefits of this on the development and maintenance of software, it has the interesting side effect of providing implicit support for higher order functions [7]. It thus provides a flexible environment for defining behaviour through time. For instance our unit delay can be specified using theories and parameterised objects. Theories contain a set of non executable assertions which may (or may not) be satisfied by other modules.

```
TH Line IS
  PROTECTING Natural .
  OP in : nat -> Bool .
ENDTH

OBJ Del[I :: Line] IS
  OP out : nat -> Bool .
  VAR T : nat .
  EQ : out (s t) = in t .
ENDO
```

where s is the successor operator. Primitive components can now be put together very naturally using module expressions in a way similar to that used for binding names to ports in structural VHDL descriptions [20]. Module expressions show how to combine, instantiate and transform existing units. For example, we can compose two unit delays to form a two unit delay. A second copy of the Del object is created by the following renaming:

```
OBJ New-Del IS
  PROTECTING Del[I] * (OP out TO new-out) .
ENDO
```

Such renamings create a new module out of an old one incorporating the syntactic changes indicated by the sort and operation mappings. Views bind the formal entities in an interface theory (Line in this case) to actual entities in a module. The two unit delay objects can now be composed as follows:

```
OBJ Del-2[I :: Line] IS
   PROTECTING Del[VIEW FROM Line TO New-Del[I] IS
                   OP : new-out TO : in .
             ENDV] .
ENDO
```

This specification can be used for simulation by providing appropriate values for in and then instantiating Del-2. More interestingly, we can use this specification for conducting formal checks in OBJ3 itself, by encoding various decision procedures in the language. An example of this is shown in [7]. This approach seems very promising and is currently under further investigation. This work is done in collaboration with Joseph Goguen.

5   RELEVANT WORK

Here we mention briefly other work involving applications of equational specifications and term rewriting techniques to the specification and verification of hardware. For a wider review see [19].

[4] addresses verification of functional correctness of combinational devices. Their design verification system is based on term rewriting techniques and supports a combination of procedures including the Kapur and Musser flavour if inductionless induction [13]. The system compares well with simulators. An 8-bit ALU slice with 200 gates was completely verified in 25 minutes compared with 270 minutes of estimated simulation time. However, the modularity of designs is not exploited, and the system cannot handle sequential circuits.

Narendran and Stillman [18] have used the AFFIRM-85 verification system [16] and the RRL theorem prover [14] for hardware verification work as part of the Interactive VHDL Workstation project. Behavioural descriptions are first-order predicate calculus sentences. Such descriptions include initialisation assumptions, operational assumptions and well as the behavioural statement. The structural specification of a circuit is then obtained by instantiating these descriptions with actual names of wires. This approach can handle combinational as well as sequential systems. However, using an automatic theorem prover such as RRL does not allow user interaction which is nearly always necessary for complicated proofs.

Finally, [17] contains an elaborate model of hardware devices tackling issues such as bidirectionality, gate capacitance and charge sharing. All these concepts are treated as abstract data types. This approach is closely related to the AFFIRM-85 and RRL work described above.

6   DISCUSSION

Specifying hardware components as abstract data types in a language such as OBJ seems to provide a viable alternative to traditional hardware description languages. This statement however, must be conditioned by the ability to satisfactorily model sequential as well as combinational devices, through the techniques outlined in Section 4. Furthermore, the efficiency of the implementation of the language is of vital importance when animating specifications. Even for this trivial adder example, the performance of UMIST OBJ was far removed from what would be considered acceptable simulation speeds.

Verifying behaviour using REVE is rather a more involved task. In common with other automatic theorem provers REVE suffers from two fundamental drawbacks:

1. The proof of many theorems requires some degree of user interaction. Such interactive facilities can make the difference between a proof being successful or not. REVE, in common with other term rewriting theorem provers such as RRL, does not allow any user interaction apart from asking user guidance in performing function symbol orderings. However, the proof optimism techniques presented in Section 3 effectively provide an implicit interactive facility.

2. It is unlikely that the first description of a circuit will be correct. It is therefore very important that the theorem prover provides diagnostic information when it falls. When a REVE proof fails there is no indication as to what might have gone wrong.

The results of using OBJ3 module expressions in specifying circuit behaviours through time are encouraging. The descriptions are succinct, readable and highly modularised. More importantly, the ability to perform formal proofs using the language itself, by axiomatising decision procedures, adds an elegant and simple dimension to theorem proving. We have so far used the propositional calculus through the well known Hsiang axiomatisation [11], and we are currently investigating extensions of these techniques to inductive proofs.

Acknowledgments

The idea of specifying behaviours through time using module expressions and performing proofs in OBJ by axiomatising decision procedures is due to Joseph Goguen. His enthusiasm and patience are gratefully acknowledged. Using proof orderings to formalise proof optimisations was suggested by Derek Coleman, who helped to shape up many of the verification ideas presented in this paper. Ursula Martin provided many useful comments. Howard Barringer, John Gurd and Doug Edwards provided support and encouragement.

This work has been sponsored by SERC Grant No. GR/D/82821.

References

[1]   E.A. Ashcroft and W.W. Wadge. Lucid - a non-procedural language with iteration. *Comm. ACM*, 20(7), July 1977.

[2]   L. Bachmair, N. Dershowitz and J. Hsiang. Orderings for Equational Proofs. In *Procs. of Symposium on Logic in Computer Science*, IEEE, Boulder, Colorado, USA, 1987.

[3]   W.F. Clocksin. *Logic Programming and the Specification of Circuits*. Technical Report 72, University of Cambridge Computer Laboratory, Corn Exchange Street, Cambridge CB2 3QG, 1985.

[4]   M.S. Chandrasekhar, J.P. Privitera and K.W. Condrat. Application of Term Rewriting Techniques to Hardware Design Verification. In *Procs. 24th Design Automation Conference*, Miami, Florida, June 1987.

[5]   K. Futatsugi, J.A. Goguen, J-P. Jouannaud and J. Meseguer. Principles of OBJ2. In *Procs. of Symposium on Principles of Programming Languages*, pages 52-66, 1985.

[6]   J.A. Goguen. How to prove algebraic inductive hypotheses without induction: with applications to the correctness of data type representations. In *Proceedings, Fifth Conference on Automated Deduction*, pages 356-373, Springer-Verlag, 1980. Lecture Notes in Computer Science, Volume 87.

[7]   J.A. Goguen. Principles of Paramterized Programming. 1987. SRI International, Menlo Park, CA 94025, USA.

[8]   M.J.C. Gordon. *HOL: A Machine Oriented Formulation of Higher Order Logic*. Technical Report 68, Computer Laboratory, University of Cambridge, Corn Exchange Street, Cambridge CB2 3QG, UK, July 1985.

[9]   G. Huet and J.M. Hullot. Proof by Induction in Equational Theories with Constructors. *JCCS*, 2(25), 1982.

[10]   G. Huet and D. Oppen. Equations and Rewrite Rules: A Survey. In R. Book, editor, *Formal Languages: Perspectives and Open Problems*, Academic Press, 1980.

[11] J. Hsiang. *Refutational Theorem Proving using Term Rewriting Systems.* Ph.D. dissertation, University of Illinois at Champaign-Urbana, 1981.

[12] D. Knuth and P. Bendix. Simple Word Problems in Universal Algebras. In J. Leech, editor, *Computational Problems in Abstract Algebra*, pages 263-297, Pergamon Press, 1970.

[13] D. Kapur and D.R. Musser. Proof by Consistency. *Artificial Intelligence Journal*, 1987. To appear.

[14] D. Kapur, G. Sivakumar and H. Zhang. RRL: A Rewrite Rule Laboratory. In *Procs. of 8th Conference on Automated Deduction*, Oxford, UK, 1986.

[15] P. Lescanne. Computer experiments with the REVE Term Rewriting System Generator. In *Proceedings of the Tenth ACM Symposium on the Principles of Programming Languages*, Austin, Texas, January 1983.

[16] D.R. Musser and D.A. Cyrluk. *Affirm-85 Reference Manual.* General Electric Corporate Research and Development Center, Schenectady, NY 12301, August 1985.

[17] D.R. Musser, P. Narendran and W.J. Premerlani. BIDS: A Method for Specifying and Verifying Bidirectional Hardware Devices. In *Proc. of Hardware Verification Workshop*, Calgary, Canada, January 1987.

[18] P. Narendran and J. Stillman. Hardware Verification in the Interactive VHDL Workstation. G.E. Corporate Research and Development Center, Schenectady, NY 12345, USA, 1986.

[19] V. Stavridou, H. Barringer and D.A. Edwards. *Formal Specification and Verification of Hardware: A Comparative Case Study.* Technical Report UMCS-87-11-1, Department of Computer Science, University of Manchester, Oxford Road, Manchester M13 9PL, UK, 1987.

[20] *VHDL Tutorial for IEEE Standard 1076 VHDL.* CAD Language Systems Inc, 51 Monroe St. Suite 606, Rockville, MD 20850, USA, draft edition, May 1987.

[21] C.D. Walter, R.M. Gallimore, D. Coleman and V. Stavridou. UMIST OBJ Manual Version 1.0, 1986. Computation Department, UMIST, Manchester M60 1QD, UK.

Chapter 3

CONSTRUCTING A GRAPHICS SYSTEM WITH OBJ2: A PRACTICAL GUIDE

Ataru T. Nakagawa
SRA, Inc.
1-1-1 Hirakawacho, Chiyoda, Tokyo 102, Japan

Kokichi Futatsugi
Electrotechnical Laboratory
1-1-4 Umezono, Tsukuba Science City, Ibaraki 305, Japan

Abstract   The output part of a graphics system functionally identical to QuickDraw, the basic graphics package of Macintosh, is described in OBJ2. The construction process and the resultant description raise some pragmatic issues in using OBJ2 as a specification language, such as the criteria for selecting a particular construction from among several alternatives. An example of checking specifications in a systematic way is also shown.

1   INTRODUCTION

To see the applicability of OBJ2 to non-trivial problem domains and to confirm the utility of its powerful features, we have described in OBJ2 the core graphics package, called QuickDraw, of Macintosh systems. The first trial, where we were faithful to the descriptions in the Macintosh Programmer's Guide (the Guide, hereafter) [15], successfully revealed that OBJ2 is indeed easy to employ, at least for problems of this kind [18]. It also helped us to detect ambiguity/omissions of software designs, and confirmed our suspicions of bad design decisions.

In the second trial, explained in this paper, we ignored details in the Guide, whether they concern design decisions or implementation biases. We already knew whether OBJ2 can be used in the manner minutely dictated by designs made elsewhere. Our principal objectives in this instance were (a) to offer a rational alternative to the designs described in the Guide, and (b) to collect pragmatics for OBJ2. As it turned out, the second objective was getting increasingly dominant.

In this paper we present a graphics system roughly identical in functionality to QuickDraw, written in OBJ2. The focus is on how to construct specifications using OBJ2. We consider, among other things, some methodologies advocated in the context of software development in general; selection from alternatives likely to be confronted in using OBJ2; and the meaning of executing specifications, as distinct from executing implemented programs. We hope this paper offers the reader a practical guidance in using OBJ2 and other languages of a similar kind.

In the next section, we give a brief overview of QuickDraw as explained in the Guide. Section 3 defines the terminology we use in the paper. Then the main part of the paper follows; the section 4 gives the overall structure of our specification; Sections 5 through 9 show the actual texts of OBJ2, combined with discussions about their characteristics in view of our concerns just stated. Section 10 exemplifies a systematic usage of reduction commands. A summary and comparison with related works, in the last section, conclude the paper.

2   OVERVIEW OF QUICKDRAW

QuickDraw is the basic 2D graphics package of the Macintosh Toolbox, consisting of procedures for generating, manipulating, and examining graphic entities widely used by other packages.[1] The Guide details, in its own way, the basic concepts, their realisation, the data types, the variables, and the interfaces and functions of the procedures. The procedures and data types are described in Pascal.

2.1   POINTS AND BITMAPS

The basic concepts of QuickDraw are founded on a *coordinate plane*, a two-dimensional grid. On the plane are *points*, defined by integral coordinates; *rectangles*, defined by a pair of its constituent diagonal points; *regions*, which are sets of arbitrary boundaries. These concepts are used to define other graphic entities and the operations upon them.

Bit images actually represent graphic images; a *bit image* is a matrix of pixels, or *bits*. A bit image coupled with a coordinate plane makes a *BitMap*; they are superposed in such a way that each pixel of the image falls between

---

[1] An important point is that QuickDraw does not contain input control.

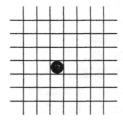

Figure 3.1   A bit map

four points of the plane (Figure 3.1).[2] BitMap is the main data type on which the definitions of drawing operations rest.

2.2   GRAFPORT

The drawing environment of QuickDraw is defined as *grafPort*, a record data type that contains such fields as the target device, the local coordinate plane, the BitMap to draw on, the drawing pattern, and the text size. There can be many grafPorts at a time, at most one of which is *current*; from the current grafPort are retrieved the crucial information at the time of drawing. Here we show the precise specifications concerning grafPort.

```
VAR thePort :  GrafPtr;
TYPE GrafPtr = ^ GrafPort;
TYPE GrafPort = RECORD
       device :  INTEGER;
       portBits :  BitMap;
       portRectangle :  Rect;
       visibleRegion :  RgnHandle;
       clippingRegion :  RgnHandle;
       backgroudPattern :  Pattern;
       fillingPattern :  Pattern;
       penLocation :  Point;
       penLineSize :  Point;
       penMode :  INTEGER;
       penPattern :  Pattern;
```

---

[2]The definitions of output primitives derived from this decision is unusual in that a pixel does not reside on a particular coordinate. In QuickDraw, the image of an output primitive, such as rectangle, is drawn *inside* the boundary. This decision probably made it easy to calculate intersections and so on, but contributed to rugged lines of such figures as ellipses [20].

```
        penVisibility :  INTEGER;
        textFont :  INTEGER;
        textFace :  Style;
        textMode :  INTEGER;
        textSize :  INTEGER;
        spaceExtra :  INTEGER;
        foregroundColour :  LongInt;
        backgroundColour :  LongInt;
        colourBit :  INTEGER;
        patternStretching :  INTEGER;
        pictureSave :  QDHandle;
        regionSave :  QDHandle;
        polygonSave :  QDHandle;
        graphicProcedures :  QDProcsPtr;
    END;
```

The variable thePort contains the pointer to the current grafPort; the pointer
grafPtr is used throughout to reach a port. We do not explain the meanings
of the fields of type GrafPort, since some of them are self-explanatory[3], and
the others are related to implementation details, which are not our concern.

2.3   DATA TYPES AND VARIABLES

In the Guide are scattered data types and global variables used in the Quick-
Draw implementation. They are described in Pascal[4].

Data Types

Most of them are of fixed record types. Among them are:

- Point — for points on a coordinate plane

- Rect — for rectangles on a coordinate plane

- BitMap — for BitMaps

- Cursor — for cursor images and their appearances

- PenState — for environments of line drawing[5]

- Region — for regions on a coordinate plane (see below)

---

[3] Actually, we expanded the original abbreviations.
[4] The terminology used in this section is that of the Guide, which we call QuickSpeak with its obvious
connotations, as the reader will be made aware as he reads on.
[5] The *pen* is an imaginary instrument to draw lines. In QuickDraw, A line has a width (size in the Guide), a
pattern (shade), and a mode that determines whether it overwrites/inverts/etc. the overlain image.

- `Picture` — for sets of drawing procedures (see below)

- `Polygon` — for polygons on a coordinate plane

- `GrafPort` — for drawing environments, as already shown

Global variables

Most important variables are pointers, including:

- `RgnHandle`, `RgnPtr`

- `PicHandle`, `PicPtr`

- `PolyHandle`, `PolyPtr`

- `thePort`

A region is, as stated in 2.1, a figure of arbitrary boundaries. QuickDraw allows defining and saving regions for future use. A picture is a collection of drawing procedures used as a macro procedure. A polygon is a polygon and needs no explanation. `RgnPtr` contains pointers to storages for regions, and `RgnHandle` is the pointer to `RgnPtr`. Similarly, `PicHandle` and `PicPtr` for pictures, and `PolyHandle` and `PolyPtr` for polygons.

2.4   QUICKDRAW ROUTINES

The procedures provided by the package are classified as:

- GrafPort Routines

- Cursor Handling

- Pen and Line Drawing

- Text Drawing

- Drawing in Colour

- Calculations with Rectangles

- Graphic Operations on Rectangles

- Graphic Operations on Ovals

- Graphic Operations on Rounded-Corner Rectangles

- Graphic Operations on Arcs and Wedges

- Calculations with Regions

- Graphic Operations on Regions

- Bit Transfer Operations

- Pictures

- Calculations with Polygons

- Graphic Operations on Polygons

- Calculations with Points

- Miscellaneous Utilities

- Customizing QuickDraw Operations

3   DEFINITIONS

The syntax and (model/proof-theoretic) semantics of OBJ2 are practically the same as those of OBJ3, which are explained concisely in "Introducing OBJ3" in this compendium. We refer the reader to that nice introduction and to articles that have appeared elsewhere [2, 4], and do not introduce OBJ2 here. We just emphasise that OBJ2/3 is *the* state-of-the-art language that is, moreover, actually implemented.

Apart from the idioms used in those papers, such as *sorts* instead of, e.g., *types*, we have to be particular as to the meanings of some words to avoid confusion in the discussions. The definitions given below are informal and not meant to be logically manipulated.

A *presentation* is a collection of actual OBJ2 texts. The *specification* denoted by a presentation is its initial model [9, 16]. An *implementation* of a specification is a specification that satisfies the specification.[6] An *implementation bias* is a tendency of a specification to restrict its possible implementations.

We *construct* a specification while we write a presentation. *Design* is a collection of activities that construct a specification. A *design decision* generates a specific design.

A *data type* is an algebra.[7] A *representation* of a data type is its structural composition, denoted in terms of other data types, or left undefined in case of *primitive* data types. *Data abstraction* is a method to define a data type without giving a representation. An *abstract data type* is a data type thus defined, and such a definition is *representation-free*. For a given data type, a definition is *representation-free relative to* another definition when the former uses a representation that structurally subsumes the latter's representation.

---

[6] We leave the meaning of satisfiability to the readers' intuition. [1], for example, gives a precise definition.
[7] This is the central tenet of abstract data type advocates.

A *constructor* of a sort s is a function with coarity s that dominates at least one irreducible term of s. An *observer* of a sort s is a function whose arity contains s and whose coarity is not s. A *characteristic observer* of a sort s is an observer of s declared in the object that declares s.

4   OVERVIEW OF THE SPECIFICATION

4.1   SPECIFICATION PROCESS

OBJ2 sees the world as a hierarchy of objects, which define a set of sorts. As befits a language originated from the method of abstract data types, specifications in OBJ2 can best be constructed from the bottom up. In most cases, such bottom-up processes have to be preceded by top-down decomposition/refinement processes. OBJ2 does accommodate refinement processes in a limited way [5], but most of the design decisions made during top-down processes are left unwritten. We feel we need an environment that supports those aspects of software processes [3, 17]; for now, let us disregard this part of our design process.

We can sketch the remainder of our design process in this way:

- Identify necessary sorts and operators.

- Define these sorts and operators using existing objects.

- Compose these definitions into new objects.

- Repeat the previous steps until completion.

This process faithfully captures the rigour of OBJ2, which can be stated as:

> Any presentation has its unique, valid specification.

Process-wise, this means:

> A presentation at any juncture of the design process has its unique, valid specification.

As long as this rigour can be maintained reasonably easily, the existing interpreter of OBJ2, or for that matter that of OBJ3, is an adequate environment. The experiments we pursued or heard of up to now suggest that, for a wide range of problems, it *is*. Needless to say, this does not mean that there is no leeway to add useful or desirable mechanisms.

4.2   COMPLETE STRUCTURE

Figures 3.2 through 3.5 show the complete module structure of our graphics system specification[8]. In these figures a trailing "+" marks a built-in module,

---

[8] Queer names abound, borrowed from QuickSpeak.

```
QUICKDRAW
        STATE
                DEVICES
                        ALIST+
                        DEVICE
                        IMAGE
                CURRENTS (continue)
                PICLIST (continue)
                RGNLIST (continue)
                PGNLIST
                        IDX
                        ALIST+
                        POLYGON
                                RECT
                                        POINT
                                LINE
                                        POINT
                                        RAT
```

Figure 3.2   Top level

and "*" a parametric module. Roughly speaking, it is such a hierarchy as (see Figure 3.6)

- The top-level object implements the equivalent of QuickDraw procedure/functions, using

- State transition functions of the object at the next level, which affect

- Images on devices, macro definitions, or values of drawing parameters, defined in the objects at the third level.

- Output primitives are defined at the lowest level and used in drawing images as well as defining functions to expand macro definitions.

- Lastly, parameterised objects are used whenever convenient.

In the sequel we ignore the top level object, which is unimportant for the purpose of this paper.

```
CURRENTS
        PATTERN
                PIXEL
                        MONOCHROME
                                COLOUR
                2TUPLE*
                INT*
                ALIST+
        DEVICE
                POINT
        POINT
                INTEXT
                        INT*
        LINESIZE
                2TUPLE*
                INT*
        PATTERNMODE
        TEXTFONT
        TEXTSTYLE
                SET+
                ASTYLE
```

Figure 3.3   Below Currents

```
PICLIST
        IDX
        ALIST+
        PICTURE
                IMAGE
                        PATTERNMODE
                        SHAPE
                                LINESIZE
                                PATTERN
                                FIGURE
```

Figure 3.4   Below PICLIST

5   COMMONPLACE OBJECTS

In this section we look into some interesting basic objects.

```
RGNLIST
        IDX
        ALIST+
        FIGURE
                BASICFIGURE
                        OVAL
                                RECT
                        WEDGE
                                RECT
                        ROUNDEDRECT
                                RECT
                        POLYGON
                        POINT
                        TRANSFORM
                                RECT
                                RAT
                                        INTEXT
                LIST+
                LINELIST
                            2TUPLE*
                            INT*
                            LINEORDER
                            LIST+
                LINEORDER
                            LIST+
                BTREE
```

Figure 3.5   Below RGNLIST

Integer

One of the most frequently used[9] objects are that of integers shown below.

```
obj INTEXT is pr INT .
  ops min max : Int Int -> Int .
  op pow2 : Int -> Int .
  vars I I' : Int .
  eq : min(I, I') = if I > I' then I' else I fi .
  eq : max(I, I') = if I > I' then I else I' fi .
  eq : pow2(I) = I * I .
jbo
```

---

[9]This is not clear from the structure shown in the figures. Even if an object is shown to be referred to only once, it may be used anywhere higher up the reference hierarchy. Or it may not. We have to look inside the objects to know.

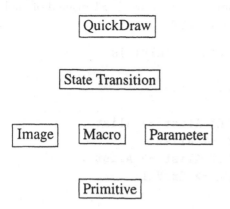

Figure 3.6   Object hierarchy

This object is an ad hoc enrichment to the built-in INT. The functions min et al. are defined here simply to avoid repetitive definitions of similar or identical functions in objects higher up. The enrichment is ad hoc in the sense that we casually added these library functions as we perceived their necessity. Clearly, judiciously enriching built-in objects *beforehand* and constructing standard library objects liberate us from this odious labour. OBJ3, an heir to OBJ2, has recognised and alleviated this inconvenience. For example, it has a built-in object for rationals, which we had to construct to calculate, e.g., geometric transformations.

Another point of discussion that arises in constructing such common objects is how to manage changes to the existing objects during design processes. On the one hand, when a change is simply an addition of functions, as in this case, the need to reflect the change in objects referring to the changed object is nil. On the other hand, for a change that affects the type of an existing function, for instance, we need carefully to trace the ripple effects of the change via reference relations, mainly but not solely upwards. OBJ2 as a language should not care about these matters; the semantics would become unnecessarily complicated. OBJ2 as an environment *should* care about these matters.

Association Lists

As a representative of parameterised objects, we show ALIST instead of such frequently (abusingly?) invoked objects as LIST.

```
obj ALIST [INDEX :: TRIV, VAL :: TRIV] is
  sort Alist ErrVal .
  subsorts Elt.VAL < ErrVal .
  op empty : -> Alist .
  op put : Elt.VAL Elt.INDEX Alist -> Alist .
  op del : Elt.INDEX Alist -> Alist .
  op chg : Elt.VAL Elt.INDEX Alist -> Alist .
  op _[_] : Alist Elt.INDEX -> ErrVal .
  op undef : -> ErrVal .
  vars I I' : Elt.INDEX .
  var V : Elt.VAL . var A : Alist .
  eq ErrVal : put(V, I, A)[ I' ] =
      if I == I' then V else A [ I' ] fi .
  eq ErrVal : empty [ I ] = undef .
  eq Alist : del(I', put(V, I, A)) =
      if I == I' then A else put(V, I, del(I', A)) fi .
  eq Alist : del(I, empty) = empty .
  eq Alist : chg(V, I, A) = put(V, I, del(I, A)) .
jbo
```

Most of this specification is standard; this object can be employed with indices and values of any sorts, providing a very general data structure. One caveat is due, however. Recall the *coherence* condition to ensure the existence of an initial algebra [8]. The subsort relation Elt.VAL < ErrVal declared to handle errors leads to the violation of this condition when a concrete sort S with S < S', where S' is not ErrVal, is bound to Elt.VAL. Similar explicit error handlings always require this consideration.[10] Anyway, existence of a universal sort eliminates this problem, and in practice this caveat can be ignored.

---

[10]Error handlings with declarations of partial domain, using NeAlist < Alist in this example, do not bring this problem.

6   OUTPUT PRIMITIVES

6.1   BASIC OUTPUT PRIMITIVES

Point

We define output primitives on a Cartesian coordinate plane[11]. Coordinates
are discrete and represented by two integrals. The first object defines points
on it.

```
obj POINT is pr INTEXT .
  sort Point .
  op (_,_) : Int Int -> Point .
  ops x y : Point -> Int .
  vars X Y : Int .
  eq Int : x(X, Y) = X .
  eq Int : y(X, Y) = Y .
  jbo
```

Here is a point of discussion. The only function of coarity Point is the
constructor (_,_). Suppose no other function of coarity Point is declared in
the objects that refer to POINT, which is in fact the case in our design. Then
we cannot change the coordinates of a point. Conceptually, this means an
element of Point denotes a particular point in the plane, and Point is the set
of actual points. Moving a point cannot occur, in the sense that changing x
or y coordinates of a point is impossible. This is the way we see things. For
presentational purposes, this means we have to denote every point with this
constructor. Additional functions such as

```
ops putx puty : Int Point -> Point .
var I : Int .
eq : putx(I, (X, Y)) = (I, Y) .
eq : puty(I, (X, Y)) = (X, I) .
```

are sometimes useful for providing "representation independent" interface.
We decided not to use them this time, since (_,_), for points, is the notation
unlikely to be forgotten or confused. Such is the power of mixfix notation.

Line

Output primitives manipulated by QuickDraw are line segments, rectangles,
polygons, wedges, rounded rectangles, and ovals (ellipses). We constructed

---

[11] We do not probe the possibility of a coordinate system-independent specification. An interesting discussion can be found in [7] in this regard.

objects for each of them, some of which are shown below. First, the object for line segments.

```
obj LINE is POINT . pr RAT .
  sorts Line .
  op (<__>) : Point Point -> Line .
  ops p1 p2 : Line -> Point .
  ops hor ver : Line -> Bool .
  ops grad ysec : Line -> Rat .
  vars P P' : Point .
  var L : Line .
  eq Point : p1(< P P' >) = P .
  eq Point : p2(< P P' >) = P' .
  eq Bool : hor(L) = y(p1(L)) == y(p2(L)) .
  eq Bool : ver(L) = x(p1(L)) == x(p2(L)) .
  cq Rat : grad(L) =
         r(y(p1(L)) - y(p2(L))) /
             r(x(p1(L)) - x(p2(L)))
      if not ver(L) .
  cq Rat : ysec(L) =
         r((y(p2(L)) * x(p1(L)) -
             y(p1(L)) * x(p2(L)))) /
         r((x(p1(L)) - x(p2(L))))
      if not ver(L) .
jbo
```

The only constructor of Line is <__>. The functions p1, p2 return end-points, hor and ver check whether segments parallel $x(y)$ axis, grad and ysec calculate gradient(y section)s, if they exist[12]. Functions necessary for transformations, point detections, and so on are not declared in this object. We distinguish them as not basic enough and relegate them to objects at higher levels.

In this object we ignore illegal attempts to calculate gradient(y section)s of vertical segments; they just create irreducible terms. In OBJ2, errors can be (a) rejected as unparsable terms, or (b) detected explicitly as errors, as in the case of ALIST. Such use of conditional equations as here can be regarded as a third class of error handlings, similar to (a) but not declaring partial sorts[13].

---

[12] The function r that appears in the last two equations is coercion of integers to rationals. We, unusually since OBJ2 supports subsort relations, treat integers and rationals separately, due to minor technicalities concerning the implementation we used.

[13] We may regard this method as error *un*handling, or error handling by stealth. The latter view is possible since when unreduced terms are presented as the results of execution, such intelligent beings as humans will not fail to detect their "illegality".

Rectangles

A rectangle of QuickDraw is a rectangle whose sides are parallel to the x- and y-axes. So is ours, whence a two-point definition is enough.

```
obj RECT is pr POINT .
  sorts Rect Junk .
  subsorts Rect < Junk .
  op make : Point Point -> Junk .
  op rect : Point Point -> Rect .
  op void : -> Junk .
  ops tl br : Rect -> Point .
  vars P P' : Point .
  cq Junk : make(P, P') = rect(P, P')
      if x(P) < x(P') and y(P) < y(P') .
  cq Junk : make(P, P') = void
      if not ( x(P) < x(P') and y(P) < y(P') ) .
  eq Point : tl(rect(P, P')) = P .
  eq Point : br(rect(P, P')) = P' .
jbo
```

This object is an example of distinguishing constructors from other functions of coarity of the sort concerned. make is a transitory function, finally turning into rect or void. We observe that we can use this technique to design a clean man-machine interface. Possibly erroneous input is regarded as a transitory function (make), translated into a valid internal meaning (rect) or rejected (void). Conditions on the first two equations are constructed so that their disjunction is always true.

Wedges

```
obj WEDGE is pr RECT .
  sort Wedge .
  op wedge : Rect Int Int -> Wedge .
  ops sec1 sec2 : Wedge -> Point .
  op sec0 : Rect Int -> Point .
  var R : Rect .
  vars I I' : Int .
  --- 0 <= I < 360, 0 < I' <= 360,
  --- I' degree clockwise from I
  eq Point : sec1(wedge(R, I, I')) = sec0(R, I) .
  eq Point : sec2(wedge(R, I, I')) =
              sec0(R, (I + I') rem 360) .
```

```
   eq Point : secO(R,    0) =
                ((x(tl(R)) + x(br(R))) quo 2, y(tl(R))) .
   eq Point : secO(R,   45) = (x(br(R)), y(tl(R))) .
   eq Point : secO(R,   90) =
                (x(br(R)), (y(tl(R)) + y(br(R))) quo 2) .
   eq Point : secO(R,  135) = br(R) .
   eq Point : secO(R,  180) =
                ((x(tl(R)) + x(br(R))) quo 2, y(br(R))) .
   eq Point : secO(R,  225) = (x(tl(R)), y(br(R))) .
   eq Point : secO(R,  270) =
                (x(tl(R)), (y(tl(R)) + y(br(R))) quo 2) .
   eq Point : secO(R,  315) = tl(R) .
jbo
```

A wedge is a portion of an ellipse. We show this object since its definition
in the Guide, whose essence we preserved in our design, is interesting. We
explain why we wrote this eerie presentation.

- An ellipse is defined by the smallest enclosing rectangle, not by its centre, width and height, as usual.[14]

- A wedge is part of an ellipse, cut by two half lines from the centre.

- The gradient of a half line is defined by the angle with an (arbitrarily defined) polar half line.

- Angles used in this way denote pseudo-angles, defined so that a half line of degree 45 cuts the top-right corner of the rectangle (see Figure 3.7)[15].

- Hence a rectangle and two integers, one for the "starting" half line and another for the "closing" one[16], uniquely define a wedge.

- For such purposes as deciding whether or not a point is in a wedge, detecting the intersections between the half lines and the rectangle is sufficient (no need to detect the intersections between the half lines and the ellipse curve, which is harder to calculate). sec1 and sec2 calculate such intersections.

---

[14] Note that since each side of a rectangle parallels a coordinate axis, each axis of an ellipse also parallels one.

[15] In the Guide no regard is taken of what happens when we use an angle of degree 30 etc. We can extrapolate to such situations in at least two ways, but let us forget about that now.

[16] The latter is defined by the relative degree from the former.

Figure 3.7   A pseudoangle

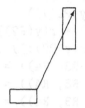

Figure 3.8   A transformation

6.2   GEOMETRIC TRANSFORMATION

QuickDraw uses scaling and parallel translation transformations and no more, so is our graphics system. Hence four parameters are enough to specify any transformation. As QuickDraw uses "definition by example", with rectangles before and after the intended transformation (see Figure 3.8), we define a function compute to get the transformation matrix from two rectangles.

```
obj TRANSFORM is pr RECT . pr RAT .
  sort Gtrans .
  op compute : Rect Rect -> Gtrans .
  op m : Rat Rat Rat Rat -> Gtrans .
  ops r1 r2 r3 r4 : Gtrans -> Rat .
  vars P1 P1' P2 P2' : Point .
  vars R1 R2 R3 R4 : Rat .
```

```
    eq Gtrans :
      compute(rect(P1, P2), rect(P1', P2')) =
      m((r(x(P1')) - r(x(P2'))) /
            (r(x(P1)) - r(x(P2))),
        ((r(x(P1)) * r(x(P2'))) -
              (r(x(P1')) * r(x(P2)))) /
            (r(x(P1)) - r(x(P2))),
        (r(y(P1')) - r(y(P2'))) /
            (r(y(P1)) - r(y(P2))),
        ((r(y(P1)) * r(y(P2'))) -
              (r(y(P1')) * r(y(P2)))) /
            (r(y(P1)) - r(y(P2)))) .
  eq Rat : r1(m(R1, R2, R3, R4)) = R1 .
  eq Rat : r2(m(R1, R2, R3, R4)) = R2 .
  eq Rat : r3(m(R1, R2, R3, R4)) = R3 .
  eq Rat : r4(m(R1, R2, R3, R4)) = R4 .
jbo
```

As we shall see, matrices thus derived are used as parameters for functions that transform. How those matrices are used — how transformations are applied, in other words — are defined separately for each output primitive. With a language that admits higher-order functions, functions instead of matrices can be given as parameters [12]. Then such functions can be understood in isolation. In general, the use of higher-order functions would enhance readability, maintainability and so on of presentations. For this particular example, however, we felt scant discomfort for lack of this mechanism.[17]

6.3   OPERATIONS ON OUTPUT PRIMITIVES

Basic Figures

Here we show a large presentation that defines some operations on output primitives we have seen. Our intention is not to daunt the readers, but to show the sweep of flexibility of OBJ2.

```
    obj BASICFIGURE is
      pr BTREE[LINELIST] *
          (sort Btree to Btr1, sort List to Lst1) .
      pr BTREE[LINEORDER] *
          (sort Btree to Btr2, sort List to Lst2) .
      pr LIST[POINT] * (sort List to Lst3) .
```

---

[17] If necessary, OBJ2 can incorporate higher-order programming [6].

```
pr POLYGON .
pr WEDGE .
pr ROUNDEDRECT .
pr OVAL .
pr TRANSFORM .
sort BasicFigure .
subsorts Line Rect Polygon Wedge RoundedRect Oval
    < BasicFigure .
subsorts Lst2 < HiddenList .
op trans : BasicFigure Gtrans -> BasicFigure .
op trans : Line Gtrans -> Line .
op trans : Rect Gtrans -> Rect .
op trans : Polygon Gtrans -> Polygon .
op trans : Point Gtrans -> Point .
op scanline : HiddenList Point Bool -> Bool .
op scanpolyg : Lst1 Point Bool -> Bool .
op createnode : Point Polygon -> 2Tuple .
op orderh : Polygon Polygon Btr1 -> Btr1 .
op orderl : Polygon Point Btr2 -> Btr2 .
op wedgevert : Rect Int Int Lst3 -> Lst3 .
op wedgepoly : Polygon Lst3 -> Polygon .
op closepoly : Polygon Polygon -> Polygon .
op _in_ : Point BasicFigure -> Bool .
vars G : Gtrans .
vars P : Point .
vars L L' L'' : Line .
vars R : Rect .
vars PG PGO : Polygon .
vars I I' : Int .
var TUP : 2Tuple .
var LST1 : Lst1 .
var BTR1 : Btr1 .
var LST2 : Lst2 .
var BTR2 : Btr2 .
var LST3 : Lst3 .
var TV : Bool .
eq Point : trans(P, G) =
    (i(r(x(P)) * r1(G) + r(y(P)) * r2(G)),
     i(r(x(P)) * r3(G) + r(y(P)) * r4(G))) .
eq Line : trans(L, G) =
    < trans(p1(L), G) trans(p2(L), G) > .
```

```
eq Rect : trans(R, G) =
   rect(trans(tl(R), G), trans(br(R), G)) .
eq Polygon : trans(frame(R), G) =
             frame(trans(R, G)) .
eq Polygon : trans(polyg(PG, L), G) =
   polyg(trans(PG, G), trans(L, G)) .
eq BasicFigure : trans(wedge(R, I, I'), G) =
   wedge(trans(R, G), I, I') .
eq BasicFigure : trans(rrect(R, I, I'), G) =
   rrect(trans(R, G), I, I') .
eq BasicFigure : trans(oval(R), G) =
                 oval(trans(R, G)) .
eq Bool : P in L =
   if ver(L)
   then x(P) == x(p1(L)) and
        (not( y(P) < min(y(p1(L)), y(p2(L))) or
              max(y(p1(L)), y(p2(L))) < y(P) ))
   else (not( x(P) < min(x(p1(L)), x(p2(L))) or
              max(x(p1(L)), x(p2(L))) < x(P) )) and
        r(y(P)) == grad(L) * r(x(P)) + ysec(L)
   fi .
eq Bool : P in R =
   (not( x(P) < x(tl(R)) or x(P) > x(br(R)) )) and
   (not( y(P) < y(tl(R)) or y(P) > y(br(R)) )) .
eq Bool : P in oval(R) =
   not(( ( (x(P) - ((x(tl(R)) + x(br(R))) quo 2))
           quo
         ( (x(br(R)) - x(tl(R))) quo 2)) *
       (( x(P) - ((x(tl(R)) + x(br(R))) quo 2))
           quo
         ( ( x(br(R)) - x(tl(R)) ) quo 2 ) )) +
       (( ( y(P) - ((y(tl(R)) + y(br(R))) quo 2 ))
           quo
         ( ( y(br(R)) - y(tl(R)) ) quo 2 ) ) *
       (( y(P) - ((y(tl(R)) + y(br(R))) quo 2 ))
           quo
         ( ( y(br(R)) - y(tl(R)) ) quo 2 ) ) )
       > 1 ) .
```

```
eq Bool : P in rrect(R, I, I') =
    P in rect((x(tl(R)) + I, y(tl(R))),
              (x(br(R)) - I, y(br(R)))) or
    P in rect((x(tl(R)), y(tl(R)) + I'),
              (x(tl(R)) + I, y(br(R)) - I')) or
    P in rect((x(br(R)) - I, y(tl(R)) + I'),
              (x(br(R)), y(br(R)) - I')) or
    P in wedge(rect(tl(R),
                    (x(tl(R)) + 2 * I,
                     y(tl(R)) + 2 * I')),
              0, -90) or
    P in wedge(rect((x(tl(R)), y(br(R)) - 2 * I'),
                    (x(tl(R)) + 2 * I, y(br(R)))),
              180, 270) or
    P in wedge(rect((x(br(R)) - 2 * I, y(tl(R))),
                    (x(br(R)), y(tl(R)) + 2 * I')),
              0, 90) or
    P in wedge(rect((x(br(R)) - 2 * I,
                     y(br(R)) - 2 * I'),
                    br(R)),
              180, 90) .
eq Bool : P in wedge(R, I, I') =
    P in oval(R) and
    P in wedgepoly(
            polyg(polyg(frame(R),
                        < sec1(wedge(R, I, I'))
                          centre(oval(R)) >),
                    < centre(oval(R))
                      sec2(wedge(R, I, I')) >),
              wedgevert(R, I + 1, I', nil)) .
eq Lst3 : wedgevert(R, I, I', LST3) =
    if ( ( I + 45 ) quo 90 ) * 90 + 45 < I + I'
    then wedgevert(R, (I + 90) rem 360, I' - 90,
            sec0(R, ((I + 45) quo 90) * 90 + 45)
            . LST3)
    else LST3
    fi .
eq Polygon : wedgepoly(PG, nil) = closepoly(PG, PG) .
eq Polygon : wedgepoly(polyg(PG, L), P . LST3) =
    wedgepoly(polyg(polyg(PG, L), < p2(L) P >),
              LST3) .
```

```
eq Polygon :
  closepoly(polyg(PG, L), polyg(frame(R), L')) =
      polyg(polyg(PG, L), < p2(L) p1(L') >) .
eq Polygon :
  closepoly(polyg(PG, L),
          polyg(polyg(PG0, L'), L'')) =
      closepoly(polyg(PG, L), polyg(PG0, L')) .
eq Bool : P in PG =
          scanpolyg(flatten(orderh(PG, PG, nil)),
                    P, false) .
eq : orderh(polyg(PG, L), PG0, BTR1) =
      orderh(PG, PG0,
              insert createnode(p1(L), PG0)
              to BTR1) .
eq : orderh(frame(R), PG0, BTR1) = BTR1 .
eq : createnode(P, PG) =
      << x(P) ; flatten(orderl(PG, P, nil)) >> .
eq : orderl(polyg(PG, L), P, BTR2) =
      if x(p1(L)) == x(p2(L)) and x(P) == x(p1(L))
      then orderl(PG, P, insert L to BTR2)
      else if ( ( x(P) ,
                  ( ( ( (y(p1(L)) - y(p2(L))) quo
                          (x(p1(L)) - x(p2(L)))
                      ) * x(P)
                    ) +
                    ( ( (x(p1(L)) * y(p2(L))) -
                        (x(p2(L)) * y(p1(L))) ) quo
                        (x(p1(L)) - x(p2(L))) )
                  ) )
              in L ) and
              (not( ( y(P) == y(p1(L))
                      and x(p2(L)) < x(p1(L))
                    ) or
                    ( y(P) == y(p2(L))
                      and x(p1(L)) < x(p2(L)) ) ))
          then orderl(PG, P, insert L to BTR2)
          else orderl(PG, P, BTR2)
          fi
      fi .
eq : orderl(frame(R), P, BTR2) = BTR2 .
```

```
      eq : scanpolyg(nil, P, TV) = false .
      eq : scanpolyg(TUP . LST1, P, false) =
           if x(P) < 1* TUP
           then false
           else scanpolyg(LST1, P, true)
           fi .
      eq : scanpolyg(TUP . LST1, P, true) =
           if x(P) < 1* TUP
           then scanline(2* TUP, P, false)
           else scanpolyg(LST1, P, true)
           fi .
      eq : scanline(nil, P, TV) = false .
      eq : scanline(L . LST2, P, false) =
           if ver(L)
           then y(P) > max(y(p1(L)), y(p2(L))) and
                   scanline(LST2, P, false)
           else y(P) > i(grad(L) * r(x(P)) + ysec(L)) and
                   scanline(LST2, P, true)
           fi .
      eq : scanline(L . LST2, P, true) =
           if ver(L)
           then not(y(P) < min(y(p1(L)), y(p2(L))))
                   or scanline(LST2, P, true)
           else not(y(P) < i(grad(L) * r(x(P)) + ysec(L)))
                   or scanline(LST2, P, false)
           fi .
  jbo
```

In essence, BASICFIGURE[18] defines geometric transformations and tests of point inclusion for each output primitive we have seen so far. The functions trans and _in_ are the main functions; others, some with unæsthetic names such as wedgevert, are meant to be hidden functions. OBJ2 does not distinguish externally visible functions and those that are internal, in that they have exactly the same semantic rôle. It is left to the user's discretion to mark such differences by lexical conventions if he so wishes, like writing the equivalent of wedgevert as wedgevertisa$hidden$function. Environmental supports may be desirable for checking such distinctions.

Declared here is BasicFigure that includes Line, Rect, Polygon, and so forth. Polymorphic functions trans and _in_ are declared on this sort. The

---

[18] We call a pure geometric entity a "figure", and a visible entity, which is a set of pixels, a "shape".

former function is declared overwrappingly on Line, Rect, and Polygon.[19] The reason is that coarities of trans's that appear in the right hand sides of equations have to be specific subsorts of BasicFigure for those terms to be well-formed. Contrarily, _in_ returns boolean values, so does not require such consideration. We can avoid these overwrapping declarations if either (a) explicit term constructs are used instead of plain variables, e.g.,

```
eq Polygon : trans(frame(rect(P,P')), G) =
                frame(trans(rect(P,P'), G)) .
```

instead of

```
eq Polygon : trans(frame(R), G) = frame(trans(R, G)) .
```

or (b) explicit coercions of BasicFigure to Line etc. are used. Note, however, that (a) somewhat contradicts the principle of data abstraction, since term constructs of sorts defined at lower levels appear in objects ever higher up[20], while (b) debauches the elegance and discipline of strong typing.

References to BTREE[LINELIST], BTREE[LINEORDER] and LIST[POINT] are necessary for deciding point inclusion. BTREE is an object that manages the sort Btree of binary trees whose nodes are of a parametric sort. LINEORDER extends LINE to order segments along y axis, and LINELIST manages pairs of integers and lists of segments thus ordered. They are used in the point inclusion algorithm for polygons.

```
obj LINEORDER is pr LINE .
  op _<_ : Line Line -> Bool .
  vars L L' : Line .
  eq Bool : L < L' =
        max(y(p1(L)), y(p2(L)))
        < max(y(p1(L')), y(p2(L'))) .
  jbo
```

---

[19] trans on Point is an unrelated function. Point is not a subsort of BasicFigure.

[20] Later we shall discuss more on this, with a meatier example.

```
obj LINELIST is
  pr 2TUPLE[INT, LIST[LINEORDER]]
        * (sort List to HiddenList,
            op (nil) to (nIL),
            op (_._) to (wow(__))) .
  op _<_ : 2Tuple 2Tuple -> Bool .
  vars X Y : 2Tuple .
  eq Bool : X < Y = (1* X) < (1* Y) .
jbo
```

The equations defining _in_ are fully shown not to argue that they are optimal, efficient, elegant, readable, or of any other positive value, but to reveal to the reader that even with the current implementation of OBJ2, which pays limited attention to performance, such complicated equations can be executed as rewrite rules in tolerable time. Anyway, the algorithms used here[21] are straightforward and declarative, except for polygons.

- A point (x_p, y_p) is in[22] a segment iff, given the definitional nonparametric equation $ax + by = c$ of the corresponding line, $ax_p + by_p = c$, and the point falls between the endpoints.

- A point is in a rectangle iff the point is bounded by the lines corresponding to the vertical sides of the rectangle and by the lines corresponding to the horizontal sides of the rectangle.

- A point (x_p, y_p) is in an ellipse iff for the definitional equation of the ellipse $(x - a)^2/c^2 + (y - b)^2/d^2 = 1$, $(x_p - a)^2/c^2 + (y_p - b)^2/d^2 \leq 1$.

- A point is in a rounded rectangle[23] iff the point is in either the largest enclosed rectangle cut vertically, in the largest enclosed rectangles of the remainders, or in the circle quadrants that remain (Figure 3.10).

- A point is in a wedge iff the point is in the ellipse that provides the curve of the wedge and in the polygons created with the half lines of the wedge and the sides of the enclosing rectangle (Figure 3.11).

The equations defining point inclusion tests seem ugly partly because we spared our labours in constructing primitive objects. For example, if we had defined `centre`, `xradius` and `yradius` in the object `OVAL` for ellipses, we could write

---

[21] Note that we are using closed boundary definitions.
[22] We mean *on* by *in*.
[23] A rounded rectangle is a rectangle rounded off at each corner by a small circle of the same size(Figure 3.9).

Figure 3.9   A rounded rectangle

Figure 3.10   Interior of a rounded rectangle

Figure 3.11   Interior of a wedge

```
var P : Point . var O : Oval .
eq Bool : P in O =
    not ( r(pow2(x(P) - x(centre(O))))
          / r(pow2(xradius(O))))
    + ( r(pow2(y(P) - y(centre(O))))
          / r(pow2(yradius(O))))
        > r(1) .
```

for ellipses.

For polygons, we resorted to a very conventional scanline algorithm (Figure 3.12).

1. Starting from a sufficiently large negative *x* coordinate, move the vertical scanline rightwards. Each time the scanline encounters a corner of the polygon, draw a vertical boundary line. Stop when the scanline does not intersect any edge of the polygon.

2. Sort vertically, for each section bounded by the drawn lines, including the left and the right half spaces, the edges which intersect its bounds. Exclude the edges that intersect only at the right bound.

Figure 3.12   Scanline

3. Find to which section the point belongs. When it is on a boundary line, it belongs to the section immediately to its left.

4. Set a flag to "out". For each sorted edge of that section, see if the point is below it, starting from the bottom edge. If it is, the point is "in" or "out", according to the flag. Otherwise, toggle the flag and continue. If no more edge is left, the point is "out".

There are other, more efficient algorithms and we may use them if we so wish.

An observation. OBJ2 is better a specification language than an implementation (programming) language[24] for reasons including (a) it is executable, but not particularly efficiently executable; (b) it has precise and simple[25] semantics against which implementations can be validated in well-defined ways, and (c) it can denote very high-level concepts, one of the benefits in using data abstraction. In this regard, presentations should be declarative, that is, equations should not define a particular procedure. In some cases, however, this is not possible. Point inclusion test for polygons is just such a case. We have to represent the problem in terms of procedures based on such strategies as divide and conquer.[26]

(2) Figures

By defining regions, we conclude the definitions of figures.

---

[24] We ignore our definitions of specification and implementation while in this paragraph and use the word implementation for the final product of software development process, and specification for all the rest.

[25] The semantics of OBJ2 is simple in that it is first-order instead of unwieldy higher-order, is restricted to equational logic instead of using full predicate calculus, and does not use partial algebra, which would complicate the meaning of equality etc.

[26] Intuitively, the most declarative definition is the one based on dividing a polyglon into the most primitive polygons — i.e., triangles — and using the disjunct of point inclusion tests within them. This strategy is not much easier to define precisely, however, considering convex/concave problems.

```
obj FIGURE is
  pr BASICFIGURE .
  sorts Region Figure .
  subsorts BasicFigure Region < Figure .
  op region : Rect -> Region .
  op rframe : Region -> Rect .
  op _and_ : Region Figure -> Region .
  op trans : Figure Gtrans -> Figure .
  op _in_ : Point Region -> Bool .
  var RE : Rect .
  vars R R' : Region .
  var C : Figure .
  var B : BasicFigure .
  var G : Gtrans .
  var P : Point .
  eq Region : R and region(RE) = R .
  eq Region : R and (R' and C) = (R and C) and R' .
  eq Region : trans(R and B, G) =
                 trans(R, G) and trans(B, G) .
  eq Region : trans(region(RE), G) =
                 region(trans(RE, G)) .
  eq Rect : rframe(R and B) = rframe(R) .
  eq Rect : rframe(region(RE)) = RE .
  eq Bool : P in region(RE) = false .
  eq Bool : P in (R and B) = (P in B) or (P in R) .
jbo
```

The sort Region is defined by the smallest enclosing rectangle (the argument to region) and the union of component figures, which may be other regions (misleadingly called _and_). When a region is used to define another, it is expanded — we are using equations as rewrite rules — with the first two equations. Geometric transformation and point inclusion for regions are defined via component transformations and point inclusions respectively.

7   SHAPES

7.1   PIXELS

Pixels and pixel patterns are defined independently of figures.

Pixels

We define colours, their mappings to monochromes, and then pixels.

```
obj COLOUR is
  sort Colour .
  ops black white red green blue cyan magenta yellow :
      -> Colour .
  op _is_ : Colour Colour -> Bool .
  vars C C' : Colour .
  eq Bool : C is C' = C == C' .
jbo

obj MONOCHROME is using COLOUR .
  op rev : Colour -> Colour .
  eq Colour : red = black .
  eq Colour : green = black .
  eq Colour : blue = black .
  eq Colour : cyan = black .
  eq Colour : magenta = black .
  eq Colour : yellow = black .
  eq Colour : rev(black) = white .
  eq Colour : rev(white) = black .
jbo

obj PIXEL is
  pr MONOCHROME * (sort Colour to Pixel) .
jbo
```

The object COLOUR defines 8 colours. We renamed builtin _==_ as _is_ for convenience. MONOCHROME collapses colours other than black and white and defines a reverse operation.

Pixel in PIXEL is the plain Colour so renamed.

Patterns

A pattern is a 2D array of pixels.

```
obj PATTERN is
  us ALIST[2TUPLE[INT, INT], PIXEL]
      * (sort Alist to Pattern) .
  ops white black grey lightGrey darkGrey :
      -> Pattern .
  op mask? : Pattern 2Tuple -> Pixel .
  ops height width : -> Int .
```

```
     vars I T : 2Tuple .
     var P : Pattern .
     var C : Pixel .
     eq Pixel : mask?(white, I) = white .
     eq Pixel : mask?(black, I) = black .
     eq Pixel : mask?(grey, I) =
           if ((1* I) - (2* I)) rem 3 == 0
           then black else white fi .
     eq Pixel : mask?(lightGrey, I) =
           if ((1* I) - (2* I)) rem 4 == 0
           then black else white fi .
     eq Pixel : mask?(darkGrey, I) =
           if ((1* I) - (2* I)) rem 2 == 0
           then black else white fi .
     eq Pixel : mask?(empty, I) = white .
     eq Pixel : mask?(put(C, T, P), I) =
         if ((1* T) == (1* I)) and ((2* T) == (2* I))
         then C
         else mask?(P, I)
         fi .
     eq : height = 8 .
     eq : width  = 8 .
   jbo
```

We define a pattern as an association list with pair of integers (meant to be row and column) as key and pixel as value. height and width define respectively the size of rows and columns, here equalised to 8. mask?(P, I) returns a pixel at row and column I of pattern P. The constants black, white, and so forth are standard patterns of shades of greyness ordered white < lightGrey < grey < darkGrey < black.[27] PATTERN does not detect whether a row(column) used in making a pattern exceeds height(width). So is an invalid reference, deemed valid with the three equations

```
     eq Pixel : mask?(white, I) = white .
     eq Pixel : mask?(black, I) = black .
     eq Pixel : mask?(empty, I) = white .
```

We decided to preclude error handling at this level, since the presentation would become ugly otherwise. We would see, for example,

---

[27] The definitions of the grey patterns are arbitrary within this order.

```
eq Pixel : mask?(white, I) =
  if 1* I < 0 or not (1* I < width) or
     2* I < 0 or not (2* I < height)
  then white
  else undef
  fi .
```

instead of

```
eq Pixel : mask?(white, I) = white .
```

for all the equations defining mask?. At a higher level, we can reject invalid setting/reference within one equation. Let us remember that we are discussing where to put error detection mechanisms. It is sometimes argued that such mechanisms are best put at lower levels, supposedly for security. Not necessarily. The crucial question is where we suppose errors occur. The answer is, of course, that they occur where their potential sources interact with the system. Then we are wiser if we define and decide how to handle errors at such places. Insistence on always concentrating on lowest levels, in fact, leads to over- and/or irrelevant specification.

This definition of arrays is very unlike those of conventional programming languages. In conventional languages, an element of an array is positionally distinguished. Take for example a 1D array v. The i-th element of v is located[28] at the i-th place of v. Given a number of elements n, an array of size n will be *allocated*. The difficulty in specifying arrays of such nature in OBJ2 lies here, in allocation. For a predetermined size of array, such a presentation as is shown below can easily be written[29].

```
obj ARRAYOFSIZE5[X :: TRIV] is
  sort Array .
  op array : Elt Elt Elt Elt Elt -> Array .
  ops 1st 2nd 3rd 4th 5th : Array -> Elt .
jbo
```

To specify an array with parametric size, we have to represent a positional indication with a symbolic or structural one, such as an association list and a plain list. As these representations are not intrinsically size-bound, out-of-bound violations have to be detected semantically, with (implicitly) parametric constants such as height and width declared here working as size specification[30].

---

[28] We are talking of definition; physical layout is not our concern.

[29] As can be seen in such builtin objects of OBJ2 as 2TUPLE and 3TUPLE.

[30] An intermediate way is to specify an array of sufficiently large size. Even in this case, the size of a specific array has to be treated in a similar way.

Note that this issue concerns how to introduce implementation biases into specifications. A tenet of data abstraction dictates that such biases should *not* be introduced, so at first glance we are discussing heresy. Let us remember, however, that specifications in software development do not constitute a mono-lithic whole, since they *cannot*. We need specifications of various levels of abstraction, which are related to each other in ways including a specification-implementation hierarchy. How to specify implementation bias, of successive restrictions is, in this regard, very important to the data abstraction mechanism.

7.2   SHAPES

We incarnate abstract figures by filling pixels, thus defining shapes. Firstly, a small housekeeping object.

```
obj LINESIZE is
  us 2TUPLE[INT, INT] * (sort 2Tuple to LineSize) .
  op inf : -> LineSize .
jbo
```

LINESIZE defines size of lines ("pen" in QuickSpeak), with width and height given in integer. The distinct constant constructor inf denotes the infinite size.

```
obj SHAPE is
  pr FIGURE .
  pr PATTERN .
  pr LINESIZE .
  sort Shape .
  op shape : Figure Pattern LineSize -> Shape .
  op rev : Shape -> Shape .
  op figure : Shape -> Figure .
  op _at_ : Shape Point -> Pixel .
  vars L : Line .
  vars F : Figure .
  vars PIX : Pixel .
  vars PAT : Pattern .
  vars PNT : Point .
  vars PG : Polygon .
  vars R : Rect .
  vars RGN : Region .
  vars SIZ : LineSize .
  vars I I' : Int .
  eq Figure : figure(shape(F, PAT, SIZ)) = F .
  eq Pixel : rev(shape(F, PAT, SIZ)) at PNT =
        rev(shape(F, PAT, SIZ) at PNT) .
```

```
eq Pixel : shape(L, PAT, SIZ) at PNT = white .
eq Pixel : shape(R, PAT, SIZ) at PNT =
    if SIZ == inf or
       not( PNT in rect((x(tl(R)) + (1* SIZ),
                         y(tl(R)) + (2* SIZ)),
                        (x(br(R)) - (1* SIZ),
                         y(br(R)) - (2* SIZ))) )
    then mask?(PAT,
           << ((x(PNT) - x(tl(R))) rem width) ;
              ((y(PNT) - y(tl(R))) rem height) >>)
    else white
    fi .
eq Pixel : shape(oval(R), PAT, SIZ) at PNT =
    if SIZ == inf or
       not(PNT in oval(rect((x(tl(R)) + (1* SIZ),
                            y(tl(R)) + (2* SIZ)),
                           (x(br(R)) - (1* SIZ),
                            y(br(R)) - (2* SIZ)))))
    then mask?(PAT,
           << ((x(PNT) - x(tl(R))) rem width) ;
              ((y(PNT) - y(tl(R))) rem height) >>)
    else white
    fi .
eq Pixel : shape(rrect(R, I, I'), PAT, SIZ) at PNT =
    if SIZ == inf or
       not( PNT in rrect(rect((x(tl(R)) + (1* SIZ),
                              y(tl(R)) + (2* SIZ)),
                             (x(br(R)) - (1* SIZ),
                              y(br(R)) - (2* SIZ))),
                        I, I') )
    then mask?(PAT,
           << ((x(PNT) - x(tl(R))) rem width) ;
              ((y(PNT) - y(tl(R))) rem height) >>)
    else white
    fi .
eq Pixel : shape(wedge(R, I, I'), PAT, SIZ) at PNT =
    if SIZ == inf or
       not(PNT in wedge(rect((x(tl(R)) + (1* SIZ),
                             y(tl(R)) + (2* SIZ)),
                            (x(br(R)) - (1* SIZ),
                             y(br(R)) - (2* SIZ))),
                      I, I') )
```

```
            then mask?(PAT,
                    << ((x(PNT) - x(tl(R))) rem width) ;
                       ((y(PNT) - y(tl(R))) rem height) >>)
         else white
         fi .
   eq Pixel : shape(PG, PAT, SIZ) at PNT =
       if SIZ == inf or
          not(PNT in
                trans(PG,
                    compute(frame(PG),
                        rect((x(tl(frame(PG))) + (1* SIZ),
                              y(tl(frame(PG))) + (2* SIZ)),
                             (x(br(frame(PG))) - (1* SIZ),
                              y(br(frame(PG))) - (2* SIZ)))
                    )     )   )
            then mask?(PAT,
                << ((x(PNT) - x(tl(frame(PG)))) rem width) ;
                   ((y(PNT) - y(tl(frame(PG)))) rem height) >>)
         else white
         fi .
   eq Pixel : shape(RGN, PAT, SIZ) at PNT =
       if SIZ == inf or
          not(PNT in
                trans(RGN,
                    compute(rframe(RGN),
                        rect((x(tl(rframe(RGN))) + (1* SIZ),
                              y(tl(rframe(RGN))) + (2* SIZ)),
                             (x(br(rframe(RGN))) - (1* SIZ),
                              y(br(rframe(RGN))) - (2* SIZ)))
                    )     )   )
            then mask?(PAT,
                << ((x(PNT) - x(tl(rframe(RGN)))) rem width) ;
                   ((y(PNT) - y(tl(rframe(RGN)))) rem height) >>)
         else white
         fi .
jbo
```

The only constructor of sort Shape is shape of arity sorts Figure, Pattern and LineSize. shape(F,PAT,SIZ) represents a shape of boundary figure F, filled with PAT up to SIZ inward from the boundary (filled completely when SIZ is inf). Then a shape can be regarded as a set of pixels thus filled. The function rev reverses a given shape, i.e., reverses whatever pixel in the set.

The characteristic observer of Shape is _at_; it gives the meaning of shapes by way of deciding which pixel is at a given point of a given shape. Take for example a definition of rectangular shapes.

```
eq Pixel : shape(R, PAT, SIZ) at PNT =
    if SIZ == inf or
      not ( PNT in rect((x(tl(R)) + (1* SIZ),
                         y(tl(R)) + (2* SIZ)),
                        (x(br(R)) - (1* SIZ),
                         y(br(R)) - (2* SIZ))) )
    then mask?(PAT,
                  << ((x(PNT) - x(tl(R))) rem width) ;
                     ((y(PNT) - y(tl(R))) rem height) >>)
    else white
    fi .
```

Here a point PNT is assumed to be in the boundary R. The equation states that the pixel at PNT is white, the background colour, if PNT is in the inner rectangle left unfilled, and a pixel at the relative position in the pattern PAT otherwise.

7.3   TEXTS

So far we ignored texts, since QuickDraw ignored them except for cursory glances at some basic ideas concerning them. Fully to incorporate texts in our drawing system is beyond this paper; we have to prepare a complete font system for that. Our conscience suggests, however, we show at least what the likely presentation would look like.

```
obj CHARCODE is pr INT .
  sort CharCode .
  op #_ : Int -> CharCode .
  var I : Int .
  cq CharCode : # I = # (I rem 128) if I > 127 .
jbo

  obj TEXTFONT is
  sort TextFont .
  ops systemFont applFont newYork geneva monaco
      venice london athens sanFran toronto : -> Font .
  jbo
```

```
obj ASTYLE is
  sort AStyle .
  ops bold italic underline outline
  shadow condense extend normal : -> AStyle .
jbo

obj TEXTSTYLE is
  us SET[ASTYLE] * (sort Set to TextStyle) .
  eq TextStyle : omega =
            bold $ italic $ underline $
            outline $ shadow $ condense $
            extend $ normal .
jbo

obj TEXTSIZE is
  pr INT * (sort Int to TextSize) .
jbo

obj CHAR is
  pr TEXTFONT .
  pr TEXTSTYLE .
  pr TEXTSIZE .
  pr CHARCODE .
  sort Char .
  op c____ : CharCode TextFont TextStyle TextSize
          -> Char .
jbo
```

CHARCODE declares a character set CharCode, supposing something similar to the ascii set. The sort TextFont of TEXTFONT contains available fonts, while AStyle of ASTYLE contains available styling parameters. TextStyle is a set of AStyle, thus making possible, e.g., italicised bold lettering. TextSize is an integer intended to denote text sizes in resolution units. Finally, CHAR declares the sort Char, constructed by c____ with fonts, styles, sizes and character codes defined above.

Note the difference between AStyle and TextStyle. Both are sets, but the former is statically defined and the latter is changeable dynamically. In general whenever a mutable set is required, a plain sort cannot be used directly, but has to be incorporated into elements of explicitly defined sets, lists, etc.

Given a complete font system for each font and a function for each styling parameter, we can treat a character as just another output primitive and decide, for example, which pixel is at a particular point affected by a character. Assuming that, the following object specifies text primitives.

```
obj TEXT is
  pr POINT .
  pr LIST[CHAR] * (sort List to String) .
  sort Text .
  op t : String Point -> Text .
jbo
```

8   DRAWING

8.1   IMAGES

Transfer Modes

To specify the way to put shapes, such as overwriting, overlaying, erasing or inverting the previous image, the object PATTERNMODE is specified.

```
obj PATTERNMODE is

  sorts BasicPatternMode PatternMode .
  subsorts BasicPatternMode < PatternMode .

  ops copy or xor bic : -> BasicPatternMode .
  op not : BasicPatternMode -> PatternMode .
jbo
```

PatternMode contains all the constants and their respective negations, eight modes in total. Their meanings shall be explained immediately, in terms of how they control the contribution of shapes to actual appearances.

Images

The specification of compositions of individual shapes, called images, is constructed out of SHAPE and PATTERNMODE.

```
obj IMAGE is pr SHAPE . pr PATTERNMODE .

  sort Image .

  op init : -> Image .
  op over : Shape PatternMode Image -> Image .
  op _at_ : Image Point -> Pixel .
  op pixel : Shape PatternMode Image Point -> Pixel .
```

```
      vars I : Image .
      vars P : Point .
      vars B : Pixel .
      vars S : Shape .
      vars M : PatternMode .

      eq Pixel : init at P = white .
      eq Pixel : over(S, M, I) at P =
          if P in figure(S) then pixel(S, M, I, P)
                                else I at P fi .
      eq Pixel : pixel(S, not(M), I, P) =
                  pixel(rev(S), M, I, P) .
      eq Pixel ; pixel(S, copy, I, P) = S at P .
      eq Pixel : pixel(S, or,   I, P) =
          if (S at P) is black then black else I at P fi .
      eq Pixel : pixel(S, xor,   I, P) =
          if (S at P) is black then rev(I at P)
                                else I at P fi .
      eq Pixel : pixel(S, bic,   I, P) =
          if (S at P) is black then white else I at P fi .
  jbo
```

An image is composed with successive addition (over) of individual shapes in ways indicated by PatternMode, starting from the initial image (init). A characteristic observer _at_ of sort Image returns the pixel of an image at a given point. The other observer, pixel, is meant to be a hidden function.

The initial image is supposed to consist of the background colour white all over. The above definition follows the following procedure. Given a point of interest P,

1. Scan the composing shapes lifo-wise.

2. If no more shape is left, the pixel is white. Otherwise, let the next shape be S.

3. If P is not in S, the pixel is that of the remaining image. Otherwise, let the mode be m. If m is a negation, reverse S and let the de-negated mode be m. Depending on m,

   (a) If m is copy, the pixel is identical to that of S at P (overwriting).

   (b) If m is or,

       i. if the pixel of S at P is black, so is the pixel of the image at P,

ii. otherwise, the pixel is that of the remaining image (overlaying).

(c) If m is xor,

i. if the pixel of S at P is black, reverse the pixel of the remaining image at P,

ii. otherwise, the pixel is that of the remaining image (exclusive or'ing).

(d) If m is bic,

i. if the pixel of S at P is black, the pixel is white,

ii. otherwise, the pixel is that of the remaining image (erasure).

A negation of a mode indicates the identical effect for the reversed shape.

8.2   DRAWING ON DEVICES

The Lilliputian DEVICE declares the available output devices to draw images on.

```
obj DEVICE is pr POINT .
  sort Device .
  ops screen laserp netdb : -> Device .
  ops size origin : Device -> Point .
  eq Point : size(screen) = (1028,1028) .
  eq Point : origin(screen) = (512,512) .
jbo
```

The characteristic observers size and origin returns the size and the coordinate origin of devices.[31] The constants and equations are exemplary. It is advisable that a separate object be specified for the sort Device, since this is clearly a sort highly susceptible to circumstantial changes. In general, altering a specification should have local *and* demarcated effects on the corresponding presentation.

For practical situations, Device should have a hierarchical structure, as shown below.

---

[31] We are abusing Point to denote *sizes*.

```
obj DEVICE' is pr POINT .
  sorts Device Screen Plotter
        HPlotter VPlotter ImageDb .
  subsorts Screen Plotter ImageDb < Device .
  subsorts HPlotter VPlotter < Plotter .
  ops s t u : -> Screen .
  ops p q : -> HPlotter .
  ops r : -> VPlotter .
  ops d e f : -> ImageDb .
  ops size origin : Device -> Point .
  var S : Screen .
  var H : HPlotter .
  var V : VPlotter .
  var D : ImageDb .
  eq Point : size(S) = (1028,1028) .
  eq Point : size(D) = (1005674,1005676) .
  --- and so forth
jbo
```

Indeed this is among the most representative usages of subsort relations that realise operator inheritance mechanism. We proceed in the following manner.

1. Define a taxonomical order of sorts.

2. Declare functions on the highest relevant[32] sorts in that order.

3. Give meanings of those functions at appropriate levels.

Next comes the specification that defines images on devices.

```
obj DEVICES is
  pr ALIST[DEVICE, IMAGE] * (sort Alist to Devices) .

  op init : -> Devices .
  op add : Shape Device PatternMode Devices
           -> Devices .
  op reset : Device Devices -> Devices .
  op _at_of_ : Device Point Devices -> Pixel .
```

---

[32] We should, that is, avoid declaring everything at *the* highest sort; sloppy specifications so constructed do not reflect design decisions, thus are hard to understand, at least mechanically.

```
var I : Device .
var D : Devices .
var S : Shape .
var P : Point .
var M : PatternMode .
eq Devices : init =
   put(init, screen,
        put(init, laserp, put(init, netdb, empty))) .
eq Devices : add(S, I, M, D) =
        chg(over(S, M, D [ I ]), I, D) .
eq Devices : reset(I, D) = chg(init, I, D) .
eq Pixel : I at P of D = (D [ I ]) at P .
jbo
```

An element of the sort `Devices`, represented by an association list with device name as index and image as value, is a complete snapshot of the output devices used. We conceive a state of a device as nothing more than the then current image on it.

The functions defined here constitute a minimal set. `init` initialises all the devices. `add` adds a shape with a rendition mode to the image of a device. `reset` resets a particular device to the initial image. `_at_of_` is the characteristic observer of `Devices`, inquiring the then current pixel of a device at a given point.

9   OBJECTS AT TOP-LEVEL

We are almost ready to define state transitions, whose specification is the eventual goal of the paper. As final preparations we need to write objects for drawing environments and macro definitions.

9.1   DRAWING PARAMETERS

For purposes such as drawing connected lines successively and defining polygons, it is useful to retain a current cursor position, line size, etc. We call them current drawing parameters and define them below.

```
obj CURRENTS is pr DEVICE .
  pr PATTERN .   pr POINT .
  pr LINESIZE .   pr PATTERNMODE .
  pr TEXTFOMT .   pr TEXTSTYLE .
  sorts Currents Varid Var .
  subsorts Device Pattern Point LineSize PatternMode
           TextFont TextStyle TextMode TextSize
             < Var .
```

```
ops dev bkp flp pnl pns pnm pnp txf txs txm txz :
    -> Varid .
op init : -> Currents .
op get : Currents Varid -> Var .
op put : Currents Varid Var -> Currents .
op crv : Device Pattern Pattern Point LineSize
         PatternMode Pattern TextFont TextStyle
         TextMode TextSize
         -> Currents .
vars DEV DEV1 : Device .
vars PT1 PT11 PT2 PT21 PT3 PT31 : Pattern .
vars PNT PNT1 : Point .
vars LSZ LSZ1 : LineSize .
vars PMD PMD1 : PatternMode .
vars FNT FNT1 : TextFont .
vars STL STL1 : TextStyle .
vars TMD TMD1 : TextMode .
vars TSZ TSZ1 : TextSize .
eq : get(crv(DEV, PT1, PT2, PNT, LSZ,
             PMD, PT3, FNT, STL, TMD, TSZ), dev)
     = DEV .
eq : get(crv(DEV, PT1, PT2, PNT, LSZ,
             PMD, PT3, FNT, STL, TMD, TSZ), bkp)
     = PT1 .
eq : get(crv(DEV, PT1, PT2, PNT, LSZ,
             PMD, PT3, FNT, STL, TMD, TSZ), flp)
     = PT2 .
eq : get(crv(DEV, PT1, PT2, PNT, LSZ,
             PMD, PT3, FNT, STL, TMD, TSZ), pnl)
     = PNT .
eq : get(crv(DEV, PT1, PT2, PNT, LSZ,
             PMD, PT3, FNT, STL, TMD, TSZ), pns)
     = LSZ .
eq : get(crv(DEV, PT1, PT2, PNT, LSZ,
             PMD, PT3, FNT, STL, TMD, TSZ), pnm)
     = PMD .
eq : get(crv(DEV, PT1, PT2, PNT, LSZ,
             PMD, PT3, FNT, STL, TMD, TSZ), pnp)
     = PT3 .
eq : get(crv(DEV, PT1, PT2, PNT, LSZ,
             PMD, PT3, FNT, STL, TMD, TSZ), txf)
     = FNT .
```

```
eq : get(crv(DEV, PT1, PT2, PNT, LSZ,
            PMD, PT3, FNT, STL, TMD, TSZ), txs)
    = STL .
eq : get(crv(DEV, PT1, PT2, PNT, LSZ,
            PMD, PT3, FNT, STL, TMD, TSZ), txm)
    = TMD .
eq : get(crv(DEV, PT1, PT2, PNT, LSZ,
            PMD, PT3, FNT, STL, TMD, TSZ), txz)
    = TSZ .
eq : put(crv(DEV, PT1, PT2, PNT, LSZ,
            PMD, PT3, FNT, STL, TMD, TSZ),
         dev, DEV1)
    = crv(DEV1, PT1, PT2, PNT, LSZ,
          PMD, PT3, FNT, STL, TMD, TSZ) .
eq : put(crv(DEV, PT1, PT2, PNT, LSZ,
            PMD, PT3, FNT, STL, TMD, TSZ),
         bkp, PT11)
    = crv(DEV, PT11, PT2, PNT, LSZ,
          PMD, PT3, FNT, STL, TMD, TSZ) .
eq : put(crv(DEV, PT1, PT2, PNT, LSZ,
            PMD, PT3, FNT, STL, TMD, TSZ),
         flp, PT21)
    = crv(DEV, PT1, PT21, PNT, LSZ,
          PMD, PT3, FNT, STL, TMD, TSZ) .
eq : put(crv(DEV, PT1, PT2, PNT, LSZ,
            PMD, PT3, FNT, STL, TMD, TSZ),
         pnl, PNT1)
    = crv(DEV, PT1, PT2, PNT1, LSZ,
          PMD, PT3, FNT, STL, TMD, TSZ) .
eq : put(crv(DEV, PT1, PT2, PNT, LSZ,
            PMD, PT3, FNT, STL, TMD, TSZ),
         pns, LSZ1)
    = crv(DEV, PT1, PT2, PNT, LSZ1,
          PMD, PT3, FNT, STL, TMD, TSZ) .
eq : put(crv(DEV, PT1, PT2, PNT, LSZ,
            PMD, PT3, FNT, STL, TMD, TSZ),
         pnm, PMD1)
    = crv(DEV, PT1, PT2, PNT, LSZ,
          PMD1, PT3, FNT, STL, TMD, TSZ) .
```

```
  eq : put(crv(DEV, PT1, PT2, PNT, LSZ,
                PMD, PT3, FNT, STL, TMD, TSZ),
           pnp, PT31)
     = crv(DEV, PT1, PT2, PNT, LSZ,
           PMD, PT31, FNT, STL, TMD, TSZ) .
  eq : put(crv(DEV, PT1, PT2, PNT, LSZ,
                PMD, PT3, FNT, STL, TMD, TSZ),
           txf, FNT1)
     = crv(DEV, PT1, PT2, PNT, LSZ,
           PMD, PT3, FNT1, STL, TMD, TSZ) .
  eq : put(crv(DEV, PT1, PT2, PNT, LSZ,
                PMD, PT3, FNT, STL, TMD, TSZ),
           txs, STL1)
     = crv(DEV, PT1, PT2, PNT, LSZ,
           PMD, PT3, FNT, STL1, TMD, TSZ) .
  eq : put(crv(DEV, PT1, PT2, PNT, LSZ,
                PMD, PT3, FNT, STL, TMD, TSZ),
           txm, TMD1)
     = crv(DEV, PT1, PT2, PNT, LSZ,
           PMD, PT3, FNT, STL, TMD1, TSZ) .
  eq : put(crv(DEV, PT1, PT2, PNT, LSZ,
                PMD, PT3, FNT, STL, TMD, TSZ),
           txz, TSZ1)
     = crv(DEV, PT1, PT2, PNT, LSZ,
           PMD, PT3, FNT, STL, TMD, TSZ1) .
jbo
```

Apart from being largish, there is nothing complicated in CURRENTS. The sort Currents consists of records of fixed size that contain all the drawing parameters. crv is its sole constructor and get its sole characteristic observer.

The sorts Var and Varid are technical devices. Var has as its subsorts all the sorts of crv's arity. Varid has constants corresponding to the elements in the arity. Then we can declare get of coarity Var, and put of arity Currents, Varid and Var, to change/retrieve any field of any sort. Alternatively, we could define get/put functions for each field, like

```
op getdevice : Currents -> Device .
op putdevice : Currents Device -> Currents .
op getbkpattern : Currents -> Pattern .
```

and so on. Standard is this alternative definition, it tends to lead to a nasty presentation, according to our taste. Note well that our presentation is possible because we are using an order-sorted language, not a mere many-sorted one.

A third alternative is to discard cvr and define put/get functions (`getdevice` and `putdevice` above) recursively:

```
eq Device : getdevice(putdevice(DEV,CVS)) = DEV .
eq Device : getdevice(putbkpattern(PAT,CVS)) =
                    getdevice(CVS) .
--- and so on
eq Device : getdevice(init) = screen .
```

where `init` denotes the initial set of drawing parameters and the initial device is assumed `screen`. This presentation is not only far less handsome than the other two, but requiring hordes of equations that degenerates efficiency in searching rewrite rules.[33]

The moral; use a distinct constructor[34] when a fixed-sized record, or a tuple, is the natural way to organise a data type. Pedantically speaking, this practice violates the principle of data abstraction, since it has more implementation biases than the ugly sister. But this is one of the situations where the need for elegant presentations wins over.

9.2   MACRO ETC. DEFINITIONS

In QuickDraw there are three kinds of definitions that require storing for future use, namely, polygons, regions, and pictures. Shown below are objects that deal with pictures.

```
obj PICTURE is
  pr IMAGE * (sort Image to Picture) .
  op transform : Picture Gtrans -> Picture .
  var M : PatternMode .
  var I : Picture .
  var F : Figure .
  var P : Pattern .
  var S : LineSize .
  var G : Gtrans .
  eq Picture :
        transform(over(shape(F, P, S), M, I), G) =
        over(shape(trans(F, G), P, S), M, trans(I, G)) .
  eq Picture : transform(init, G) = init .
jbo
```

A picture is a macro definition that is a composition of shapes. In this regard a picture is similar to an image, except that it may be transformed when used

---

[33] The tendency of the terms to grow inexorably in size also contributes to loss of efficiency.

[34] Such a constructor is sometimes called a *canonical* constructor.

to draw actual images. Hence PICTURE imports IMAGE, renames Image to Picture, and defines transform on Picture. Transformation is successively applied to component shapes.

The reader may notice that the terms of these equations are over-minute. The constructor shape of the sort Shape as well as over of Image appear in the presentation. This is chiefly because we have not defined adequate functions on Shape. It is not easy to tell whether we have defined adequate functions for a given sort. We are safe if we observe *sufficient completeness* criterion [11], but it is tedious — indeed. A better way is to be a little skimpy at first and gradually to enrich objects as needed. However, as we stated already, this may cause problems of ripple effects and we have to be very careful.

A collection of Picture is again defined in terms of ALIST.

```
obj IDX is
   sorts Idx SubIdx .
   subsorts SubIdx < Idx .
   op 0 : -> SubIdx .
   op s : SubIdx -> SubIdx .
   op e : -> Idx .
jbo

obj PICLIST is
   pr ALIST[IDX, PICTURE] *
        (sort Alist to PicList, sort Idx to PicId) .
jbo
```

Idx is supposed to contain indices, including an illegal index denoted e.[35] PicList is an association list of Picture indexed by Idx, renamed PicId.

RGNLIST for region definitions and PGNLIST for polygon definitions are defined similarly.

9.3   STATE TRANSITION FUNCTIONS

Armed with DEVICES for output devices, CURRENTS for drawing parameters, and PICLIST etc. for definition storage, we can now construct the top-level specification[36].

```
obj STATE is pr DEVICES .
   pr CURRENTS . pr PICLIST .
   pr RGNLIST . pr PGNLIST .
   sorts State Constituent ConstituentName .
```

---

[35] Viewed otherwise, Idx contains pointers, where SubIdx contains valid references and e is a null pointer.
[36] As stated earlier, we are ignoring the truly top-level object that defines QuickDraw routines.

```
subsorts Devices Currents PicList RgnList PgnList
           < Constituent .
op init : -> State .
op st : Devices Currents PicList RgnList PgnList
           -> State .
op get : State ConstituentName -> Devices .
ops dev cur pic rgn pgn -> ConstituentName .
op replace : State ConstituentName Constituent
               -> State .
vars D D' : Devices . vars C C' : Currents .
vars P P' : PicList . vars R R' : RgnList .
vars G G' : PgnList .
eq : init = st(init,init,empty,empty,empty) .
eq : get(st(D,C,P,R,G),dev) = D .
eq : get(st(D,C,P,R,G),cur) = C .
eq : get(st(D,C,P,R,G),pic) = P .
eq : get(st(D,C,P,R,G),rgn) = R .
eq : get(st(D,C,P,R,G),pgn) = G .
eq : replace(st(D,C,P,R,G),dev,D') = st(D',C,P,R,G) .
eq : replace(st(D,C,P,R,G),cur,C') = st(D,C',P,R,G) .
eq : replace(st(D,C,P,R,G),pic,P') = st(D,C,P',R,G) .
eq : replace(st(D,C,P,R,G),rgn,R') = st(D,C,P,R',G) .
eq : replace(st(D,C,P,R,G),pgn,G') = st(D,C,P,R,G') .
jbo
```

The structure is quite similar to that of CURRENTS. The sort State has a constructor st and a characteristic observer get. State transitions are realised by replace, a polymorphic function over constituents of states. If error handling mechanism is required, it is best ingrained in this object, since it is here that the system interacts with the outside world.

10   EXECUTING THE SPECIFICATION

10.1   ANALYSIS VERSUS EXECUTION

We have written the presentations of a graphics output system in OBJ2. We then would like to see if our specification is complete and/or correct [37] in some well-defined senses. There are analytical techniques, coupled with corresponding semantic definitions, to check completeness of specifications. For example, the following procedure ascertains a kind of completeness that relies on sort dependency.

---

[37] Let us disregard the potent undertone of completeness, correctness and what not and subject them to loose arguments in this section.

1. For each sort s, assemble the constructor set K.

2. From each $\kappa \in K$, retrieve a multiset μ, consisting of sorts other than s, in coarity of κ.

3. Take the union M of all μs.

4. For each characteristic observer of s, subtract from M (the singleton of) its arity sort.

5. If M remains nonempty, more observers are needed for s.

This is a very weak completeness in that it only assures that an adequate number of functions is declared for each sort, with no in-depth analysis of definitional parts (i.e., equations). We can be more demanding and require, e.g., sufficient completeness as defined in [11].

The advantage of these analytical techniques is that they are based on well-defined semantic characteristics. The disadvantage is that they are exhaustive. In particular, if deep reasonings, such as inductive proof, are needed, ensuring completeness and/or correctness in this way is practically impossible, either automatically or interactively. At least we have to restrict our attention to a manageable chunk of a specification.

Once we admit the impossibility of exhaustive analysis, execution arises as the least bad alternative to check completeness, to say nothing of correctness. An executable specification is propounded for variegated purposes, but its essence is that

> There is no way to validate a specification against the "true" intent of the designing agents, other than to believe their say-so.

In different contexts, such as rapid prototyping [19], informative arguments on this subject can be found.

In OBJ2, a specification is executed by term rewriting system [13]. The terms are reduced with equations as rewrite rules. An inadequate set of equations give inadequately reduced terms, and incorrect equations make incorrect terms. So we can say that, given a sufficient[38] set of terms to be reduced,

> The specification is complete and correct if all those terms are reduced to the expected — i.e., correct — terms.

Unexpected results are useful assistants in adding or modifying signatures and equations as required, just in the way symbolic execution indicates the nature and location of errors in programming codes.

---

[38] Sufficiency is determined by designing agents. We do have some techniques to help check that, similar to those for measuring test coverage, but do not elaborate here.

10.2   EXECUTING A GRAPHICS SYSTEM SPECIFICATION

Our graphics system is composed of devices, drawing parameters, and macro definitions, which are unrelated with each other except at the top-level. So the natural way to check the system is to reduce terms in each of them in turn. The latter two components are uninteresting for the present purpose, since (a) with drawing parameters, all we have to see is whether each parameters are set or retrieved as intended, and (b) macro definitions works correctly, if a parametric object ALIST works correctly, thus no complication is expected.

The most interesting, and most important, matter is whether an image is correctly constructed. In dealing with machine codes, invoke routines (operators in OBJ2) and we literally see what happens on the screen. An executable specification is not executable in such a way.[39] Instead, we indirectly observe the equivalent effects by inquiring

> Which kind of pixel is at a given location of a given device at a given time.

So we perform the following procedure:

1. Select a representative set of images.

2. Make terms that get pixels at sampling points of those images.

3. Attatch expected pixels to each of them.

4. Reduce terms and check the results against those pixels.

Representative Set of Images

Faced with an infinite number of images, we perforce establish a criterion for selecting a comprehensive yet manageable set of images. For that purpose we first make the following observations.

- An image is a sequence of pairs of shapes and rendition modes.

- A rendition mode is either overwriting, overlaying, etc.

- A shape is a triple of a figure, a pattern, and a line size.

- A figure is a composition of basic figures.

- A basic figure is either a line, or a rectangle, etc.

Assume patterns, composite figures, and line sizes are correctly defined. Then a basic set B of shapes consists of the cross product of the set of basic figures and the set of rendition modes (Figure 3.13).

---

[39] In fact, we can execute just in such a way, by replacing equations with those that invoke builtin lisp codes; a futile exercise, we suspect.

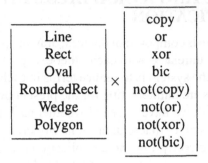

Figure 3.13   The basic set B

With this basic set, we shall use a kind of induction on images, for which we enrich the object IMAGE slightly.

```
obj IMAGE' is us IMAGE .
  op animage : -> Image .
endo
```

A constant animage is declared, to be used as an arbitrary image.

The induction base uses a set of images created by adding shapes in B to the initial blank image, one at a time. We check if all those images are correctly defined. The induction hypothesis is that animage is correctly defined. If all the images created by adding to animage shapes in B, again one at a time, are correctly defined, we can say that any image is correctly defined.

Sampling points

Sampling points can be chosen by mimicking conventional test data selection methods. We use a boundary analysis, which we summarise as

1. Determine equivalence classes of (tuples of) input data, using either specifications or programmes.

2. Detect bounds between such classes.

3. Choose test data on or near the bounds for each class.

Equivalence classes classifies data according to various characteristics, depending on the criteria. Typical characteristics include (a) normal or abnormal (error), and abnormal in what ways; (b) which paths are taken during execution; (c) what functions are invoked. For trivial example, with integers as input, $\{i|i \leq 0 \quad or \quad i \geq 127\}$ is the invalid class and $\{i|0 \leq i \leq 127\}$ is the valid class.

If input data are totally ordered and equivalence classes are contiguous over the orders, the bounds are automatically determined once the equivalence classes are determined. With the above example, 0 and 127 are the bounds. When input data are well-ordered in such a manner, we can choose boundary data matter-of-factly; 0 and 127 for the valid class and -1 and 128 for the invalid class.

Let us adapt these notions to our situation. We have an infinite set of points as input data, and have to consider their relation to shapes[40].

- There are two equivalence classes, one for points possibly affected by shapes and the other for the rest.

- The bounds of shapes are the bounds of the classes.

- The boundary data are points on the bounds of shapes (for the affectable class) and immediately adjacent outside points (for the unaffectable class).

It is impractical to use all these boundary points. Because there is no good rationale to choose particular points among them, we randomly choose some points.

Expected Pixels

Given an arbitrary image, it is hard to know what pixel is at a particular point. With images we need to check, however, the task is so much simpler. Those images fall into two types, one for the induction base and the other for the induction conclusion. An image for the induction base is of the form

```
over(shape(F,P,S),M,init)
```

where F is a figure, P a pattern, S a size and M a rendition mode. Given such an image, if a point PT is in F and its distance from the bounds is within S, the pixel at PT is determined by P and M; otherwise, it is the same as that of the initial blank image, white.

Similarly, an image for the induction conclusion is of the form

```
over(shape(F,P,S),M,animage)
```

Given such an image, if a point PT is in F and its distance from the bounds is within S, the pixel at PT is determined by P and M; otherwise, it is the same as that of animage. An expected pixel may be such terms as

```
rev(animage at (0,5))
```

---

[40] We are checking images, but as things stand, we only have to think of shapes.

meaning "the reverse of whatever pixel is at (0,5) of animage". We can say that this is the expected pixel, from the induction hypothesis.

Reduction Commands

A tiny subset of the resultant reduction commands are shown below.

```
reduce in IMAGE' as Pixel :
  (over(shape(< (10,10) (20,20) >, black, << 5 ; 5 >>),
                copy, init)
     at (15,18))
   ---> white
  (over(shape(< (10,10) (20,20) >, black, << 5 ; 5 >>),
                xor, init)
     at (15,18))
   ---> white
  (over(shape(< (10,10) (20,20) >, black, << 5 ; 5 >>),
                bic, init)
     at (15,18))
   ---> white
  (over(shape(< (10,10) (20,20) >, black, << 5 ; 5 >>),
                copy, animage)
     at (15,18))
   ---> animage at (15,18)
  (over(shape(< (10,10) (20,20) >, black, << 5 ; 5 >>),
                not(bic), animage)
     at (15,12))
   ---> animage at (15,12) .
```

11   SUMMARY AND CONCLUSIONS

We have shown in some detail the specification of a graphics system roughly identical in functionality to QuickDraw. We have articulated some pragmatics along the way, which we summarise here. Mutatis mutandis, they are relevant to algebraic specifications in general.

- In defining operators, take a moment to observe which are and should be constructors and observers of each sort. Looking from this angle, you have a clear idea of the adequacy of specifications. Also, remember what functions are or are not meant to be hidden.

- Supply adequate observers to give representation independent interfaces to modules, but do not attempt always to be exhaustive. Overspecification may result.

- Put error detection and handling mechanisms in appropriate places. Otherwise, the construction process is excessively tedious and often over-specification may result.

- Choose appropriate error handling mechanisms. OBJ offers a couple of options, with respective pros and cons.

- Think of higher-order functions if necessary, then translate them into first-order ones. This translation is not difficult in practice.

- Do not give up if declarative definitions do not come up. Algorithms can be written as recursive equations, if sometimes complicated. If the efforts arenot worth the results, however, you may shy away; even inadequately reduced terms are informative.

- Implementation biases are bad, but not always. If you want to introduce them, make the reasons clear.

- Distinguish, normally by allocating to them a distinct object, operators susceptible to changes. The resultant presentations are easier to revise.

- Use execution mechanisms cleverly, and you have a satisfactory way to be assured of correct, complete specifications.

Lastly, we would like to refer the reader to the similar experimentations reported in some literature, for comparison. [12] shows an algebraic specification of a system for drawing structured pictures. [14] is a comprehensive attempt to use algebraic techniques in designing graphics systems, incorporating user interactions as well as manipulating pictures.

Because both experiments do not intend to create executable specifications and in general not stick to a particular language, they have more freedom. For example, [14] uses procedures, instead of functions, for certain input operations. [12] uses higher-order functions to define geometric transformations. Also, to what extent and in what way their specifications are complete is unclear, since they have no way to state the completeness, correctness, etc. Our definitions concerning such properties, based on executions, has a fragile theoretical foundation but at least provide a way to evaluate specifications in concrete terms.

References

[1]   Rod Burstall and Joseph Goguen. The Semantics of Clear, A Specification Language. *Proc. of 1979 Copenhagen Winter School*, Lecture Notes in Computer Science 86, Springer-Verlag, 1980, pp.292–332.

[2]   Kokichi Futatsugi. An Overview of OBJ2. Proc. of Franco-Japanese Symp. on Programming of Future Generation Computers, Tokyo, Oct.

1986, published as *Programming of Future Generation Computers*, ed. Fuchi,K. and Nivat,M., North-Holland, 1988, pp.139–160.

[3]   Kokichi Futatsugi. Experiences in Algebraic Specification/Programming Language Systems. Internal Report, Electrotechnical Laboratory, 1989.

[4]   Kokichi Futatsugi, Joseph Goguen, Jean-Pierre Jouannaud and José Meseguer. Principles of OBJ2. *Proc. 12th Symp. on Princ. ProgLang.* 1985, pp.52–66.

[5]   Kokichi Futatsugi, Joseph Goguen, José Meseguer and K. Okada. Parameterized Programming in OBJ2. *Proc. of 9th Int. Conf. Soft. Eng.*, March, 1987, pp.51–60.

[6]   Joseph Goguen. Higher Order Functions Considered Unnecessary for Higher Order Programming. Tech. Rep. CSL-88-1, SRI International, 1988.

[7]   Joseph Goguen. Modular Algebraic Specification of Some Basic Geometric Constructions. *Artificial Intelligence*, Vol.37, 1988, pp.123–153.

[8]   Joseph Goguen and Joseé Meseguer. Order-Sorted Algebra I: Partial and Overloaded Operators, Errors and Inheritance. Technical Report, SRI International, Computer Science Lab., 1987.

[9]   Joseph Goguen, James Thatcher and Eric Wagner. An initial algebra approach to the specification, correctness, and implementation of abstract data types, In Raymond Yeh, editor, *Current Trends in Programming Methodology, IV*, pages 80–149. Prentice-Hall, 1978.

[10]   Joseph Goguen and Timothy Winkler. Introducing OBJ3, in this compendium.

[11]   John Guttag. The Algebraic Specification of Abstract Data Types. Acta Informatica Vol.10, 1978, pp.27–52.

[12]   John Guttag and J.J. Horning. Formal Specification As a Design Tool. *Proc. of Symp. on Princ. Prog. Lang.*, ACM, 1980, pp.251–261.

[13]   Gérard Huet and D.C. Oppen. Equations and rewrite rules: a survey. Technical Report CSL-111, SRI International, Jan. 1980.

[14]   W.R. Mallgren. *Formal Specification of Interactive Graphics Programming Languages*. MIT Press, 1982.

[15]   *Macintosh Programmer's Guide*, also available as *Inside Macintosh*, Addison-Wiesley, 1985.

[16]   José Meseguer and Joseph Goguen. Initiality, induction and computability. In M. Nivat (ed.), *Algebraic Methods in Semantics*, Cambridge University Press, 1984, pp.459-541.

[17]   Ataru Nakagawa and Kokichi Futatsugi. Stepwise Refinement Process with Modularity: An algebraic Approach. *Proc. of 11th Inter. Conf. Soft. Eng.*, IEEE, 1989, pp.166–177.

[18] Ataru Nakagawa, Kokichi Futatsugi, S. Tomura and T. Shimizu. Algebraic Specification of Macintosh's QuickDraw using OBJ2. *Proc. of 10th Inter. Conf. Soft. Eng.*, IEEE, 1988, pp.334–343.

[19] Special Issue on Rapid Prototyping, ACM *Software Engineering Notes*, Vol.7, No.5, 1982.

[20] J.R. Van Aken. An Efficient Ellipse-Drawing Algorithm. *IEEE Computer Graphics and Applications*, Vol.4 No.9, 1984, pp.24–35.

Chapter 4

APPLICATIONS OF OBJ TO THE SPECIFICATION OF STANDARDS FOR COMPUTER GRAPHICS

David A. Duce

Rutherford Appleton Laboratory,
Chilton, Didcot, Oxon OX11 0QX, UK

Abstract   There are now three International Standards for application program interfaces for computer graphics programming, GKS, GKS-3D and PHIGS. In this paper a simplified model GKS-like system is described and a 2D PHIGS-like system is then described in terms of this and a centralised structure store. Formal specifications of the systems are given illustrating how the specification of a system can be built up from a hierarchy of simple components. The purpose of the paper is to illustrate one approach to the description of a compatible family of graphics standards and the use of formal specification techniques in this process.

1   INTRODUCTION

Considerable effort has been devoted to the development of international standards for computer graphics, since the Seillac I Workshop in 1976, which marked the beginning of the formal moves to achieve a set of standards for computer graphics by consensus amongst experts in the field. In 1985, the first international standard for computer graphics, the Graphical Kernel System [4] was published by the International Organization for Standardization (ISO).

GKS addresses the needs of applications which require to output 2D graphics and perform graphical input, for example draightling systems. An extension of GKS to provide facilities for output and input of 3D graphics, the Graphical Kernel System for three dimensions, GKS-3D, was published in 1988 [5]. GKS-3D provides application programs with the capability to define and display 3D graphics in a framework very similar to that provided by GKS. In June 1989, a third application program interface standard, the Programmer's

Hierarchical Interactive Graphics System, PHIGS [6] was published. PHIGS, like GKS-3D, provides facilities for 3D output and input, but is aimed at applications which manipulate models of complex objects, which can be described as hierarchical structures. The classical example is a robot arm that can be articulated about the various joints.

Other standards for the storage and transfer of picture description information and for dialogues with graphical devices have been defined, or are in the process of definition, but these are not considered in this paper.

GKS, GKS-3D and PHIGS are described in self-contained documents but there are many concepts in common between the three systems. Each system is defined independently of any particular programming language, in terms of a collection of data structures (which have some familiarity with Fortran COMMON blocks) and functions which modify or inquire the contents of the data structures and generate graphical output or input. The function definitions are given in English.

The remainder of this paper explores the application of OBJ to the specification of a simplified model GKS-like system and a 2D PHIGS-like system is then defined using the components of the GKS system. It is worth stressing that the relationship between GKS-3D and PHIGS is not quite so exact as that between the models described here, in part because the coordinate systems in the two standards do not exactly coincide and also because they have different mechanisms for operator attribute control (highlighting parts of a picture, for example). However, this way of viewing the relationship is interesting in that it allows "reuse" of the GKS description in the descriptions of PHIGS. Such an approach greatly simplifies the descriptions of the two systems.

The purpose of this paper is to illustrate one approach to the description of a compatible family of graphics standards. For the purposes of illustration, the starting point is a simple systems which captures the essense of GKS. Of necessity the model systems are simplifications of the full standards, but the models chosen capture the concepts of GKS and PHIGS essential for the discussion.

The specifications are given in the ObjEx [3, 1] dialect of OBJ.

2   THE GKS MODEL SYSTEM

2.1   GKS

GKS provides a functional interface between an application program and a configuration of graphical input and output devices at a level of abstraction that hides the peculiarites of device hardware. It achieves device independence by means of the concepts of abstract input, abstract output and abstract workstations. The concept of abstract input will not be discussed, but the specifications attempt to capture the other two concepts.

Firstly, the concept of abstract output is described. In GKS, pictures are constructed from a number of basic building blocks, called **output primitives**, which are abstractions of the basic actions that a graphical output device can perform (eg. drawing a line). There are six output primitives in GKS: polyline, polymarker, text, fill area, cell array and generalized drawing primitive (GDP); each of which has associated with it a set of **parameters**, which defines a particular instance of the primitive. This paper considers the polyline primitive, which draws a connected sequence of line segments and has the coordinates of its vertices as parameters.

The concept of an abstract **workstation** in GKS is an abstraction from the physical device hardware and maps abstract output primitives to physical output primitives and physical input primitives to abstract input primitives. It represents zero or one display surfaces and zero or more input devices as a configurarion of abstract devices. An application program may direct output to more than one workstation simultaneously; however, the specification will aim to model only a system with a single workstation.

The application program specifies coordinate data in the parameters of an output primitive in **world coordinates** (WC), a Cartesian coordinate system. World coordinates are then transformed to a uniform coordinate system for all workstations, called **normalised device coordinates** (NDC) by a window to viewport mapping termed **normalisation transformation**. A second window to viewport mapping, called the **workstation transformation** accomplishes the transformation to the **device coordinates** (DC) of the display surface.

In order to simplify the specification, WC coordinate space will be ignored and it will be assumed that polyline coordinate data are supplied in the NDC coordinates. Primitives can optionally be clipped to the boundary of the viewpoint of the normalization, but clipping too, will be ignored.

An application often requires the capability of structuring a picture, such as the ability to define a graphical object, for example, a tree by a sequence of polyline primitives, and the abulity to re-use this definition. GKS allows output primitives to be grouped together into units termed **segments** which are stored, conceptually at the NDC level, and which may be manipulated in certain ways as a single entity. Segments are not considered in this specification.

The appearance of a primitive displayed on a workstation is determined by its parameters and additional data termed **aspects**. The aspects of a polyline are: linetype, which in GKS may be solid, dashed, dashed-dotted or an implementation-dependent type; linewidth scale factor, which is applied to the nominal linewidth provided by the workstation to give a value which is then mapped to the nearest available linewidth; and polyline colour index which is an index into a workstation dependent colour table. For simplicity, it will be assumed in the specifications that follow that the value for linewidth can be specified directly, rather than as the product od a scale factor and a nominal width. It is also assumed that the workstation supports any linetype and linewidth requested, as, although it is a simple matter to map the requested value onto the nearest available value, this adds needless complexity for the present purposes. Colour will also not be considered.

The value of aspects are determined by **attributes**. There are two basic schemes for specifying aspects, termed **individual specification** and **bundled specification**. In the individual scheme the value of each aspect is determined by a different attribute; the linetype aspect by the linetype attribute and the linewidth scale factor aspect by the linewidth scale factor attribute. For each of the attributes there is an operation to set its value. In this scheme, the setting of the value of an attribute, such as linetype, applies to all subsequently created polyline primitives until it is reset. The individual scheme will not be further considered here.

In the bundled mode of specifying polyline aspects, the values of all the aspects are determined by a single attribute, called the **polyline index**. A polyline index defines a position in a table, the **polyline bundle table**, each entry in which is termed a **bundle** and specifies the values for each of the aspects. The bundle corresponding to a particular polyline index is termed the **representation** of the index. There is an operation which sets the value of polyline index modally, as well as as operation to set the representation of a bundle index. When a polyline primitive is created, the current value of the polyline index is bound to the primitive and cannot subsequently be changed. Bundles are bound to primitives when they are displayed. If a representation of a particular polyline index has not been defined, the representation for polyline index 1 is used instead, and GKS is initialised such that there will always be a representation defined for polyline index 1.

In GKS each workstation has its own polyline bundle table, which allows the application to control the appearance of polylines with the same polyline index independently on each workstation on which they are displayed, using the capabilities of the workstation. If a representation of a polyline index is changed, the appearance of polylines already created with that polyline index may also be changed to the new representation. Thus although the value of the polyline index with which a polyline is created cannot subsequently be changed, the representation with which the polyline is displayed can be changed. GKS admits that some workstations are able to perform changes dynamically (for example a colour table can be dynamically changed on most raster devices affecting the appearance of all primitives displayed), whilst for other devices the picture has to be redrawn to effect the change (for example changing colour on a pen plotter). This act of redrawing the picture is called **regeneration**. The complexities of regeneration are ignored in this paper as they do not contribute to understanding the relationship between GKS and PHIGS. The specification of regeneration is discussed in [2].

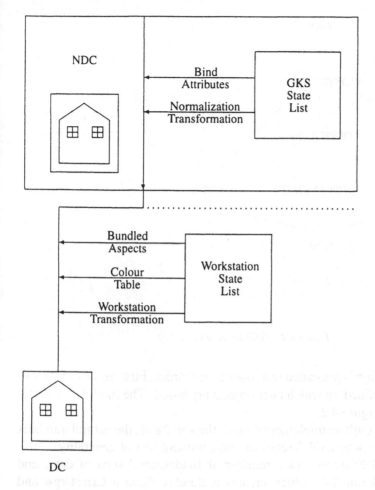

Figure 4.1   GKS architecture

The architecture of GKS is described in Figure 4.1.

2.2   THE SPECIFICATION

For the present purposes, it suffices to consider a small subset of GKS which includes the following concepts:

1. a picture in NDC space in which primitives are created and attributes are bound to them;

2. a workstation including a picture in DC space which displays primitives with their representations bound to them and primitive bundle tables.

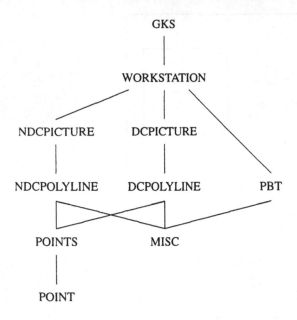

Figure 4.2   GKS module hierarchy

The specification is presented in a 'bottom-up' order. First, some fundamental objects are defined on which later objects are based. The module hierarchy is illustrated in Figure 4.2.

As there is no built-in implementation of the sort Real, the natural numbers are used in places where GKS requires reals, without loss of generality.

The object MISC introduces a number of fundamental sorts of data, and the operation mkBundle, which creates a Bundle from a Linetype and Linewidth (used as an abbreviation for the GKS aspect linewidth scale factor). The third component of the GKS polyline bundle, polyline colour index, is omitted as colour specification is not considered here. To do so would complicate the specification without adding any new principles.

The object POINT defines the data type representing points (in NDC space), and the object POINTS defines lists of points.

```
obj MISC
   sorts Window Viewport PolylineIndex
         Linetype Linewidth Bundle
   ops mkBundle: Linetype Linewidth -> Bundle
   jbo
```

```
obj POINT
  sorts Point
  ops mkPoint : nat nat -> Point
jbo
```

```
obj POINTS/ POINT
  sorts Points
  ops emptyPoints : -> Points
      addPoints : Point Points -> Points
jbo
```

Polylines in NDC space are represented by objects of sort NDCPolyline.
A polyline is represented by a list of points (the vertices of the polyline) and a
polyline index.

```
obj NDCPOLYLINE / POINTS MISC
  sorts NDCPolyline
  ops create : Points PolylineIndex -> NDCPolyline
jbo
```

The sort DCPolyline represents polylines as displayed on the workstation
display surface. This is an abstraction which records both the geometric and
aspect data from which a visible image might be rendered and so describes the
appearance of the primitive to be displayed. Polylines are represented as a list
of vertices and a bundle.

```
obj DCPOLYLINE / POINTS MISC
  sorts DCPolyline
  ops display: Points Bundle -> DCPolyline
jbo
```

Figure 4.3 illustrates an NDC polyline between points P_1, P_2, P_3 (of sort
Points) with polyline index I_1 (sort PolylineIndex); this is represented by
the term:

```
create(addPoints(P_1,
                 addPoints(P_2,
                           addPoints(P_3,
                                     emptyPoints))),
       I_1) .
```

Suppose the polyline transformed to DC coordinates (see Figure4.3) has vertices Q_1, Q_2, Q_3 (of sort Points), and is displayed with linetype LT_1 (sort
Linetype) and linewidth LW_1 (sort Linewidth), the DC polyline would be
represented by the term

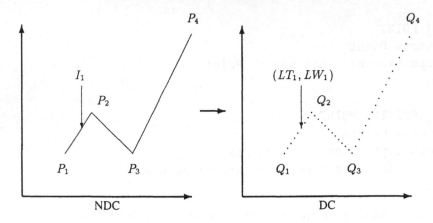

Figure 4.3   Relationship between NDC and DC polylines

$$display(addPoints(Q_1,$$
$$addPoints(Q_2,$$
$$addPoints(Q_3,$$
$$emptyPoints))),$$
$$mkBundle(LT_1, LW_1)) \ .$$

The concepts of an NDC picture and a DC picture are captured by the objects NDCPICTURE and DCPICTURE. These two objects have a set structure, the first being a set of NDC polylines and the second a set of DC polylines. They are defined as instances of the generic object PICTURE. The **image** construct is used for this purpose. In the first example of its usage below, the object NDCPICTURE is defined, based on PICTURE, and importing the object NDCPOLYLINE. The sort Picture is replaced ('⇒') by the sort NDCPicture, and the sort Primitive by NDCPolyline. The operator

    empty : -> Picture

is replaced by emptyNDCP which will have the signature:

    emptyNDCP : -> NDCPicture

The object PICTURE is defined as follows:

```
obj PICTURE
   sorts Picture Primitive
   ops empty : -> Picture
       _U_ : Picture Picture -> Picture
             (ASSOC COMM ID: empty)
       {_} : Primitive -> Picture
```

```
      vars p : Picture
      eqns ( p U p = p )
   jbo

   image ( PICTURE => NDCPICTURE ) / NDCPOLYLINE
      sorts ( Picture => NDCPicture )
            ( Primitive => NDCPolyline )
      ops ( empty : -> Picture => emptyNDCP )
   endim

   image ( PICTURE => DCPICTURE ) / DCPOLYLINE
      sorts ( Picture => DCPicture )
            ( Primitive => DCPolyline )
      ops ( empty : -> Picture => emptyDCP )
   endim
```

The next part of the specification characterizes a polyline bundle table. Essentially a bundle table is a finite function from polyline indices to bundles. The details are not important for what follows.

```
obj PBT/ MISC
   sorts Pbt
   ops emptyPbt : -> Pbt
       _U_ : Pbt Pbt -> Pbt (ASSOC  COMM  ID: emptyPbt)
       [_%_] : PolylineIndex Bundle -> Pbt
       _\_ : Pbt PolylineIndex -> Pbt
       _+_ : Pbt Pbt -> Pbt
       _[_] : Pbt PolylineIndex -> Bundle
   vars pbt, pbt1 : Pbt
        i, dj: PolylineIndex
        b, b1, b2: Bundle
   eqns ( pbt  U  pbt = pbt )
        ( [ i % b ] \ i = emptyPbt )
        ( [ j % b ] \ i = [ j % b ] IF  not  i==j )
        ( (pbt U pbt1) \ i = (pbt \ i ) U ( pbt \ i ) )
        ( pbt + [ i % b1 ] = (pbt \ i ) U ( [ i % b1 ] ) )
        ( (pbt U [ i % b1 ]) [i] = b1 )
        ( (pbt U [ i % b1 ]) [j] = pbt [ j ]
          IF not i == j )
   jbo
```

The object WORKSTATION models a GKS workstation, which is characterised by a workstation transformation defined by a window and viewport and a polyline bundle table, together with a DC picture.

The operation t transforms the vertices of the polyline by the workstation transformation (which is not further defined here). The operation redisplay generates a DC picture from an NDC picture.

```
obj WORKSTATION / DCPICTURE PBT NDCPICTURE
  sorts Workstation
  ops mkWs : Window Viewport Pbt DCPicture
              -> Workstation
      t : Window Viewport Points -> Points
      redisplay : Window Viewport Pbt NDCPicture
                  -> DCPicture
  vars ndcp1, ndcp2 : NDCPicture
       pts : Points
       pi : PolylineIndex
       pbt : Pbt
       w : Window
       v : Viewport
  eqns ( redisplay(w,v,pbt,ndcp1 U ndcp2 ) =
           redisplay(w,v,pbt,ndcp1)
           U redisplay(w,v,pbt,ndcp2) )
       ( redisplay(w,v,pbt,emptyNDCP) = emptyDCP )
       ( redisplay(w,v,pbt, { create(pts,pi) } ) =
         { display(t(w,v,pts),pbt [ pi ]) } )
jbo
```

For the polyline example given earlier, if the workstation transformation has window w_1 and viewport v_1, and the representation of polyline index I_1 is mkBundle(LT_1, LW_1), the DC polyline will be represented by the term

```
display(
  t($w_1,v_1$,
    addPoints($P_1$,
               addPoints($P_2$,
                          addPoints($P_3$,
                                     emptyPoints)))),
  mkBundle($LT_1,LW_1$)) .
```

Finally the object GKS is defined. It defines the GKS operations:

```
POLYLINE
SET POLYLINE INDEX
```

```
SET POLYLINE REPRESENTATION
SET WORKSTATION WINDOW
SET WORKSTATION VIEWPORT
CLEAR WORKSTATION
```

The sort GKS is a tuple with components of sorts PolylineIndex, NDC-Picture and Workstation. The specification only considers a single workstation. Expanding the specification to include multiple workstations is in principle straightforward, but adds unnecessary complexity for the present purposes.

```
obj GKS / WORKSTATION
  sorts GKS

  ops mkGKS : PolylineIndex  NDCPicture  Workstation
                 -> GKS
      Polyline : Points  GKS -> GKS
      SetPlIndex : PolylineIndex  GKS -> GKS
      SetPlRepresentation :
         PolylineIndex  Linetype  Linewidth GKS -> GKS
      SetWsWindow : Window GKS -> GKS
      SetWsViewport : GKS -> GKS
      ClearWs: GKS -> GKS

  vars i, j : PolylineIndex
       ndcp : NDCPicture
       ws : Workstation
       lt : Linetype
       lw : Linewidth
       w, w1 : Window
       v, v1 : Viewport
       pbt : Pbt
       dcp : DCPicture
       pts : Points

  eqns

  ( SetPlIndex(i,mkGKS(j,ndcp,ws)) = mkGKS(i,ndcp,ws) )
  ( Polyline(pts, mkGKS(j, ndcp, mkWs(w,v,pbt,dcp))) =
    mkGKS(j, { create(pts,j) } U ndcp,
       mkWs(w, v, pbt,
              { display(t(w,v,pts), pbt[ j ]) }
              U dcp)) )
```

```
( SetPlRepresentation(
        i, lt, lw, mkGKS(j, ndcp, mkWs(w,v,pbt,dcp))) =
    mkGKS(j, ndcp,
          mkWs(w, v, pbt + [ i % mkBundle(lt,lw) ],
              redisplay(w, v,
                          pbt + [ i % mkBundle(lt,lw) ],
                          ndcp))) )
( SetWsWindow(w, mkGKS(j,ndcp,mkWs(w1,v,pbt,dcp))) =
    mkGKS(j, ndcp,
          mkWs(w, v, pbt, redisplay(w,v,pbt,ndcp))) )
( SetWsViewport(v, mkGKS(j, ndcp,
                            mkWs(w,v1,pbt,dcp))) =
    mkGKS(j, ndcp, mkWs(w, v, pbt,
                          redisplay(w,v,pbt,ndcp))) )
( ClearWs(mkGKS(j,ndcp,mkWs(w,v,pbt,dcp))) =
    mkGKS(j, emptyNDCP, mkWs(w,v,pbt,emptyDCP)) )
  jbo
```

The effect of the `Polyline` operation is to create a new NDC polyline in the NDC picture and display the corresponding DC polyline in the DC picture. The result is modelled by an object of sort GKS, whose NDC picture component is that of the initial state with the addition of the new NDC polyline, and whose workstation component is that of the initial state with the addition of the new DC polyline to the DC picture component. Other components of the object remain unchanged. This is what the equations defining the `Polyline` operation state. The operation `SetPlIndex` generates a new state with values corresponding to the parameter of the operation.

The `SetPlRepresentation` operation adds the representation for the specified polyline index to the polyline bundle table, overriding any definition already present in the table for the specified index. The workstation is assumed to have a dynamic modification accepted capacity for changing polyline representations, and so the DC picture resulting from the operation is that obtained by redisplaying the NDC picture with the new bundle table. The operations `SetWsWindow` and `SetWsViewport` are defined similarly. A dynamic modification accepted capability is also assumed for the workstation transformation.

That completes the specification of the model GKS system.

3   THE MODEL PHIGS SYSTEM

3.1   PHIGS

The major difference between GKS and PHIGS is that in GKS output is displayed immediately on all active workstations, whereas in PHIGS graphical data are stored in a Centralised Structure Store (CSS), which can be thought of as a database, and nothing is displayed until a structure is explicitly posted to a workstation.

Graphical information is organized in the CSS in named units called structures. A structure is a sequence of structure elements. Structure elements represent graphical entities such as the parameters of a polyline or the value of a polyline index.

Posting a structure to a workstation causes the structure to be **traversed**, generating graphical output for display on the workstation. Traversal consists of interpreting each structure element in the structure and performing the appropriate operations.

Once a structure has been posted, changes made to the structure are reflected on the workstation until the structure is unposted. Unposting a structure does not cause it to be removed from the centralised structure store.

Particular features of the structure facility are:

1. **Hierarchy:** structures can call other structures and the same structure may be called more than once from a higher level. Thus a car may need only a single wheel structure which is called four times.

2. **Modelling coordinates:** structure elements contain positional information in modelling coordinates. Each structure has a global and local modelling transformation which are concatenated to produce the transformation to be applied to points to turn the modelling coordinates into the coordinates to be passed to the viewing pipeline.

3. **Inheritance:** substructures inherit attributes from the calling structure. Thus, the global modelling transformation is the one passed by the calling structure. Similarly, attributes such as polyline index can be passed to the substructure. On completion of traversing a structure, control reverts to the higher structure that called it and the attributes are reset to those in force on entry to the substructure. Thus the substructure can have no effect on the calling structure.

4. **Editing:** there is a structure element pointer and functions akin to those of a simple line editor are provided. It is possible to move around a structure and edit it after initial creation.

In GKS, visibility, highlightling and detectability, may be controlled for primitives stored in segments. PHIGS controls these values on a per primitive basis using the idea of name sets and filters. Because the mechanisms are different and neither is central to the principles being illustrated here, segments and attributes are not considered in the GKS-model and name sets are not considered in the PHIGS-model.

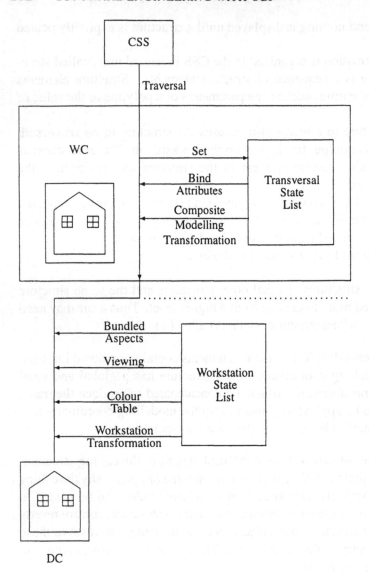

Figure 4.4   PHIGS architecture

The architecture of PHIGS is illustrated in Figure 4.4. The relationship between the model PHIGS system and the model GKS system described in Section 2 is that traversal of the PHIGS CSS generates invocations of the GKS operations to produce graphical output. The application thus creates and modifies structures in the CSS and traversal invokes GKS operations as shown in Figure 4.5.

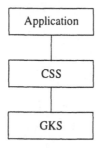

Figure 4.5   Relationship between PHIGS and GKS systems

3.2   THE SPECIFICATION

The module hierarchy is illustrated in Figure 4.6. The first part of the PHIGS specification is the definition of the centralised structure store. This is built up in stages starting with the definition of structure names, lists of names, modelling coordinates and the modelling transformation and structure elements.

The object NAMELIST defines the sort Name and the sort NameList which represents lists of names. This data type is used later to represent the list of structures posted to a workstation. For illustration, a limited range of names (5 in total) is defined here. Constants are denoted by operators with a null arity. The semantics of OBJ ensures that these operators denote different values of the sort. The constant NULL represents "no name".

```
obj NAMELIST
  sorts Name NameList
  ops NULL, N1, N2, N3, N4 : -> Name
      emptyNL : -> NameList
      _&_ : Name NameList -> NameList
jbo
```

The objects MCPOINT and MCPOINTS define points in modelling coordinates and lists of points in modelling coordinates respectively. They are analogous to the objects POINT and POINTS in the GKS specification. A generic object could have been used to define all types of points and point lists.

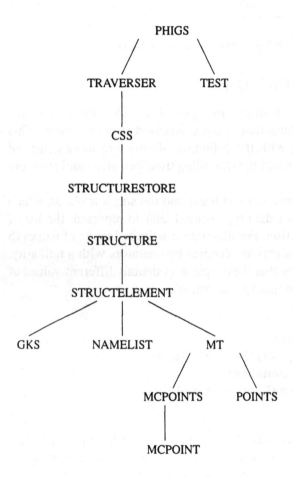

Figure 4.6   PHIGS module hierarchy

```
obj MCPOINT
  sorts MCPoint
  ops mkMCPoint : nat  nat  -> MCPoint
jbo
```

```
obj MCPOINTS / MCPOINT
  sorts MCPoints
  ops emptyMCPoints : -> MCPoints
      addPoints : MCPoint MCPoints -> MCPoints
jbo
```

The next object defines the modelling transformation. The sort Comptype represents the different combining modes for the local modelling transformation provided by the system. The meaning of these modes is given in the object TRAVERSER. The operation _o_ is the composition operation for modelling transformations. The operation _[_] applies a modelling transformation to a list of points in modelling coordinates and produces a list of points in normalized device coordinates. It is not further defined here. For illustration, four modelling transformations are declared as constants. The constant, IDENT, denotes to identity transformation.

```
obj MT / MCPOINTS POINTS
  sorts MTComptype
  ops PRECONCAT : -> Comptype
  POSTCONCAT : -> Comptype
  REPLACE : -> Comptype
  IDENT : -> MT
  MT1, MT2, MT3, MT4 : -> MT
  _o_ : MT MT -> MT (ASSOCID: IDENT)
  _[_] : MT MCPoints -> Points
jbo
```

The object STRUCTELEMENT defines the sort StructElement, representing the possible types of structureelement considered here. The constructors pise, plse, exse, loct and globt make structure elements corresponding to the "set polyline index", "polyline", "execute structure", "set local modelling transformation" structure elements respectively. As will be seen shortly, these constructors hold the arguments of the PHIGS functions by which they are created, in order that they can be passed to the corresponding GKS operations when the structure is traversed.

```
obj STRUCTELEMENT / GKS NAMELIST MT
  sorts StructElement
  ops pise : PolylineIndex -> StructElement
      plse : MCPoints -> StructElement
      exse : Name -> StructElement
      loct : MTComptype -> StructElement
      globt : MT -> StructElement
jbo
```

Structures are now represented as sequences of structure elements (where the sequence number is of sort nat and the structure element is of sort StructElement). The operation size returns the number of structure elements in a structure, inse inserts a structure element at a specified place in the structure. Elements beyond that position are renumbered accordingly. The operation __ removes an element from a structure and _[_] delivers the element as a specified position in the structure. Errors are not treated in this specification.

```
obj STRUCTURE / STRUCTELEMENT
  sorts Structure
  ops emptystruct : -> Structure
      _U_ : Structure Structure -> Structure
              (ASSOC COMM ID: emptystruct)
      mkStruct : nat StructElement -> Structure
      inse : nat StructElement Structure -> Structure
      _\_ : Structure nat -> Structure
      _[_] : Structure nat -> StructElement
      size : Structure -> nat
  vars ep, ep1 : nat
       nos, n, m : Name
       s, s1, s2 : Structure
       se, se1 : StructElement
       i : PolylineIndex
       pts : Points
  eqns
      ( s U s = s )
      ( inse(succ(ep), se, emptystruct) = emptystruct )
      ( inse(0, se, emptystruct) = mkStruct(1,se) )
      ( inse(ep, se, s1 U s2) =
        inse(ep,se,s1) U inse(ep,se,s2) )
      ( inse(ep, se, mkStruct(ep1,se1)) =
          mkStruct(succ(ep1), se1)
        IF (ep < ep1) )
```

```
          ( inse(ep, se, mkStruct(ep1,se1)) =
              mkStruct(ep1,se1)
              IF (ep1 < ep) )
          ( inse(0, se, mkStruct(1,se1)) =
              mkStruct(1,se) U mkStruct(2,se1) )
          ( inse(ep, se, mkStruct(ep,se1)) =
              mkStruct(ep,se1) U mkStruct(succ(ep),se) )
          ( (s1 U s2) \ ep =
              (s1 \ ep) U (s2 \ ep) )
          ( emptystruct \ ep = emptystruct )
          ( mkStruct(ep,se) \ ep = emptystruct )
          ( mkStruct(ep1,se) \ ep = mkStruct(ep1,se)
              IF (not((ep1 == ep))) )
          ( (s U mkStruct(ep,se)) [ ep ] = se )
          ( (s U mkStruct(ep1,se)) [ ep ] = s [ ep ]
              IF (not((ep1 == ep))) )
          ( (s U emptystruct) [ ep ] = s [ ep ] )
          ( size(emptystruct) = 0 )
          ( size(s1 U s2) = size(s1) + size(s2) )
          ( size(mkStruct(ep,se)) = 1 )
  jbo
```

A structure generating a polyline with vertices P_1 and P_2, with polyline index I_1, and a polyline with vertices P_3, P_4, with polyline index I_2 would be represented by the term

```
mkStruct(1, pise(I₁)) U
mkStruct(2, plse(addPoints(P₁,
                          addPoints(P₂,
                                   emptyMCPoints)))) U
mkStruct(3, pise(I₂)) U
mkStruct(4, plse(addPoints(P₃,
                          addPoints(P₄,
                                   emptyMCPoints))))
```

The structure store is represented in a similar way to the polyline bundle table, as a finite function from a structure identifier (of sort Name) to a structure (sort Structure) and the element pointer associated with the structure (sort nat). Strictly speaking, PHIGS only requires a global element pointer; however, it makes the specification neater to associate an element pointer with each structure. The operation get retrieves a named structure and its size from the structure store, and addstruct adds another structure element to the specified structure. The sort Emode represents the two modes for adding structure elements, REPLACE which replaces the element pointed at by the element pointer and INSERT which inserts the element after the element pointed to by the element pointer. The operation uep updates the element pointer associated with a named structure. os opens a named structure, if a structure of the specified name already exists in the structure store, it is opened. If not, an empty store with the specified name is created and opened.

The operations uep, add and os have similar definitions. To bring out the similarities and to illustrate another specification technique, they are defined in terms of an operation map. This operation essentially applies a specified operation to all structures in the structure store. The operation applied is the first parameter to the operation. Because OBJ is a first order language, map cannot be described as a true higher-order function; instead the functions to which map can be applied have to be enumerated and this is the purpose of the auxiliary operations fadd, fuep, fos.

```
obj STRUCTURESTORE / STRUCTURE

    sorts StructureStore FSS
          Emode NS

    ops INSERT : -> Emode
        REPLACE : -> Emode
        emptyss : -> StructureStore
        mkSS : Name nat Structure -> StructureStore
        _U_ : StructureStore StructureStore
                -> StructureStore
                (ASSOC COMM ID: emptyss)
        map : FSS StructureStore -> StructureStore
        addstruct :
                Name Emode StructElement StructureStore
                -> StructureStore
        mkNS : nat Structure -> NS
        get : Name StructureStore -> NS
        uep : nat Name StructureStore -> StructureStore
        _in_ : Name StructureStore -> BOOL
        os : Name StructureStore -> StructureStore
        fadd : Name Emode StructElement -> FSS
        fuep : nat Name -> FSS
        fos : Name -> FSS
```

```
vars ss1, ss2, ss : StructureStore
     ep, ep1 : nat
     em, em1 : Emode
     nos, n, m : Name
     s, s1, s2 : Structure
     se, se1 : StructElement
     i: PolylineIndex
     pts : Points
     f : FSS
eqns
( ss U ss = ss )
( map(f, emptyss) = emptyss )
( map(f, ss1 U ss2) = map(f,ss1) U map(f,ss2) )
( get(n, emptyss) = mkNS(0, emptystruct) )
( get(n, mkSS(n,ep,s) U ss) = mkNS(size(s),s) )
( get(n, mkSS(m,ep,s) U ss) = get(n,ss)
  IF (not((n == m))) )
( uep(ep,nos,ss) = map(fuep(ep,nos), ss) )
( map(fuep(ep,nos), mkSS(nos,ep,s)) = mkSS(nos,ep,s) )
( map(fuep(ep,nos), mkSS(nos,ep1,s)) = mkSS(nos,ep,s)
  IF (ep $<$ size(s)) )
( map(fuep(ep,nos), mkSS(nos,ep1,s)) = mkSS(nos,ep1,s)
  IF (size(s) $<$ ep) )
( map(fuep(ep,nos), mkSS(m,ep1,s)) = mkSS(m,ep1,s)
  IF (not((nos == m))) )
( n in emptyss = F)
( n in (ss1 U ss2) = (n in ss1) or (n in ss2) )
( n in mkSS(n,ep,s) = T )
( n in mkSS(nos,ep,s) = F IF (not((n == nos))) )
( addstruct(nos,em,se,ss) = map(fadd(nos,em,se), ss) )
( addstruct(nos,em,se,ss) = map(fadd(nos,em,se), ss) )
( map(fadd(nos,em,se), mkSS(m,ep,s)) = mkSS(m,ep,s)
  IF (not((m == nos))) )
( map(fadd(nos,INSERT,se), mkSS(nos,ep,s))
  = mkSS(nos, succ(ep), inse(ep,se,s)) )
( map(fadd(nos,REPLACE,se), mkSS(nos,ep,s))
  = mkSS(nos, ep, (s \ ep) U mkStruct(ep,se)) )
( os(n,ss) = map(fos(n), ss) )
( map(fos(nos), mkSS(nos,ep,s)) = mkSS(nos,size(s),s) )
( map(fos(nos), mkSS(n,ep,s)) = mkSS(n,ep,s)
  IF (not((n == nos))) )
jbo
```

The next object describes the centralised structure store. This is presented as a tuple, the first component represents the name of the open structure, the second the current editing mode (REPLACE or INSERT) and the third the structure store itself. The operations open, close, sem and sep open the specified structure, close the open structure, set editing mode and set the element pointer in a named structure, respectively. add adds a structure element in the current editing mode to the open structure.

```
obj CSS / STRUCTURESTORE
  sorts CSS
  ops mkCSS : Name Emode StructureStore -> CSS
      open : Name CSS -> CSS
      close : CSS -> CSS
      sem : Emode CSS -> CSS
      sep : nat CSS -> CSS
      add : StructElement CSS -> CSS
  vars ss1, ss2, ss : StructureStore
      ep, ep1 : nat
      em, em1 : Emode
      nos, n, m : Name
      s, s1, s2 : Structure
      se, se1 : StructElement
      i : PolylineIndex
      pts : Points
  eqns
    ( open(n,mkCSS(nos,em,ss))
      = mkCSS(n,em,ss U mkSS(n,0,emptystruct))
      IF (not)((n in ss))) )
    ( open(n,mkCSS(nos,em,ss)) = mkCSS(n,em,os(n,ss))
      IF ((n in ss)) )
    ( close(mkCSS(nos,em,ss)) = mkCSS(NULL,em,ss) )
    ( sem(em,mkCSS(nos,em1,ss)) = mkCSS(nos,em,ss) )
    ( add(se,mkCSS,(NULL,em,ss)) = mkCSS(NULL,em,ss) )
    ( add(se,mkCSS,(nos,em,ss))
      = mkCSS(nos,em,addstruct(nos,em,se,ss))
      IF (not((nos == NULL))) )
    ( sep(ep,mkCSS(NULL,em,ss)) = mkCSS(NULL,em,ss) )
    ( sep(ep,mkCSS(nos,em,ss))
      = mkCSS(nos,em,uep(ep,nos,ss))
      IF (not((nos == NULL))) )
  jbo
```

The object TRAVERSER is the structure store traverser. The operation `tstruc` traverses a structure. When a structure is traversed, the appropriate GKS operation is invoked for each class of structure element. Thus for example the polyline structure element causes the GKS `Polyline` operation to be invoked. In the case of an execute element (`exse`), the referenced structure is traversed in an environment inherited from the parent. When the traversal is completed, the environment of the parent is restored. This is described by the operation `rest`, which in this case sets the polyline index to the value obtaining when the execute structure element was invoked and resets the modelling transformations.

Two modelling transformations are defined in the traversal state. The first is the global modelling transformation, set by the structure element `globt` and inherited by a child structure from its parent. The second is the local modelling transformation, set by the structure element `loct` and also inherited. The co-ordinate data associated with a `plse` structure element is transformed by the composite modelling transformation (the product of the global and local modelling transformations). When a new posted structure is interpreted, the global and modelling transformations are initialized to the identity transformation.

```
obj TRAVERSER / CSS TEST
   sorts Tr
   ops mkTr : CSS PolylineIndex MT MT GKS -> Tr
       tstruc : nat NS Tr -> Tr
       t : StructElement Tr -> Tr
       trav :  NameList Tr -> Tr
       tinit : Name Tr -> Tr
       rest :  PolylineIndex MT MT Tr -> Tr
   vars tr, tr1 : Tr
        css, css1 : CSS
        ns : NS
        gks : GKS
        n, nos : Name
        nl : NameList
        ep, ep1 : nat
        em : Emode
        ss : StructureStore
        i, pi : PolylineIndex
        lmt, lmt1, gmt, gmt1 :   MT
        s : Structure
        p : MCPoints
```

```
      eqns
        ( tstruct(ep,mkNS(0,s), tr) = tr )
        ( tstruc(0,ns,tr) = tr )
        ( tstruc(ep1, mkNS(succ(ep),s),tr)
            = tstruc(succ(ep1), mkNS(ep,s), t(s [ ep1 ],tr)) )
        ( t(pise(i), mkTr(css,pi,gmt,lmt,gks))
            = mkTr(css, i, gmt, lmt, SetPlIndex(i,gks)) )
        ( t(plse(p),mkTr(css,pi,gmt,lmt,gks))
            = mkTr(css, pi, gmt, lmt,
                    Polyline((gmt o lmt) [ p ], gks)) )
        ( t(exse(n),
            mkTr(mkCSS(nos,em,ss), pi, gmt, lmt, gks))
          = rest(pi, gmt, lmt,
                    tstruc(1, get(n,ss),
                        mkTr(mkCSS(nos,em,ss),
                            pi,gmt,lmt,gks))) )
        ( t(globt(gmt1), mkTr(css,pi,gmt,lmt,gks))
            = mkTr(css,pi,gmt1,lmt,gks) )
        ( t(loct(lmt1,REPLACE), mkTr(css,pi,gmt,lmt,gks))
            = mkTr(css,pi,gmt,lmt1,gks) )
        ( t(loct(lmt1,PRECONCAT), mkTr(css,pi,gmt,lmt,gks))
            = mkTr(css, pi, gmt, lmt o lmt1, gks) )
        ( t(loct(lmt1,POSTCONCAT), mkTr(css,pi,gmt,lmt,gks))
            = mkTr(css,pi,gmt,lmt1 o lmt,gks) )
        ( trav(emptyNL,tr) = tr )
        ( trav(n & nl, tr) = trav(nl, tinit(n,tr)) )
        ( tinit(n, mkTr(mkCSS(nos,em,ss), pi,gmt,lmt,gks))
            = tstruc(1, get(n,ss),
                    mkTr(mkCSS(nos,em,ss),
                    I1, IDENT, IDENT, SetPlIndex(I1,gks))) )
        ( rest(i, gmt1, lmt1, mkTr(css,pi,gmt,lmt,gks)) =
          mkTr(css, i, gmt1, SetPlIndex(i,gks)) )
      jbo
```

The object PHIGS defines the PHIGS-like operations available to the application program. The sort PHIGS is a tuple whose components represent the list of structures posted to the workstation, the centralised structure store and the underlying GKS system.

OpenStructure adds an empty structure of the specified name to the structure store and sets the name of the currently open structure. CloseStructure clears the name of the open structure. SetEditMode sets the editing mode to REPLACE or INSERT. The operation SetElementPointer sets the element pointer in the openstructure. The operations SESetPlIndex, SEPolyline, SEExecute, SEGlobalMT and SELocalMT add structure elements of the specified types to the open strucutre. PostStrucutre adds a strucutre indentifier to the list of strucutres to be traversed. The operations PSetPlRepresentation, PSetWsWindow and PSetWsViewport set polyline representations and the workstation window and workstation viewport, respectively.

```
obj PHIGS / TRAVERSER TEST

   sorts PHIGS

   ops mkPHIGS :  NameList Tr -> PHIGS
       OpenStrucutre : Name PHIGS -> PHIGS
       CloseStructure : PHIGS -> PHIGS
       PostStructure : Name PHIGS -> PHIGS
       SetEditMode : Emode PHIGS -> PHIGS
       SetElementPointer : nat PHIGS -> PHIGS
       SESetPlIndex : PolylineIndex PHIGS -> PHIGS
       SEPolyline : MCPoints PHIGS -> PHIGS
       SEExecute : Name PHIGS -> PHIGS
       SEGlobalMT : MT PHIGS -> PHIGS
       SELocalMT : MT Comptype PHIGS -> PHIGS

       PSetPlRepresentation :
           PolylineIndex Linetype Linewidth PHIGS
           -> PHIGS
       PSetWSWindow :  Window PHIGS -> PHIGS
       PSetWsViewport : Viewport PHIGS -> PHIGS

   vars phigs : PHIGS
       tr : Tr
       gks, gks1 : GKS
       listps, listps1 : NameList
       nl, nl1 : NameList
       n, nos, nos1 : Name
       ep : nat
       em : Emode
       css, css1 : CSS
       i, pi, pi1 : PolylineIndex
       lt : Linetype
       lw : Linewidth
       ctype : Comptype
       p : MCPoints
```

```
      mt, gmt, lmt : MT
      s, s1, s2 : Structure
      w : Window
      v : Viewport

eqns

  ( OpenStructure(n,
              mkPHIGS(listps,
                      mkTr(css,pi,gmt,lmt,gks)))
    = mkPHIGS(listps,
            mkTr(open(n,css), pi, gmt, lmt, gks)) )
  ( CloseStructure(mkPHIGS(listps,
                      mkTr(css,pi,gmt,lmt,gks)))
    = mkPHIGS(listps,
            mkTr(close(css), pi, gmt, lmt, gks)) )
  ( PostStructure(n,
              mkPHIGS(listps,
                      mkTr(css,pi,gmt,lmt,gks)))
    = mkPHIGS(n & listps,
            trav(n & listps,
                mkTr(css, pi, gmt, lmt,
                    ClearWs(gks)))) )
  ( SetEditMode(em,
              mkPHIGS(listps,
                      mkTr(css,pi,gmt,lmt,gks)))
    = mkPHIGS(listps,
            mkTr(sem(em,css), pi, gmt, lmt, gks)) )
  ( SetElementPointer(ep,
              mkPHIGS(listps,
                      mkTr(css,pi,gmt,lmt,gks)))
    = mkPHIGS(listps,
            mkTr(sep(ep,css), pi, gmt, lmt, gks)) )

  ( SESetPlIndex(i,
              mkPHIGS(listps,
                      mkTr(css,pi,gmt,lmt,gks)))
    = mkPHIGS(listps,
            trav(listps,
                mkTr(add(pise(i),css), pi,gmt,lmt,
                    ClearWs(gks)))) )
```

```
( SEPolyline(p,
              mkPHIGS(listps,
                        mkTr(css,pi,gmt,lmt,gks)))
   = mkPHIGS(listps,
              trav(listps,
                    mkTr(add(pise(p),css), pi,gmt,lmt,
                        ClearWs(gks)))) )

( SEExecute(n, mkPHIGS(listps,
                        mkTr(css,pi,gmt,lmt,gks)))
   = mkPHIGS(listps,
              trav(listps,
                    mkTr(add(exse(n),css), pi,gmt,lmt,
                        ClearWs(gks)))) )
( SEGlobal(mt,
            mkPHIGS(listps,
                      mkTr(css,pi,gmt,lmt,gks)))
   = mkPHIGS(listps,
              trav(listps,
                    mkTr(add(globt(mt),css),
                        pi, gmt, lmt,
                        ClearWs(gks)))) )
( SELocalMT(mt, ctype,
              mkPHIGS(listps,
                        mkTr(css,pi,gmt,lmt,gks)))
   = mkPHIGS(listps,
              trav(listps,
                    mkTr(add(loct(mt,ctype),css),
                        pi, gmt, lmt,
                        ClearWs(gks)))) )


( PSetPlRepresentation(i, lt, lw,
                        mkPHIGS(listps,
                                  mkTr(css,pi,gmt,lmt,gks)))
   = mkPHIGS(listps,
            mkTr(css, pi, gmt, lmt,
                SetPlRepresentation(i,lt,lw,gks)))) )
```

```
( PSetWsWindow(w, mkPHIGS(listps,
                           mkTr(css,pi,gmt,lmt,gks)))
  = mkPHIGS(listps,
             mkTr(css, pi, gmt, lmt,
                  SetWsWindow(w,gks))) )


( PSetWsViewport(v,
                 mkPHIGS(listps,
                          mkTr(css,pi,gmt,lmt,gks)))
  = mkPHIGS(listps,
             mkTr(css, pi, gmt, lmt,
                  SetWsViewport(v,gks))) )
jbo
```

3.3   EXAMPLES OF EXECUTION

OBJ specifications can be executed by using the data type equations as rewrite rules, to reduce an expression to normal form. The specifications given here were exercised using the ObjEx [1] OBJ interpreter. Suppose:

```
PHIGS0 = MKPHIGS(emptyNL,
                 mkTr(mkCSS(NULL,INSERT,emptyss),
                      I1,IDENT,IDENT,GKS0))
GKS0 = mkGKS(I1, emptyNDCP,
             mkWs(W1, V1, [ I1 % mkBundle(LT1,LW1) ],
             emptyDCP))
```

The sequence of functions

```
OPEN STRUCTURE(N1)
SEPOLYLINE(MCPTS1)
SEPOLYLINE(MCPTS2)
SEPOLYLINE(MCPTS3)
CLOSE STRUCTURE
```

can be executed on this specification by evaluating the expression:

```
CloseStructure(
  SEPolyline(MCPTS3,
    SEPolyline(MCPTS2,
      SEPolyline(MCPTS1,
        OpenStructure(N1,
          PHIGS0)))))
```

The result is the term:

```
mkPHIGS(emptyNL,
        mkTr(mkCSS(N1, INSERT,
                   mkSS(N1, 3,
                        mkStruct(1,plse,(MCPTS1))
                        U mkStruct(2,plse(MCPTS2))
                        U mkStruct(3,plse(MCPTS3))))),
                   I1, IDENT, IDENT,
                   mkGKS(I1, emptyNDCP,
                         mkWs(W1, V1,
                              [ I1 % mkBundle(LT1,LW1) ],
                              emptyDCP))))
```

The sequence of functions

```
OPEN STRUCTURE(N2)
SEPOLYLINE(MCPTS1)
CLOSE STRUCTURE
OPEN STRUCTURE(N1)
SEEXECUTE(N2)
SEPOLYLINE(MCPTS2)
CLOSE STRUCTURE
POST STRUCTURE(N1)
```

can be executed on this specification by evaluating the expression:

```
PostStructure(N1,
   CloseStructure(
     SEPolyline(MCPTS2,
        SEExecute(N2,
           OpenStructure(N1,
              CloseStructure(
                 SEPolyline(MCPTS1,
                    OpenStructure(N2,
                       PHIGSO))))))))
```

The structure hierarchy is shown in Figure 4.7.

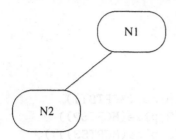

Figure 4.7   Structure hierarchy

The result is the term:

```
mkPHIGS(N1 & emptyNL,
        mkTr(mkCSS(NULL, INSERT,
                 mkSS(N2, 1, MkStruct(1,plse,MCPTS1))
                 U mkSS(N1, 2,
                         mkStruct(1,exse(N2))
                         U mkStruct(2,plse(MCPTS2)))),
             I1, IDENT, IDENT,
             mkGKS(I1,
                 { create(IDENT [ MCPTS2 ], I1 }
                 U { create(IDENT [ MCPTS1 ], I1) },
                 mkWs(W1, V1,
                     [ I1 % mkBundle(LT1,LW1) ],
                     { display(t(W1, V1,
                                 IDENT [ MCPTS2 ]),
                               mkBundle(LT1,LW1)) }
                     U { display(t(W1, V1,
                                 IDENT [ MCPTS1 ]),
                               mkBundle(LT1,LW1))
                 } ))))
```

which represents the state of the system after the operations have been applied. The structure store contents are:

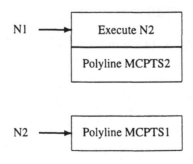

The NDC picture contains two polylines with coordinates `IDENT[MCPTS1]` and `IDENT[MCPTS2]` respectively. Both have polyline index `I1`. The DC picture contains the corresponding DC polylines whose coordinates correspond to the coordinates of the NDC polyline transformed to DC coordinates by the workstation transformation:

`t(W1,V1, ···)`

and representation `mkBundle(LT1,LW1)`, which is the representation corresponding to polyline index `I1`.

3.4   CONCLUSIONS

This paper has demonstrated how a PHIGS-like structure store and traverser could be defined on top of GKS and has shown how such a system can be formally described. It is important to remember that the fact that the final system is defined in terms of simpler components does not mean that the system has to be implemented as a layered system. There is no reason for the GKS interface to exist in an implementation of the PHIGS-like system. The specification concentrates on the essential concepts in GKS and PHIGS and shows clearly how they are related. The benefits of being able to execute OBJ specifications were considerable. In particular, the availability of a type checker for OBJ was invaluable.

References

[1] *ObjEx Reference Manual*, Gerrard Software Ltd, UK (1987).

[2] D.A. Duce, E.V.C. Fielding and L.S. Marshall. Formal Specification of a Small Example Based on GKS, *Transaction on Graphics* 7(3) pp. 180–197, 1988.

[3] R.M. Gallimore, D. Coleman and V. Stavridou. UMIST OBJ: a Language for Executable Program Specification, *Computer Journal* 32(5) pp. 413–421, 1989.

[4] ISO. Information processing systems — Computer graphics — Graphical Kernal System (GKS) functional description, ISO 7942, ISO Central Secretariat, August 1985.

[5] ISO. Information processing systems — Computer graphics — Graphical Kernal System (GKS) for three dimensions (GKS-3D) functional description, ISO/IEC 8805, 1988.

[6] ISO. Information processing systems — Computer graphics — Programmer's Hierarchical Interactive Graphics System functional description, ISO/IEC 9592:1, 1989.

III
SEMANTICS IN OBJ

III

SEMANTICS IN O.E.I

Chapter 5

SEMANTIC SPECIFICATIONS FOR THE REWRITE RULE MACHINE

Joseph A. Goguen

Department of Computer Science and Engineering
University of California at San Diego

Abstract   This paper presents three semantic specifications for the Rewrite Rule Machine.
This machine consists of a large number of parallel rewrite processors operating
independently, each implemented as a VLSI chip. The first specification, called
parallel rewriting, provides an abstract operational semantics for the rewrite
processor. The second specification, called the **cell machine** model, provides a
more concrete operational semantics for this processor, using algebraic semantics
(in OBJ) and set theory. The third specification, called **concurrent rewriting**,
gives an abstract semantics for the Rewrite Rule Machine as a whole.

1   INTRODUCTION

The goal of the Rewrite Rule Machine (RRM) project is

> to design, build and test a prototype multi-grain, massively parallel computer
> architecture especially suited for executing non-homogeneous programs written
> in declarative ultra high level languages.

The RRM architecture is a **multi-grain hierarchy**, with several different levels of organization, each having a different structure. These levels may be described as follows:

1. A **cell** stores one item of data and pointers to two other cells.

2. A **tile** provides shared communication resources for a small number of cells.

3. An **ensemble** consists of many tiles executing instructions broadcast from a common central controller.

4. A **cluster** interconnects many ensembles to cooperate in a larger computation.

5. A **network** interconnects several clusters to give a complete RRM.

This paper concentrates on the third level, the ensemble. A single ensemble consists of a controller which broadcasts instructions to its array of cells; hence it executes in SIMD (Single Instruction Multiple Data) mode. A complete RRM consists of many such ensembles, each executing its own independent instruction stream; hence it operates in MIMD (Multiple Instruction Multiple Data) mode[1]. In this paper, the Rewrite Rule Machine is presented as an *abstract architecture* that is not committed to any particular number or structure for the units at each of these levels, and that deliberately fails to model many lower level details. However, a concrete prototype RRM, which of course does make particular choices for these parameters is being constructed at SRI international, as described in [27, 15] and [2].

The RRM project began in 1985, and its first paper is [12]. An early description of RRM architecture is given in [34], and some early simulation results are reported in [26]. Intermediate stages of the project are documented in [19, 27] and [15], and its current state is described in [1] and [2]. The present paper was drafted in early 1988 to help initiate ensemble design by giving a precise semantics for some basic features, and was put in its present form in 1990. Its style is informal, but its content can (I hope) be made completely precise.

1.1   MODELS OF COMPUTATION

A model of computation defines the major interface between the hardware and the software aspects of a computing system. This interface determines both what the hardware must provide, and what the software can rely upon. It therefore plays a basic role in the design of any computing system, even if it is not made explicit. Most current machines are based upon the classical von Neumann model of computation, which is inherently sequential, and is characterized by enormously long streams of fetch/compute/write cycles. We regard a clear statement of desired semantics as essential for design; indeed, the RRM is a *"Semantics First"* machine.

It is important to distinguish the levels of architectural organization that were described above from models of computation. Both may be hierarchically organized, but models of computation should be stratified by level of abstraction rather than by the aggregation of parts into wholes. In fact, we could develop semantic models for any of the architectural levels, and these models could range from the very abstract to the very concrete. This paper considers the following semantic models:

---

[1] Actually, the terms MIMD and SIMD are somewhat misleading when applied to the RRM, because of its multi-grain architecture, and also because of its autonomous processes.

1. In **concurrent rewriting**, many different rules can be applied simultaneously at many different sites; this is an abstract MIMD operational semantics.

2. In **parallel rewriting**, many instances of the *same* rewrite rule are applied simultaneously at many different sites; this is an abstract SIMD operational semantics.

3. A **cell machine** is an abstract array of cells; it can be used to implement either parallel or concurrent rewriting.

The second and third models are for the third hierarchical level of the RRM, that of ensembles, whereas the first provides a semantics for the RRM as a whole. The first two models are more abstract than the third. More concrete levels would take account of resource limitations, such as the unavailability of cells and communication paths. The present paper does not address these issues. The first two models are especially suitable for the semantics of functional and logic programming languages, because they do not directly model storage; however, the third model does model storage, and is suitable for object oriented languages, as well as for functional and logic programming languages.

1.2   LANGUAGES

The languages that we are developing for the RRM include the object-oriented, functional, and logic programming paradigms; they also support parameterized programming, graphical programming, sophisticated error handling, and flexible type systems. The declarative character of these languages makes their programs easier to read, write, debug, verify, modify, and maintain. All of these languages are extensions of OBJ [10, 7, 4, 5], a first order functional language based on (order sorted) equational logic. Eqlog [16, 17] is a logic programming extension of OBJ which also supports so-called constraint based programming. A major discovery of the RRM project is a way to view object oriented programming as a declarative paradigm. This insight is embodied in the language FOOPS [18], which is an object-oriented extension of OBJ, and in FOOPlog [18], which combines all three paradigms. The suitability of OBJ for the RRM is discussed in [14], while a graphical programming interface for FOOPS is described in [8]. See [23] for more on FOOPS and on types.

Rewrite rules provide a link between the abstract mathematical semantics of our languages and the operational semantics of the RRM. For example, the most abstract mathematical semantics of OBJ is initial algebra semantics for order sorted equational logic, but equations in OBJ programs are interpreted operationally as left-to-right rewrite rules [4, 22, 5]. Rewrite rules are the highest level of modelling considered in this paper.

Term rewriting, whether parallel or concurrent, is ideal for implementing functional languages, and can also be used to implement relational languages. But it is not very well suited to implementing the object oriented paradigm. However, the RRM actually implements *graph rewriting*, not just term rewriting, and this provides an excellent way to implement objects and methods. Moreover, extended term rewriting and other techniques greatly extend the expressive capability. See [19] for further discussion of such issues.

1.3   ARCHITECTURE

The RRM implements *true concurrent* rewriting, in which many different instances of many different rules can be rewritten asynchronously at many different sites. However, the cell machine model described in this paper implements *parallel* rewriting, in which one rewrite rule at a time is simultaneously applied at many different sites. Compilers can first convert programs into sets of rewrite rules, and then into machine level instruction streams for RRM ensemble execution.

The intended applications of the RRM include symbolic processing, such as: simulation of hardware and other complex systems; software development environments, including specification, rapid prototyping, development, debugging, verification, and testing; and Artificial Intelligence applications, such as natural language processing, planning, expert systems, and reasoning. The RRM can also efficiently implement (arbitrary precision) arithmetic [33], and thus is very suitable for mixed symbolic/numeric computation.

The RRM is a **multi-grain** machine: fine-grain SIMD at the ensemble level, but large-grain MIMD at higher levels of organization. This allows it to take advantage of the fact that many important computations are *locally homogeneous* but not *globally homogeneous*; that is, the data items to which the same operations can be applied tend to occur in local clusters, each of which requires different operations. Neither pure SIMD nor pure MIMD machines can take advantage of this characteristic property of large and complex computations. Another significant architectural property of the RRM is that it does not separate processors from memory, and thus is not subject to the so-called "von Neumann bottleneck," whereby data items must be fetched and stored sequentially over a low bandwidth channel; in fact, an RRM ensemble processes data where it is stored, possibly rearranging storage by a dynamic autonomous process, to ensure that data items that are logically related are also physically contiguous.

The RRM ensemble is an associative processor, but not in the old fashioned sense which required either enormous bandwidth or else was very slow; rather, it is a SIMD machine, whose content addressing is largely internal. The cells in an ensemble only connect to their nearest neighbors[2]. Some cells serve as buffers to the outside world, and there is also a one bit feedback line to the controller, which returns the disjunction across all cells of special one bit status registers. The models in this paper deliberately omit such details, and also avoid commitment to any particular ALU design for cells, except to assume an equality test for tokens. See [15, 2] for architectural details of the SRI prototype.

Our performance estimate[3] for a single ensemble chip is 150 MIPS, based on today's off-the-shelf technology, at a modest 20 MHz, for a 12-by-12 grid of tiles with 8 cells each [27]. Of course, this figure will scale up with improvements in technology, yielding performance in the tera-op range for an RRM prototype with 10,000 ensembles completed in 1995.

In comparison with fine-grain dataflow machines, the RRM avoids the overhead and latency involved in moving many small packets over large distances. In fact, data tends to stay in one place in the RRM. Shared memory machines try to avoid the von Neumann bottleneck with elaborate cache hierarchies and clever caching strategies, but are limited in the number of processors that they can effectively support, and can also be very difficult to program, if they require explicit programming for each processor. Massively parallel SIMD machines are only maximally effective for homogeneous applications that have massive data parallelism; their resources are largely wasted for complex non-homogeneous problems, such as circuit simulations, expert systems, and natural language processing. The RRM combines the advantages of these two classes of machine, because of its multi-grain architecture.

There are some other architecture that resemble the RRM, although they are not yet very well known. These include the ASP machine of Lea [25], and the IUA [32] from Hughes Research Labs, which has a processor called CAAP [31] that plays a role similar to that of the ensemble in the RRM. Both of these machines, like the RRM, have a hierarchical MIMD/SIMD structure, using custom VLSI associative processors. However, these machines were designed for homogeneous applications, particularly signal processing, and cannot be expected to achieve optimum performance for non-homogeneous applications. Also, both machines are programmed with fairly conventional low level languages, and hence can be expected to have difficulties with software reliability, portability and maintenance.

---

[2] The prototype ensemble being constructed at SRI actually has the topology of a torus; however, many different structures could have been chosen to realize the abstract ideas in this paper.

[3] This is a conservative estimate based on simulating small but realistic problems, rather than a misleading "raw peak power" estimate assuming that all processers always do useful work.

1.4   SUMMARY

Sections 2.1 and 2.2 briefly review the algebra that we need, and then Section 2.3 presents new simplified definitions of parallel and concurrent rewriting. Section 3 gives the cell machine model, including its structure and its instruction set, using OBJ and set theory. Section 4 describes *extended* rewriting, in which variables may match open terms, rather than just ground terms, as in *standard* rewriting. Section 5 describes some topics for future work, including robustness under failures due to resource limitations.

Acknowledgements

I owe an enormous debt to my collegues who have done so much to realize the dreams expressed by the models given in this paper. These include Dr Jose Meseguer, who is now leading the project at SRI, and who has done exciting recent work on the semantics of concurrency and on RRM compiler correctness; Dr Sany Leinwand, who is doing the actual VLSI layout, as well as much work on design and simulation; Mr Timothy Winkler, for his many useful comments on this paper, as well as for his valuable work on simulation, algorithms, compilation and design; Dr Hitashi Aida, who wrote an RRM compiler for (a subset of) OBJ, and who also contributed greatly to the simulators; Mr Patrick Lincoln, who contributed significantly to compiler technology and ensemble design; and Prof Ugo Montanari, for his work on compiler technology and some useful discussions of concurrency. Finally, I wish to thank Healfdene Goguen and Peter Sewell for their careful readings of a draft of this paper, which uncovered several bugs.

This research has been supported in part by Office of Naval Research Contracts N00014-90-C-0086 and N00014-90-C-0210.

2   PARALLEL AND CONCURRENT REWRITING

For expository simplicity, this section only develops unsorted rewriting; however, order sorted rewriting is needed to fully capture our declarative languages for the RRM. The first two subsections review some basic concepts from algebra. More detail on this material (or its generalizations to many sorted and order sorted algebra) can be found, for example, in [3, 29, 11, 24] and [20].

2.1   SIGNATURES AND TERMS

Let ω denote the set $\{0, 1, 2, ...\}$ of all natural numbers.

Definition 1 A **signature** is a family Σ_n of sets, for $n \in \omega$. An element $f \in \Sigma_n$ is called a **function symbol** of **arity** n, and in particular, an element of Σ_0 is called a **constant symbol**.

Given two signatures, Σ and Φ, we say that $\Sigma \subseteq \Phi$ iff $\Sigma_n \subseteq \Phi_n$ for each $n \in \omega$, and we define their **union** by

$$(\Sigma \cup \Phi)_n = \Sigma_n \cup \Phi_n.$$

Given a set X and a disjoint signature Σ, we define the signature $\Sigma(X)$ by

$$\Sigma(X)_0 = \Sigma_0 \cup X, \text{ and}$$
$$\Sigma(X)_n = \Sigma_n \text{ for } n > 0.$$

This notation views X as a ground signature of variable symbols. $\square$

Definition 2 The set T_Σ of all **(ground)** Σ-**terms** is the smallest set of *strings* over the alphabet $\Sigma \cup \{(,)\}$ (where (and) are special symbols disjoint from Σ) such that

- $\Sigma_0 \subseteq T_\Sigma$ and

- given $t_1, ..., t_n \in T_\Sigma$ and $\sigma \in \Sigma$, then $\sigma\underline{(}t_1 ... t_n\underline{)} \in T_\Sigma$.

The underlined parantheses are a pedagogical device that is only used occasionally to improve clarity. $\square$

Terms that have variables, e.g., $t \in T_{\Sigma(X)}$, will be called **open terms**.

2.2   ALGEBRAS, INITIALITY AND SUBSTITUTION

We first show that the Σ-terms form a Σ-algebra, and then state a simple property that characterizes this algebra.

A Σ-**algebra** is a set A with a function $A_\sigma \colon A^n \to A$ for each $\sigma \in \Sigma_n$; note that if $\sigma \in \Sigma_0$, then A_σ is essentially an element of A, since A^0 is a one point set. Given Σ-algebras A and B, a Σ-**homomorphism** $h \colon A \to B$ is a function h such that

$$h(A_\sigma(a_1, ..., a_n)) = B_\sigma(h(a_1), ..., h(a_n)),$$

for all $a_1, ..., a_n \in A$. We may view T_Σ as a Σ-algebra as follows:

- For $\sigma \in \Sigma_0$, let $(T_\Sigma)_\sigma$ be the string σ.

- For $\sigma \in \Sigma_n$ with $n > 0$, let $(T_\Sigma)_\sigma$ be the function that sends $t_1, ..., t_n \in T_\Sigma$ to the string $\sigma\underline{(}t_1 ... t_n\underline{)}$.

Thus, $\sigma(t_1, ..., t_n) = \sigma\underline{(}t_1 ... t_n\underline{)}$, and from here on we prefer to use the first notation. The key property of T_Σ is its *initiality*:

Theorem 3 For any Σ-algebra A, there is a unique Σ-homomorphism $T_\Sigma \to A$. $\square$

Definition 4 Given a set X of variable symbols and a Σ-algebra A, an **interpretation** of X in A is a function $a \colon X \to A$. Notice that any such function a determines a unique $\Sigma(X)$-homomorphism $\bar{a} \colon T_{\Sigma(X)} \to A$ by Theorem

3 for $\Sigma(X)$-algebras, i.e., a unique Σ-homomorphism that extends a. When $A = T_{\Sigma(Y)}$ such an a is called a **substitution**, and if $X = \{x_1, ..., x_n\}$, then the notation
$$t[x_1 \leftarrow t_1, ..., x_n \leftarrow t_n]$$
is used for $\overline{a}(t)$ when $a(x_i) = t_i$ for $i = 1, ..., n$; this is called the **result** of substituting t_i for x_i in t. $\square$

Notice that the order in which the variables x_i are substituted for does not matter, as long as they are distinct.

2.3   REWRITING

Definition 5 Given a signature Σ, a **Σ-rewrite rule** is a triple $\langle X, l, r \rangle$ where X is a set of **matching variables** disjoint from Σ, and l and r are $\Sigma(X)$-terms. We write such rules in the form
$$(\forall X) \, l \rightarrow r$$
and more concretely in forms like
$$(\forall x, y) \, l \rightarrow r$$
when (for example) $X = \{x, y\}$. $\square$

The following definition captures the semantics of rewriting multiple instances of a single rule in parallel. In the formula for t_1 below, $y_1, ..., y_n$ mark n sites in a term t_1 where the rule $(\forall X) \, l \rightarrow r$ applies, and the corresponding formula for t_2 gives the result of applying this rule at all n sites in parallel.

Definition 6 A **parallel rewrite** using the Σ-rule $(\forall X) \, l \rightarrow r$ is a pair $\langle t_1, t_2 \rangle$ of ground Σ-terms, where
$$t_1 = t_0[y_1 \leftarrow \overline{a_1}(l)] \ldots [y_n \leftarrow \overline{a_n}(l)]$$
for some $n > 0$, where $t_0 \in T_{\Sigma(X \cup Y)}$ with $Y = \{y_1, ..., y_n\}$ disjoint from $\Sigma(X)$, where $a_i \colon X \rightarrow T_{\Sigma(X \cup Y)}$ for $i = 1, ..., n$, where each term $t_0[y_1 \leftarrow \overline{a_1}(l)] \ldots [y_k \leftarrow \overline{a_k}(l)]$ for $k = 1, ..., n$ has at most one occurrence of each y_i, and where
$$t_2 = t_0[y_1 \leftarrow \overline{a_1}(r)] \ldots [y_n \leftarrow \overline{a_n}(r)].$$
In this case, we may write $t_1 \overset{P}{\rightarrow} t_2$. Ordinary, i.e., sequential, rewriting is the special case where $n = 1$. $\square$

It is easy to generalize Definition 6 to any number of rules applied at any number of sites; parallel rewriting is then the special case where just one rule is involved. Let us assume that we are given a finite set R of Σ-rewrite rules, say $(\forall X) \, l_i \rightarrow r_i$ for $i = 1, ..., N$, where we may assume without loss of generality that all rules are quantified over the same set of variables, say X.

Definition 7 A **concurrent rewrite** using a rule set R as above is a pair $\langle t_1, t_2 \rangle$ of ground Σ-terms, where

$$t_1 = t_0[y_1 \leftarrow \overline{a_1}(l_{j_1})] \ldots [y_n \leftarrow \overline{a_n}(l_{j_n})]$$

for some $n > 0$, with $t_0 \in T_{\Sigma(X \cup Y)}$ where $Y = \{y_1, \ldots, y_n\}$ is disjoint from $\Sigma(X)$, where $a_i : X \rightarrow T_{\Sigma(X \cup Y)}$ for $i = 1, \ldots, n$, where each term $t_0[y_1 \leftarrow \overline{a_1}(l_{j_1})] \ldots [y_k \leftarrow \overline{a_k}(l_{j_k})]$ for $k = 1, \ldots, n$ has at most one occurrence of each y_i, where $1 \leq j_i \leq N$ for $i = 1, \ldots, n$, and where

$$t_2 = t_0[y_1 \leftarrow \overline{a_1}(r_{j_1})] \ldots [y_n \leftarrow \overline{a_n}(r_{j_n})].$$

In this case, we may write $t_1 \xrightarrow{C} t_2$. □

A more complex explication of these two concepts is given in the appendix of [13]. Note that the sites where rewriting occurs are non-overlapping in the above definitions. Also, only term rewriting is treated, whereas sharing, i.e., graph rewriting, can easily be implemented on cell machines (and the real RRM), with gains in efficiency that may be quite considerable. Everything in this section generalizes easily to the many sorted case, and the order sorted case is only slightly more difficult.

2.4   AN EXAMPLE

Here is a simple rule set R for computing Fibonacci numbers:

```
f(0) = 0
f(s 0) = s 0
f(s s N) = f(N) + f(s N)
```

(Some further rules are needed for addition.)

A sequential implementation of this functional program takes time exponential in N to compute f(N), whereas a parallel rewriting execution can take only linear time. Of course, one can write a different functional program for Fibonacci numbers that does run in linear time. But the point of this simple example is that even naive programs can often be executed in optimal or near optimal time on the RRM, so that it really is reasonable to use ultra high level declarative languages in a straightforward way with this machine and model of computation; see [14, 19] for further discussion and more substantial examples.

3   CELL MACHINES

The cell machine models an RRM ensemble as an array of (small) processors, each of which can contain a token, two pointers to other cells, and some (Boolean) flags. Rewriting is implemented on a cell machine by broadcasting machine level instructions which initiate elementary actions in parallel in each cell. This level of description is more concrete than parallel rewriting, and indeed is a form of graph rewriting. The models in this section ignore resource limitations, assuming that an unbounded number of cells is available, and that communication always succeeds.

3.1   CELLS, STATES AND TERMS

We first describe cells and cell machine states without flags, using set theory; the main result characterizes when a cell machine state represents a term. Let Σ be a fixed unsorted signature with $\Sigma_n = \emptyset$ for $n > 2$; this is no loss of generality because an n-ary operation with $n > 2$ can be expressed as a composition of $n - 1$ binary operations. (Also, note that high arity operations are rare in practice.) We use natural numbers for the addresses of cells, and hence also as pointers to cells; $\perp$ represents the null pointer. Let $\omega_\perp = \omega \cup \{\perp\}$.

Definition 8 A **cell state** c is a triple $\langle op, l, r \rangle$, where $op \in \Sigma$ and $l, r \in \omega_\perp$. If $c = \langle o, l, r \rangle$ then let $op(c) = o$, $lpt(c) = l$ and $rpt(c) = r$. Call c **nullary** and write $\#c = 0$ if $lpt(c) = rpt(c) = \perp$; call c **unary** and write $\#c = 1$ if $lpt(c) \neq \perp$ and $rpt(c) = \perp$; call c **binary** and write $\#c = 2$ if $lpt(c) \neq \perp$ and $rpt(c) \neq \perp$; otherwise, let $\#(c) = \perp$. Let C denote the set of all cell states. □

Definition 9 A **cell machine state** is a partial function $s: \omega \to C$. The **domain** of s is $D(s) = \{n \in \omega \mid s(n) \text{ is defined}\}$. Given a cell machine state s and $n \in D(s)$, let $op(n) = op(s(n))$, let $lpt(n) = lpt(s(n))$, and let $rpt(n) = rpt(s(n))$. □

Definition 10 The **graph** of a cell machine state s is defined as follows:

1. Its **node set** is the domain of s.

2. Its **edges** are the pairs $\langle m, n \rangle$ with $m, n \in D(s)$ such that $lpt(m) = n$ or $rpt(m) = n$.

3. Node n is labelled by $op(n)$.

This is a directed labelled graph whose edges are not ordered. □

Definition 11 A cell machine state s is **well formed** iff

1. its domain $D(s)$ is finite,

2. if $n \in D(s)$, then $lpt(n) = \perp$ implies $rpt(n) = \perp$,

3. if $n \in D(s)$, then $lpt(n) = \perp$ or $lpt(n) \in D(s)$,

4. if $n \in D(s)$, then $rpt(n) = \perp$ or $rpt(n) \in D(s)$,

5. if $n \in D(s)$, then $op(n) \in \Sigma_{\#s(n)}$, and

6. the graph of s is acyclic, with a single root node from which all other nodes are reachable.

□

Definition 12 The **term** of a well formed cell machine state s at node $n \in D(s)$ is defined as follows:

0. $term(s, n) = op(n)$ if $\#s(n) = 0$.

1. $term(s, n) = op(n)\underline{(}term(s, lpt(n))\underline{)}$ if $\#s(n) = 1$.

2. $term(s, n) = op(n)\underline{(}term(s, lpt(n)), term(s, rpt(n))\underline{)}$ if $\#s(n) = 2$.

(Here $\underline{(}$ and $\underline{)}$ are the special symbols used in the strings that represent terms.)
□

Fact 13 The term of a well formed cell machine state is a ground Σ-term. □

3.2 CELLS AND STATES

The following algebraic specification for cell machines assumes familiarity with OBJ; see [22, 4, 5] for more information on OBJ. We first describe the structure of cell machines; the instruction set is described in Section 3.3. The ARRAY and 5TUPLE data types used here were taken from my library of predefined OBJ modules, and their definitions are given in Appendix A. The first specification defines two auxiliary data types, representing tokens as (quoted) identifiers and addresses as natural numbers; 0 is used as a null address, so that proper addresses are positive numbers.

```
obj DATA is
  dfn Tkn is QID .
  dfn Adr is NAT *(sort NzNat to PAdr, op 0 to null).
endo
```

We will define flags as an array of Booleans, and cells as 5-tuples with components for a token, a flag array, two addresses (i.e., pointers to other cells), and a reference count. The constant "*" names the default value in an array (see the Appendix); for the flag array, its value is false. The operations whose names end with "*" are selectors for the four components of cells (except for just "*" by itself). nullc will serve as the default value for cells in the cell machine, when it is defined as an array of cells. The line "psort Cell" says that the "principal sort" of CELL is Cell; this is needed to make the default view in the second line of CELLM0 come out as intended.

```
obj CELL is ex DATA .
  dfn FlagA is ARRAY[NAT, view from TRIV* to BOOL is
                          op * to false .
                      endv] .
  dfn Cell is 5TUPLE[Tkn,FlagA,Adr,Adr,INT]
                *(op (1*_) to (tkn*_),
                  op (3*_) to (lpt*_),
                  op (4*_) to (rpt*_),
                  op (5*_) to (rfc*_)).
  let nullc = << 'null ; initial ; null ; null ; 0 >> .
  op flag* : Nat Cell -> Bool .
  var N : Nat . var C : Cell .
  eq flag*(N,C) = (2* C)[N] .
  psort Cell .
endo

obj CELLMO is ex DATA .
  dfn Cellm is (ARRAY *(op initial to initialCm,
                        op * to nullc))[Adr,CELL].
  var A1 : PAdr . var T : Tkn . vars A2 A3 : Adr .
  var Cm : Cellm . var N : Nat .
  op mkcell : PAdr Tkn Adr Adr Cellm Nat -> Cellm .
  eq mkcell(A1,T,A2,A3,Cm,N)
      = put(<< T ; initial ; A2 ; A3 ; N >>,A1,Cm) .
endo
```

The mkcell operation is for initializing a cell machine. Note that the cell machine model given here omits the details needed for allocating and deallocating cells; this facility is not difficult to specify, but the details would cloud the overall picture. Also note that reference counts must be explicitly incremented and decremented, as illustrated in the program in Section 3.4.

3.3   CELL INSTRUCTIONS

The cell machine is an abstraction of the ensemble chip. Hence, it does not have the complete instruction set of the real RRM ensemble, but rather a smaller set sufficient to show the principles involved, given by the following BNF grammar:

Pgm := *Act* | *Ins* | *Act* ; *Pgm* | *Ins* ; *Pgm*
Ins := if *Cond* then *Act*
Cond := *Acond* | *Acond* & *Cond* | *Bool*
Acond := *Tkn* eq *Tkn* | flag(*Nat, Path*)
Tkn := tkn(*Path*) | *Id*

Path := nil | l | r | l *Path* | r *Path*
Act := settkn(*Tkn, Path*) | setflag(*Nat, Path*) |
      unsetflag(*Nat, Path*) | skip | clear(*Path*) |
      clear | reset | setlpt(*Path, Path*) |
      setrpt(*Path,Path*) | inc(*Path*) | dec(*Path*)

Programs in this language are streams of actions and instructions. An instruction is a condition-action pair, written with if_then_ syntax. This way of structuring the grammar prevents the recursive nesting of condition-action pairs. Conditions may be conjoined using _&_, and they include the Booleans, equality testing on tokens, and testing whether a given flag, accessed down a given path, is "up" (i.e., has value true). A path is a string of l and r symbols, indicating whether a left or right branch should be taken in passing from a cell where the instruction is executed to the designated cell; the empty path is nil. The token in the cell down the path P is indicated tkn(P).

There are eleven actions: settkn(T,P) sets the token of the cell down the path P to the value T, setflag(N,P) sets the Nth flag of the cell down path P to true, unsetflag(N,P) sets the Nth flag down path P to false, skip has no effect, clear(P) clears all the flags in the cell down the path P, clear clears every flag in the machine, and reset returns the entire machine to its initial state. Also, setlpt(P,P') and setrpt(P,P') respectively set the value of the left and the right pointers of the cell down the path P' to the address of the cell down the path P, while inc(P) and dec(P) respectively increment and decrement the reference count of the cell down the path P.

The OBJ version of this grammar is more satisfactory, because it allows the declaration of associative syntactic operations, and it also conveys some semantic information, including that the skip instruction has no effect, that nil obeys the identity law for __, and that _&_ and _;_ obey the associative law. This OBJ code could be used to drive an ensemble simulator, by using OBJ's facility for "building in" Lisp code to attach efficient underlying implementations to the high level syntax. Here, it is used as the initial part of a specification for the RRM ensemble chip.

```
obj PGM is sorts Cond Pgm Act Path .
  including DATA + NAT .
  subsort Bool < Cond .
  subsorts Act < Pgm .
  ops skip clear reset : -> Act .
  op _;_ : Pgm Pgm -> Pgm [assoc idr: skip prec 50] .
  op if_then_ : Cond Act -> Pgm .
  op _&_ : Cond Cond -> Cond [assoc idr: true] .
  op flag : Nat Path -> Cond .
```

```
  op tkn : Path -> Tkn .
  op _eq_ : Tkn Tkn -> Cond .
  op nil : -> Path .
  op __ : Path Path -> Path [assoc idr: nil] .
  ops l r : -> Path .
  op settkn : Tkn Path -> Act .
  ops inc dec : Path -> Act .
  ops setflag unsetflag : Nat Path -> Act .
  ops setlpt setrpt : Path Path -> Act .
  op clear : Path -> Act .
endo
```

The following specification for instructions builds on the cell machine and program specifications given above. In it, ev is the main evaluation function, specifying the effects of programs on cell machines. As usual in denotational definitions, there are several auxiliary denotation functions: Cev evaluates a condition at a given cell in a cell machine, Pev returns the address of the cell pointed to by a path, starting from a given cell, and Tev returns the token at the end of a path from a cell at a given address.

```
  obj CELLM is ex CELLMO + PGM .
    op ev : Pgm Cellm -> Cellm .
    var A : Act . var P P1 : Pgm . var Cm : Cellm .
    var B : Bool . var Ad : PAdr . var N : Nat .
    vars Pa Pa1 : Path . vars C C1 C2 : Cond .
    vars T T1 T2 : Tkn . var I : Tkn . *** was Id
    eq ev(P1 ; P,Cm) = ev(P,ev(P1,Cm)) .
    eq ev(skip,Cm) = Cm .
    eq ev(reset,Cm) = initialCm .
    op Cev : Cond Adr Cellm -> Bool .
    op Pev : Path Adr Cellm -> Adr .
    op Tev : Tkn Adr Cellm -> Tkn . *** was Id
    eq Cev(B,Ad,Cm) = B .
    eq Cev(flag(N,Pa),Ad,Cm)
         = flag*(N,Cm[Pev(Pa,Ad,Cm)]) .
    eq Cev(C1 & C2,Ad,Cm)
         = Cev(C1,Ad,Cm) and Cev(C2,Ad,Cm) .
    eq Cev(T1 eq T2,Ad,Cm)
         = Tev(T1,Ad,Cm) == Tev(T2,Ad,Cm) .
    cq ev(if C then A,Cm)[Ad] = ev(A,Cm)[Ad]
         if Cev(C,Ad,Cm).
    cq ev(if C then A,Cm)[Ad] = Cm[Ad]
         if not Cev(C,Ad,Cm).
```

```
   eq Pev(nil,Ad,Cm) = Ad .
   eq Pev(l Pa,Ad,Cm) = lpt*(Cm[Pev(Pa,Ad,Cm)]) .
   eq Pev(r Pa,Ad,Cm) = rpt*(Cm[Pev(Pa,Ad,Cm)]) .
   eq Tev(I,Ad,Cm) = I .
   eq Tev(tkn(Pa),Ad,Cm) = tkn*(Cm[Pev(Pa,Ad,Cm)]) .
   eq tkn*(ev(settkn(T,Pa),Cm)[Pev(Pa,Ad,Cm)]) = T .
   eq rfc*(ev(inc(Pa),Cm)[Pev(Pa,Ad,Cm)])
      = rfc*(Cm[Ad]) + 1 .
   eq rfc*(ev(dec(Pa),Cm)[Pev(Pa,Ad,Cm)])
      = rfc*(Cm[Ad]) - 1 .
   eq flag*(N,ev(setflag(N,Pa),Cm)[Pev(Pa,Ad,Cm)])
      = true .
   eq flag*(N,ev(unsetflag(N,Pa),Cm)[Pev(Pa,Ad,Cm)])
      = false .
   cq lpt*(ev(setlpt(Pa,Pa1),Cm)[Pev(Pa1,Ad,Cm)])
      = Pev(Pa,Ad,Cm)
      if Pa =/= nil and Pa1 =/= nil .
   cq rpt*(ev(setrpt(Pa,Pa1),Cm)[Pev(Pa1,Ad,Cm)])
      = Pev(Pa,Ad,Cm)
      if Pa =/= nil and Pa1 =/= nil .
   eq lpt*(ev(setlpt(nil,nil),Cm)[Pev(nil,Ad,Cm)])
      = null .
   eq rpt*(ev(setrpt(nil,nil),Cm)[Pev(nil,Ad,Cm)])
      = null .
   eq 2*(ev(clear,Cm)[Ad]) = initial .
   cq ev(clear,Cm)[Ad] = nullc
      if rfc*(Cm[Ad]) == (0).Nat .
   eq 2*(ev(clear(Pa),Cm)[Pev(Pa,Ad,Cm)]) = initial .
 endo
```

For example, the third to last equation says that after a `clear` instruction has been broadcast, the flag component of each cell in the machine is the initial flag array (in which all flags are "down", i.e., `false`). The last equation says that after a `clear(Pa)` instruction, the cell which is down the path `Pa` from a cell at address `Ad` has its flag array cleared (i.e., set to `initial`). This equation may look a little strange; the fourth from last equation may show more clearly why. It says that after a `setrpt(Pa,Pa1)` instruction has been broadcast, the right pointer of the cell down the path `Pa1` from a cell at address `Ad` will have the address of the cell down the path `Pa` from `Ad`. Although this will usually occur as part of a condition-action pair, it is still possible that a given cell will be down the `Pa1` path of more than one other cell, and consequently there can be contention about which address it gets. Note that the instructions `setlpt(nil,nil)` and `setrpt(nil,nil)` are used to set a (left or right) pointer in the current cell to `null`.

It should not be surprising that this specification is not Church-Rosser, because it defines a non-deterministic process. This means that forward chaining by rewriting cannot be used to animate a standard initial algebra semantics[4]. Intuitively, this is because of the need to determine for each cell which other cells are pointing at it down a given path. However, the "rewriting logic" of Meseguer [28] can provide a standard denotation for this specification. This logic admits non-determinism by dropping the symmetry law from equational logic, and has an initial category of proofs instead of an initial model. Also, unification and backward chaining could be used to animate this specification, as provided for example by Eqlog [16, 17]. Nevertheless, the code given above is syntactically correct OBJ3 which has been run and tested.

It is exciting that ordinary equational deduction can be used, plus induction over the data type constructors, to prove things about this cell machine model. For example, we could prove that a given machine instruction sequence correctly implements a given rewrite rule, or that a given compiler is correct. No such proofs are given here, but [1] and [30] (which builds on the 1988 draft version of this paper) show the correctness of compilers for more realistic models of the RRM.

3.4   FIBONACCI NUMBERS ON THE CELL MACHINE

This subsection gives a program for computing the Fibonacci numbers in Peano notation[5] on the cell machine given in Sections 3.2 and 3.3 above. This code does not use all the power of cell machines, in order to be more like the programs that are needed for the real RRM.

```
if tkn(nil) eq 'z then setflag(0,nil);
if tkn(nil) eq 's then setflag(1,nil);
if tkn(nil) eq 'f then setflag(2,nil);
if flag(2,nil) & flag(0,1) then settkn('z,nil);
if flag(2,nil) & flag(0,1) then dec(1);
if flag(2,nil) & flag(0,1) then setlpt(nil,nil);
if flag(2,nil) & flag(0,1 1) then settkn('z,nil);
if flag(2,nil) & flag(0,1 1) then dec(1);
if flag(2,nil) & flag(0,1 1) then setlpt(nil,nil);
if flag(2,nil) & flag(1,1) then setflag(3,nil);
```

---

[4] [6] proves that rewriting correctly animates the initial algebra semantics approach to abstract data types in [21], provided that the equations are Church-Rosser and terminating as rules.

[5] That is, the constructors are 0 and s, with 1 represented by s 0, with 2 represented by s s 0, etc.

```
if flag(2,nil) & flag(1,1) then dec(1);
if flag(3,nil) then settkn('p,nil);
if flag(3,nil) then setlpt(1 1,nil);
if flag(3,nil) then inc(1 1);
if flag(3,nil) then dec(1);
if flag(3,nil) then setrpt(1 1 1,nil);
if flag(3,nil) then inc(1 1 1);
clear .
```

Here 'z, 's, 'f and 'a indicate 0, successor, Fibonacci and addition, respectively. (This code has been checked using OBJ3.)

3.5   ASSOCIATIVE SEARCH

This subsection indicates how associative search can be implemented on the RRM. Given an alphabet A, we can represent its elements as functions $a: A^* \rightarrow A^*$ which append the given element on the left of a list; then we can represent the list $a_1 a_2 ... a_n$ as the term

$$a_1(a_2(...(a_n(nil))...)),$$

and by using prefix notation for the a_i we can even get the usual list notation,

$$a_1 a_2 ... a_n \ nil.$$

The fact that concatenation in A^* is associative corresponds to the fact that the composition of unary functions is associative.

Implementing this term representation on the cell machine gives the linked list data representation, in which each a_i is a cell with a pointer to a_{i+1}, and a_n finally points to nil. Using this data representation, we can program the cell machine to search[6] for a given element, by setting a certain flag in each cell if it contains the given element; on the RRM, the disjunction of all these bits can then be read out of the machine, or used internally. This gives a *constant time* search algorithm that is very natural on the RRM.

4   EXTENDED REWRITING

We now discusses *extended term rewriting*, in which variables can match open terms as well as ground terms. This extension can be very useful in practice, e.g., in verifying VLSI circuits [9]. Although it is a special case of second order rewriting, it should be seen as taking first order rewriting to its limit, rather than as a part of proper second order rewriting; for the terms themselves are first order, and so is the associated equational logic [11].

---

[6] It is amusing that the associativity of composition is so closely related to associative search; in Section 4, we will see that it is also related to rewriting modulo associativity!

An example of extended rewriting arises in giving a denotational style semantics for expressions, where one can avoid having to write many rules of the form

$$(\forall e, e') \; [[e + e']](\rho) \to [[e]](\rho) + [[e']](\rho)$$
$$(\forall e, e') \; [[e - e']](\rho) \to [[e]](\rho) - [[e']](\rho)$$
$$(\forall e, e') \; [[e \times e']](\rho) \to [[e]](\rho) \times [[e']](\rho)$$

....

by instead writing the following much simpler rule which uses matching over the binary function symbol $*$,

$$(\forall e, e') \; (\forall\!\!\!/ *) \; [[e * e']](\rho) \to [[e]](\rho) * [[e']](\rho).$$

There is a somewhat subtle point here. Although it is easy to implement the matching of function symbol variables to function symbols, it can be hard to implement the matching of function symbol variables to open terms, as is required by full second order rewriting. Let us use the symbol $\forall$ to indicate the variables that match terms, whether open or ground, and let us use $\forall\!\!\!/$ to indicate the variables that only match individual function symbols. The latter can be regarded as a special case of the former by imposing a conditional equation (provided the signature is finite).

Definition 14 Given a signature Σ, then an **extended rewrite rule** is a quadruple $\langle \Phi, \Psi, l, r \rangle$ where Φ and Ψ are signatures of **matching variables**, and where l and r are $(\Sigma \cup \Phi \cup \Psi)$-terms. Let us write such rules abstractly in the form

$$(\forall \Phi) \, (\forall\!\!\!/ \Psi) \, l \to r$$

and concretely in forms like

$$(\forall x, y, f, g) \, (\forall\!\!\!/ h) \, l \to r$$

where we might for example have $\Phi = \{x, y, f, g\}$ and $\Psi = \{h\}$, with arities that can (presumably) be inferred from their uses in l and r. (Note that no ordering of the matching process is implied by the ordering of the quantifiers.) $\square$

Standard rewriting is the special case where only Φ_0 is non-empty. In many cases, we can get the effect of second order rewriting using just $\forall\!\!\!/$ and first order $\forall$; one such case is homomorphic equations like those given above for $[[\,]]$.

We can now give definitions similar to those in Section 2.3 for sequential, parallel and concurrent extended rewriting. However, the details are somewhat complex, and are omitted here[7]. Instead, let us consider the example of Section 3.5. The following extended rewrite rules produce *true* iff the symbol $a \in A$ occurs in a list in the unary function representation:

$$(\forall \Phi) \; searcha(f \, a \, f' \; nil) \to true$$

---

[7] This is because notation is needed for substituting open terms into other open terms.

$(\forall \Phi)\ searcha(a\ f'\ nil) \to true$

$(\forall \Phi)\ searcha(f\ a\ nil) \to true$

$(\forall \Phi)\ searcha(a\ nil) \to true,$

where $\Phi_1 = \{f, f'\}$ and $\Phi_i = \emptyset$ for $i \neq 1$. The essential idea is that the variables in Φ match open unary terms. For example, if $A = \{a, b, c, d, e\}$, then $searcha(b\ c\ a\ d\ nil)$ rewrites to *true* by the first rule with f matching b c and f' matching d. This shows how rewriting modulo associativity can be implemented with extended rewriting[8].

5   DISCUSSION AND FUTURE RESEARCH

The models in this paper do not address the resource limitations that necessarily occur in real machines. One important limitation is that a given cell can connect directly to only a relatively small number of other cells. Although communication cannot be entirely local, particularly when executing an object-oriented language, the systematic exploitation of the locality of communication involved in the rewriting model of computation allows us to get more computational power from a given amount of silicon than is possible with conventional designs.

An important topic that could be studied using more detailed models of computation is the *robustness* of various ways to implement rewriting: we would like to guarantee that if a rewrite is aborted because of resource failure (e.g., if there is no free communication link), then the machine is still in a correct state, and will be able to execute that rewrite at some future time. This goes beyond the compiler correctness issues discussed in Section 3.3.

Appendix A : Auxiliary Specifications

The following specifications are used in Section 3.2. The first two define interfaces for the two parameterized objects that follow, defining arrays and 4-tuples, respectively.

```
th TRIV is sort Elt .
endth

th TRIV* is sort Elt .
    op * : -> Elt .
endth
```

---

[8] By allowing the identity function to match a variable, we can also implement rewriting modulo associativity and identity; then only the first rule above for *searcha* is needed. This case is actually the most natural to implement on the RRM

```
obj ARRAY[INDEX :: TRIV, VAL :: TRIV*] is sort Array .
  op initial : -> Array .
  op put : Elt.VAL Elt.INDEX Array -> Array .
  op _[_] : Array Elt.INDEX -> Elt.VAL .
  var V : Elt.VAL .  var I I' : Elt.INDEX .
  var A : Array .
  eq put(V,I,A)[I'] = if I == I' then V else A[I'] fi .
  eq initial[I] = * .
endo

obj 5TUPLE[C1 C2 C3 C4 C5 :: TRIV] is sort 5Tuple .
  op <<_;_;_;_;_>> : Elt.C1 Elt.C2 Elt.C3 Elt.C4 Elt.C5
                        -> 5Tuple .
  op 1*_: 5Tuple -> Elt.C1 .
  op 2*_: 5Tuple -> Elt.C2 .
  op 3*_: 5Tuple -> Elt.C3 .
  op 4*_: 5Tuple -> Elt.C4 .
  op 5*_: 5Tuple -> Elt.C5 .
  var e1 : Elt.C1 .  var e2 : Elt.C2 .
  var e3 : Elt.C3 .  var e4 : Elt.C4 .
  var e5 : Elt.C5 .
  eq 1* << e1 ; e2 ; e3 ; e4 ; e5 >> = e1 .
  eq 2* << e1 ; e2 ; e3 ; e4 ; e5 >> = e2 .
  eq 3* << e1 ; e2 ; e3 ; e4 ; e5 >> = e3 .
  eq 4* << e1 ; e2 ; e3 ; e4 ; e5 >> = e4 .
  eq 5* << e1 ; e2 ; e3 ; e4 ; e5 >> = e5 .
endo
```

The modules 5TUPLE and ARRAY are from the library, while the natural numbers (NAT), the Booleans (BOOL), and quoted identifiers (QID) are part of the standard prelude. (The standard prelude includes 2-, 3- and 4-tuples, but not 5-tuples.)

References

[1]   Hitoshi Aida, Joseph Goguen, and Josè Meseguer. Compiling concurrent rewriting onto the Rewrite Rule Machine. Technical Report SRI-CSL-90-03, Computer Science Lab, SRI International, February 1990. To appear in *Proceedings, International Workshop on Conditional and Typed Rewriting Systems*, Montreal, Canada, 1990.

[2]   Hitoshi Aida, Sany Leinwand, and Josè Meseguer. Architectural design of the Rewrite Rule Machine ensemble. Technical Report to appear, Computer Science Lab, SRI International, 1990. Also, to appear in

Proceedings, International Workshop on VLSI for Artificial Intelligence and Neural Nets, edited by Will Moore and A. Delgado-Frias, Oxford, 1990.

[3] Rod Burstall and Joseph Goguen. Algebras, theories and freeness: An introduction for computer scientists. In Martin Wirsing and Gunther Schmidt, editors, *Theoretical Foundations of Programming Methodology*, pages 329–350. Reidel, 1982. Proceedings, 1981 Marktoberdorf NATO Summer School, NATO Advanced Study Institute Series, Volume C91.

[4] Kokichi Futatsugi, Joseph Goguen, Jean-Pierre Jouannaud, and José Meseguer. Principles of OBJ2. In Brian Reid, editor, *Proceedings, Twelfth ACM Symposium on Principles of Programming Languages*, pages 52–66. Association for Computing Machinery, 1985.

[5] Kokichi Futatsugi, Joseph Goguen, José Meseguer, and Koji Okada. Parameterized programming in OBJ2. In Robert Balzer, editor, *Proceedings, Ninth International Conference on Software Engineering*, pages 51–60. IEEE Computer Society, March 1987.

[6] Joseph Goguen. How to prove algebraic inductive hypotheses without induction: with applications to the correctness of data type representations. In Wolfgang Bibel and Robert Kowalski, editors, *Proceedings, Fifth Conference on Automated Deduction*, pages 356–373. Springer, 1980. Lecture Notes in Computer Science, Volume 87.

[7] Joseph Goguen. Parameterized programming. *Transactions on Software Engineering*, SE-10(5):528–543, September 1984.

[8] Joseph Goguen. Graphical programming by generic example. In Steven Kartashev and Svetlana Kartashev, editors, *Proceedings, Second International Supercomputing Conference, Volume I*, pages 209–216. International Supercomputing Institute, Inc. (St. Petersburg FL), 1987.

[9] Joseph Goguen. OBJ as a theorem prover, with application to hardware verification. In V.P. Subramanyan and Graham Birtwhistle, editors, *Current Trends in Hardware Verification and Automated Theorem Proving*, pages 218–267. Springer, 1989. Also Technical Report SRI-CSL-88-4R2, SRI International, Computer Science Lab, August 1988.

[10] Joseph Goguen. Principles of parameterized programming. In Ted Biggerstaff and Alan Perlis, editors, *Software Reusability, Volume I: Concepts and Models*, pages 159–225. Addison-Wesley, 1989.

[11] Joseph Goguen. Proving and rewriting. In *Proceedings, Second International Conference on Algebraic and Logic Programming*, pages 1–24. Springer, 1990. Lecture Notes in Computer Science, Volume 463.

[12] Joseph Goguen, Claude Kirchner, Sany Leinwand, José Meseguer, and Timothy Winkler. Progress report on the Rewrite Rule Machine. *IEEE*

Computer Architecture Technical Committee Newsletter, March:7–21, 1986.

[13] Joseph Goguen, Claude Kirchner, and José Meseguer. Concurrent term rewriting as a model of computation. In Robert Keller and Joseph Fasel, editors, *Proceedings, Graph Reduction Workshop*, pages 53–93. Springer, 1987. Lecture Notes in Computer Science, Volume 279.

[14] Joseph Goguen, Claude Kirchner, José Meseguer, and Timothy Winkler. OBJ as a language for concurrent programming. In Steven Kartashev and Svetlana Kartashev, editors, *Proceedings, Second International Supercomputing Conference, Volume I*, pages 195–198. International Supercomputing Institute, Inc. (St. Petersburg FL), 1987.

[15] Joseph Goguen, Sany Leinwand, José Meseguer, and Timothy Winkler. The Rewrite Rule Machine, 1989. Technical Report Technical Monograph PRG-76, Programming Research Group, Oxford University, 1989.

[16] Joseph Goguen and José Meseguer. Eqlog: Equality, types, and generic modules for logic programming. In Douglas DeGroot and Gary Lindstrom, editors, *Logic Programming: Functions, Relations and Equations*, pages 295–363. Prentice-Hall, 1986. An earlier version appears in *Journal of Logic Programming*, Volume 1, Number 2, pages 179–210, September 1984.

[17] Joseph Goguen and José Meseguer. Models and equality for logical programming. In Hartmut Ehrig, Giorgio Levi, Robert Kowalski, and Ugo Montanari, editors, *Proceedings, 1987 TAPSOFT*, pages 1–22. Springer, 1987. Lecture Notes in Computer Science, Volume 250.

[18] Joseph Goguen and José Meseguer. Unifying functional, object-oriented and relational programming, with logical semantics. In Bruce Shriver and Peter Wegner, editors, *Research Directions in Object-Oriented Programming*, pages 417–477. MIT, 1987. Preliminary version in *SIGPLAN Notices*, Volume 21, Number 10, pages 153–162, October 1986.

[19] Joseph Goguen and José Meseguer. Software for the Rewrite Rule Machine. In *Proceedings, International Conference on Fifth Generation Computer Systems 1988*, pages 628–637. Institute for New Generation Computer Technology (ICOT), 1988.

[20] Joseph Goguen and José Meseguer. Order-sorted algebra I: Equational deduction for multiple inheritance, overloading, exceptions and partial operations. Technical Report SRI-CSL-89-10, SRI International, Computer Science Lab, July 1989. Given as lecture at Seminar on Types, Carnegie-Mellon University, June 1983; many draft versions exist.

[21] Joseph Goguen, James Thatcher, and Eric Wagner. An initial algebra approach to the specification, correctness and implementation of abstract

data types. Technical Report RC 6487, IBM T.J. Watson Research Center, October 1976. In *Current Trends in Programming Methodology, IV*, Raymond Yeh, editor, Prentice-Hall, 1978, pages 80–149.

[22] Joseph Goguen *et al.* Introducing OBJ3. This volume.

[23] Joseph Goguen and David Wolfram. On types and FOOPS. In *Proceedings, IFIP TC2 Conference on Object Oriented Databases*. IFIP, to appear 1990.

[24] Gérard Huet and Derek Oppen. Equations and rewrite rules: A survey. In Ron Book, editor, *Formal Language Theory: Perspectives and Open Problems*, pages 349–405. Academic, 1980.

[25] R.M. Lea. ASP: A cost-effective parallel microcomputer. *IEEE Micro*, 8(5):10–29, 1988.

[26] Sany Leinwand and Joseph Goguen. Architectural options for the Rewrite Rule Machine. In Steven Kartashev and Svetlana Kartashev, editors, *Proceedings, Second International Supercomputing Conference, Volume I*, pages 63–70. International Supercomputing Institute, Inc. (St. Petersburg FL), 1987.

[27] Sany Leinwand, Joseph Goguen, and Timothy Winkler. Cell and ensemble architecture of the Rewrite Rule Machine. In *Proceedings, International Conference on Fifth Generation Computer Systems 1988*, pages 869–878. Institute for New Generation Computer Technology (ICOT), 1988.

[28] José Meseguer. Rewriting as a unified model of concurrency. In *Proceedings, Concur'90 Conference*, number 458 in Lecture Notes in Computer Science, pages 384–400, Amsterdam, August 1990. Springer. Also, Technical Report SRI-CSL-90-02R, Computer Science Lab, SRI International.

[29] José Meseguer and Joseph Goguen. Initiality, induction and computability. In Maurice Nivat and John Reynolds, editors, *Algebraic Methods in Semantics*, pages 459–541. Cambridge, 1985.

[30] Peter M. Sewell. Cell machine correctness via parallel jungle rewriting, 1990. MSc Thesis, Programming Research Group, University of Oxford.

[31] David Shu, Lap-Wai Chow, Greg Nash, and Charles Weems. A content addressable, bit-serial associative processor. In *Proceedings, IEEE Workshop on VLSI Signal Processing*, pages 120–128. IEEE Computer Society, 1988.

[32] David Shu, Greg Nash, and Charles Weems. Image understanding architecture and applications. In Jorge Sanz, editor, *Machine Vision*. Springer, 1988.

[33] Timothy Winkler. Numerical computation on the RRM. Technical report, SRI International, Computer Science Lab, November 1988. Technical Note SRI-CSL-TN88-3.

[34] Timothy Winkler, Sany Leinwand, and Joseph Goguen. Simulation of concurrent term rewriting. In Steven Kartashev and Svetlana Kartashev, editors, *Proceedings, Second International Supercomputing Conference, Volume I*, pages 199–208. International Supercomputing Institute, Inc. (St. Petersburg FL), 1987.

Chapter 6

OBJ FOR OBJ

Claude Kirchner
INRIA Lorraine & CRIN

Hélène Kirchner
CRIN & INRIA Lorraine

Aristide Mégrelis
INRIA Lorraine & CRIN
615 rue du jardin botanique, BP 101,
54602 Villers-lès-Nancy Cedex, France

Abstract   An interpreter for OBJ3 implemented in Common LISP has been designed using the language OBJ. This formal design is both an effective support of the programming task and a means of communication between different programmers and designers. In the light of this experiment, we propose some extensions to the language and also give a reflexive version of the interpreter.

1   INTRODUCTION

Software engineers use tools, methods and theories to produce software systems as efficiently and safely as possible. The growing need for very large software systems has been, for more than a decade, the motivation for intense research in the field of software engineering. Although various techniques are now available, many of them have not yet been fully tried out on real, full-sized systems to determine their actual usefulness.

Here we report how OBJ can be used to design a complex piece of software, namely an OBJ3 interpreter. We emphasize that we do not describe the exact state of the current OBJ3 interpreter, but rather a method of formal design. This chapter is therefore not meant to be as the work of the OBJ3 team. Note that since we report on a joint work, we write the word "team" to designate the 85-56 OBJ3 group of SRI International, namely Joseph Goguen, José Meseguer, Tim Winkler and the three authors, and the words "we" and "us" to designate, as usual, the authors.

OBJ is a programming language based on equational logic and (versions 2 and 3) on order-sorted algebra [13]. OBJ was developed first at UCLA [6, 10, 21], then at SRI International by Joseph Goguen, José Meseguer and their group [9, 4, 7]. OBJ3 is version number 3 of the language [7, 11]; its operational semantics is described in [15]. We shall assume that the reader has an elementary knowledge of it.

Faced with the task of writing a complex piece of software, the team agreed on the need of a formal and abstract design phase, and looked for a powerful design technique. Several features were required:

- *Mathematical semantics* — Mathematics was a common reference, so by means of a language having a mathematical semantics, unambiguous communication and formal reasoning were possible.

- *Ease of change* — The software development process is most often not straightforward: the various parts of the system are not produced simultaneously, so that changes are unavoidable. A modular design was necessary to control this as much as possible.

- *Organization of the program from general to particular* ('top-down') — We wanted to introduce new data and functions only *by need* to avoid unnecessary planning and unnecessary work.

- *Verification* — A strongly-typed language allowed simple syntactic checks and thus helped to avoid many errors.

- *Documentation* — If the code is kept to comply with the design, debugging and addition of new functions are easier. The design was intended to be a clear documentation of the LISP code.

With respect to these criteria, OBJ itself was a good candidate, and was chosen. The formal design of the OBJ3 interpreter, written in OBJ, appeared to be both useful in the designing task, and a means of communication between different programmers. Design decisions were taken at the appropriate time (not too early), so that, eventually, the team quickly produced a program, written in Common LISP [20]. Moreover, it was quite challenging and interesting to use OBJ itself; we were able to understand precisely its features and to discover possible improvements.

In Section 2, we argue for the choice of OBJ and describe more precisely how to use it. We then present the high-level design of the interpreter and give several examples of OBJ text in Section 3. In Section 4, we suggest some syntactic extensions to the language, that we would have appreciated when designing the interpreter. In Section 5, we show how we can make the design of the OBJ3 interpreter *reflexive*, i.e. an executable OBJ program.

2   OBJ FOR OBJ

OBJ was chosen as design language because of several powerful features:

- *Mathematical semantics.* The mathematical semantics of OBJ3 is based on order-sorted algebra [13]. The language also supports the theory of abstract data types, which enforces a rigorous description of objects and operators.

- *Modularity.* Moreover, OBJ provides the concepts of modules, hierarchy of modules, and parameterization. The relationships between modules are made explicit via declarations such as 'using', 'extending' or 'protecting'. Because of this "controlled" modularity, some proofs of correctness reduce to local validations. Currently, these validations are left to the programmer and are done by hand.

- *Readability and accuracy.* The general structure of an OBJ program is easy to understand and the program itself can be read at different levels of detail, depending on the choice of the reader: one can either get a general overview of the program, i.e. how the different pieces are combined, or have a precise description of one part and of the objects it manipulates.

The usual method for programming in OBJ is to follow a bottom-up process which consists of building more and more complex data and operators from elementary ones. This discipline allows an incremental interpretation (or compilation) of the program. However, the development of a program is usually an alternating sequence of top-down and bottom-up refinements.

Moreover, the intent was not to have an executable program at each step, except possibly the last one. Dropping this requirement allowed ignoring at first some parts of the design, leaving them unspecified, and completing them later on.

As already emphasized, different layers of the language can be used in the development process as well as for documentation. Which parts of the language were used at different stages in the design are described below.

1. *Division of work.* Modularity was used from the very beginning of the design. Of course, the first step was to determine the hierarchy of

modules in order to identify the different parts of the program and the shared objects. At that point, the team was able to divide the work between the different designers. The following subtasks were identified:

- The installation of modules and views, which is decomposed into a MODULE EVALUATOR, a VIEW EVALUATOR and a MODULE EXPRESSION EVALUATOR. This creates new objects in the environment of the interpreter.

- The RULE-GENERATION module encapsulates the part of the interpreter that transforms the equations given by the user within an OBJ program, into rewrite rules used by the REWRITE-ENGINE module.

- The REWRITE-ENGINE itself deals with the command **reduce**. It is a black box encapsulating the operator normalize, that is applied to a parsed term and a module, and returns the normal form of this term.

- The PARSER transforms a character stream into a correctly-typed term.

- The SPACE is in some sense the data-base of the OBJ interpreter. It contains the environment in which the OBJ commands are evaluated.

2. *Interface.* In the second stage, the signatures of modules were specified, which provided a syntactical description of the data. Moreover, it allowed identifying operators that are used to build the data, and special procedures shared by other parts of the program. Since OBJ is based on the notion of modules which encapsulate all the procedures and objects, some modules only provide one main operator.

Example 15 The RULE-GENERATION module defines a procedure called *rule-generation* whose rank is:

```
op rule-generation : Module Space -> Space .
```

□

At that point some very simple and syntactic checks can be performed, which justifies the choice of a strongly-typed language such as OBJ.

The reader should realize that this effort of listing all the input and output data for each operator is not only necessary on a rigorous mathematical basis (functions with hidden arguments are unknown in mathematics), but also crucial for a careful design: these are *not* details to be omitted. Later, the low-level design or implementation will determine which data to handle as explicit procedure parameters, which data to treat as global variables, etc. This is a different concern.

3. *Functionality.* At the third stage, the functionality of operators is described by equations. Through equations, one is able to grasp the dynamic part of the design process: equations introduce new operators which lead naturally (by need) to new modules at a lower level, until a state is reached where implementation is straightforward. For example, if one ends up with a module specifying a stack or a queue, one would say that its implementation is straightforward. This top-down design process will be illustrated in Section 3.

4. *LISP programming.* The last use of OBJ was to comment the LISP code. Such a documentation is crucial for software maintenance and improvement. It is intended to be updated throughout the life of the program.

3   AN EXPERIMENT—HIGH-LEVEL DESIGN OF AN INTERPRETER

We describe the top-level design of the interpreter by introducing a few OBJ modules; headers, variable declarations, and a few other items are omitted. This is not the original design but a simplified one.

3.1   THE INTERPRETER

The first design-decision is to declare what data, including files and input-output channels, the operating system (OS) passes to the interpreter, and what data the interpreter returns to the OS

Example 16

```
sort CharacterStream .

op session :
   CharacterStream  --- standard input
   CharacterStream  --- standard output
   CharacterStream  --- standard error output
   ->
      [ .input ] CharacterStream
      [ .output ] CharacterStream
      [ .err-output ] CharacterStream .
```

```
eq
session ( INPUT , OUTPUT , ERR-OUTPUT )
= interpreting-loop ( nil , INPUT , OUTPUT ,
                          ERR-OUTPUT , initial-space ) .
```

□

This OBJ module consists of three[1] parts: sorts ('sort'), operators ('op') and equations ('eq'). Any text written at the right of '---' is a comment.

3.1.1   Sorts. The first introduced sort is CharacterStream. Character streams are the only data that the OS and the interpreter exchange. We do not mention a possible saving and restoring of the working space on a disk file.

3.1.2   Operators. The first operator introduced is session. What is a real session like?

Entry — The OS gives the interpreter *control* of the standard input-output channels. At execution time, the interpreter repeatedly reads data from the keyboard, returns data to the screen, and issues error messages if needed.

Exit — At the end of the session, the OS is given back control of the input-output channels, so that it gets what input comes next, and writes its output messages.

The input sorts (sort symbols appearing before the arrow '->') represent the types of data the process reads or modifies; the output sorts (symbols appearing after the arrow) represent the types of data the process modifies or produces.

Because we choose, for convenience, to consider "multi-valued" operators, we need a notation to designate a particular coordinate. First, we prefix output-sort symbols by named indices; we write for instance:

```
[ .input ] CharacterStream
```

Then, we denote the first coordinate of the multi-valued session operator by

```
session [ .input ] .
```

In this way, we also avoid possible mistakes: to be able to speak about the *first, second, etc.,* value, one has to choose a particular ordering, and to remember it as one writes a possibly large text; on the contrary, the meaning of 'session [.input]' does not depend on any ordering on the output sorts of session.

---

[1] A general module consists of four parts. Here, we omit *importation* declarations.

3.1.3   Equations.   Variables are written in upper-case letters; whereas constant symbols are written in lower-case letters, e.g. 'nil'. Variables are not declared when it is immediate to guess their types. Constants are declared as *nullary* operators, that is operators without any input sort.

Through the above equation defining `session`, we introduce the operator `interpreting-loop`, which is described next.[2]

3.2   THE INTERPRETING LOOP

This second module is related to the interpreting loop, which interacts with the user until he terminates the session.

Example 17

```
op
interpreting-loop :
  Signal
  CharacterStream
  CharacterStream
  CharacterStream
  Space
  ->
      [ .input ]  CharacterStream
      [ .output ]  CharacterStream
      [ .err-output ]  CharacterStream
  .

eq
interpreting-loop ( SIGNAL , INPUT , OUTPUT ,
                    ERR-OUTPUT , SPACE )
= if is-exit-signal ( SIGNAL )
  then ( INPUT , OUTPUT , ERR-OUTPUT )
  else interpreting-loop
          ( interpreting-step ( INPUT , OUTPUT ,
                                ERR-OUTPUT , SPACE ) ) .
```

☐

There are two new sorts: `Signal` and `Space`. We choose not to declare them here, because they logically belong to other modules.[3] `Signal` is a

---
[2]Fully understanding this equation requires looking alternately at two modules. This is the usual way of reading an OBJ text.

[3]These modules are not described here.

sort of signal values, i.e. values which are to be interpreted as brief reports of abnormal execution of some procedure; this is a way of handling exceptions. In this case, when the user terminates the session, some "exit" message will be sent by `interpreting-step` to `interpreting-loop`.

`Space` is the sort of the different states of the working-space. The working-space is indeed implemented as a complex structured data. At this stage, we just handle it abstractly: we do not know yet what it is precisely. Only *by need* will this dense sort progressively be broken down, as the design is refined.

3.3   THE READ-EVAL-PRINT STEP

The next module is the main one of this top-level design. It is related to the real interpreting work: getting a message from the user, evaluating it (in the more general sense), and possibly returning a message to the user.

Example 18

```
op
interpreting-step :
  CharacterStream
  CharacterStream
  CharacterStream
  Space
  ->
    [ .signal ]  Signal
    [ .input ]  CharacterStream
    [ .output ]  CharacterStream
    [ .err-output ]  CharacterStream
    [ .space ]  Space
    .


eq
interpreting-step ( INPUT , OUTPUT ,
                    ERR-OUTPUT , SPACE )
= let PARSING-SIGNAL be
        read-item [ .signal ]
        ( INPUT , ERR-OUTPUT , SPACE )
    in
```

```
if null ( PARSING-SIGNAL )
   --- parsing was without trouble
then
   let INPUT-ITEM be
         read-item [ .item ]
           ( INPUT , ERR-OUTPUT , SPACE )
       EVALUATION-SIGNAL be
         eval [ .signal ]
           ( ERR-OUTPUT , INPUT-ITEM , SPACE )
   in
   if null ( EVALUATION-SIGNAL )
      --- evaluation was without trouble
   then
      [ .signal ] = if is-exit-item ( INPUT-ITEM )
                      then exit-signal
                          --- to signal loop termination
                      else nil .
      [ .input ] = read-item [ .input ]
                      ( INPUT , ERR-OUTPUT , SPACE ) .
      [ .output ] =
        print-term
        ( OUTPUT, eval [ .term ]
                    ( ERR-OUTPUT, INPUT-ITEM, SPACE ) ) .
      [ .err-output ] = ERR-OUTPUT .
      [ .space ] =
        eval [ .space ]
        ( ERR-OUTPUT , INPUT-ITEM , SPACE ) .

   else  --- Parsing was all right but an exception
         --- arose at evaluation time
   ---   More
else  --- An exception arose at parsing,
      --- e.g. ambiguous or incomplete parse
   --- More according to case, e.g.
   ---   if ambiguous or incomplete parse,
   ---   give the user what has been obtained so far
```

□

Error handling is not described, only hinted by comments between curly braces '{' and '}'. We write "let" before declaring abbreviations, although this notation is foreign to the present OBJ3 language.

The above equation is split according to the five co-ordinates of the operator `interpreting-step`. We introduce the three main procedures involved in the read-eval-print process: `read-item`, `eval`, and `print-term`. Everything correctly typed by the user is called an *item*, whether

- a *command*, i.e., an OS-like request, e.g. a listing request,

- a *declaration*, i.e., a request to modify the working environment, e.g. declaring and adding a new object,

- or an *expression for computation*, i.e., an *OBJ term* to reduce.

This module is a good example of what we were able to get. We feel that one can meticulously apply this method of formal design from start to end, before writing the first line of code.

3.4   THE READER

The operator `read-item` has just been introduced in the equation above defining `interpreting-step`. Its refinement amounts to designing the parser.

Example 19

```
op
read-item :
  CharacterStream
  CharacterStream
  Space
  ->
    [ .input ]  CharacterStream
    [ .err-output ]  CharacterStream
    [ .signal ]  Signal  --- to signal abnormal parsing
    [ .item ]  Item
    .
```

□

3.5   EVALUATING AND PRINTING

We show below the profiles of `eval` and `print-term`.

Example 20

```
op
eval :
  CharacterStream
  Item
  Space
  ->
    [ .err-output ] CharacterStream
    [ .signal ] Signal --- to signal abnormal evaluation
    [ .term ] Term      --- evaluated term
    [ .space ] Space    --- modified working space
  .

op
print-term :
  CharacterStream
  Term
  ->
    [ .output ] CharacterStream
  .
```

□

4   IMPROVING OBJ

OBJ already appears as an appropriate design language for large-scale programming. However, during our extensive use of OBJ, some additional features appeared as helpful. In order to improve the practical use of the language, we added a few syntactical constructs, some of which have already appeared in the examples above. Some extensions to OBJ are listed below. None is absolutely necessary, but altogether they ought to provide a better design language.

4.1   IMPORTATION AND EXPORTATION

The interface between modules, described through parameterization and "`using`", "`extending`" or "`protecting`" relations, was not precise enough in the design process: they did not provide the capability of limiting the interface between two modules to a subset of operators in the imported module. We found helpful to add export and import declarations, in order to ease checks between imported and exported operators. These declarations are similar to constructs available in modular programming languages such as ADA [2] or CLU [18]. The rule is that any operator declared as imported from a given submodule must be exported by this submodule.

In the extended BNF notation used for the OBJ3 syntax, these new commands are expressed as follows:

```
<export-command> ::= exporting  <operator-identifier> ...
<import-command> ::= importing
          { from  <module-identifier>: ( <operator-identifier> ...)
          | all  }...
```

Example 21 The RULE-GENERATION module begins with these import and export commands:

```
obj RULE-GENERATION is

exporting rule-generation .

importing
  from REWRITE-ENGINE : ( normalize )
  from MODULE : ( get-equations , get-imported-modules ,
                  is-compiled , add-rule, delete-rule ,
                  get-rules , get-sort-relation ,
                  get-coregularity-table )
  from REWRITE-RULE : all
  from OPERATOR : ( get-rules , add-rule )
  from VARIABLE : ( get-sort )
  .

--- etc.

jbo
```

□

4.2   ABBREVIATIONS

A completely functional language is sometimes difficult to read and cumbersome to manipulate. In writing down some equations, we felt the need to introduce abbreviations.

The syntax of an abbreviation is:

```
<abbreviation> ::= let {<variable-identifier> be <expression>}...
             in <expression>.
```

This feature is illustrated in the definition of `interpreting-step` in Example 18. Of course, the definition of this operator could be written without this trick, but would then lose readability.

4.3 MULTIPLE VALUES

We frequently encountered operators that modify several objects. The pure way to handle them is to introduce a new composite object with the different modified objects as components. But that can lead to a drastical increase of the kinds of objects that are actually meaningless, since for each such operator, a new tuple must be introduced to record the modified objects. In order to limit that effect, we introduced multi-valued operators, as in Common LISP. Actually, to manipulate an operator `f` taking its value in a product of two sorts `s1` and `s2`, we just write `f : s -> s1, s2`. We already mentioned how output sorts are prefixed in order to access to the different coordinates.

Section 3 provides several examples, for instance in the definitions of the operator `read-item` in Example 19 and the operator `interpreting-step` in Example 18. The operator `interpreting-step` modifies simultaneously the input and output character streams as well as the space of evaluation of the interpreter.

4.4 EXCEPTION HANDLING

Error handling in OBJ needs to explicitly introduce error super-sorts and additional constants for error values. This can greatly increase the size of the signature and thus the complexity of the modules. A part of this task could be automatically handled in the language itself by adding an exception mechanism.

One possibility is to use multiple-valued operators and to keep one field for a signal. This is illustrated in the definition of the operator `read-item` in Example 19. The operators calling it (for instance `interpreting-step` in Example 18) can then appropriately handle that exception. The advantage of this method is that it is straightforward to translate the OBJ equation into LISP code, thus providing the same exception handling mechanism in LISP.

However, it seems important for the practical use of the programming language OBJ to have a flexible exception mechanism. For example, the CLU error handling mechanism [18] provides `signal`, `resignal` and `except when` statements.

Example 22 By use of these statements, the operator `interpreting-step` in Example 18 can be written in a different way. First the operator `eval` can signal an evaluation error.

```
op eval :
   CharacterStream
   Item
   Space
   -> [ .err-output ] CharacterStream
      [ .term ] Term        --- evaluated term
      [ .space ] Space      --- modified working space
      signals ( evaluation-signal )
                        --- to signal abnormal evaluation
      .
```

The operator read-item can signal either a parsing error or an exit command.

```
op read-item :
   CharacterStream
   CharacterStream
   Space
   ->
      [ .input ]  CharacterStream
      [ .err-output ]  CharacterStream
      [ .item ]  Item
      signals( parsing-signal --- to signal abnormal parsing
               exit-signal    --- to signal an exit command
         )
      .
```

The exit-signal message is propagated to interpreting-step via the resignal statement.

The evaluation-signal and parsing-signal messages are handled in the definition of interpreting-step, where a special action is performed if and only if the error is detected, via the except when statement.

```
op interpreting-step :
   CharacterStream
   CharacterStream
   CharacterStream
   Space
   -> [ .input ]  CharacterStream
      [ .output ]  CharacterStream
      [ .err-output ]  CharacterStream
      [ .space ]  Space
      signals ( exit-signal )
```

```
eq
interpreting-step( INPUT , OUTPUT , ERR-OUTPUT , SPACE )
= let INPUT-ITEM
  be read-item [ .item ] ( INPUT , ERR-OUTPUT , SPACE )
  in
    [ .input ] = read-item [ .input ]
                     ( INPUT , ERR-OUTPUT , SPACE ) .
    [ .output ] =
      print-term
      ( OUTPUT , eval [ .term ]
                     ( ERR-OUTPUT , INPUT-ITEM , SPACE ) ) .
    [ .err-output ] = ERR-OUTPUT .
    [ .space ] = eval [ .space ]
                     ( ERR-OUTPUT , INPUT-ITEM , SPACE ) .

  except when  evaluation-signal :
  --- Parsing was all right but an exception arose
  ---     at evaluation time.
  --- {More}

  except when parsing-signal :
  --- An exception arose at parsing,
  ---     e.g. ambiguous or incomplete parse.
  --- {More according to case, e.g. if ambiguous
  ---   e.g. if ambiguous or incomplete parse,
  ---   give the user what has been obtained so far}.

  resignal ( exit-signal ) .
```

□

4.5   ITERATORS

On some structures, such as sets, the notion of iterators as defined in CLU, is helpful. For example a useful iterator would be an operator that enumerates all the elements of the set. That would avoid repeatedly handling two cases in writing equations: the basic case where the set is empty, and the recursive case where the set is the union of an element and a set.

Example 23 To handle the set of equations in RULE-GENERATION, we need to write:

```
op
install-module-equations :
  Module EquationSet RuleSet -> RuleSet Module .

eq
install-module-equations ( MOD , E union ES , RULE-SET )
---recursive case
= let ( R , MOD1 ) be install-one-equation ( E , MOD )
  in
  install-module-equations
  ( MOD1 , ES , R union RULE-SET )
  except when no-specialization :
          install-module-equations ( MOD1, ES, RULE-SET )
```
.

```
install-module-equations
( MOD , empty-equation-set , RULE-SET )
---basic case
= ( RULE-SET , MOD ) .
```

By contrast, using an iterator 'for each in do', we could write the following equation.

```
eq
install-module-equations ( MOD , ES ,  RULE-SET )
= for each E in ES do
  let ( R , MOD1 ) be install-one-equation ( E , MOD )
  in
  (R union RULE-SET, MOD1)
  except when no-specialization :
          ( RULE-SET, MOD1 )
```
.

□

However, one can argue that the first style of programming (without iterator) is very close to the definition of a LISP function, so that we decided not to introduce the notion of iterator, losing perhaps some clarity and brevity in the design.

To conclude this section, it is worth emphasizing that the enhancements proposed here do not need any extra semantics: they are only "syntactic sugar" that considerably facilitated the use of OBJ as a design language.

5   A REFLEXIVE POINT OF VIEW—OBJ *IN* OBJ

The design of the OBJ3 interpreter program in OBJ suggests the idea of directly using it as an executable text. This is a bootstrapping problem.

As shown hereafter, this idea leads to a very concise, efficient and clear design by factorizing the common parts and expressing both the program and the specified objects in the same formalism.

5.1   FACTORIZING

Let us first show which parts of the system can be factorized.

The two main tasks of the OBJ system are first to parse and create an object or a theory, second to parse and normalize a term in the context of a given object. Both actions are quite similar, except that the contexts in which they are performed are not the same.

For example, to reduce the term `factorial(6)` in the object `NAT`, the string `factorial(6)` has first to be parsed with respect to the syntax declared in `NAT`, and then the rules of `NAT` are used to reduce it.

On the other hand, to install the module `NAT` in the current environment, it first must be parsed with respect to the OBJ syntax and then installed in the current environment.

Since parsing an object is nothing else but parsing it with respect to a given module, hereafter called `OBJECT`, it is similar to the parsing of a term, such as `factorial(6)`. Furthermore, the actions to be applied on a parsed module can be described in *OBJ* itself, using rewrite rules. The module `OBJECT` is given below. Note that, for more readability, the self-explanatory sorts are not declared and thus the specification is not intended to be complete.

Example 24

```
obj OBJECT is

sort
OkCompiledObject CompiledBody Body .

subsort
OkCompiledObject < OkObject .
CompiledBody < Body .
```

```
--- operations for building bodies
op empty-body :                 -> Body .
    _ . _        : Body Body -> Body [ assoc ] .
--- object building
op obj _ is _ jbo : ObjectId Body -> OkCompiledObject .
    obj _ [ _ ] is _ jbo :
    Name ParameterDeclaration Body -> OkCompiledObject .
--- importation
op protecting _ : ModuleExpression -> Body [ 1 0 ] .
    extending _  : ModuleExpression -> Body [ 1 0 ] .
    using _      : ModuleExpression -> Body [ 1 0 ] .
--- sorts
op sort _         : SortList -> Body .
op subsort _ < _ : SortList SortList -> Body .
--- operators
op op _ : _ -> _ : OperatorId Arity CoArity -> Body .
op op _ : _ -> _ [ _ ] :
    OperatorId Arity CoArity Attribute -> Body .
--- variables
op var _ : _ : VariableId SortId -> Body .
--- equations
op _ eq _ = _ :
    Module CharacterStream CharacterStream -> Body .
--- Note that the first argument of the previous
--- operator indicates in which module the equation
--- will be parsed. It does not correspond to the
--- current syntax of OBJ and is introduced to give
--- a simpler description of reflexivity.

var C-STREAM1, C-STREAM2 : CharacterStream,
    MOD : Module .

eq ( MOD eq C-STREAM1 = C-STREAM2 )
    =
    ( MOD eq parse-for-term [ .term ] ( C-STREAM1, MOD )
        =
        parse-for-term [ .term ] ( C-STREAM2 , MOD ) ) ) .
```

```
--- parameters
op ( _ : _ ) :
    ParameterId Theory -> ParameterDeclaration .
op ( _ , _ ) :
    ParameterDeclaration ParameterDeclaration
    -> ParameterDeclaration [assoc] .
--- attributes
op ( _ , _ ) : Attribute Attribute -> Attribute
                [assoc] .
op assoc : -> Attribute .
op comm : -> Attribute .
op id _ : Operator -> Attribute .
op memo : -> Attribute .
op strat _ : NatList -> Attribute .
op prec _ : Nat -> Attribute .

jbo
```

Note that we are using the local strategy[4] [1 0] in order to specify that the argument of the operator protecting has to be evaluated before applying rules to the term itself. The operator parse-for-term will be defined in the next example. □

This shows that the parser for terms can be used to parse modules and that the rewrite engine can be used to install a module in its environment, so that these main parts of the OBJ system are in fact factorized. Moreover, this presentation gives the syntax of OBJ3 in a concise and clear way, quite different from an usual BNF description. In addition, one can easily change the basic syntax of the language, which is quite useful in an experimental design and implementation.

This seems rather obvious, except that the reader may be anxious about the behavior of a system that runs by executing itself. Of course, some bootstrapping is needed in order to initialize the process.

5.2   HOW TO INITIALIZE THE WORLD?

The fundamental step is to initialize the universe on which OBJ operates. What is the minimum needed? In fact, the whole knowledge of the system is in a table of symbols. If the system is able to find in this table the previous object OBJECT and *if there exist a parser for terms and a rewrite engine*, then

---

[4] More on local strategies is given in [4] and extensions of this notion are given in [8].

the system is able to parse and install modules, as well as to parse and reduce terms.

Thus, in order to create an OBJ system, one only needs to write a parser and a rewrite engine so that the system will run when an environment containing the internal representation of OBJECT is provided. The next step is to describe the parser and the rewrite engine themselves in OBJ. A very similar approach has been followed by G. Cousineau and his group, in the design and the implementation of CAML, an implementation of ML based on the *Categorical Abstract Machine* [1].

Following this process, we obtain a second version of the top-level design (see Section 3) which is reflexive:

Example 25 The read-item operator introduced in Example 18 in the definition of interpreting-step of is simply replaced by the following operator:

```
op
read-term :
  CharacterStream
  CharacterStream
  Module
  ->
    [ .input ]  CharacterStream
    [ .err-output ]  CharacterStream
    [ .signal ]  Signal  --- to signal abnormal parsing
    [ .term ]  Term
    .

  eq
read-term ( INPUT , ERR-OUTPUT , MODULE )
  = parse-for-term ( INPUT , ERR-OUTPUT , MODULE ) .
```

□

Anything, whether a command, a declaration, or an expression for evaluation, given to the interpreter will eventually be parsed as a term or be rejected. This unifies the top-level design of the interpreter through a unique format, and allows a unique parser.

Now, the parse-for-term operator is described as:

Example 26

```
op
parse-for-term :
  CharacterStream
  Module              --- parsing is relative to a module
  ->
      [ .input ]  CharacterStream
      [ .err-output ]  CharacterStream
      [ .signal ]  Signal --- to signal abnormal parsing
      [ .term ]  Term
```

□

Note that parsing is parameterized by information available in the given module. Modules are either built-in, or added to the working space (during the session) according to declarations given to the interpreter.

Any expression given by the user to the interpreter is parsed within the appropriate context: an object is parsed in the module OBJECT, a term is parsed either in the module in which it appears, or in the module specified by the command containing this term. The "boot-strapped" module OBJECT is built in the initial-space given at starting time and remains available during the session. This characterizes a reflexive interpreter.

In that context, the eval operator of Example 20 can simply be implemented as the normalization for an appropriate set of rewrite rules.

This approach has many advantages. They include:

- Factorized code and thus a unified conception mechanism, a uniform design of both the top level interface and the program evaluation step.

- A uniform semantics for the module and the term (i.e. the program) to be reduced.

Finally, note that the argument of inefficiency that may be applied against such a reflexive approach holds only in the case of an interpreted version. The example of the CAML implementation shows clearly that a compiled version of a reflexive definition of the interpreter is at least as efficient as a non-reflexive one.

6   CONCLUSION

Two main advantages are to be emphasized concerning the design phase:

- A formal design enforces clarification of the implementation choices, and their justification, both theoretically and practically.

- A careful design leads to successful coding. The different pieces of Common LISP code, based on a common design, were written *independently*. It took only *one* day to put them together and to make the complete system begin to work.

In the opinion of the authors, this initial work is not a throw-away item: the design *must be maintained* during the entire life-time of the system. Certainly, this rule has a drawback: it takes more work to correct bugs, since the design and the program have to be modified simultaneously. But it also has two great advantages: up-to-date documentation of the code is always available; and modifications are first validated at an abstract level.

For this application, we proposed extensions of the OBJ language: importation and exportation, variable binding, multiple values, exception handling, iterators. For a large design, we think that these features are essential. On the other hand, there are a few features of OBJ that were not used, for example sort constraints [4]. Also, we did not follow a method of bottom-up development since we wanted to hide many implementation details (e.g. implementation of terms). Thus, our design was an incomplete OBJ program that was not executable.

A design language must be delivered with a set of methods and tools, if it is to be used safely and comfortably. Particularly, we felt the need of a version manager, editing facilities, a type-checking mechanism that remains usable on incomplete programs, and a mechanism to validate assertions (such as Church-Rosser or termination properties of term-rewriting systems [14, 3, 17]). These are topics of further research.

Related works: Ten years after its completion, this work can now be connected with several other research topics, in particular with the development of the rewriting logic as a logical framework by José Meseguer [19]. In this direction, we have designed and implemented a framework, called ELAN [16], that allows the specification and execution of computational logics. In the same vein, the 2OBJ [12] system provides metalangage facilities for extending OBJ3. Let us also mention that a specification method similar to the one described here has been used to design a completion-based theorem prover for OBJ3 [5].

Acknowledgments

Many thanks to Joseph Goguen, José Meseguer and Tim Winkler for their support and for many fruitful discussions and remarks on previous versions of this paper and to Joseph Goguen and José Meseguer for giving us the opportunity to work on OBJ at SRI during the academic year 85-86.

References

[1] G. Cousineau, P.-L. Curien, and M. Mauny. The categorical abstract machine. In *Proceedings 2nd Conference on Functional Programming Languages and Computer Architecture, Nancy (France)*, volume 201 of *Lecture Notes in Computer Science*, pages 50–64. Springer-Verlag, 1985.

[2] Department of Defense. Reference manual for the ADA programming language. Technical Report ANSI/MIL-STD-1815A, United States Government, 1980.

[3] N. Dershowitz. Termination. In *Proceedings 1st Conference on Rewriting Techniques and Applications, Dijon (France)*, volume 202 of *Lecture Notes in Computer Science*, pages 180–224, Dijon (France), May 1985. Springer-Verlag.

[4] K. Futatsugi, J. A. Goguen, J.-P. Jouannaud, and J. Meseguer. Principles of OBJ-2. In B. Reid, editor, *Proceedings 12th ACM Symp. on Principles of Programming Languages*, pages 52–66. ACM, 1985.

[5] I. Gnaedig. ELIOS-OBJ: Theorem proving in a specification language. In B. Krieg-Brückner, editor, *Proceedings of the 4th European Symposium on Programming*, volume 582 of *Lecture Notes in Computer Science*, pages 182–199. Springer-Verlag, February 1992.

[6] J. A. Goguen. Some design principles and theory for OBJ-0, a language for expressing and executing algebraic specifications of programs. In *Proceedings of International Conference on Mathematical Studies of Information Processing*, pages 429–475. IFIP Working Group 2.2, Kyoto, Japan, 1978.

[7] J. A. Goguen, Claude Kirchner, Hélène Kirchner, A. Mégrelis, J. Meseguer, and T. Winkler. An introduction to OBJ-3. In J.-P. Jouannaud and S. Kaplan, editors, *Proceedings 1st International Workshop on Conditional Term Rewriting Systems, Orsay (France)*, volume 308 of *Lecture Notes in Computer Science*, pages 258–263. Springer-Verlag, July 1987. Also as internal report CRIN: 88-R-001.

[8] J. A. Goguen, Claude Kirchner, and J. Meseguer. Concurrent term rewriting as a model of computation. In R. Keller and J. Fasel, editors, *Proceedings of Graph Reduction Workshop*, volume 279 of *Lecture Notes in Computer Science*, pages 53–93, Santa Fe (NM, USA), 1987. Springer-Verlag.

[9] J. A. Goguen, J. Meseguer, and D. Plaisted. Programming with parameterized abstract objects in OBJ. *Theory And Practice of Software Technology*, pages 163–193, 1982.

[10] J. A. Goguen and J. Tardo. An introduction to OBJ: A language for writing and testing software specifications. In M. K. Zelkowitz, editor, *Specifica-*

tion of Reliable Software, pages 170–189. IEEE Press, Cambridge (MA, USA), 1979. Reprinted in *Software Specification Techniques*, N. Gehani and A. McGettrick, editors, Addison-Wesley, 1985, pages 391-420.

[11] J. A. Goguen and T. Winkler. Introducing OBJ3. Technical Report SRI-CSL-88-9, SRI International, 333, Ravenswood Ave., Menlo Park, CA 94025, August 1988.

[12] Joseph Goguen, Andrews Stevens, Keith Hobley, and Hendrick Hilberdink. 2OBJ, a metalogical framework based on equational logic. *Philosophical Transactions of the Royal Society, Series A*, (339):69–86, 1992.

[13] Joseph A. Goguen and José Meseguer. Order-sorted algebra I: equational deduction for multiple inheritance, overloading, exceptions and partial operations. *Theoretical Computer Science*, 2(105):217–273, 1992.

[14] J.-P. Jouannaud and Hélène Kirchner. Completion of a set of rules modulo a set of equations. *SIAM Journal of Computing*, 15(4):1155–1194, 1986. Preliminary version in Proceedings 11th ACM Symposium on Principles of Programming Languages, Salt Lake City (USA), 1984.

[15] Claude Kirchner, Hélène Kirchner, and J. Meseguer. Operational semantics of OBJ-3. In *Proceedings of 15th International Colloquium on Automata, Languages and Programming*, volume 317 of *Lecture Notes in Computer Science*, pages 287–301. Springer-Verlag, 1988.

[16] Claude Kirchner, Hélène Kirchner, and M. Vittek. Designing constraint logic programming languages using computational systems. In P. Van Hentenryck and V. Saraswat, editors, *Principles and Practice of Constraint Programming. The Newport Papers.*, pages 131–158. The MIT press, 1995.

[17] Donald E. Knuth and P. B. Bendix. Simple word problems in universal algebras. In J. Leech, editor, *Computational Problems in Abstract Algebra*, pages 263–297. Pergamon Press, Oxford, 1970.

[18] B. H. Liskov, R. Atkinson, T. Bloom, E. Moss, J. Schaffert, B. Scheifler, and A. Snyder. *CLU Reference Manual*, volume 114 of *Lecture Notes in Computer Science*. Springer-Verlag, New York, 1981.

[19] J. Meseguer. Conditional rewriting logic as a unified model of concurrency. *Theoretical Computer Science*, 96(1):73–155, 1992.

[20] G. L. Steele. *Common Lisp: The Language*. Digital Press, 1984.

[21] J. Tardo. *The Design, Specification and Implementation of OBJT: A Language for Writing and Testing Abstract Algebraic Program Specifications*. PhD thesis, UCLA, Computer Science Department, 1981.

Chapter 7

OBJSA NETS:
OBJ AND PETRI NETS FOR SPECIFYING CONCURRENT SYSTEMS

E. Battiston

F. De Cindio

G. Mauri

Dipartimento di Science dell'Informazione
Universitá di Milano
via Comelico 39, 120135 Milano (Italy)
email: { battiston,decindio,mauri } @dsi.unimi.it

Abstract   This paper provides an intuitive presentation of OBJSA nets, a specification language which combines a specific class of Petri nets, namely Superposed Automata nets, and the well-known algebraic specification language OBJ. The presentation is particularly addressed to people confident with algebraic specification techniques and focuses on the composition mechanism which allows the designer to obtain the OBJSA specification of a system by combining the specifications of the system components.

1 COMBINING PROCESS ABSTRACTION AND DATA ABSTRACTION FOR REAL SYSTEM SPECIFICATION

When using formalisms based on abstract data type techniques [14, 16, 23, 32] for real system specification, a major limitation turns out to be the lack of features for treating concurrency, synchronization, mutual exclusion and other analogous situations. These points of weakness are outlined both in the literature (see, e.g. [1]) and in concrete experiences of use of algebraic languages.

On the other hand, the most popular formalisms which allow an appropriate handling of concurrency and support process abstraction, such as (high-level) Petri nets [15, 19], Milner's CCS [27] or specialized specification languages such as SDL for telecommunication applications, are weak in supporting data abstraction.

The increasing awareness of the limitations of both families of formalisms has given rise in recent years to several attempts of defining new theories, formalisms and languages, integrating both data abstraction and process abstraction for concurrency handling. [1] and [20] survey the most of them.

In order to overcome both limitations, in [4] we defined, in both graphical and matricial form, a new class of high-level nets, called OBJSA net systems, or OBJSA nets for short. OBJSA nets are couples consisting of a Superposed Automata (SA) net [10] and of an algebraic specification, that we give using OBJ3 [17], plus the inscription function which associates the net elements with the corresponding algebraic entities. The attention is focused, on the one hand, as in CSP [18], CCS [27], and COSY [22], on the possibility of building the net system model through composition of its (sequential non-deterministic) components: this is the reason of the choice of SA nets among the various classes of Petri nets [6]. On the other hand, we stress the use of algebraic specification techniques for describing the individual tokens flowing in the net: here the choice is in favour of a well defined and supported specification language such as OBJ3.

The resulting specification language takes full advantage of the best features of Petri Nets and algebraic specification techniques. On the one hand the integration of the algebraic specification formalism into the net model allows the definition of a new class of high-level nets, equipped with a formalism for modelling the data handled by the concurrent processes which is more powerful than in the classical classes of high-level nets. More precisely, in regard to OBJSA nets, we feel very satisfied with our choice of adopting one well developed algebraic specification language such as OBJ3 instead of redefining on nets all the algebraic notations. The major advantages consist in genericity, compositionality, reusability, executability and support tools, as discussed below.

On the other hand, the net formalism gives to the algebraic specifications a way for modelling concurrency and synchronization constraints.

This mutual advantage takes its full form when combined with the modularization and compositionality features, which are recognized as a major need in the specification of concurrent systems [7, 13].

Furthermore, in order to reduce the difficulty that system designers operating in industrial framework usually find in the autonomous development of formal specifications, the definition of OBJSA nets is tightly coupled with the development of a support environment, called ONE (OBJSA Nets Environment).

ONE consists of different modules, each one of which combines a 'graphic engine', based on DesignML [24], with an 'algebraic engine', i.e. the OBJ3 Interpreter [31].

To generate an OBJSA net using ONE, (i) the user specifies the elementary components of the system and their interactions; then, (ii) s/he builds the whole system model by merging (through transition fusion) the models of its elementary components; finally, (iii) the user can validate either the whole system model or its components at different levels by simulating the specification, i.e. by playing the token game and by rewriting the associated specification.

In particular in the steps above mentioned, OBJ and its Interpreter assume a fundamental role:

(i) they strongly support the specification incremental development through different importing modalities (*protecting*, *extending*, *using* and *including*) and through genericity; both techniques are exploited to build up the algebraic specification of an OBJSA net incrementally by using a set of built-in parameterized modules, hidden from users.

(ii) the notions of *theory* and *view* allow, as shown below (cf. Section 3.4), the extension to the algebraic part of the specification of the composition mechanism through transition fusion typical of SA nets.

(iii) OBJ specifications can be effectively executed using equations as rewriting rules; this allows the extension to OBJSA nets of the net token game (cf. Section 3.5).

In Section 2 a first overview of the proposed approach is given, through the developement of an example, where attention is given to the presentation of the composition mechanism of OBJSA components, so as to support intuition. In Section 3 some built-in objects and theories are specified and tested on the previous example, to highlight the use of OBJ in the specification, composition and simulation of OBJSA nets. Section 4 presents the state-of-art of the overall project on OBJSA nets.

2 OVERVIEW OF THE APPROACH

We said in the introduction that the main idea of our approach is to specify a system by specifying, and then composing, its elementary components, each one in turn specified through a couple of elements, namely a net and an associated object. The aim of this section is to sketch, in an informal and intuitive way, the relationships mutually binding these two ingredients, while the next section will show how OBJ modules are associated with net elements (places, markings, transitions and arcs).

An example will support the intuition also for those who are not familiar with Petri nets. It consists of a simplified version of a real case, namely, the mechanism of message exchange between SDL processes. It is taken into consideration for three reasons: this non trivial mechanism requires concurrency; the basic objects it requires to specify (queues and buffers) are familiar to everybody; and finally SDL is largely used for specifying switching systems. Nevertheless, since the goal here is to present OBJSA net systems, we will use a simplified model, disregarding some features of SDL, such as priorities and save signals.

2.1   ELEMENTARY COMPONENTS

Let us begin by considering the two parameterized objects BUFFER and QUEUE whose definitions are given below and which introduce the usual operators for building the type, for inserting a new element (operator fill for the buffer and append for the queue), for removing an element (operator empty for the buffer and consume for the queue). Note that in the given specification the queue operators together with the equations characterize the usual FIFO mechanism, while the SDL queue consuming mechanism is more complex in order to deal with priorities and save signals.

```
obj BUFFER[Elem :: TRIV] is sort Buffer .
    subsorts Elt.Elem < Buffer .
    op eb : -> Buffer .
    op no-elem : -> Elt.Elem .
    ops buffer-busy  buffer-empty : -> Buffer .
    ops is-busy  is-empty : Buffer -> Bool .
    op fill : Elt.Elem  Buffer -> Buffer .
    op empty : Buffer -> Buffer .
    op get : Buffer -> Elt.Elem .
    var s : Elt.Elem .     var b : Buffer .
    eq is-empty (b) = (b == eb) .
    eq is-busy (b) = (b =/= eb) .
    cq empty (b) = buffer-empty if is-empty(b) .
    cq empty (b) = eb if is-busy(b) .
    cq fill (s,b) = s if is-empty(b) .
    cq fill (s,b) = buffer-busy if is-busy(b) .
    cq get (b) = no-elem if is-empty(b) .
    cq get (fill (s,b)) = s if is-empty(b) .
endo
```

```
obj QUEUE[Elem :: TRIV , Bound :: NUMTH] is
   sort Queue .
   op eq : -> Queue .
   op no-elem : -> Elt.Elem .
   ops queue-busy  queue-empty : -> Queue .
   ops is-busy  is-empty : Queue -> Bool .
   op append : Queue Elt.Elem -> Queue .
   op consume : Queue -> Queue .
   op front : Queue -> Elt.Elem .
   op len : Queue -> Nat .
   var x : Elt.Elem .
   var q : Queue .
   eq len (eq) = 0 .
   cq len (q) = 1 + len(consume(q))
      if not(is-empty(q)) .
   eq is-empty (q) = (q == eq) .
   eq is-busy (q) = (len(q) >= ub) .
   eq front (eq) = no-elem .
   eq front (append (eq,x)) = x .
   cq front (append (q,x)) = front(q)
      if not(is-empty(q)) .
   cq append (q,x) = queue-busy if is-busy(q) .
   cq consume(q) = queue-empty if is-empty(q) .
   eq consume(append(eq,x)) = eq .
   cq consume(append(q,x)) = append(consume(q),x)
      if not(is-empty(q)) .
endo
```

where the theories TRIV* and NUMTH require that the actual parameters of
the objects BUFFER and QUEUE, given above, have to provide, respectively, a
sort with at least a constant operator, and a value of sort Nat to specify the
upperbound of the QUEUE size.

```
th TRIV* is
   sort Elt .
   op * : -> Elt .
endth

th NUMTH is
   protecting NAT .
   op ub : -> Nat .
endth
```

The two (state-machine) nets in Figures 7.1 and 7.2 can be, respectively, associated with the two previous objects.

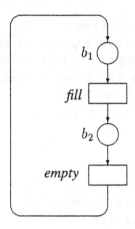

Figure 7.1 Buffer.

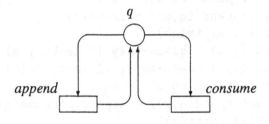

Figure 7.2 Queue.

We can imagine marking both nets by a single token (initially in place b_1 and in q, respectively) representing the state of the object. Then the structure of the net represents synchronization constraints among the various operators. In fact in Petri nets a transition can occur when it has all its preconditions marked. The transition occurrence moves the tokens from the input places to the output ones.

Therefore Figure 7.1 says that the filling and the emptying of the buffer must be in sequence: transition *empty* can occur only when the token is in place b_2. This happens as a consequence of the firing of transition *fill*, which moves the tokens from b_1 to b_2. If we agree on respecting the constraints modelled by the net, we can in accordance simplify the BUFFER data specification. In fact it is no longer necessary, before emptying, to test if the buffer is full, and so forth before filling. Then the two conditional equations at the end of the object

BUFFER, as shown in the following specification, become simple equations. In the following, references to the object BUFFER are intended to follow this specification.

Let us notice that the idea that errors in a sequential framework become waiting conditions in a distributed one has been already suggested, in the context of concurrent object-oriented languages, for instance in [26] and in [21].

```
obj BUFFER [Elem :: TRIV] is sort Buffer .
    subsorts Elt.Elem < Buffer .
    op eb : -> Buffer .
    op fill : Elt.Elem Buffer -> Buffer .
    op empty : Buffer -> Buffer .
    op get : Buffer -> Elt.Elem .
    var s : Elt.Elem .  var b : Buffer .
    eq fill (s,b) = s .
    eq empty (fill (s,b)) = eb .
    eq get (fill (s,b)) = s .
endo
```

2.2   NON-ELEMENTARY COMPONENTS

Both the Buffer and the Queue must not be thought of as isolated, but as components of a more complex system. As a consequence we introduce, consistently for the nets and for the associated objects, a mechanism allowing one to obtain more complex components by composing more elementary ones.

The basic idea for the composition is the same as in a number of languages and theories for concurrency, such as CSP, CCS, COSY. As the behaviour of a system results from the composition of the behaviours of its autonomous components as constrained by their mutual interactions, the composition of the models of the various components results from the identification of their interactions (input/output command in CSP, corresponding actions in CCS and in COSY).

2.2.1   The net composition mechanism.   In terms of nets, this composition mechanism yields the superposition of the transitions which, in the models of the elementary components, represent the same interaction, as shown in Figure 7.3.

The structure of nets built in such a way has the following characteristics: each transition is balanced, i.e. it has the same number of incoming and outcoming arcs; if this number is equal to one, then the transition models an action *local* to an elementary component; otherwise, it represents an interaction between two (or more) components, or among more instances of the same

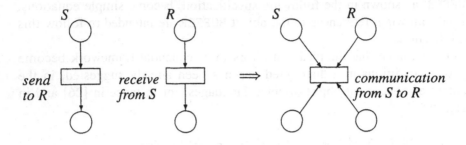

Figure 7.3   Composition of nets.

component. The places of the resulting net can then be partitioned into disjoint sets, each set representing the possible states of an *elementary* component. The occurrence of a token in a place gives the state of the component; and the overall state, represented by the *marking* of the net, results from the composition of the component states. This structure is what characterizes Superposed Automata Nets, as introduced in [10].

In the case of our previous example, one has to consider that the operations on the two objects are not at all performed by the object itself. There should be in the overall system some other component which fills the buffer, and some other which empties it, and the like for the Queue. That is, we can see the transitions *fill*, *empty*, *append* and *consume* as open transitions and the Buffer and the Queue as two *open* components which change their state by interacting with other components.

In particular we can imagine that the two components interact mutually; for instance, if the buffer emptying coincides with the queue appending. This can be interpreted as follows: the last message received by the buffer is appended to the queue as soon as possible depending on the occurrence of a conflicting consuming action. Figure 7.4 shows the net obtained from the nets of Figure 7.1 and 7.2 by *superposing* the transitions *empty* of Buffer and *append* of Queue into the transition *enqueue*.

This net models the behaviour of a new and more complex component, which is still open: in fact while the transition *enqueue*, generated by superposition, is local (internal) to it, the transitions *fill* and *consume* still look for partners.

The net models in a natural way that in this more complex data structure obtained combining the Buffer and the Queue:

- the transitions *fill* and *enqueue* can occur only in sequence;

- *enqueue* and *consume* can occur in whatever order, but not concurrently;

- *fill* and *consume* can occur in whatever order, even concurrently.

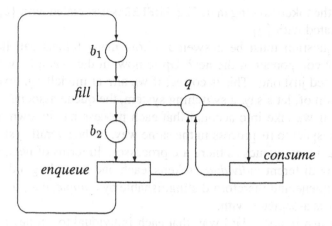

Figure 7.4 SDLQueue.

This net is adequate for modelling the semantic of the mechanism of message exchange between SDL processes, as discussed in [12]. Therefore in the following we will call the new component SDLQueue.

As the object BUFFER, with the mentioned simplifications, is associated with the (state-machine) net in Figure 7.1, and the object QUEUE is associated with the (state-machine) net in Figure 7.2, in the same way an algebraic specification must be associated with the net in Figure 7.4 resulting by their composition through superposition. That is, accordingly with the net composition mechanism, a consistent composition mechanism for the associated algebraic specifications must be introduced.

3 CORRESPONDENCE BETWEEN NET ELEMENTS AND OBJ MODULES

In order to introduce the algebraic specification composition mechanism consistent with the already sketched net composition, we need first to give more hints about the correspondence in OBJSA nets between net elements and OBJ modules.

3.1 PLACES AND PARAMETERIZED OBJECT
COMP-DOM

In regard to places, we have already seen that they are partitioned into disjoint sets preserving the elementary component membership relation. A (different) object is associated with each set of places in order to characterize the structure of the token flowing in it. E.g. BUFFER is associated with $\{b_1, b_2\}$; QUEUE is associated with $\{q\}$.

But now a question must be answered: How many tokens can flow in each elementary component of the net? Up to now, in the example, we have implicitly assumed just one. This is correct if we aim at modelling, given the SDL specification of, let's say, a switching system, the queue associated with a process. But if we take into account that each process has its own queue, behaving with respect to its process in the same way, in the overall system we should model as many queues as there are processes. In terms of nets, this is grasped by using different *individual* tokens, each one modelling a different instance of the queue and therefore distinguishable by a *name*, e.g., the name of the process it is associated with.

In order to grasp in a standard way that each individual token has its own structure and represents a different instance of the object flowing in the associated net, and for facilitating the user task, a predefined (built-in) parameterized object is provided. Since it characterizes the individual tokens of a component it is called COMP-DOM for COMPonent DOMain. It is defined, as follows, by means of the OBJ3 built-in parameterized object 2TUPLE, where the first field is for the name part, and the second field for the data part of the tokens.

```
obj COMP-DOM[N :: TRIV, D :: TRIV] is
    dfn Dom is 2TUPLE[N,D] *(
        op <<_;_>> to <_;_>,
        op 1*_ to name,
        op 2*_ to data ) .
endo
```

The ground terms of sort Dom are the individual tokens flowing in the corresponding component, and determining its *marking*. They then consist of two parts: a name part which distinguishes (through an identifier, which is not modified by transition occurrence) different instances of the same component, and a data part, which represents the data structure belonging to the component and can be modified by transition occurrence.

Let us note that the trivial theory TRIV*, given in 2.1, just requires that a constant operator is defined. If both the actual parameters of the instantiation of COMP-DOM are the most trivial object satisfying this theory, let's say the object

```
obj  LAMBDA is sort Lambda .
    op λ : -> Lambda .
endo
```

then there is a single individual token $<\lambda;\lambda>$ turned into the not structured token, which stands for one instance without any relevant data structure.

Example 27 By instantiating the object COMP-DOM we can define the objects BUFFERDOM and QUEUEDOM associated, respectively, with the set of places $\{b1, b2\}$ of the elementary component Buffer and with $\{q\}$ of the elementary component Queue.

As actual parameters, we use, for the name part, the object PROCESS which defines the various processes constituting a given SDL application, and, for the data part, the instantiations of the two parameterized objects BUFFER and QUEUE suitable for dealing with the messages exchanged between the processes. The object MSG is used as an actual parameter for instantiating BUFFER and QUEUE. It is defined as an instantiation of the built-in object 2TUPLE consisting of two fields, one for the message and the other for the identifier of the destination process. Consistently with the initial option for simplification, we omit here a field for the priority of each message.

The second actual parameter used for instantiating QUEUE is the view BOUND6, which says that actual queues can have, let's say, at most six elements.

```
obj BUFFERDOM is
   dfn BufferDom is COMP-DOM [
      view to PROCESS is sort Elt to Process .endv,
      view to BUFFER [MSG] is sort Elt to Buffer .endv ]
   op get1 : BufferDom -> Msg .
   var y : BufferDom .
   eq get1(y) = get(data(y)) .
endo

obj QUEUEDOM is
   dfn QueueDom is COMP-DOM [
      view to PROCESS is sort Elt to PROCESS . endv,
      view to QUEUE [MSG,BOUND6] is
         sort Elt to Queue . endv ] .
   var y : QueueDom .
endo
```

where:

```
view BOUND6 from NUMTH to NAT is
   op ub to 6 .
endv
```

```
obj PROCESS is
   sort PROCESS .
   ops p1 p2 p3 .... pm : -> Process .
endo

obj BODY is
   sort Body .
   ops m1 m2 m3 m4 m0 : -> Body .
endo

obj MSG is
   dfn Msg is 2TUPLE [
      view to PROCESS is sort Elt to Process . endv ,
      view to BODY is sort Elt to Body . endv ]* (
      op 1*_ to header(_) ,
      op 2*_ to body(_) ,
      op <<_;_>> to [_;_] ) .
endo
```

Let us notice that the individual tokens which flow in the net in Figure 7.1 and which, together with the net, model the Buffer associated with each process, are

$$<p_1 ; buffer_1 > .... <p_m ; buffer_m >$$

where $buffer_1$ ... $buffer_m$ are terms of the main sort Buffer of the object BUFFER [MSG] (e.g. the empty buffer eb or the term $[p_3 ; m_3]$ which represents the Buffer containing the message m_3 for the process p_3) and p_1 ... p_m are the constant operators defined in the object PROCESS, i.e. the names of the processes by which we can distinguish the different instances of the Buffer.

Analogously the individual tokens which flow in the net in Figure 7.2 are

$$<p_1 ; queue_1> .... <p_m ; queue_m>$$

where $queue_1$ ... $queue_m$ are terms of the main sort Queue of the object QUEUE [BOUND6,MSG] (e.g. the empty queue eq or the term

```
append (append (append (eq,[p1; m3]),
                  [p2 ; m3]), [p3 ; m3 ])
```

which represents the Queue containing the message m_3 sent to the processes p_1, p_2 and p_3, in that order).□

3.2 TRANSITIONS AND THE PARAMETERIZED MODULES TRANS_K AND TTH_{K-O}

Let us now consider transitions. As usual in Petri nets, the occurrence of the transitions, moving tokens from input to output places, models the dynamic behaviour of the system. In all the classes of high-level Petri nets, a transition can occur when all its input places contain some individual tokens, such that the *predicate* associated with the transition is satisfied. The transition occurrence takes away from each input place the involved tokens and puts them, *changing* their data part, in the correspondent output place. Therefore to formalize the predicate and the change of value of the (data part of the) individual tokens a suitable labelling is associated to arcs and transitions.

In OBJSA nets each transition is associated with an OBJ module. Depending on the *arity* of the transition (i.e., the number of tokens involved in its occurrence) and on its opening degree (i.e., the number of not yet identified partners) this OBJ module specifies variables and operators used for labelling the transition surrounding arcs. In particular, denoting by o the transition opening degree and by k the number of the already specified tokens involved, $k + o$ gives the arity of the transition, and the OBJ module specifies:

- k variables y and o variables x for labelling input arcs; in particular, y represent the already specified tokens involved, and x the not yet identified partners.

- k operators y' for labelling output arcs;

- k operators ch, each one of which makes explicit how the data part of each individual token involved in the transition occurrence is modified (y' and ch are bound by an equation which makes the first ones depend on the second);

- a boolean operator pr which, if necessary, introduces a further restriction for transition occurrence (it is used in the condition of the equations which define the operators

These modules operate on the individuals flowing in their input and output places, i.e. on the main sorts of some objects obtained as instantiation of COMP-DOM. Since these sorts are in general different for each sm-component, they must be taken as parameters. It is necessary to define a theory CDTH which retains the main characteristics of the object COMP-DOM. The theory CDTH is defined as follows:

```
th CDTH is
  sort CDSort .
  sorts NSort DSort .
  op <_;_> : NSort DSort -> CDSort .
  op name : CDSort -> NSort .
  op data : CDSort -> DSort .
  var n : NSort .
  var d : DSort .
  eq name (< n ; d >) = n .
  eq data (< n ; d >) = d .
endth
```

In order to associate a transition with an OBJ module, there are two possibilities:

- if the transition is *closed*, i.e. it is already fully characterized as the transition *enqueue* in Figure 7.4 is, then the module is an object (e.g. the object ENQUEUE, defined in the next section);

- if the transition is *open*, i.e., it is only partially characterized as the transitions *fill* and *consume* in Figure 7.4 are, then the module is a theory (e.g. the theories FILLTH and CONSUMETH, defined in the next section), which defines constraints for transition superposition being possible. Theories become objects when a set of corresponding open transitions are superposed giving rise to a closed transition.

In order to introduce a standard notation, both objects and theories associated with transitions are obtained by instantiation of one of the following built-in parameterized modules, the objects $TRANS_k$ and the theories TTH_{k-o} (for Transition THeory).

Their instantiation by the user actually consists simply in defining the actual operators which capture how the transition firing modifies the data part of the individual token moved from input to output places (i.e. in defining pr and change).

Here we show the modules $TRANS_2$ and TTH_{1-1} which correspond to the transitions we have to specify (see Examples 28 and 30). In particular the parameterized object $TRANS_2$ is associated with all the closed transitions having two already specified involved tokens.

```
obj TRANS₂ [A₁ :: CDTH , A₂ :: CDTH] is sort Trans₂ .
   subsorts CDSort.A₁ < Trans₂ .
   subsorts CDSort.A₂ < Trans₂ .
   op no-enabled : -> Trans₂ .
   op pr : CDSort.A₁ CDSort.A₂ -> Bool .
   op ch₂ : CDSort.A₁ CDSort.A₂ -> DSort.A₂ .
   op ch₁ : CDSort.A₁ CDSort.A₂ -> DSort.A₁ .
   op-as y'₂ : CDSort.A₁ CDSort.A₂ -> CDSort.A₂
           for y'₂(y₁,y₂) if pr(y₁,y₂) .
   op-as y'₂ : CDSort.A₁ CDSort.A₂ -> Trans₂
           for y'₂(y₁,y₂) if not(pr(y₁,y₂)) .
   op-as y'₁ : CDSort.A₁ CDSort.A₂ -> CDSort.A₁
           for y'₁(y₁,y₂) if pr(y₁,y₂) .
   op-as y'₁ : CDSort.A₁ CDSort.A₂ -> Trans₂
           for y'₁(y₁,y₂) if not(pr(y₁,y₂)) .
   var y₂ : CDSort.A₂ .
   var y₁ : CDSort.A₁ .
   cq y'₂(y₁,y₂) = <(name(y₂));(ch₂(y₁,y₂))>
       if pr(y₁,y₂) .
   cq y'₂(y₁,y₂) = no-enabled
       if not(pr(y₁,y₂)) .
   cq y'₁(y₁,y₂) = <(name(y₁));(ch₁(y₁,y₂))>
       if pr(y₁,y₂) .
   cq y'₁(y₁,y₂) = no-enabled
       if not(pr(y₁,y₂)) .
endo
```

The choice of introducing the error operator no-enabled guarantees the "no junk" property when one rewrites the labels of output arcs of a transition which cannot occur in a certain mode because its predicate is not verified. Let us notice that the codomain of the operators y'_k $(1 \leq k \leq 2)$ in successful situations, i.e. when the predicate is satisfied, is Asort.A_k; whereas, when the predicate is not satisfied, the result consists of the error message no-enabled.

On the other hand the parameterized theory TTH_{1-1} is associated with all the open transitions t which have two involved tokens: one is already specified and the other corresponds to a not yet specified component.

```
th TTH₁₋₁[A₁ :: CDTH , A₂ :: CDTH] is
    including TRANS₂ [A₁ , A₂ ] .
endth
```

In the case of the parameterized object $TRANS_2$ the two formal parameters A_k $(1 \leq k \leq 2)$ are instantiated by objects obtained as instantiation of COMP-DOM;

they correspond to the domains of the tokens flowing in the input/output arcs. In regard to the parameterized theories TTH_{1-1}, one of the two formal parameters A_k ($1 \leq k \leq 2$) is an object obtained as instantiation of COMP-DOM (it corresponds to the already identified component), while the theory of the other A_k is replaced by a theory, which can be more restrictive than CDTH, imposing constraints on the domains associated with not yet identified components (see Examples 28 and 30).

The instantiation of $TRANS_2$ and TTH_{1-1} consists in selecting the actual parameters and in mapping operators y'_k, ch_k (corresponding to the already specified components) and pr into corresponding actual operators, defined by suitable equations ($1 \leq k \leq 2$). These operators are often inherited by the modules used as actual parameters which specify the domains of the involved tokens, but, if necessary, further (hidden) operators, variables and equations can be introduced (see Examples 28 and 30).

Example 28 Let us consider the transitions of the SA nets in Figure 7.1 and Figure 7.2. All of them are open transitions since their complete characterization requires interaction with another component, denoted by the small places in Figure 7.5, and involve one token already specified. They are therefore to be associated with a parameterized theory obtained by instantiating TTH_{1-1}.

For instance the parameterized theory EMPTYTH associated with the open transition *empty* of the Buffer is defined below. The corresponding net is now enriched with the labelling of arcs and transitions by variables (yb) and terms (true and $y'_b(y_b, x_c)$) defined in the module EMPTYTH (see Figure 7.5).

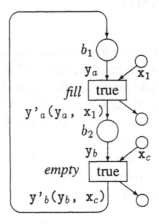

Figure 7.5   Buffer (labelled net).

```
th EMPTYTH [BufferConsumer :: CDTH] is
  including TTH₁₋₁ [
    view to BUFFERDOM is
      sort CDSort to BufferDom .
      sort NSort to Process .
      sort DSort to Buffer . endv,
                     BufferConsumer] *(
      op no-enabled to Empty-no-enabled ,
      op ch₁ to ch_b ,
      op y'₁ to y'_b ) .
  var y_b : BufferDom .
  var x_c : CDSort.BufferConsumer .
  eq pr (y_b,x_c) = true .
  eq ch_b (y_b,x_c) = empty(data(y_b)) .
endth
```

Let us notice that the conditional equations defined in TTH_{1-1} are inherited in EMPTYTH as

$$y'_b \ (y_b,x_c) = \ < \ name(y_b) \ ; \ empty(data(y_b)) \ > \quad \text{if true .}$$
$$y'_b \ (y_b,x_c) = \text{Empty-no-enabled} \qquad\qquad \text{if not true .}$$

where the renaming of the operators is given in EMPTYTH and the renaming of the variable is: y_b for y_1 and $_xc$ for y_2.

The first equation shows that the labelling $y'_b(y_b,x_c)$ of the output arc of the transition *empty* belonging to the Buffer component does not depend on x_c, i.e. on the not yet identified BufferConsumer component. Let us notice that, in this case, the constraint needed on the domain associated with not yet identified input/output places of transition *empty*, is that the partner must retain the same structure of a component domain (COMP-DOM) and this is captured by the built-in theory CDTH.

Let us consider the Queue component. The labelled net in Figure 7.6 corresponds to the specification of the parameterized theories APPENDTH and CONSUMETH associated with the open transitions *append* and *consume* of the Queue.

The theory APPENDTH associated with transition *append* is defined as follows.

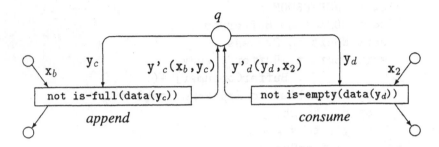

Figure 7.6   Queue (labelled net).

```
th APPENDTH [QueueFiller :: CTH] is
  including TTH₁₋₁ [QueueFiller,
    view to QUEUEDOM is
      sort CDSort to QueueDom .
      sort NSort to Process .
      sort DSort to Queue . endv] *(
        op no-enabled to Append-no-enabled ,
        op ch₂ to chc ,
        op y'₂ to y'c ) .
  var yc : QueueDom .
  var xb : CDSort.QueueFiller .
  eq pr (xb,yc) = not(is-busy(data(yc))) .
  eq chc(xb,yc) = append(data(yc),AMsgIn(xb)) .
endth
```

In APPENDTH the conditional equations defined in TTH_{1-1} take the form

```
y'c(xb,yc) = < name(yc) ; append(data(yc),AMsgIn(xb)) >
  if  not(is-busy(data(yc))) .
y'c(xb,yc) = Append-no-enabled    if is-busy(data(yc)) .
```

where the renaming of the operators is given in APPENDTH and the renaming of the variables is: y_c for y_2 and x_b for y_1.

The first equation shows that the labelling $y'_c(x_b, y_c)$ of the output arc of the transition *append* belonging to the Queue depends on x_b, i.e. on the not yet specified QueueFiller component.

Let us notice that, in this second case, we need to impose some further constraint on the domain associated with the not yet specified input/output places of *append*. In particular the partner has to provide the message to be appended to its corresponding queue. Therefore the theory CTH, given below, in order to retain the same structure of a component domain (COMP-DOM), is defined by means of the built-in theory CDTH. Furthermore it must contain the sort Process, to select the appropriate queue, and the sort Msg, to specify the item which must be appended in the queue. Finally it must contain an extraction operator for each sort (in this case AMsgIn and AProcessIn) which guarantee the possibility of selecting in the data structure of the QueueFiller process a part of the corresponding sort.

```
th CTH is
   including CDTH .
   including PROCESS .
   including MSG .
   op AMsgIn : CDSort -> Msg .
   op AProcessIn : CDSort -> Process .
endth
```

In a similar way we define (see below) the parameterized theories FILLTH, associated with the transition *fill* of the Buffer component, and CONSUMETH, associated with the transition *consume* of the Queue component.

```
th FILLTH [BufferFiller :: CTH] is
   including TTH₁₋₁ [
   view to BUFFERDOM is
      sort CDSort to BufferDom .
      sort NSort to Process .
      sort DSort to Buffer . endv,
               BufferFiller] *(
      op no-enabled to Fill-no-enabled ,
      op ch₁ to chₐ ,
      op y'₁ to y'ₐ ) .
   var yₐ : BufferDom .
   var x₁ : CDSort.BufferFiller .
   eq pr (yₐ,x₁) = true .
   eq cha (yₐ,x₁) = fill (AMsgIn(x₁),data(yₐ)) .
endth
```

```
th CONSUMETH [QueueConsumer :: CDTH] is
  including TTH₁₋₁ [
    view to QUEUEDOM is
      sort CDSort to QueueDom .
      sort NSort to Process .
      sort DSort to Queue . endv,
                        QueueConsumer] *(
        op no-enabled to Consume-no-enabled ,
        op ch₁ to ch_d ,
        op y'₁ to y'_d ) .
  var y_d : QueueDom .
  var x₂ : CDSort.QueueConsumer .
  eq pr (y_d,x₂) = not(is-empty(data(y_d))) .
  eq chd (y_d,x₂) = consume(data(y_d)) .
endth
```

□

3.3   COMPONENTS AND OBJECTS

In the previous section we have seen that a transition is said to be open if it requires, in order to be completely specified, the superposition with some open transition of other components. Then, in an analogous way, we define as open those components which have at least one open transition.

In the case of our example, the Buffer and the Queue are both open components. The Buffer component, in order to be completely specified, must interact with a BufferFiller and a BufferConsumer. Analogously the Queue component must interact with a QueueFiller and a QueueConsumer.

With a component **c** is associated an object defined as follows:

- if **c** is open then the object is parameterized and has, as formal parameters, the theories, instantiations of TTH_{k-o} and associated with the open transitions of **c**, which specify the interface of **c**;

- if **c** is closed then such object is not parameterized;

- *protecting* the objects obtained as instantiation of the parameterized object COMP-DOM and associated with the disjoint sets of places into which the places of **c** are partitioned; they specify the structure of the tokens flowing in these set of places;

- *protecting* the objects obtained as instantiations of the parameterized objects $TRANS_k$ and associated with the closed transitions of **c**; they specify the labels of the input/output arcs of each closed transition and its inscription.

Example 29 In order to fully define the elementary open component Buffer, we associate with the net in Figure 7.1 the object BUFFERCOMP defined as follows.

```
obj BUFFERCOMP [BufferConsumer :: CTH,
        BufferFiller :: CDTH,
        EmTh :: EMPTYTH [BufferConsumer],
        FiTh :: FILLTH [BufferFiller]] is
    including BUFFERDOM .
endo
```

where BUFFERDOM is given in Example 27 , FILLTH and EMPTYTH are in Example 28.

In an analogous way the elementary open component Queue in Figure 7.2 is associated with the object QUEUECOMP defined as follows.

```
obj QUEUECOMP [QueueFiller :: CTH,
        QueueConsumer :: CDTH,
        ApTh :: APPENDTH [QueueFiller],
        CoTh :: CONSUMETH [QueueConsumer]] is
    including QUEUEDOM .
endo
```

where QUEUEDOM is given in Example 27, APPENDTH and CONSUMETH are in Example 28. □

3.4   THE ALGEBRAIC SPECIFICATION COMPOSITION MECHANISM THROUGH THEORY SUPERPOSITION

In order to introduce the algebraic specification composition mechanism consistent with the already sketched net composition, we have first to state when such an operation is possible. The interaction of some open components through the superposition of a tuple of n open transitions is possible if the theories, obtained as instantiations of TTH_{k-o} and associated with them, mutually correspond. This means that there must exist an object, instantiation of $TRANS_k$, of which we can specify n *views*, one for each theory.

Example 30 The non-elementary net component in Figure 7.4 results by transition superposition, starting from the elementary net components in Figures 7.1 and 7.2. We are now in the position to sketch how we can obtain, in a similar and consistent way, the object SDLQUEUECOMP, associated with the non-elementary component SDLQueue in Figure 7.4, by composing the objects BUFFERCOMP and QUEUECOMP, respectively associated with the two elementary net components Buffer and Queue.

First of all we must verify that the two transitions *empty* of Buffer and *append* of Queue can be superposed, i.e., that the parameterized theories EMPTYTH and APPENDTH mutually correspond. This is the case since we are able to define an object which is an instantiation of TRANS$_2$, such that there exist two views to it, one from the instantiation of EMPTYTH obtained using QUEUEDOM as the actual parameter, and the other from the instantiation of APPENDTH obtained using BUFFERDOM as actual parameter.

Such an object is defined as follows.

```
obj ENQUEUE is
  including TRANS₂ [
    view to BUFFERDOM is
      sort CDSort to BufferDom .
      sort NSort to Process .
      sort DSort to Buffer . endv ,
    view to QUEUEDOM is
      sort CDSort to QueueDom .
      sort NSort to Process .
      sort DSort to Queue . endv ] *(
      op no-enabled to Enqueue-no-enabled ,
      op ch₁ to ch_b ,
      op ch₂ to ch_c ,
      op y'₁ to y'_b ,
      op y'₂ to y'_c ) .
  var y_b : BufferDom .
  var y_c : QueueDom .
  eq pr (y_b,y_c) = (name(y_b) == name(y_c))
                    and not(is-busy(data(y_c))) .
  eq chb (y_b,y_c) = empty(data(y_b)) .
  eq chc (y_b,y_c) = append(data(y_c),get(data(y_b))) .
endo
```

Let us notice that we define ENQUEUE starting from the two theories involved in the composition (EMPTYTH and APPENDTH). This object formalizes the fact that the occurrence of the transition *enqueue* in Figure 7.4 causes both the emptying of the Buffer and the appending to the Queue of the element which was in the Buffer. In other words, this object realizes a *composition* of the operator empty defined in the object BUFFER and of the operator append defined in the object QUEUE so that they can be viewed as *projections* on the corresponding components of a more complex operator defined by the new object.

The two required views to the object ENQUEUE from EMPTYTH and from APPENDTH are defined as follows.

```
view BUFFERENQUEUE from EMPTYTH [
   view to QUEUEDOM is
      sort CDSort to QueueDom .
      sort NSort to Process .
      sort DSort to Queue . endv ] to ENQUEUE is
   op ch₂ to ch_c .
   op y'₂ to y'_c .
endv

view QUEUEENQUEUE from APPENDTH [
   view to BUFFERDOM is
      sort CDSort to BufferDom .
      sort NSort to Process .
      sort DSort to Buffer .
      op AMsgIn to get₁ .
      op AHeaderIn to name . endv ] to ENQUEUE is
   op ch₁ to ch_b .
   op y'₁ to y'_b .
endv
```

Since the two open transitions *empty* and *append* can be superposed, we can then compose the components Buffer and Queue and obtain the new component SDLQueue in Figure 7.7, which is still open in the transitions *fill* and *consume*.

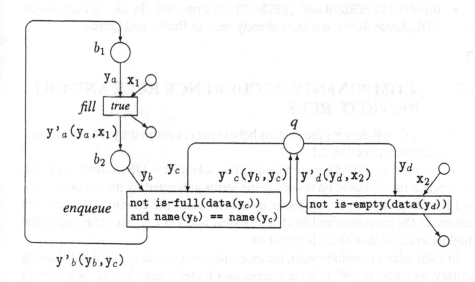

Figure 7.7 SDLQueue (labelled net).

With this component is associated the object SDLQUEUECOMP defined as follows.

```
obj SDLQUEUECOMP [BufferFiller :: CTH,
                  QueueConsumer:: CDTH,
                  CoTh :: CONSUMETH [QueueConsumer],
                  FiTh :: FILLTH [QueueFiller]] is
     including BUFFERDOM .
     including QUEUEDOM .
     including ENQUEUE .
endo
```

It is obtained by merging the objects BUFFERCOMP and QUEUECOMP in Example 30, where in particular:

- the theories APPENDTH and EMPTYTH are composed giving rise to the object ENQUEUE. Let us note that the actualization of predicate pr gives the rule for combining the various instances of the two components when they mutually interact. In fact the first part of the condition, name(y_b) == name(y_c), says that the transition *enqueue* can occur if in its input places there are two tokens having the same name, i.e., associated with the same process;

- the two remaining theories CONSUMETH and FILLTH represent the interface of the new component which is still open;

- objects BUFFERDOM and QUEUEDOM are imported. In fact in component SDLQueue flow the tokens already seen in Buffer and Queue.

□

3.5   COMPONENTS OCCURRENCE RULE AND OBJ REWRITE RULE

In general in Petri nets the system behaviour is captured by the occurrence rule, sketched in Section 2.1.

In the case of OBJSA components, the tokens are OBJ terms; then the occurrence rule is based on rewriting the terms generated by the operators y'_k and labelling the output arcs using as rewrite rules the conditional equations defined in the parameterized modules $TRANS_k$ and TTH_{k-o}, and inherited in the module associated with each transition.

In particular a transition with, for example, δ input and δ output arcs having unitary weights, is said to have **concession** under a marking M in a certain mode $(y_1, \ldots, y_\delta)$ if in each of its input places there is a token such that the predicate associated with the transition holds.

This predicate, in the module associated with the transition, is (maybe renamed) the operator pr defined in $TRANS_k$ and TTH_{k-o}.

If such a predicate is not satisfied by the tokens involved in the transition occurrence, then the rewriting of the δ terms y'_k $(y_1, \ldots, y_\delta)$ $(1 \leq k \leq \delta)$ gives rise to the error message that, in the actual module associated with the transition, renames the operator no-enabled.

On the other hand, if the transition has concession to occur in a certain mode, the tokens, which satisfy the predicate, are taken away by the transition occurrence from the input places. The occurrence puts in the output places the individual tokens obtained by the rewriting of the term labelling each output arc and defined, in the actual module associated with the transition, by renaming the operators y'$_k$ and ch$_k$.

Therefore the occurrence of a transition modifies the marking of the involved components and so models the system behaviour.

Remark 31 Let us notice that in OBJ3 theories and parameterized objects are not executable. Nevertheless OBJSA theories, associated with open transitions and obtained as instantiation of the parameterized theory TTH_{k-o}, have to be executable because even open transitions can occur, though the involved tokens are not yet completely specified, as shown in the next example. □

Example 32 Let us again consider the component SDLQueue and the object SDLQUEUECOMP associated with it (see Example 30). As initial marking let us suppose that the Buffers, one for each process, are empty and ready to be filled (in place b_1), and that the Queues, again one for each process, are empty (in place q). Under this marking, only transition *fill* of the net in Figure 7.7 has concession for whatever of the m individual tokens is in its initial place b_1.

In fact for whatever individual token < p_k ; eb > $(1 \leq k \leq m)$ the rewriting of the condition pr(y_a,x_1) of the equation that defines the term y'$_a$(y_a,x_1), as inherited in the corresponding theory FILLTH (see Example 28), holds true.

On the other hand, the transition *enqueue* has no concession since it has no individual tokens in its input place b_2, while transition *consume* cannot occur because its initial place q contains m tokens but none of them constitutes an occurrence mode which satisfies the predicate associated with it and defined in the corresponding theory CONSUMETH .

In fact for whatever individual token < p_k ; eq > $(1 \leq k \leq m)$, the rewriting of the condition of the equation in the corresponding theory CONSUMETH returns false, as shown below.

```
pr (< pk ; eq >, x2) = not is-empty(data(< pk ; eq >))
```

where

```
is-empty(data(< pk ; eq >)) → is-empty(eq) → true
```

and then if we rewrite the terms $y_d(< p_k ; eq >, x_2)$ $(1 \leq k \leq m)$, we obtain as result the error message Consume-no-enabled.

The firing of transition *fill*, let's say with the individual token < p₁ ; eb >, takes it away from place b_1 and puts in place b_2 the individual token obtained by the following rewriting:

```
ya(< p1 ; eb >, x1) →
< name(< p1 ; eb >) ; cha(< p1 ; eb >, x1) > →
< p1 ; fill(AMsgIn(x1),data(ya)> →
< p1 ; AMsgIn(x1)>
```

Since all the other tokens are not involved in the firing, the new marking is such that:

- place b_1 is marked by: < p₂ ; eb > . . . . < p_m ; eb >

- place b_2 is marked by: < p₁ ; AMsgIn(x₁) >

- place q is marked by: < p₁ ; eq > . . . . < p_m ; eq >

This new marking says that now the buffer identified by p₁, i.e., the instance of the Buffer component belonging to the process p₁, contains a message taken from the data structure of the not yet identified BufferFiller component.

Now again we can use condition rewriting for verifying that under this marking have concession:

- transition *fill* in whatever mode involving one of the individual tokens in its input place;

- transition *enqueue* in the mode involving the couple of the individual tokens having p₁ as name;

and then use rewriting for deriving the new possible markings. □

4   CONCLUSIONS

Modern formal specification languages require suitable mechanisms for supporting, in an integrated way, both process abstraction and data abstraction. The definition of various classes of algebraic high-level nets (see [20] for a survey) goes in this direction.

OBJSA nets indeed can be seen and have been defined as a class of *algebraic* or *SPEC-inscribed nets* (in the sense of [29]) provided with modularity facilities (a similar effort has been done in [8]). This foundamental feature perfectly copes with the intrinsic modularity provided by OBJ and is the basis for the incremental development of a specification.

OBJSA nets have different well defined semantics, behind the occurrence rule above sketched. As usual for high-level nets [30], first we developed in

[5] a net semantics by defining an unfolding function *Unf* which transforms an OBJSA net into a 1-safe SA net. In [3], Meseguer's concurrent rewriting techniques [28], [25] are applied to give OBJSA nets an operational and a denotational semantics. We are now extending the same categorical framework to open components too, yielding a compositional semantics: a composition can be obtained as the colimit of a diagram in the category of specifications.

Another specific effort we have done to achieve the actual usability of our specification formalism has been the development of the OBJSA Net Environment, ONE, and of a real case studies (see, e.g. the 'Hydroelectric Power Plant Control System'; [2], proposed by the ENEL S.p.A., the major italian electricity supplier).

The OBJSA Net Environment actually supports the user in the whole specification process of a concurrent distributed system: from the analisys, to the incremental development of the specification, to its verification. ONE consists of different modules, each one interacting with the OBJ interpreter and supporting a different step in the specification process:

- **ONESyst** supports the user in the identification of the system elementary components and in the automatic generation of the OBJ objects which specify the data associated with them.

- **ONEGen** guides the user in the specification of an OBJSA component: it provides, on the one hand, a graphical net editor, and, on the other one, supports the user in developing the algebraic specification associated with the net elements (cf. the OBJ modules shown in the Examples in Section 3 and obtained as instantiations of the predefined built-in OBJSA modules COMP-DOM, CDTH, TRANS$_k$ and TTH$_{k-o}$).

- **ONERed** supports two transformations, Redp and Redt, which transfer the information contained in an OBJSA component from the net, i.e. from places and transitions respectively, to the associated algebraic specification, preserving its semantics. These transformations, originally introduced to give a net semantics to OBJSA nets (cf. [5]), in the practice have been proved to be very useful in the incremental development of the specification.

- **ONEComp** supports the composition mechanism of OBJSA open components. It is based for the net part, on transition superposition and, for the algebraic part, on the definition of an object, obtained as instantiation of TRANS$_k$, such that there exists a view to it from the theories associated with the open transitions which have to be superposed (cf. Section 3.4).

- **ONESim** is the module which allows the simulation of an OBJSA component by applying the usual occurrence rule for high-level Petri nets.

It interacts with the OBJ interpreter to perform the rewriting specified in the transition outcoming arcs on the data part of the tokens involved before putting them in the output places (cf. Section 3.5).

- **ONEUnf** proceeds in the reversed direction with respect to ONERed implementing the Unfolding operation. That is it transfers to the net all the information contained in the algebraic specification of an OBJSA component. This module is very useful since it allows the use of several different tools available on basic net models which support verification features, as shown by the two following modules.

- **ONEInv** calculates s- and t- invariants of the SA net obtained as the Unfolding of an OBJSA specification. To this end we have incorporated in ONE the tool INVARI realized by A. Stuebinger. The main task performed by ONEInv is the suitable format conversion. Let us recall that s- and t- invariant calculus is a specific technique of Petri nets which allows to find properties of the system (e.g. deadlock freeness and mutual exclusion) by avoiding th state space generation thanks to linear system solution techniques.

- **ONEVer** allows the user to verify on an OBJSA specification temporal logic properties expressed in the ACTL logic [11], by integrating some features of the tool JACK (Just Another Concurrency Kit) [9].

References

[1] E. Astesiano, G. Reggio.   Algebraic Specification of Concurrency, in:*Recent Trends in Data Type Specification*, LNCS 655, (M. Bidoit, C. Choppy eds.), pp. 1-39, Springer Verlag, 1993.

[2] E. Battiston, O. Botti, E. Crivelli, F. De Cindio. An Incremental Specification of a Hydroelectric Power Plant Control System using a class of modular algebraic nets, in: Proc. of the "16th Int. Conference on Application and Theory of Petri nets, Torino, I, 28à30 June 1995", LNCS 935, (G. De Michelis, M. Diaz eds.), pp. 84-102, Springer Verlag,1995.

[3] E. Battiston, V. Crespi, F. De Cindio, G. Mauri. Semantics frameworks for a class of modular algebraic nets, in*Proc. of the "3rd Int. Conference on Algebraic Methodology and Software Technology, AMAST '93, Enschede, NL, 21-25 June 1993"*, Workshops in Computing, (M. Nivat, C.Rattay, T.Rus and G.Scollo eds.), pp. 271-280, Springer-Verlag, 1993.

[4] E. Battiston, F. De Cindio, G. Mauri. OBJSA nets: a class of high level nets having objects as domains, in "Advances in Petri Nets 88", LNCS 340, (G. Rozenberg ed.), pp. 20-43, Springer Verlag,1988. Also in [20].

[5] E. Battiston, F. De Cindio, G. Mauri, L. Rapanotti. Morphisms and Minimal Models for OBJSA Nets, in Proc. of the "12th Int. Conference on Application and Theory of Petri nets, Gjern, DK, 26à28 June 1991", pp. 455-476.

[6] L. Bernardinello, F. De Cindio. A survey of basic net models and modular net classes. in*Advances in Petri Nets 1992*, LNCS 609, (G.Rozenberg ed.), pp. 304-351, Springer Verlag, 1992.

[7] E.Best. DEMON (Design Methods Based on Nets): Aims, Scope and Achievements. in*Advances in Petri Nets 1992*, LNCS 609, (G.Rozenberg ed.), pp. 1-20, Springer Verlag, 1992.

[8] D. Bouchs, N. Guelfi. CO-OPN: A Concurrent Object Oriented Petri Net Approach. in Proc. of the "12th Int. Conference on Application and Theory of Petri nets, Gjern, DK, 26à28 June 1991", pp. 432-454.

[9] A. Bouali, S. Gnesi, S. Larosa. The Integration Project for the JACK Environment. in Bulletin of EATCS, 54, pp. 207-223, October 1994.

[10] F.De Cindio, G. De Michelis, L. Pomello, C. Simone. Superposed Automata Nets. in "Application and Theory of Petri Nets", IFB 52, (C. Girault and W. Reisig eds.), pp. 269-279, Springer Verlag, 1982.

[11] R. De Nicola, A. Fantechi, S. Gnesi, G. Ristori. An action-based framework for verifying logical and behavioural properties of concurrent systems. in Computer Network and ISDN systems, 25, 7, pp. 761-778, North Holland, 1993.

[12] F.De Cindio, G.A. Lanzarone, A. Torgano. An SA Net Model of SDL. in Proc. of "5th European Workshop on Applications and Theory of Petri Nets, Aarhus, DK,1984".

[13] R. De Nicola and U.Montanari (eds.). Selected Papers of "Second Workshop on Concurrency and Compositionality, San Miniato, I, March 1990", TCS 96, 1,1992.

[14] H. Ehrig, B. Mahr. Fundamentals of algebraic specification 1. Springer-Verlag, Berlin, 1985.

[15] H. Genrich. Predicate/Transition nets. in "Advances in Petri Nets 86, Part I", LNCS 254, (W. Brauer, W. Reisig, G. Rozenberg eds.), pp. 207-247, Springer-Verlag, 1987.

[16] J.A. Goguen, J.W. Thatcher, E.G. Wagner. An initial algebra approach to the specification, correctness and implementation of abstract data types. in "Current Trends in Programming Methodology IV: Data structuring", (R. Yeh, Ed.), pp. 80-144, Prentice Hall, 1978.

[17] J.A. Goguen, T. Winkler. Introducing OBJ3. Report SRI-CSL-88-9, August 1988.

[18] C.A.R. Hoare. Communicating sequential processes. in CACM, 21, pp. 666-677, 1978.

[19] K. Jensen. Coloured Petri nets. in "Advances in Petri Nets 90", LNCS 483, (G. Rozenberg ed), pp. 342-416, Springer Verlag, 1990. Also in [20].

[20] K. Jensen and G. Rozenberg (eds). High-level Petri Nets. Theory and Application. ISBN: 3-540-54125 X or 0-387-54125 X, Springer Verlag,1991.

[21] K.P.Lohr. Concurrency annotations for reusable software. in CACM, 36, 9, pp. 81-89, 1993.

[22] P.E. Lauer, P.R. Torrigiani, M.W. Shields. COSY- A System Specification Language Based on Paths and Processes. in Acta Informatica, 12, pp.109-158, 1979.

[23] B. Liskov, S. Zilles. An introduction to Formal Specifications of Data Abstractions. in "Current Trends in Programming Methodology I: Software Specification and Design", (R. Yeh ed.), pp. 1-32, Prentice-Hall, 1978.

[24] J. Malhotra. DesignML. Reference Manual. Meta Software Co., Cambridge, MA, USA,1990.

[25] J. Meseguer. Rewriting as a unified model of concurrency. in [13], 1992.

[26] B. Meyer. Sequential and Concurrent Object-Oriented Programming. in CACM, 36, 9, pp. 56-80, 1993.

[27] R. Milner. A calculus for communicating systems. LNCS 92, Springer Verlag,1980.

[28] J. Meseguer, U. Montanari. Petri nets are monoids. in Information and Computation, 88, 2, 1990.

[29] W. Reisig. Petri Nets with Algebraic Specifications. in TCS, 80, pp. 1-34, 1991. Also in [20].

[30] W.Reisig, E. Smith. The semantics of a net is a net. An exercise in general net theory. in "Concurrency and Nets", (K. Voss, H. Genrich, G. Rozenberg eds.), pp. 269-286, Springer Verlag, 1987.

[31] T. Winkler. Introducing OBJ3's New Features. Report SRI-CSL, 1992.

[32] S.N. Zilles. Algebraic specification of data types. Project MAC Progress Report 11, pp. 28-52, MIT, Cambridge, Mass., 1974.

IV
PARAMETERIZED PROGRAMMING

Chapter 8

A LOTOS SIMULATOR IN OBJ

Kazuhito Ohmaki

Koichi Takahashi

Kokichi Futatsugi
Electrotechnical Laboratory
1-1-4 Umezono, Tsukuba, Ibaraki 305, JAPAN
E-mail: {*ohmaki*|*takahashi*|*futatsugi*}*@etl.go.jp*

Abstract   In this paper, we show how to write a LOTOS simulator using OBJ. Both syntax rules and their inference rules (axioms) of LOTOS can be formally specified by operator definition part and equation definition part in OBJ, respectively.

When writing the simulator using a term rewriting system, we need a lazy evaluation mechanism, because rewriting operations for recursive process definitions in LOTOS would not terminate without lazy evaluation. We use this lazy evaluation mechanism of OBJ to realize the simulator. Powerful features like **theory**, **view**, and **parameterized modules** of OBJ are fruitfully used to write the simulator.

Using OBJ as an implementation language, we can also use the power of the abstract data type features of OBJ. This leads to the enhancement of LOTOS in future, especially for abstract data type enhancement. The introduction of **subsort** is one of the most distinguished point of using OBJ. This point is discussed using simple examples.

We also show an example to prove properties of a LOTOS specification.

1   INTRODUCTION

We have implemented a LOTOS [1] simulator using OBJ [2, 3, 4].

LOTOS is a specification language for the formal specification of the OSI (Open System Interconnection) architecture [5], and is also applicable to distributed and concurrent systems, in general [6]. LOTOS was standardized as

ISO 8807 in the beginning of 1989. A concise tutorial can be found in [7]. Several OSI protocols have been specified using LOTOS [8, 9, 10, 11]. Most of these activities were carried out in SEDOS project of ERPIT program in Europe[12].

LOTOS's formal semantics consists from two components. The first one is to specify process behavior based on algebraic methods introduced in Milner's calculus of communicating systems (CCS)[13]. The second component concerns the description of data structures and value expressions. This is based on abstract data types (ADT, for short) used in ACT ONE [14].

Several LOTOS simulators have been proposed in the literature [8, 12, 15, 16]. The reasons why we use OBJ as an implementation language for the simulator are:

1. The process definition part in LOTOS is based on a process algebra. We wish to show how the term rewriting system can be applied to write semantics for the language which is based on a process algebra.

2. The OBJ system behaves as a theorem prover [17]. Therefore, the simulator written in OBJ can be used to check behavioral properties of specifications written in LOTOS.

3. The data type part of LOTOS does not employ state of the art technology from ADT research [18]. It is possible to introduce the powerful ADT features of OBJ, such as **subsort, theory, view**, and **parameterized modules**, into LOTOS when using OBJ as an implemetation language.

In this paper, we show how to write a LOTOS simulator using OBJ. Both syntax rules and their inference rules (axioms) of LOTOS can be formally specified by operator definition part and equation definition part in OBJ, respectively.

There has been a proposal to specify the algebraic semantics of LOTOS [19]. In contrast with this approach, we are investigating the way to use a term rewriting system to give structural operational semantics of LOTOS's behavior expressions. We will show the usefulness of the features such as **subsort, theory, view**, and **parameterized modules**. Neither these features nor lazy evaluations are employed in [19].

Using OBJ as an implementation language, we can also use the power of ADT features of OBJ. This leads to the enhancement of LOTOS in future, especially for ADT enhancement. The introduction of **subsort** is one of the most distinguished point of OBJ. This point is discussed using simple examples in this paper.

We also show an example to prove properties of a LOTOS specification.

```
specification two-slot-buffer [input, output] :  noexit
   type NatNum is
      sorts Nat
      opns
         0 :  -> Nat
         succ :  Nat -> Nat
   endtype

   behavior
      hide middle in
         buffer[input, middle]
         |[middle]| buffer[middle, output]
      where
         process buffer[inp, outp] :  noexit :=
            inp?x:Nat; outp!succ(x); buffer[inp, outp]
         endproc
endspec
```

Figure 8.1   Specification of two-slot-buffer in LOTOS

2   LOTOS DEFINITIONS

We give a rough illustration of the language LOTOS. Readers can find the precise definitions of LOTOS in the document [1].

Figure 8.1 shows a very simple but complete specification of a two-slot-buffer written in LOTOS. Following the keyword **specification**, the name of the specification, two-slot-buffer, is declared. input and output denote the interaction points of two-slot-buffer with its environment, i.e., an observer of two-slot-buffer. We call these interaction points "gates."

In this example, an ADT part is defined in between keywords **type** and **endtype**. A process definition part begins with **behavior**. This definition contains a subprocess buffer. The definition of buffer is in **process** through **endproc**.

In the following subsections, we will explain this example more in detail.

2.1   ADT DEFINITION PART

We show the ADT facilities "renaming" and "actualization" in LOTOS.

Figure 8.2 shows a formal queue type FormalQueue. Sort Data and operator d0 are formal in the sense that these are actualized when actually used. Figure 8.3 shows to actualize FormalQueue by using data type Char and

```
type FormalQueue is
    formalsorts Data
    formalopns d0 :   -> Data
    sorts Queue
    opns
        create :   -> Queue
        add :  Data, Queue -> Queue
        first :  Queue -> Data
        remove :  Queue -> Queue
    eqns forall x,y:Data, z:Queue
        ofsort Data
            first(create) = d0;
            first(add(x,create)) = x;
            first(add(x,add(y,z))) = first(add(y,z));
        ofsort Queue
            remove(create) = create;
            remove(add(x,create)) = create;
            remove(add(x,add(y,z))) = add(x,remove(add(y,z)));
endtype
```

Figure 8.2   Formal type FormalQueue

to get type CharQueue as an actualized result. In the figure, formal sort Data in FormalQueue is actualized by Char and d0 by bottom. Figure 8.4 shows to rename sort names and operator names in CharQueue and to get AnotherCharQueue. Queue, add, and first are renamed by CharQueue, append, and char, respectively.

The ADT facilities of LOTOS are weak in comparison with the state of the art technologies in the ADT research area [18]. These facilities are covered by OBJ. We will discuss the data type definition part of LOTOS in comparison with OBJ in a later section.

2.2   PROCESS DEFINITION PART

In LOTOS, distributed systems are described in terms of processes. A system is a single process that may consist of several interacting subprocesses.

To express the interaction between different processes, each process can only communicate with others through "gates" where its environment can only observe this process. The atomic form of interaction, which may occur at gates, is an "event." An event is a unit of synchronized communication that

```
type Char is
   sorts Char
   opns a,b,c,bottom :   -> Char
endtype

type CharQueue is FormalQueue actualizedby Char using
   sortnames Char for Data
   opnnames bottom for d0
endtype
```

Figure 8.3 Actualized type CharQueue

```
type AnotherCharQueue is CharQueue renamedby
   sortnames CharQueue for Queue
   opnnames append for add
           car for first
endtype
```

Figure 8.4 Renamed type AnotherCharQueue

may exist between two processes that can both perform that event. We often call events as "actions."

We can consider that "behavior expression" represents some "process", and vice versa. We, therefore, use terminologies "behavior expression" and "process" interchangeably.

2.2.1 "Basic" LOTOS. To simplify the explanation, we show the syntax and semantics of a "basic" LOTOS in this subsection, which is a subset of LOTOS. Basic LOTOS does not use ADT features, and processes interact with each other by pure synchronizations without exchanging values.

(1) Syntax

Table 8.1 shows syntactic constructs of a basic LOTOS. Each construct means as follows:

Inaction: An inaction **stop** is a basic behavior expression, and cannot perform any event.

Action prefix: Let B be a behavior expression and a be an event. Then, the expression $a; B$ is called an action prefix construct. This means if an event takes place then the resulting behavior is given by B. From the

Name	Syntax
inaction	**stop**
action prefix	
- unobservable(internal)	$i; B$
- observable	$a; B$
choice	$B_1 [] B_2$
parallel composition	
- general case	$B_1 \| [g_1, ..., g_n] \| B_2$
- pure interleaving	$B_1 \|\|\| B_2$
- full synchronization	$B_1 \|\| B_2$
hiding	$\mathbf{hide} g_1, ..., g_n \mathbf{in} B$
process instantiation	$P[g_1, ..., g_n]$

Table 8.1   Syntax of behavior expressions in basic LOTOS

viewpoint of an observer, the event a is accepted (or offered) by the system and the next behavior is determined by B.

An invisible event, which cannot be observed by the environment, is denoted by **i**. This is called an iternal event. This observability is controlled by **hide** operator.

Choice: Let B_1 and B_2 be behavior expressions. $B_1 [] B_2$ denotes an expression that behaves either like B_1 or like B_2. If the environment provides an initial event of B_1 then B_1 may be selected. If an initial event of B_2 is provided then B_2 may be selected.

Pure interleaving: In the case of two independent process given by behavior expressions B_1 and B_2, we can write $B_1 \|\|\| B_2$ for their independent composition. That is, if an event is offered by either B_1 or B_2, then this event is also offered by $B_1 \|\|\| B_2$.

Full synchronization: We can write $B_1 \|\| B_2$ for their independent composition. That is, if an event is offered by B_1, then this event should also be offered by B_2, and vice versa. Otherwise, $B_1 \|\| B_2$ does not offer this event.

General parallel: Let $g_1, ..., g_n$ be gate names. The behavior expression $B_1 \| [g_1, ..., g_n] \| B_2$ defines the expression where any events in $g_1, ..., g_n$ should be offered by both B_1 and B_2 at the same moment. Other events than $g_1, ..., g_n$ can be offered independently. In the case of $\|\|\|$, these gates alphabets are empty. In the case of $\|\|$, these alphabets are complete gates alphabets in B_1 and B_2.

Hiding: To hide events $g_1, ..., g_n$ in B form its environment, we can write

hide $g_1, ..., g_n$ **in** B

Then these events become internal ones. These events cannot be observed by the outer environment. An unobservable event is denoted by **i**. This hiding operator corresponds to the notion of restriction of CCS [13].

Process instantiation: Each process definition is in the following format:

process *process-identifier parameter-list* :=
behavior- expression
endproc

parameter-list may include gate list. Let

process $P[g_1', ..., g_n'] := B_p$ **endproc**

be a process definition. The expression $P[g_1, ..., g_n]$ is treated as the same expression as $B_p[g_1/g_1', ..., g_n/g_n']$, where $[g_1/g_1', ..., g_n/g_n']$ denotes substitution of gate names. This corresponds to the relabeling of CCS [13].

To express an infinite behavior, the recursive occurrences of *process-identifier* are used in *behavior-expression*.

(2) Semantics

We show the operational semantics of the basic LOTOS to derive the actions which a process (behavior expression) may perform from the structure of the expression.

Let B be a behavior expression. We call the following triple as a labeled transition:

$B - \mu \rightarrow B'$, where μ is an action and B' is another behavior expression. This labeled transition denotes that B may perform (offer) action μ and transform into B'. Using this transition, the operational semantics of the basic LOTOS is defined as in Table 8.2.

The axiom for the action prefix states that process ' μ; B ' can perform action μ and transform into process B.

Two axioms for the choice construct state that, once an action is chosen from one component (either B_1 or B_2), the other component does not affect the resulting expression.

As for parallel operators, $B_1|[g_1, ..., g_n]|B_2$ denotes a process where B_1 and B_2 are synchronized only when the offered event is in the set $\{g_1, ..., g_n\}$. $B_1|||B_2$ is the same case when the set $\{g_1, ..., g_n\}$ is empty. $B_1||B_2$ is the

Syntax	Axiom
stop	none
$i; B$	$i; B - i \rightarrow B$
$g; B$	$g; B - g \rightarrow B$
$B_1 [] B_2$	(i) $B_1 - \mu \rightarrow B_1' \vdash B_1 [] B_2 - \mu \rightarrow B_1'$
	(ii) $B_2 - \mu \rightarrow B_2' \vdash B_1 [] B_2 - \mu \rightarrow B_2'$
$B_1 |[g_1, ..., g_n]| B_2$	(i) $B_1 - \mu \rightarrow B_1' \wedge \mu \notin \{g_1, ..., g_n\}$
	$\vdash B_1 |[g_1, ..., g_n]| B_2 - \mu \rightarrow B_1' |[g_1, ..., g_n]| B_2$
	(ii) $B_2 - \mu \rightarrow B_2' \wedge \mu \notin \{g_1, ..., g_n\}$
	$\vdash B_1 |[g_1, ..., g_n]| B_2 - \mu \rightarrow B_1 |[g_1, ..., g_n]| B_2'$
	(iii) $B_1 - \mu \rightarrow B_1' \wedge B_2 - \mu \rightarrow B_2' \wedge \mu \in \{g_1, ..., g_n\}$
	$\vdash B_1 |[g_1, ..., g_n]| B_2 - \mu \rightarrow B_1' |[g_1, ..., g_n]| B_2'$
$B_1 ||| B_2$	(i) $B_1 - \mu \rightarrow B_1' \vdash B_1 ||| B_2 - \mu \rightarrow B_1' ||| B_2$
	(ii) $B_2 - \mu \rightarrow B_2' \vdash B_1 ||| B_2 - \mu \rightarrow B_1 ||| B_2'$
$B_1 || B_2$	$B_1 - \mu \rightarrow B_1' \wedge B_2 - \mu \rightarrow B_2' \vdash B_1 || B_2 - \mu \rightarrow B_1' || B_2'$
$\text{hide} g_1, ..., g_n \text{ in} B$	(i) $B - \mu \rightarrow B' \wedge \mu \notin \{g_1, ..., g_n\}$
	$\vdash \text{hide} g_1, ..., g_n \text{ in} B - \mu \rightarrow \text{hide} g_1, ..., g_n \text{ in} B'$
	(ii) $B - \mu \rightarrow B' \wedge \mu \in \{g_1, ..., g_n\}$
	$\vdash \text{hide} g_1, ..., g_n \text{ in} B - i \rightarrow \text{hide} g_1, ..., g_n \text{ in} B'$
$P[g_1, ..., g_n]$	If
	$\text{process} P[g_1', ..., g_n'] := B_p \text{endproc}$
	is a process definition then
	$B_p[g_1/g_1', ..., g_n/g_n'] - \mu \rightarrow B' \vdash P[g_1, ..., g_n] - \mu \rightarrow B'$
	where $[g_1/g_1', ..., g_n/g_n']$ denotes gate renaming.

Table 8.2   Axioms of behavior expressions in basic LOTOS

same case when the set $\{g_1, ..., g_n\}$ is including all observable events in B_1 and B_2.

By a hiding construct **hide**$g_1, ..., g_n$**in** B, gates actions in the set $\{g_1, ..., g_n\}$ are hidden from the environment of this expression and all events in the set $\{g_1, ..., g_n\}$ are treated as internal envets i from the environment.

Process instantiation defines how formal gates (i.e., $g_1', ..., g_n'$) are replaced by actual gates (i.e., $g_1, ..., g_n$).

2.2.2   "Full" LOTOS.   The processes of the full LOTOS (i.e., ISO 8807) can interact by synchronizations with exchanging values which are defined as ADT. Therefore, the events are structured with these values.

process A	process B	Sync. condition	Interaction sort	Effect
g!E1	g!E2	value(E1)=value(E2)	value matching	synchronization
g!E	g?x:t	value(E)∈domain(t)	value passing	after synchronization x=value(E)
g?x:t	g?y:u	t=u	value generation	after synchronization x=y=v for v∈domain(t)

Table 8.3 Interaction types

(1) Structured event

A structured event consists of a gate name with a finite list of attributes. The gate name identifies the point of interaction between different processes. Two types of attributes are possible: a value declaration and a variable declaration.

A value declaration is a value expression, i.e., a term describing a data value preceded by an exclamation mark. Examples of value declarations are !(3+5) or !(x+1). These values must be in sorts defined in type declarations.

A variable declaration has the form ?x:T, where x is the name of the variable and T is its sort identifier. The sort identifier indicates the domain of values over which x ranges. Examples of variable declarations are ?x:Integer or ?text:String.

For example, gate?x:Integer!(3+5) is a valid structured event.

(2) Event matching

We can define interactions between processes. Interaction between two processes can take place if both processes have enabled one or more identical events. Table 8.3 lists the different possibilities. The effects are summarized as follows:

> An event containing a variable declaration is an implicit choice ranging over the value domain indicated, with the side-effect that after synchronization the value of the variable is defined as the value that resulted as part of the synchronization event.

Events can be structured with several attributes. These attributes must meet the conditions of Table 8.3. For example, gate?x:Nat?text:String synchronizes with gate?x:Nat!some_string and gate!0!another_string but not with gate!0 or gate!0!3.

2.3   EXPLANATION OF TWO-SLOT-BUFFER

Now we can explain the specification of two-slot-buffer in Figure 8.1. The process buffer can offer the following event sequence as an example:

```
inp!0; outp!0; inp!succ(0); outp!succ(0); ...
```

Therefore, the specification `two-slot-buffer` can offer the following event sequences:

```
input!0; i;
    ( output!0; two-slot-buffer...
    [] input!succ(0);
       output!0; i;
           ( output!succ(0); two-slot-buffer...
           [] input...
```

That is, this example specifies a shift register. Note that two processes `buffer[input,middle]` and `buffer[middle,output]` are synchronized via the gate `middle`.

3   WHAT IS THE SIMULATOR?

We state the standpoint of our simulator.

Semantics of LOTOS consists of both static and dynamic semantics [1]. The static semantics defines scope rules of identifiers for processes or type definitions, and also defines the consistency in between parameters used in process definitions. On the other hand, the dynamic semantics defines inference rules corresponding to each syntactic structure of behavior expressions.

Our simulator written in OBJ is an implementation of the dynamic semantics of LOTOS. The static semantics is realized as hierarchical structures of modules in OBJ.

3.1   IN CASE OF THE BASIC LOTOS

Figure 8.5 shows the specification of `two-slot-buffer` in LOTOS (actually, basic LOTOS).

Using OBJ, we write the same specification as shown in Figure 8.6. In this figure, the operator `2-buffer` in the object `2BUFFERwithoutVALUE` corresponds to the process `two-slot-buffer` in Figure 8.5. `#Gate` is used to represent "nil" gate list.[1] `2BUFFERwithoutVALUE` is extending `BUFFERwithoutVALUE`. This extension corresponds to the "**where**" hierarchy in LOTOS. The operator `buffer` is defined in `BUFFERwithoutVALUE` and used in `2BUFFERwithoutVALUE`. Note that relabeling operations are performed as term rewritings.

---

[1] In this paper, #... is used for the "nil" list.

```
process two-slot-buffer[inp, outp] : noexit :=
  hide mid in
    buffer[inp, mid] |[mid]| buffer[mid, outp]

    where
    process buffer[inp, outp] : noexit :=
      inp; outp; buffer[inp, outp]
  endproc
endproc
```

Figure 8.5 Specification of two-slot-buffer in a basic LOTOS

```
obj BUFFERwithoutVALUE is
  extending LOTOS-BEXP[SIMPLE-VALUE , GATE-EX] .
  op buffer[_,_] : Gate Gate -> Bexp [strat (0)] .
  vars a b : Gate .
  eq buffer[ a , b ] =
    a ; ( b ; buffer[ a , b ]) .
endo
obj 2BUFFERwithoutVALUE is
  extending BUFFERwithoutVALUE .
  vars in out mid : Gate .
  op 2-buffer[_,_,_] : Gate Gate Gate -> Bexp
                       [strat (0)] .
  eq 2-buffer[ in , mid , out ] =
    hide ( mid , #Gate ) in
      ( buffer[ in , mid ]
        |[ (mid , #Gate) ]| buffer[ mid , out ] ) .
endo
```

Figure 8.6 Specification of a two slot buffer in OBJ

```
theory GATE is
  sort Gate .
endth

theory VALUE is
  sort Value .
  sort Variable .
  subsort Variable < Value .
  sort Binding .
  op _/_ : Variable Value -> Binding .
  op value-of : Value Binding -> Value .
  op element-of-sort-p : Value Variable -> Bool .
endth
```

Figure 8.7   Theories GATE and VALUE for action representation

3.2   TO TREAT VALUES

We explain the objects which are used in BUFFERwithoutVALUE.

In order to define actions (events) with value attributes, we use two theories GATE and VALUE. These theories are shown in Figure 8.7. The theory GATE only defines the sort Gate which is used for gates in the sense of LOTOS. The theory VALUE defines the features of values variables. In our simulator, we treat each variable used as a LOTOS variable to be a constant. The subsort relation Variable < Value defines each variable to be an element of a value.

Figure 8.8 shows the object ACTION which defines actions for LOTOS. Each action consists of a gate name and an attribute list. Each attribute is either a variable declaration or a value declaration. The operator "!" is for the value declaration and "?" is for the variable declaration.

In the example we show in subsection 3.1, we do not use any attributed actions. We will explain attributed actions in the following section.

3.3   SYNTAX DEFINITION OF BEHAVIOR EXPRESSIONS

Figure 8.9 shows a syntax of behavior expressions used in a LOTOS program.

By prec 30 or prec 32, we define the precedence of operators.

By strat, we control the order of evaluation of the operator. In this case, [strat(0)] states that the operator ";" should be lazily evaluated. This lazy

```
obj ACTION[V :: VALUE , G :: GATE] is
  sort Attribute .
  --- for value and variable declarations
  op ! : Value -> Attribute . --- value declaration
  op ? : Variable -> Attribute . --- variable declaration

  sort AttList . --- list of attributes
  op #Att : -> AttList . --- empty attribute.
  op (_,_) : Attribute AttList -> AttList .

  sort Action . --- sort for action
  subsort Gate < Action . --- Any gate is an action.
  op <_,_> : Gate AttList -> Action .
    --- Normal action consists of a gate and attributes.
  op i : -> Action . --- internal action

  vars G : Gate .
  vars AtSt : AttList .

  op attribute : Action -> AttList .
  --- returns attributes of an action
  eq attribute( i ) = #Att .
  eq attribute( G ) = #Att .
  eq attribute( < G , AtSt > ) = AtSt .

  op gate : Action -> Gate .
  --- returns a gate name of an action
  eq gate(i) = i .
  eq gate(G) = G .
  eq gate( < G , AtSt > ) = G .

  sort GateList . --- list of gates.
  op #Gate : -> GateList .
  op (_,_) : Gate GateList -> GateList .
endo
```

Figure 8.8   Definition of actions with value attributes

```
obj LOTOS-BEXP[X :: VALUE , Y :: GATE ] is
  extending ACTION[ X , Y ] .
  sort Bexp . --- sort of behavior expressions.
  op stop : -> Bexp .
  op  _;_ : Action Bexp -> Bexp [ prec 30 strat(0) ] .
  ops (_[]_) (_||_) (_|||_) : Bexp Bexp -> Bexp
                                    [ prec 32 ] .
  op (_|[_]|_) : Bexp GateList Bexp -> Bexp [ prec 32 ] .
  op (hide_in_) : GateList Bexp -> Bexp  .
endo
```

Figure 8.9   Syntax definition of behavior expressions

evaluation is used to prevent rewriting operations repeating infinitely in the case of recursive process definition.

3.4   BASIC FUNCTIONS MENU AND NEXT

Basic functions of the simulator are menu and next.

Menu shows a pair of next possible actions and resulted behavior behavior expression list which a given behavior expression can offer.

Next takes three arguments. The first one is a result of menu operation. The second one is a natural number to select one of pairs listed in the first first argument. The last argument is a list of values to be fulfilled in variables in a selected behavior expression. The operator next gives a resulted behavior expression for these three arguments.

We will give the exact definitions for these two operators in subsection 4.4.

3.5   AN EXECUTION OF THE SIMULATOR FOR THE TWO SLOT BUFFER

We use objects GATE-EX and SIMPLE-VALUE, shown in Figure 8.10, to instantiate our example of a two slot buffer.

Figure 8.11 shows an object SAMPLE1 of the instantiation of the simulator for the two slot buffer by GATE-EX and SIMPLE-VALUE. SIMULATOR is an object to realize dynamic semantics of LOTOS. It will be explained in the following section.

By this instantiation, we can simulate operator 2-buffer in the object 2BUFFERwithoutVALUE as shown in in Figure 8.12. In this figure, the action input is resulted by the reduction of

```
menu(2-buffer[ input , dummy , output ] )
```

```
obj GATE-EX is
  sort Gate .
  ops input output dummy : -> Gate .
endo

obj SIMPLE-VALUE is
  sort Value .
  sort Variable .
  subsort Variable < Value .
  sort Binding .
  op _/_ : Variable Value -> Binding .
  op value-of : Value Binding -> Value .
  op element-of-sort-p : Value Variable -> Bool .
endo
```

Figure 8.10   Examples of objects for gates and values

after 59 rewrites. This result is named as ed1 by the call-that command of OBJ.

By the reduction red next(ed1 , O , #Val), we get the next behavior expressions after 8 rewrites. This behavior expression is named as b1 by a call-that.

Then red menu(b1) shows us an internal event i as an only possible action with a resulted behavior expression.

In this figure, we can see operators bound-bexp and protect-binding. Each of them has the following role:

- bound-bexp makes a pair of a behavior expression and variable binding list, and

- protect-binding protects a behavior expression from illegal binding information.

In the following sections, we will explain the object SIMULATOR appeared in Figure 8.11. This object is a realization of inference rules of dynamic semantics of LOTOS. Up to now, we have not been concerned with value passing between "!" and "?". We will show inference rules with value passing in the following section as well.

```
obj SAMPLE1 is
  extending SIMULATOR[SIMPLE-VALUE , GATE-EX] .
  extending 2BUFFERwithoutVALUE .
endo
```

Figure 8.11   Instantiation of the simulator for the two slot buffer

4   WRITING DYNAMIC SEMANTICS IN OBJ

4.1   DATA REPRESENTATION

One of our main purposes is to demonstrate that the ADT facilities in OBJ such as subsorts or parameterizations are quite useful for LOTOS.

In order to use sorts defined in a part of OBJ program as data in a LOTOS simulator, we have to treat *sort names* in OBJ as a data object for OBJ because synchronization conditions for parallel operators have to check the equality of sort names. Since OBJ is based on a first order logic, we cannot directly use sort names in OBJ as data. Our solution for this problem is to treat all variables as constants. And these constants are to be a subset of their values.

VALUE in Figure 8.7 is a theory which should be satisfied by all variables and values. Sort Value is for values and sort Variable is for variables. User should define each variable as a constant operator. The subsort relation Variable < Value makes Variables to have the same structures as in Value. The operator element-of-p checks whether a given value is in a sort of some variable. The equations for element-of-p is defined by users. This operator checks whether a value is in a sort of variable.

The operator / is used to keep binding information between variables and their values. All variables appearing in a value are replaced by the value associated with binding information of the sort Binding. The operator value-of instantiates Value by Binding, e.g., value-of(f(x), x/3) = f(3).

4.2   ACTION REPRESENTATION

Figure 8.8 shows actions with value attributes. The operators ! and ? are used to value and variable declarations. Sort Attribute is for value or for variables attributed at the gate. According to the object ACTION, actions are one of the following three types:

- gate without attributes,

- <gate, *value or variables*, ...>, or

- internal action i.

```
OBJ> red menu(2-buffer[ input , dummy , output ] ) .
reduce in SAMPLE1 : menu(2-buffer[input,dummy,output])
rewrites: 59
result EdgeSet:
  (- input ->
      (hide dummy,#Gate in
          bound-bexp(dummy ; buffer[input,dummy]
                      ,#Bind)
          |[dummy,#Gate]|
          protect-binding(
            bound-bexp(dummy ;
                        (output ; buffer[dummy,output])
                        ,#Bind))))
 ,#Edge
OBJ> call-that ed1 .
OBJ> red next(ed1 , 0 , #Val) .
reduce in SAMPLE1 : next(ed1,0,#Val)
rewrites: 8
result Bexp:
 bound-bexp(hide dummy,#Gate in
                bound-bexp(dummy ; buffer[input,dummy]
                            ,#Bind)
                |[dummy,#Gate]|
                protect-binding(
                  bound-bexp(dummy ;
                              (output ; buffer[dummy,output])
                              ,#Bind))
            ,#Bind)
OBJ> call-that b1 .
OBJ> red menu(b1) .
reduce in SAMPLE1 : menu(b1)
rewrites: 86
result EdgeSet:
  (- i ->
      (hide dummy,#Gate in
          bound-bexp(input ; (dummy ; buffer[input,dummy])
                      ,#Bind)
          |[dummy,#Gate]|
          bound-bexp(output ; buffer[dummy,output]
                      ,#Bind)))
 ,#Edge
OBJ> ...
```

Figure 8.12   Execution of the simulator for the two slot buffer

```
type ...
sort S1
...
endtype
...
process some-process[a, b] := a?x:S1; b!x; ...
...
```

(a) A fragment of a pure LOTOS program

⇓ (is treated as)

```
obj ...
  sort S1 .
  ops a b : Gate .
  op x : -> S1 .
  ...
  eq  some-bexp [a, b] = <a, ?(x)> ; <b, !(x)> ; ...
  ...
endo
```

(b) Corresponding OBJ program

Figure 8.13　Variable declarations in the LOTOS simulator

In the object ACTION, operators gate and attribute are defined to extract a gate name or attributes from a given action.

In order to use sorts defined in OBJ as for variables, we slightly change a syntax of variable declaration. Figure 8.13 shows a LOTOS program and its corresponding OBJ program. In stead of the syntax like a?x:S1, we use <a, ?(x)> as an action. Note that the sort S1 is declared in the OBJ framework in Figure 8.13(b). By this convention, we can directly use sorts in OBJ just like as sorts in LOTOS programs.

4.3　CONDITIONS OF ACTION SYNCHRONIZATION

Figure 8.14 shows a part of object UTILITY to test synchronization conditions. The meaning of main operators are as follows:

- match-able tests whether given actions are satisfying conditions of synchronization or not,

- att-match-able tests whether given attributes are satisfying conditions of synchronization or not,

- matching gives variable binding information for given attributes, and

- matched gives the resulted action after synchronized.

The operator element-of-sort-p is defined in 8.7 to check whether a value is in a sort of variable.

Note that we have already been able to use the subsort in the sort Action. In Figure 8.14, the operator matching are extended to handle the subsort relations. For example, for given two variable declarations such as ?x:Sort1 and ?y:Sort2, the operator matching checks whether Sort1 < Sort2 or Sort1 > Sort2. If one of these conditions is satisfied, these two actions can be synchronized. The original LOTOS (i.e., ISO 8807) does not include these conditions. We can say that we have already extended synchronizing conditions to include subsort relations in Figure 8.14.

4.4   INFERENCE RULES FOR BEHAVIOR EXPRESSIONS

In this subsection, we mainly show key operators menu and next. These operators reflect the dynamic semantics of LOTOS appeared in Section 7 of [1].

Using the object UTILITY defined in the previous subsections, SIMULATOR is defined as shown in Figure 8.15. In this figure, the operators menu and next are defined. The sort Edge represents a possible transition, which is a pair of an action and a behavior expression.

The operator menu gives all possible transitions, i.e., EdgeSet, for a given behavior expression.

The operator next gives a next behavior expression. The first argument EdgeSet of next represent all possible transitions, which will be given by menu operator. The second argument Nat of next select one of these transitions. The last argument ValList gives a list of values to be fulfilled to variables appeared in EdgeSet.

In Figure 8.15, parallel operators or others are extended to be ranging over EdgeSet and Bexp. In the figure, we have only listed a part of equations of menu on a general parallel operator | [] |. In these equations, match-able, matched, or matching are used to test the synchronizing conditions.

```
obj UTILITY[ VX :: VALUE , VY :: GATE ] is
  ...
  op match-able : Action Action -> Bool .
  op att-match-able : AttList AttList -> Bool .
  op matching : AttList AttList -> BindList .
  op matched : Action Action -> Action .
  op matched-sub : AttList AttList -> AttList .

  eq match-able( A1 , A2 ) =
    if gate(A1) == gate(A2)
    then att-match-able(attribute(A1) , attribute(A2))
    else false
    fi .
  ...
  eq matching( (!(V1) , AtSt1) , (!(V2) , AtSt2) ) =
    matching( AtSt1 , AtSt2 ) .
  eq matching( (!(V1) , AtSt1) , (?(Var2) , AtSt2) ) =
    ( Var2 / V1 ) , matching( AtSt1 , AtSt2 ) .
  eq matching( (?(Var1) , AtSt1) , (!(V2) , AtSt2) ) =
    ( Var1 / V2 ) , matching(AtSt1 , AtSt2) .
  eq matching( (?(Var1) , AtSt1) , (?(Var2) , AtSt2) ) =
    if (element-of-sort-p(Var1 , Var2) == true)
    then (( Var2 / Var1 ) , matching(AtSt1 , AtSt2))
    else (( Var1 / Var2 ) , matching(AtSt1 , AtSt2))
    fi .
  ...
  eq matched( i , i ) = i .
  eq matched( G1 , G1 ) = G1 .
  eq matched( < G1 , AtSt1 > , < G1 , AtSt2 > ) =
    < G1 , matched-sub( AtSt1 , AtSt2 ) > .
  ...
endo
```

Figure 8.14   A part of synchronization conditions for attributed actions

```
obj SIMULATOR[ XM :: VALUE , YM :: GATE] is
  extending UTILITY[XM , YM] .
  sort Edge .
  op (-_->_) : Action Bexp -> Edge .
  op menu : Bexp -> EdgeSet .
  op next : EdgeSet Nat ValList -> Bexp .
  ...
  eq menu(stop) = #Edge .
  eq menu( A1 ; Be )
     = menu(bound-bexp(( A1 ; Be ) , #Bind)) .
  ...
  eq (- A1 -> Be1) |[ GtSt ]| (- A2 -> Be2 , EdSt2) =
     if (gate(A1) == gate(A2)) and (gate(A1) isIn GtSt)
     then if (match-able(A1 , A2) == true)
           then adjoin(
                  (- matched(A1 , A2) ->
                    bound-bexp(
                      Be1 ,matching(attribute(A1),
                                    attribute(A2)))
                    |[ GtSt ]|
                    bound-bexp(
                      Be2 ,matching(attribute(A1),
                                    attribute(A2))))
                  , ((- A1 -> Be1) |[ GtSt ]| EdSt2) )
           else ((- A1 -> Be1) |[ GtSt ]| EdSt2)
           fi
     else ((- A1 -> Be1) |[ GtSt ]| EdSt2)
     fi .
  ...
  eq next( EdSt1 , N , VS1 ) =
     bound-bexp(edge-bexp(nth( EdSt1 , N )) ,
        make-bind-set( edge-attribute(nth( EdSt1 , N ))
                  , VS1)) .
  ...
endo
```

Figure 8.15 The object SIMULATOR with menu and next

```
obj STACK[X::ANY] is
  sort NeStack Stack .
  --- Non-empty stack and stack.
  op empty : -> Stack .
  op push : Any Stack -> NeStack .
  op top : NeStack -> Any .
  op pop : NeStack -> Stack .
  var A : Any .
  var S : Stack .
  eq top(push(A, S)) = A .
  eq pop(push(A, S)) = S .
endo
```

Figure 8.16   Object STACK with subsort

5   EXAMPLE WITH VALUE PASSING

In Figure 8.18, we show an example of two slot buffer with value passing. Figure 8.17 defines values passed between two buffers. These are of sort Stack. Stacked elements are defined as d1, d2, and d3 in the object DATA.

EX-VALUE2 is extending STACK[DATA]. STACK is the same object as in Figure 8.16. The object EX-VALUE2 has to obey the conditions listed in the theory VALUE in Figure 8.7. Therefore, there are so many subsort declarations in EX-VALUE2. We omit further explanation of EX-VALUE2 for brevity.

The object 2BUFFERwithVALUE in Figure 8.18 specifies the two operators buffer and 2-buffer. The operator buffer is treated as the same process as

```
process buffer [a, b] : noexit :=
  a?x:NeStack; b!pop(x); buffer[a, b]
endproc
```

in the original LOTOS. Therefore 2-buffer specifies a two slot buffer to pass the stacks in between two buffers. Note that the variable x is sort NeStack and pop(x) at gate b does not cause any errors such as to take top of the stack empty.

Figure 8.19 shows a dialog of the simulator with this example. The current implementation of OBJ system gives a number of messages, but we omit most of them in Figure 8.19. At the line 01, by menu operator, the possible action < input , ?(x) > is listed at the line 02. This action is named buf1 at 03 by call-that command in OBJ. Then, at 04, the variable x is set to be push(d1, push(d2 , empty) by the operator next. At 15, x is set to be push(d3 , empty). In this case, the poped stack becomes empty. The stack

```
obj DATA is
  sort Data .
  ops d1 d2 d3 : -> Data .
endo

obj EX-VALUE2 is
  sort Value .
  sort Variable .
  subsort Variable < Value .
  sort Binding .
  op _/_ : Variable Value -> Binding .
  op value-of : Value Binding -> Value .
  op element-of-sort-p : Value Value -> Bool .

  extending STACK[DATA] .

  subsort Data < Value .
  sort DataVar .
  subsort DataVar < Variable .
  subsort DataVar < Data .
  subsort Stack < Value .
  sort StackVar .
  subsort StackVar < Variable .
  subsort StackVar < Stack .
  subsort NeStack < Value .
  sort NeStackVar .
  subsort NeStackVar < Variable .
  subsort NeStackVar < NeStack .
  ...
endo
```

Figure 8.17   Value definitions of stacks for a two slot buffer

```
obj BUFFERwithVALUE is
  extending LOTOS-BEXP[EX-VALUE2 , GATE-EX] .
  op buffer[_,_] : Gate Gate -> Bexp [strat (0)] .
  vars a b : Gate .
  op x : -> NeStackVar .
  --- variables in LOTOS are declared like this.
  eq buffer[ a , b ] =
      < a , ?(x) , #Att > ;
      (< b , !(pop(x)) , #Att > ; buffer[ a , b ]) .
endo

obj 2BUFFERwithVALUE is
  extending BUFFERwithVALUE .
  vars in out mid : Gate .
  op 2-buffer[_,_,_] : Gate Gate Gate -> Bexp [strat (0)] .
  eq 2-buffer[ in , mid , out ] =
      hide ( mid , #Gate ) in
        ( buffer[ in , mid ]
          |[ (mid , #Gate) ]| buffer[ mid , out ] ) .
endo

obj SAMPLE2 is
  extending 2BUFFERwithVALUE .
  extending SIMULATOR[EX-VALUE2 , GATE-EX] .
endo
```

Figure 8.18   Two slot buffer with Stack value passing

```
01    OBJ> red menu(2-buffer[ input , dummy , output ] ) .
02      ---> - < input , ?(x) > ->
03    OBJ> call-that buf1 .
04    OBJ> red next( buf1 , 0 ,
                      push( d1, push( d2 , empty) , #Val ) .
05    OBJ> call-that be1 .
06    OBJ> red menu( be1 ) .
07      ---> - i ->
08    OBJ> call-that buf2 .
09    OBJ> red next( buf2 , 0 , #Val ) .
10    OBJ> call-that be2 .
11    OBJ> red menu( be2 ) .
12      ---> - < input , ?(x) > ->
13      ---> - < output , !(empty) > ->
14    OBJ> call-that buf3 .
15    OBJ> red next( buf3 , 0 , push(d3 , empty) , #Val ) .
16    OBJ> call-that be3 .
17    OBJ> red menu( be3 ) .
18      ---> - < output , !(empty) > ->
19    OBJ> call-that buf4 .
20    OBJ> red next( buf4 , 0 , #Val ) .
21    OBJ> call-that be4 .
22    OBJ> red menu( be4 ) .
23      ---> #
24    OBJ>
```

Figure 8.19   Dialog by the object SAMPLE2 in the previous figure

empty is not in the sort NeStack. Therefore, menu(be4) returns an empty list at the line 23. This type checking is done by a subsort handling mechanism of OBJ.

6   A PROPERTY CHECKER

We can use our simulator as a property checker of behavior expressions. Again, we use the example shown in Figure 8.5. Process

```
two-slot-buffer[inp, outp]
```

offers the following set of event sequences:

```
inp; i; ( outp; two-slot-buffer
       [] inp; outp; i; (outp; two-slot-buffer
                              [] inp; ...
```

Note that event mid is hidden by **hide** operator and observed as event **i** for the environment.

Let w be a first finite portion of an event sequence in this set, and $\bar{I}$ and $\bar{O}$ be the numbers of occurrences of inp and outp in w, respectively.

We can show that for any w, one of the following condition is satisfied:

1. $\bar{I} = \bar{O}$

2. $\bar{I} = \bar{O} + 1$

3. $\bar{I} = \bar{O} + 2$

In other words, the the number of events inp cannot exceed the number of events outp more than two nor be less than it, at any moment. This is an "intuitive" specification of two-slot-buffer. We will show this property holds on the specification two-slot-buffer by our simulator.

Let $< BE, I >$ be a pair of a behavior expression and an integer. We have implemented the procedure in Figure 8.20 using OBJ. Note that the operator 2-buffer is defined in Figure 8.6. The key issue of this procedure is as: For a given pair $< BE, I >$,

- if BE can offer inp then I is incremented, and

- if BE can offer $outp$ then I is decremented.

If this procedure terminates and all integers of second element in pairs are 0, 1, or 2, then we can say that the number of events inp cannot exceed the number of events $outp$ more than two nor be less than it, at any moment. This is an "intuitive" specification of a two slot buffer.

We have implemented objects to perform this procedure by importing the modules SIMULATOR (in Figure 8.15), 2BUFFERwithoutVALUE (in Figure 8.6), and INT. The key object is PAIR-BEXP in Figure 8.21. In PAIR-BEXP, "<_,_>" is defined as a constructor of sort Pair. The operator next-pair is used to increment or decrement the second element of pair. Operator isIn, menu, and next are imported from the module SIMULATOR. inp and outp are from GATE-EX.

By using the kernel object PAIR-BEXP, we define several other objects to perform the procedure. An operator all-states appeared in Figure 8.22 performs this procedure. results in Figure 8.22 is a list of pairs $< BE, I >$. This result shows "intuitive" specification is satisfied by the specification

$InputList = < 2 - buffer[inp, mid, outp], 0 >$
$OutputList = \phi$
repeat
    select $< BE_0, I > \in InputList$
    remove $< BE_0, I >$ from $InputList$
    if $< BE_0, I > \notin OutputList$
        then add $< BE_0, I >$ to $OutputList$
        if there is an expression BE_1 such that $BE_0 - inp \rightarrow BE_1$
            then add a pair $< BE_1, I + 1 >$ to $InputList$
        if there is an expression BE_2 such that $BE_0 - outp \rightarrow BE_2$ **then**
            add a pair $< BE_2, I - 1 >$ to $InputList$
until $InputList = \phi$
print $OutputList$

Figure 8.20   A procedure to check property

```
obj PAIR-BEXP is
  sort Pair .
  extending SIMULATOR[SIMPLE-VALUE , GATE-EX] .
  extending 2BUFFERwithoutVALUE .
  protecting INT .
  op <_,_> : Bexp Int -> Pair .
  op next-pair : Pair -> Pair .
  var B : Bexp .
  var I : Int .
  eq next-pair(<B,I>) =
      if inp  isIn menu(B) then <next(B), I+1> fi .
  eq next-pair(<B,I>) =
      if outp isIn menu(B) then <next(B), I-1> fi .
endo
```

Figure 8.21   Key object PAIR-BEXP of a properties checker

```
OBJ> reduce all-states(<2-buffer[inp, mid, outp], 0>) .
results:
  (<hide mid in mid ; buffer[inp,mid] |[mid|
                 mid ; (outp ; buffer[mid,outp])
    , 1>,

   <hide mid in mid ; buffer[inp,mid] |[mid]|
                 outp ; (mid ; (out ; buffer[mid,outp]))
    , 2>,

   <hide mid in inp ; (mid ; buffer[inp,mid]) |[mid]|
                 mid ; (outp ; buffer[mid,outp])
    , 0>,

   <hide mid in inp ; (mid ; buffer[inp,mid]) |[mid]|
                 outp ; (mid ; (outp ; buffer[mid,outp]))
    , 1>,

   <hide mid in mid ; (inp ; (mid ; buffer[inp,mid]))
                   |[mid]|
         mid ; (outp ; (mid ; (outp ; buffer[mid,outp])))
    , 1>,

   <hide mid in buffer[inp,mid] |[mid]| buffer[mid,outp]
    , 0>)
```

Figure 8.22   After execution of the property checker

2BUFFERwithoutVALUE written in OBJ. The number of possible behavior expressions is six. Each expression has either 0, 1, or 2 as its second element. This result shows the "intuitive" specification is satisfied by the specification 2BUFFERwithoutVALUE.

7   DISCUSSIONS

7.1   INTRODUCING SUBSORTS INTO LOTOS

In this subsection, we compare the original LOTOS (i.e., ISO 8807) and an "enhanced" LOTOS from the viewpoint of subsort.

In Figure 8.23, the sort Int has its subsorts NInt and PInt. Int represent integers. Its subsorts are for negative integers and positive integers. Figure

8.24 shows an example of value passing for stacks. In both cases, if we could use the facility of subsort, guard expressions were avoidable, since exception handling is performed as a role of ADT part.

7.2   PROBLEMS TO BE RESOLVED

OBJ employs a first order logic to handle each operator. To use any sorts of OBJ in the LOTOS simulator, variables have to be treated as constants in the simulator. This makes the simulator complicate.

We introduced binding operators between variables and values. Our simulator is explicitly keeping this environmental information during execution. If we can define a generic object for the extended labeled transition system including variables in their states, then the simulator for process algebras, like CCS or ACP, are instantiated from this generic object, since operational semantics of these languages are normally defined by extended labeled transition system.

8   CONCLUSION AND FUTURE WORKS

All samples of OBJ programs listed in the paper have already been tested by the OBJ3 system [4].

Both syntax and semantics of LOTOS has been written by OBJ just as their original definitions. We can state that OBJ is a good tool for rapid prototyping for this type of language processor, especially, towards the enhancement of the LOTOS language.

We fully use parameterization facility in OBJ. This fairly large sample program written in OBJ shows that parameterization mechanism is a powerful tool to specify language processors.

As future works, inductive verification method for this type of language should be developed as shown in [17]. The way we have shown is traversing all possible transitions. But if we can apply inductive way, we can use OBJ system as a "calculator" for inductive prover.

Our trial is an implementation of a process algebra using a term rewriting system. LOTOS is considered to be a language of CCS+ADT. It is known that some family of ACP can be interpreted by a term rewriting system [20]. Our implementation can easily be extensible to a language of ACP+ADT.

Acknowledgments

The authors wish to thank Drs. J. Meseguer and T. Winkler for their helpful discussions to improve our simulator.

References

[1]   ISO 8807. Information Processing Systems - Open System Interconnec-

```
specification EX1

    type Integer is Boolean
    sorts Int
    opns _<_ : Int, Int -> Bool
         _>_ : Int, Int -> Bool
         -_  : Int -> Int
    ...
    endtype

    behavior
    inp?x:Int;
        (
          [x>0] -> sap!x; P[...](x,...)
        []
          [x<0] -> sap!-x; P[...](x,...)
        )
    endspec
```

(a) Original LOTOS

```
specification NEW-EX1

    type Integer is Boolean
    subsort PInt < Int
    subsort NInt < Int
    ...
    endtype

    behavior
      inp?x:PInt; sap!x;
    []
      inp?x:NInt; sap!-x;
    endspec
```

(b)If we could use subsort in LOTOS,...

Figure 8.23   Example of subsort in Integers

```
specification EX2
  type Stack is
    sort Stack
    ...
  endtype

  behavior
    inp?x:Stack;
    (
        [x eq empty] -> sap!pop(x);...
        []
        sap!push(e,x);...
    )
endspec
```

(a) Original LOTOS

```
specification NEW-EX2

  type Stack is
    subsort NeStack < Stack
    eqns
    ...
  endtype

  behavior
    inp?x:NeStack; sap!pop(x);...
    []
    inp?x:Stack; sap!push(e,x);...
endspec
```

(b) If we could use subsort in LOTOS,...

Figure 8.24   Example of subsort in Stack

tion - LOTOS - A formal description technique based on the temporal ordering of observational behavior. 1989-02-15.

[2]   Kokichi Futatsugi, Joseph Goguen, Jean-Pierre Jouannaud and José Meseguer. Principles of OBJ2. Proc. 12th ACM Symp. on POPL, pp. 52–66, 1985.

[3]   Kokicji Futatsugi, Joseph Goguen, José Meseguer and K. Okada. Parameterized Programming in OBJ2. Proc. 9th Int'l Conference on Software Engineering, pp. 51–60, 1987.

[4]   Joseph Goguen *et al*. Introducing OBJ3. This volume.

[5]   ISO 7498. Information Processing Systems - Basic Reference Model for Open System Interconnection. 1983.

[6]   Kazuhito Ohmaki and Kokichi Futatsugi. Specifications of Library and Lift Problems in LOTOS. Technical Report of Information Processing Society of Japan, SE 64-12, 1989.

[7]   T. Bolognesi and Ed Brinksma. Introduction to the ISO Specification Language LOTOS. Computer Networks and ISDN Systems, Vol. 14, pp. 25–59, 1987.

[8]   M. Diaz and C. Visser. SEDOS:Designing Open Distributed Systems. *IEEE Software*, November, pp. 24–33, 1989.

[9]   2nd DP, ISO/IEC DP 10026-1,2,3. Information processing systems - Open systems interconnection - Distributed transaction processing, Part 1 (Model), Part 2 (Service definition), Part 3 (Protocol specification). ISO/IEC JTC 1/SC 21/WG5, 1988.

[10] I. Ajubi and M. van Sinderen. High level synchronization services of OSI - Commitment, Concurrency and Recovery. University of Twente MEMORANDUM INF-88-35, 1988.

[11] M. van Sinderen and I. Widya. On the Design and Formal Specification of a Transaction Protocol. Proc. Third International Conference of Formal Description Techniques (FORTE'90), pp. 515–532, November 1990.

[12] P.H.J. van Eijk, C.A. Vissers and M. Diaz (eds.). *The Formal Description Technique LOTOS*. North-Holland, 1989.

[13] Robin Milner. A Calculus of Communicating Systems. Lecture Notes in Computer Science, 92, Springer-Verlag, 1980.

[14] Hartmut Ehrich and Bernd Mahr. *Fundamentals of Algebraic Specification*. Springer Verlag, Berlin, 1985.

[15] Software Environment for Design of Open Distributed Systems, HIPPO-LOTOS Simulator. University of Twente, The Netherlands.

[16] P.H.J. van Eijk. Software tools for the specification language LOTOS. PhD. thesis, University of Twente, 1988.

[17] Joseph Goguen. OBJ as a Theorem Prover with Applications to Hardware Verification. Technical report SRI-SCL-88-4R2, August 1988.

[18] Giuseppe Scollo. Some facilities for concise data type definition in LOTOS, Draft Version 1. ISO/TC 97/SC 21/N2015, Potential enhancements to LOTOS, 1987.

[19] H. Ehrig, J. Buntrock, P. Boehm, K.-P. Hasler and F. Nuernberg. Towards an Algebraic Semantics of the ISO-Specification Language LOTOS," in [12] pp. 249–268.

[20] J.A. Bergstra and J.W. Klop. Process algebra for Synchronous Communication. *Information and Control*, Vol. 60, pp. 109–137, 1984.

Chapter 9

MORE HIGHER ORDER PROGRAMMING IN OBJ

Joseph A. Goguen
Department of Computer Science and Engineering
University of California at San Diego

Grant Malcolm
Department of Computer Science
University of Liverpool

1   INTRODUCTION

This paper discusses the use of OBJ3's parameterized modules for higher order programming, giving examples beyond those in [8, 3, 4] and showing some capabilities that may seem surprising. We also discuss parameterized views, which are not yet implemented, but which we hope soon will be. We assume familiarity with [8], which appears as the first paper in this book.

2   PARAMETERIZED MODULES AS PARAMETERS

A feature of OBJ3 not discussed in [8] allows the use of parameterized modules as parameter theories of other modules. The example below follows one suggested by Yatsu and Futatsugi [9] in connection with their design work on the CafeOBJ system [2].

The parameterized LIST object defines lists, with a comma syntax for concatenation. The theory FUN defines an interface requesting a (unary) function f between two possibly different sorts. Then MAP extends f to a function between lists of those sorts, parameterized by the sorts and the funciton. Finally, a function double is defined on natural numbers, and f is instantiated to it.

```
obj LIST[X :: TRIV] is
  sorts List NeList .
  subsorts Elt < NeList < List .
  op nil : -> List .
  op _,_ : List List -> List [assoc id: nil] .
endo

th FUN[X Y :: TRIV] is
  op f_ : Elt.X -> Elt.Y .
endth

obj MAP[X Y :: TRIV, F :: FUN[X,Y]] is
  pr (LIST * (sort List to List1))[X] .
  pr (LIST * (sort List to List2))[Y] .
  op map_ : List1 -> List2 .
  var E : Elt.X .
  var L : List1 .
  eq map nil = nil .
  eq map (E,L) = (f E),(map L) .
endo

obj DOUBLE is pr NAT .
  op double_ : Nat -> Nat .
  var N : Nat .
  eq double N = N + N .
endo

make MAP-double is
  MAP[NAT,NAT, view to DOUBLE is
                 op f_ to double_ .
               endv]
endm
```

Although this code runs in OBJ3, the recursion equation in the MAP module does not parse. This is because the OBJ3 parser erroneously gives f the rank Elt.X -> Elt.X; we hope to fix this bug in a new implementation of the OBJ3 module system. However, similar examples work correctly in the present OBJ3, including the modified version below, which shows that in principle the original should have worked.

```
th TRIV1 is sort Elt1 . endth

th FUN[X :: TRIV, Y :: TRIV1] is
  op f_ : Elt -> Elt1 .
endth

obj MAP[X :: TRIV, Y :: TRIV1, F :: FUN[X,Y]] is
  pr (LIST * (sort List to List1))[X] .
  pr (LIST * (sort List to List2))[Y] .
  op map_ : List1 -> List2 .
  var E : Elt.X .
  var L : List1 .
  eq map nil = nil .
  eq map(E,L) = (f E),(map L) .
endo

make MAP-double is
  MAP[NAT,NAT, view to DOUBLE is
                op f_ to double_ .
              endv]
endm
```

We could also have added L1 :: LIST[X], L2 :: LIST[Y] to the parameters of MAP, as in [9], but the above is more natural to OBJ3. It would have been even more natural to have the two sorts in the body of FUN instead of as parameters. It is interesting to notice that nesting parameterized modules in this way corresponds to a kind of dependent type [5].

3   RECURSIVE DEFINITION OVER THE NATURAL NUMBERS

The example below was inspired by work of Feng, Sakabe and Inagaki [1] on their dynamic term rewriting calculus. We do not follow their code, but instead seek to accomplish the same objective in a way that is natural to OBJ3. This objective is to mechanize recursive definitions of functions over the natural numbers, i.e., to produce a reusable specification that encapsulates a general scheme for recursive definitions.

The module REC gives the general scheme for recursive definitions, parameterized by an interface that requires one unary and one binary function (p M is the predecessor of M). The module NAT1 then introduces some functions that are needed for the particular recursive functions defined later in the module NAT2; these are addition, multiplication and exponentiation, and each is defined as an instantiation of REC.

```
    th NATF1 is pr NAT .
      op b : Nat -> Nat .
    endth

    th NATF2 is pr NAT .
      op c : Nat Nat -> Nat .
    endth

    obj REC[X :: NATF1, Y :: NATF2] is pr NAT .
      op f : Nat Nat -> Nat .
      vars N M : Nat .
      eq f(N,0) = b(N).
      cq f(N,M) = c(N,f(N,p M)) if M > 0 .
    endo

    obj NAT1 is pr NAT .
      ops id 0 1 : Nat -> Nat .
      op s2 : Nat Nat -> Nat .
      vars N M : Nat .
      eq id(N) = N .
      eq 0(N) = 0 .
      eq 1(N) = 1 .
      eq s2(N,M) = s(M) .
    endo

    obj NAT2 is pr NAT1 .
      pr (REC * (op f to add)) [id.NAT1, s2.NAT1] .
      pr (REC * (op f to mult)) [0.NAT1, add.NAT2] .
      pr (REC * (op f to exp)) [1.NAT1,mult.NAT2] .
    endo
```

This code runs just as you would expect, and of course we could define other functions in the same way. The "self-referential" use of NAT2 in the last module seems not to be mentioned in [8].

4   INDUCTIVE PROOF OVER THE NATURAL NUMBERS

The example in this section was also inspired by [1]. The objective in this case is to mechanize induction by encapsulating the structure of standard inductive proofs over the natural numbers into a reusable specification.

The code below proves associativity of addition for natural numbers. For induction, we cannot use OBJ3's built in numbers, but must axiomatize the natural numbers. The first module, TERM, does this in the usual way, at the same time introducing terms that involve addition and variables x, y, z. The parameterized modules GOAL and HYP respectively introduce equations to be proved and equations to be used as hypotheses. These are instantiated in the module IND to give the entire proof structure, which is then executed with a red command.

```
obj TERM is
  sort Nat .
  op 0 : -> Nat .
  op s_ : Nat -> Nat .
  op _+_ : Nat Nat -> Nat .
  vars M N : Nat .
  eq 0 + N = N .
  eq s M + N = s(M + N) .
  ops x y z : -> Nat .
endo

th NATFO is pr TERM .
  op a : -> Nat .
endth

obj GOAL[A :: NATFO] is pr TERM .
  let goal = (a +(y + z)) == ((a + y)+ z) .
endo

obj HYP[A :: NATFO] is pr TERM .
  eq a +(y + z) = (a + y)+ z .
endo

make IND is
  (GOAL * (op goal to base))[(0).TERM]
  + HYP[(x).TERM]
  + (GOAL * (op goal to step))
     [view to TERM is op a to s x . endv]
endm

red base and step .    ***> should be: true
```

In executing this reduction, OBJ3 goes through all the steps of an inductive proof of the associative law, and confirms this by printing true. Clearly this technique could be used to prove other results about natural numbers in the same way, just by changing the expressions in GOAL and HYP (although of

course it may be necessary to first prove and then introduce some lemmas).
However, it would be nice if this could instead be achieved by providing a view
that selects any two terms to be proved equal. A way to do this is suggested in
Section 6 below.

5   INDUCTIVE PROOF OVER BINARY TREES

This section shows that the approach of the previous section applies to
inductive proofs over other data structures, in this case binary trees. We prove
that a certain inductively defined function is in fact the identity function. This
uses the HYP module twice, because the induction hypothesis is needed once
for each of two subtrees.

```
obj TERM is pr NAT .
  sort Tree .
  op tip_ : Nat -> Tree .
  op _++_ : Tree Tree -> Tree .
  op id_ : Tree -> Tree .
  var N : Nat .
  vars T U : Tree .
  eq id tip N = tip N .
  eq id(T ++ U) = (id T)++(id U) .
  op y : -> Nat .
  ops t u : -> Tree .
endo

th TREEFO is pr TERM .
  op a : -> Tree .
endth

obj GOAL[A :: TREEFO] is
  let goal = (id a == a) .
endo

obj HYP[A :: TREEFO] is
  eq id a = a .
endo
```

```
make IND is
  (GOAL * (op goal to base))
   [view to TERM is
      op a to tip y .
    endv]
 + HYP[(t).TERM]
 + HYP[(u).TERM]
 + (GOAL * (op goal to step))
     [view to TERM is
        op a to t ++ u .
      endv]
endm
```

```
red base and step .   ***> should be: true
```

6   PARAMETERIZED VIEWS

Parameterized views are not implemented in OBJ3, but Sections 4.7 and C.8 of [8], on higher order programming and on category theory, respectively, present parameterized views asserting certain properties of parameterized modules.

The code below is again for proving associativity of addition, but now using a parameterized view. Because of this, the code does not run in the current OBJ3 implementation. The module TERM defines terms involving addition and variables x, y, z over the naturals. The constant required by NATF0 represents the induction variable, and PTERM gives terms that may involve that variable; this parameterized module will be the target of the parameterized view. The next theory is for picking out the two terms to be proved equal. Then goal and hypothesis modules are defined; these are much as before, except for the parameterization. The parameterized view ASSOCV gives the left and right sides of the associativity law as terms using the induction variable a from NATF0. Because this variable is a parameter to ASSOCV, it can be instantiated in different ways in the proof. The module IND gives the proof structure for induction over naturals, using the parameterized view three times, once instantiating a to 0 for the base case, then to x for the inductive hypothesis, and finally to s x for the goal of the induction step.

```
obj TERM is
  sort Nat .
  op 0 : -> Nat .
  op s_ : Nat -> Nat .
  op _+_ : Nat Nat -> Nat .
  vars M N : Nat .
  eq 0 + N = N .
  eq s M + N = s(M + N) .
  ops x y z : -> Nat .
  let sx = s x .
endo

th NATFO is pr TERM .
  op a : -> Nat .
endth

obj PTERM[A :: NATFO] is
  ex TERM .
endo

th 2TERM[A :: NATFO] is pr PTERM[A] .
  ops t1 t2 : -> Nat .
endth

obj GOAL[A :: NATFO, T :: 2TERM[A]] is
  let goal = t1 == t2 .
endo

obj HYP[A :: NATFO, T :: 2TERM[A]] is
  eq t1 = t2 .
endo

view ASSOCV[A :: NATFO]
    from 2TERM[A] to PTERM[A] is
  op t1 to a + (y + z) .
  op t2 to (a + y) + z .
endv
```

```
make IND is
  (GOAL * (op goal to base))
    [(0).TERM, ASSOC[(0).TERM]]
  + HYP[(x).TERM,ASSOC[(x).TERM]
  + (GOAL * (op goal to step))
    [(sx).TERM, ASSOC[(sx).TERM] .
endm
```

```
red base and step .   ***> should be: true
```

The final module and the reduction do not get executed, because OBJ fails when it reaches the parameterized view. However, we have written an executable version of the above code by replacing ASSOCV with three views corresponding to its three instantiations in IND.

The semantics of parameterized views is discussed in [5], using the notion of pushout from category theory. It would not be difficult to give a semantics using the more concrete approach introduced in [7].

The technique of the proof above could also be used to prove other properties of numbers, just by replacing ASSOCV with a view picking out the two new terms to be proved equal. This suggests an exciting extension to parameterized programming allowing IND to be parameterized by the parameterized view ASSOCV. This would give a fully general inductive proof structure that could be reused for any equational property by suitably instantiating the parameterized view. The semantics of theories parameterized by parameterized views seems a natural extension of the semantics of parameterized views in [5], and we hope to investigate this subject soon.

7   SOME UNDOCUMENTED FEATURES OF PARAMETERIZATION

Anyone who wants to do further experiments with higher order programming in OBJ3 may find the following remarks useful:

1. Proper terms cannot be used as parameters of modules. For example, M[(s 0).NAT] does not work, but M[(1).NAT] does, where M has parameter theory NATFO; an explicit view could also be used. (This explains the constant sx in the second associativity proof.)

2. A single variable cannot be used as target in an operation map in a view. For example, "op f(N) to N" does not parse (assuming of course that the variable N has been declared in the view).

3. A list of terms cannot be used as an argument for a parameterized module having a theory requiring multiple operations. For example,

M[(O).NAT, (s_).NAT] will not work when M has a parameter theory requiring one constant and one unary function; however, an explicit view showing how the two operation symbols are to be instantiated can be used, e.g.,

M[view to NAT1 is op b to O . op c to s_ .endv].

4. The import mode declarations, pr, ex and us, can be used in the parameter declarations of parameterized modules, but not in module expressions.

The last point is illustrated in the code below. The two theories are just for set up; then the first three makes work as expected, but things like the last two produce error messages:

```
th A is sort A . endth

th B is sort B . endth

make T1[ex P :: A, ex Q :: B] is A + B endm

make T2[us P :: A, pr Q :: B] is A + B endm

make T3[ex P :: A, us Q :: B] is A + B endm

make T4 is (pr A) + (ex B) endm

make T5 is us A + us B endm
```

8   DISCUSSION AND FUTURE WORK

Parameterized views would add a great deal of power to a module system like that of OBJ3, probably allowing nearly everything one might want to do in practice. However, it would often be convenient to have available the even more general feature of *view expressions*, which are analogous to module expressions, and allow constructing new views from components using operations similar to those of module expressions. Another feature that would be interesting to implement and experiment with is the *synchronized concurrent connection* introduced in [6] for specification of concurrent object oriented systems. We feel it should be very exciting to explore this new area of parameterized programming, and hope to do so in the not too distant future.

Acknowledgments

We thank Prof. Futatsugi for organizing the "10th Anniversay of OBJ2" seminar in Itoh, Japan, which stimulated the work in this paper, and Prof. Futatsugi and Dr. Yatsu for valuable conversations concerning some of the topics in this paper at that seminar.

The research reported in this paper has been supported in part by the Science and Engineering Research Council, the CEC under ESPRIT-2 BRA Working Groups 6071, IS-CORE (Information Systems COrrectness and REusability) and 6112, COMPASS (COMPrehensive Algebraic Approach to System Specification and development), Fujitsu Laboratories Limited, and a contract under the management of the Information Technology Promotion Agency (IPA), Japan, as part of the Industrial Science and Technology Frontier Program "New Models for Software Architectures," sponsored by NEDO (New Energy and Industrial Technology Development Organization).

References

[1]   Su Feng, Toshiki Sakabe, and Yasuyoshi Inagaki. Mechanizing explicit inductive equational reasoning by DTRC. In Kokichi Futatsugi, editor, *Proceedings, Workshop on Tenth Anniversary of OBJ2, Itoh, Japan, 21–22 October 1995.* Unisys, 1995.

[2]   Kokichi Futatsugi and Toshimi Sawada. Design considerations for Cafe specification environment. In Kokichi Futatsugi, editor, *Proceedings, Workshop on Tenth Anniversary of OBJ2, Itoh, Japan, 21–22 October 1995.* Unisys, 1995.

[3]   Joseph Goguen. Principles of parameterized programming. In Ted Biggerstaff and Alan Perlis, editors, *Software Reusability, Volume I: Concepts and Models*, pages 159–225. Addison Wesley, 1989.

[4]   Joseph Goguen. Higher-order functions considered unnecessary for higher-order programming. In David Turner, editor, *Research Topics in Functional Programming*, pages 309–352. Addison Wesley, 1990. University of Texas at Austin Year of Programming Series; preliminary version in SRI Technical Report SRI-CSL-88-1, January 1988.

[5]   Joseph Goguen. Types as theories. In George Michael Reed, Andrew William Roscoe, and Ralph F. Wachter, editors, *Topology and Category Theory in Computer Science*, pages 357–390. Oxford, 1991. Proceedings of a Conference held at Oxford, June 1989.

[6]   Joseph Goguen and Răzvan Diaconescu. Towards an algebraic semantics for the object paradigm. In Hartmut Ehrig and Fernando Orejas, editors, *Proceedings, Tenth Workshop on Abstract Data Types*, pages 1–29. Springer, 1994. Lecture Notes in Computer Science, Volume 785.

[7]   Joseph Goguen and William Tracz. An implementation-oriented semantics for module composition. In Gary Leavens and Murali Sitaraman,

editors, *Foundations of Component-based Systems*. Cambridge, 1999. To appear.

[8] Joseph Goguen, Timothy Winkler, José Meseguer, Kokichi Futatsugi, and Jean-Pierre Jouannaud. Introducing OBJ. This volume.

[9] Hirokazu Yatsu and Kokichi Futatsugi. Modular specification in CafeOBJ. In Kokichi Futatsugi, editor, *Proceedings, Workshop on Tenth Anniversary of OBJ2, Itoh, Japan, 21–22 October 1995*. Unisys, 1995.

Index

algebra, 25
apply, 85, 89
arity, 13
assoc, 34
at, 89
attribute, 33

built-in rule, 131
built-in sorts, 128

canonical, 30
category theory, 123
cd, 55
ceq, 19
Church-Rosser property, 30
close, 52
combinatory algebra, 118
comm, 34
context, 42, 70
cq, 19

define, 71
denotational semantics, 24, 58
dfn, 71
do, 8, 95–96
do clear memo, 39
do restore, 42
do save, 42

eof, 55
eq, 17
equality operator, 23
equation, 17
  built-in, 128, 131
  conditional, 19, 89
  in theory, 58
Erastosthenes' sieve, 117
ev, 97
evaluation strategy, 38
evq, 97
extending, 44, 46

Fermat's little theorem, 114

gathering, 36

id, 34
idem, 35
idr, 35
if, 19
including, 44, 46
initial algebra, 25
instantiation, 57, 67

label, 19
lazy evaluation, 117
let, 18, 20, 86
ls, 55

make, 68
memo, 39
memoization, 39
mixfix syntax, 12–13
module, 7, 41
  expression, 57, 68, 71
  importation, 42, 44
  parameterized, 61, 68
  redefinition, 47
  sum, 72
multiple inheritance, 11

normal form, 22

obj, 9
object, 7, 9
of, 88
op, 12–13
open, 52
openr, 53
operator mapping, 63, 71
ops, 14
order sorted algebra, 10
overloading, 16

parse, 15